Rethinking Intuition

Studies in Epistemology and Cognitive Theory
Series Editor: *Paul K. Moser, Loyola University of Chicago*

Rethinking Intuition

*The Psychology of Intuition
and Its Role in Philosophical Inquiry*

edited by
Michael R. DePaul
and William Ramsey

ROWMAN & LITTLEFIELD PUBLISHERS, INC.
Lanham • Boulder • New York • Oxford

ROWMAN & LITTLEFIELD PUBLISHERS, INC.

Published in the United States of America
by Rowman & Littlefield Publishers, Inc.
4720 Boston Way, Lanham, Maryland 20706

12 Hid's Copse Road
Cumnor Hill, Oxford OX2 9JJ, England

British Library Cataloguing in Publication Information Available

Library of Congress Cataloging-in-Publication Data

Rethinking intuition : the psychology of intuition and its role in
  philosophical inquiry / edited by Michael R. DePaul and William Ramsey.
      p.   cm. — (Studies in epistemology and cognitive theory)
    Includes bibliographical references and index.
    ISBN 0-8476-8795-3 (alk. paper). — ISBN 0-8476-8796-1 (pbk.:
  alk. paper)
    1. Intuition. 2. Methodology. 3. Intuition (Psychology)
  I. DePaul, Michael R. (Michael Raymond), 1954- . II. Ramsey,
  William (William M.). III. Series: Studies in epistemology and
  cognitive theory (Unnumbered)
  BD181.R47   1998
  121'.3—dc21   98-23794
                                      CIP

Printed in the United States of America

♾™ The paper used in this publication meets the minimum requirements of American
National Standard for Information Sciences—Permanence of Paper for Printed Library
Materials, ANSI Z39.48–1984.

Contents

Preface

Perhaps more than any other intellectual discipline, philosophical inquiry is driven by intuitive judgments, that is, by what "we would say" or by what seems true to the inquirer. For most of philosophical theorizing and debate, intuitions serve as something like a source of evidence that can be used to defend or attack particular philosophical positions.

One clear example of this is a traditional philosophical enterprise commonly known as *conceptual analysis*. Anyone familiar with Plato's dialogues knows how this type of inquiry is conducted. We see Socrates encounter someone who claims to have figured out the true essence of some abstract notion, be it piety, justice, or knowledge. Characteristically, the person puts forward a definition or analysis of the notion in the form of necessary and sufficient conditions that are thought to capture all and only instances of the concept in question. Socrates then refutes his interlocutor's definition of the concept by pointing out various *counterexamples*, that is, situations where the proposed definition yields a result that conflicts with our intuitive judgments about the concept in question. For example, in Book I of the *Republic*, when Cephalus defines justice in a way that requires the returning of property and total honesty, Socrates responds by pointing out that it would be *un*just to return weapons to a person who had gone mad or to tell the whole truth to such a person. What is the status of these claims that certain behaviors would be unjust in the circumstances described? Socrates does not argue for them in any way. They seem to be no more than spontaneous judgments representing "common sense" or "what we would say." So it would seem that the proposed analysis is rejected because it fails to capture our *intuitive* judgments about the real nature of justice. After a proposed analysis or definition is overturned by an intuitive counterexample, the idea is to revise or replace the analysis with one that is not subject to the counterexample. Counterexamples to the new analysis are sought, the analysis revised if any counterexamples are found, and so on, with the ultimate goal of the process being an analysis or definition of the concept in question that is immune to intuitive counterexample.

Refutations by intuitive counterexamples figure as prominently in today's philosophical journals as they did in Plato's dialogues. In recent times, efforts to provide philosophical analyses of knowledge, the nature of meaning and reference, the human mind, and moral right and wrong—to name only a few examples—have been both defended and attacked by appeal to what is considered to be intuitively obvious. Even philosophers who do not advertise themselves as engaged in the search for necessary and sufficient conditions nevertheless lean heavily upon our intuitive judgments and counterexamples to support or criticize positions. While there have always been a few philosophers who have been skeptical of the search for precise analyses, this type of philosophy is still very widely practiced. For many, appealing to our intuitions is the only available option for uncovering the true nature of the many things that occupy philosophers.

While a good deal of philosophical inquiry seems to presuppose that acceptable definitions and accounts must be completely immune to intuitive counterexamples, and treats intuitive judgments as more or less infallible, a very sizable group of contemporary philosophers hold a more qualified view of the reliability of intuitions as a source of philosophical truth. These philosophers are committed to what we might loosely describe as a more Aristotelian understanding of philosophical method. Aristotle cautioned that we should not expect all branches of human knowledge to have the same degree of precision that we find in mathematics. While Aristotle also tested the accounts he developed against "what we commonly say," that is, against our intuitive judgments, his aim was not to construct a definition that agrees with every single intuitive judgment we make. Instead, he sought an account that agrees with our intuitive judgments *for the most part*, and, at least ideally, provided some understanding of why we make the intuitive judgments that disagree with the account. Many analytic philosophers employ essentially the same method. They "test" their theories against the "data" of what we say about real and hypothetical examples, that is, against our intuitive judgments. But they hold intuitive judgments to be revisable, both in the face of apparently contradictory intuitive judgments about analogous cases and in the face of theories that are well established or intuitively plausible on their own. The idea is that philosophers must seek to mold a philosophical analysis, theory or account of the target subject matter together with the totality of their relevant intuitive judgments, along with their background philosophical, scientific, political, and even their theological beliefs—in effect, virtually all of their beliefs—into a coherent whole. In order to do this, philosophical definitions or theories will often have to be revised because they conflict with intuitive judgments. In other cases it will be the intuitive judgment that will be revised, for example, when they conflict not only with a developing philosophical view, but with various background beliefs as well. The method of *reflective equilibrium* is perhaps the best known and most fully articulated contemporary example of this approach.

While there are many other ways in which philosophers employ and appeal to intuitions, these two approaches serve to illustrate a central point: from its beginning in Greek philosophy right through to the present, intuitions have always played an extremely important role in Western philosophy. Of course, the use of intuitions has been criticized from time to time, but in spite of the criticisms, philosophers have continued to rely heavily upon intuitive judgments in pretty much the way they always have. And they continue to use them in the absence of any well articulated, generally accepted account of intuitive judgment—in particular, an account that establishes their epistemic credentials. However, what appear to be serious new challenges to the way intuitions are employed have recently emerged from an unexpected quarter—empirical research in cognitive psychology. With the weight of these empirical findings added to the more traditional philosophical criticisms of intuition and the lack of a good positive account of intuitive judgment, we feel it is fair to say that unease about the use of intuitions is growing among philosophers. It is convenient to call attention to two areas of empirical research that, respectively, challenge one of the two uses of intuitive judgments in philosophical inquiry identified above.

With respect to the tradition of seeking definitions or conceptual analyses that are immune to counterexample, the challenge is based on the work of psychologists studying the nature of concepts and categorization judgments. (See, e.g., Rosch 1978; Rosch and Mervis 1975, reprinted in this volume; Rips 1975; and Smith and Medin 1981.) Psychologists working in this area have been pushed to abandon the view that we represent concepts with simple sets of necessary and sufficient conditions. The data seem to show that, except for some mathematical and geometrical concepts, it is not possible to use simple sets of conditions to capture the intuitive judgments people make regarding what falls under a given concept. A few psychologists and philosophers have argued that these empirical results throw into doubt analytic philosophy's efforts to define concepts by providing necessary and sufficient conditions that also accord with our intuitions. (See, e.g., Ramsey 1992, reprinted in this volume.) In conversation philosophers respond to this challenge in various ways: for example, they suggest that psychologists work with a different notion of concepts than philosophers or they attempt to explain away the data upon which psychologists rely. But the literature contains next to nothing in the way of a detailed response to this challenge. (One exception is provided by Rey 1983.)

With regard to the use of intuitive judgments exemplified by reflective equilibrium, the challenge from cognitive psychology stems primarily from studies of inference strategies and belief revision. (See, e.g., Nisbett and Ross 1980; and Kahneman, Slovic, and Tversky 1982.) Numerous studies of the patterns of inductive inference people use and judge to be intuitively plausible have revealed that people are prone to commit various fallacies. Moreover, they continue to find these fallacious patterns of reasoning to be intuitively acceptable upon reflection. It is arguable, therefore, that the rules of inductive inference that best capture our intuitive judgments, that is, the rules that are in reflective equilibrium for us, are simply unacceptable. Similarly, studies of the "intuitive" heuristics ordinary people accept reveal various gross departures from empirically correct principles. Once again, although the system of principles that best captures intuitive judgments might be psychologically interesting, there seems to be no reason to place a strong credence in it. In the light of such results, some philosophers have come to question the widely accepted method of reflective equilibrium, suggesting that it cannot lead us to a rational, coherent method of belief formation. (See, e.g., Stich 1988, reprinted in this volume.) Most philosophers would agree that this psychological research presents a serious prima facie challenge to the sort of standard philosophical methodology that reflective equilibrium represents, and there have been a couple of efforts on the part of more traditionally inclined philosophers to respond (e.g., Sosa 1991: ch. 15; and Cohen 1981). It is still true, however, that there has been surprisingly little effort either to meet the challenge or to articulate a plausible method for philosophical inquiry that does not run foul of current empirical research.

Two points are worth emphasizing: (1) In a certain sense these challenges to traditional philosophical methods are not new. Wittgenstein (1953), for example, criticized conceptual analysis on the basis of a view of concepts that is very similar to the theories now being developed by psychologists. And there have always been philosophers who feared that intuitive judgments were unreliable, reflecting little more than the superstitions of one's society. But since these criticisms were grounded in nothing more solid than more philosophical speculation, traditional philosophy was able to roll along its old course for the most part unperturbed. What is new about the challenges being raised by the psychologists is the empirical support behind them. This time around the challenges seem to be rooted in something firmer than other intuitive judgments, so there is reason to hope that traditional philosophy will have to take them more seriously than it has when similar challenges were raised in the past. (2) There is reason to think this hope is not idle. The sparse literature directly addressing these challenges does not indicate that philosophers are unaware of the challenges or that they regard them as uninteresting or unimportant. Quite the contrary. One commonly hears these matters being informally discussed with considerable fervor. There is a growing consensus among philosophers that there is a serious and fundamental problem here that needs to be addressed. In fact, we do not think it is an overstatement to say that Western analytic philosophy is, in many respects, undergoing a crisis where there is considerable urgency and anxiety regarding the status of intuitive analysis. It is becoming increasingly clear that philosophers need to provide a clear and strong justification for the important role intuitions play in their research; otherwise, there needs to be a significant change in the way a great deal of philosophy gets done.

Our goal is to initiate a self-examination of philosophical method that we believe is long overdue. We took the first step toward this goal by organizing a conference on the psychology of intuitions and their role in philosophical inquiry at the University of Notre Dame in April of 1996. This conference provided a setting where psychologists and philosophers had an opportunity to explore and debate the nature of intuitions and their significance for contemporary philosophy. In order to make progress on this topic, we brought together (a) psychologists whose research sheds light on the nature of intuitive judgment, concepts, inference strategies, and other relevant matters, (b) philosophers who are critical of traditional philosophical methods in part because of empirical results, and (c) philosophers who employ traditional analytic methods and who can help clarify the methodological and epistemological role intuitions play in philosophical inquiry. While scholars from the first two groups have been interacting frequently, more traditional philosophers had largely been left out of the debate. One thing that was significant about the conference, therefore, was that it brought influential cognitive psychologists and philosophers who were already talking to each other together with leading representatives of the much larger, more traditionally oriented community of analytic philosophers.

This volume is the second step toward our goal. The papers presented at the conference constitute the bulk of the volume. Specifically, the chapters by Edward Wisniewski, Eldar Shafir, Alison Gopnik and Eric Schwitzgebel, Robert Cummins, Hilary Kornblith, Tamara Horowitz, Alvin Goldman and Joel Pust,

George Bealer, Richard Foley, and Ernest Sosa are all revised versions of papers originally presented at the conference. Chapter 1 originated in the conference as well. We ended the conference with a panel discussion, the panelists being Gary Gutting, Andreas Kemmerling, and Helen Longino. These three accepted the difficult task of presenting brief remarks that responded to the papers that had been presented and the discussions that had taken place over the course of the conference in a way that would help bring our conversations to an appropriate close. The task was complicated because the panelists had to prepare their remarks after the last paper was presented on the last full day of the conference. The remarks of all three panelists were excellent, even ignoring the circumstances under which they had to be prepared, but because Gutting sought to place the papers presented at the conference into a historical context, it was obvious that with just a little expanding his comments would make a very natural introduction for this volume.

At the conference, we wanted the discussions to be informed by a familiarity with the relevant psychological research even if the papers did not directly address these findings, so we began with the papers by the cognitive psychologists. This volume begins in the same way for the same reason, with part I devoted to papers by cognitive psychologists. In addition to the chapters derived from conference papers, we have reprinted, as chapter 2, one of the early papers by Eleanor Rosch and Carolyn Mervis presenting now famous experimental evidence for the Wittgensteinian position that concepts have a family resemblance structure. While the paper involves a great deal of experimental detail, we wanted to include it for three reasons: first, the findings discussed here have been important for criticisms of the classical view of concepts; second, because Rosch's work on the nature of concepts has been of such importance for the development of the field; and third, it provides a taste of the type of experimental work that lies behind the psychological findings that are, in the rest of the volume, discussed and applied more abstractly.

Chapter 3, by Edward Wisniewski, is a revised version of the lead-off paper from the conference. It provides a general survey of some of the psychological results that are relevant to the nature and epistemological status of intuitive judgments. In particular, Wisniewski demonstrates how very strong intuitions can prove, in various ways, highly unreliable. Chapters 4 and 5 go into more detail regarding the two areas of research described above. Eldar Shafir, the author of chapter 4, works primarily on human reasoning and decision making. In his contribution he describes ways in which intuitive judgments—regarding, for example, the preferability of outcomes or the rationality of bets—have been found to shift systematically as a result of seemingly inconsequential manipulations. He goes on to consider some of the implications these findings about intuitive judgments might have for the stability and significance of philosophical theorizing. Chapter 5, jointly authored by a psychologist, Alison Gopnik, and philosopher, Eric Schwitzgebel, returns to issues regarding the nature of concepts. But because Gopnik, a developmental psychologist, studies the ways in which the conceptual structures of children change over time, this chapter presents a somewhat different perspective on the nature of concepts than chapter 2. In addition, Gopnik and Schwitzgebel seek to apply the psychological findings both negatively, by challenging some philosophical uses of intuition, and positively, by suggesting ways in which intuition-driven philosophical inquiry might be relevant to empirical psychology.

The chapters in part II represent work by philosophers who find the results being attained by psychologists extremely significant for philosophy and accord these results a prominent place in their own research. The result is very often a critique of either the methods or some specific conclusions of traditional philosophy. Chapter 6 reprints a paper by Stephen Stich that raises a practical epistemological question: supposing cognitive diversity is possible—that we could go about forming and revising beliefs in various ways—how should we decide among the alternatives? Stich uses empirical research on human inference to argue that reflective equilibrium cannot answer this question. He does not think analytic epistemology will fare any better, since mere conceptual analysis cannot be counted on to reveal why we should prefer those modes of conducting our cognitive affairs that our positive epistemic concepts sanction rather than those that might be approved by alternative epistemic concepts. In chapter 7, Robert Cummins criticizes reflective equilibrium as well. He argues that the authority of this method depends upon the intuitive judgments on which it relies, but that these judgments are derived from either an "explicit" theory, in which case they may be reliable (if the theory is independently supported) but are unnecessary, or a "tacit" theory, in which case their reliability is highly dubious.

Hilary Kornblith strikes a more positive tone in chapter 8. He does not hold that appeals to intuitive judgments can or should be eliminated from philosophy. Yet he is a naturalist, so he aims to show that, contrary to what Bealer (1987, 1993) and others have argued, it is possible to give a naturalistic account of the epistemology of intuitive judgments. According to Kornblith, intuitive judgments are neither a priori nor produced by some nonnatural faculty. They are instead a posteriori, corrigible, and mediated by background belief and theory. Moreover, they are properly understood as providing prima facie evidence regarding the natures of real things in the world and not merely our concepts. He suggests that we can understand intuitive judgments in philosophy as analogous to the most obvious judgments we make regarding natural kinds.

After three chapters devoted to rather general discussions of philosophical methodology, Tamara Horowitz provides a detailed consideration of a particular philosophical use of intuitive judgments in chapter 9. Her target is Warren Quinn's (1993) discussion of the Doctrine of Doing and Allowing. She argues that we should not accept Quinn's conclusion that people (perhaps tacitly) accept this moral doctrine because the intuitive judgments he relies on to support it are better explained by Prospect Theory, which was developed by Kahneman and Tversky (1979) as a general descriptive theory of decision making that was supposed to predict the decisions people actually make better than classical Expected Utility Theory.

Chapter 10 reprints a paper by Bill Ramsey that again focuses on a general aspect of philosophical practice: the effort to define significant concepts with sets of necessary and sufficient conditions that capture all our intuitive judgments applying the concepts. Ramsey reviews some of the psychological research that has challenged the view that we represent concepts by means of necessary and sufficient conditions and introduces the prototype models of concept representation that have replaced this classical view. He then argues that if the prototype models are on the right track, the efforts of philosophers to analyze significant concepts with simple sets of necessary and sufficient conditions that are immune to counterexample are doomed to fail.

In the last chapter of part II Alvin Goldman and Joel Pust consider how intuitive judgments could possibly provide evidence in support of philosophical analyses, focusing most of their attention on the claim that intuitive judgments are a basic source of prima facie evidence. In order to evaluate this claim we need to know what intuitions are supposed to provide evidence about—what, that is, philosophical analyses tell us about. Goldman and Pust consider and reject several forms of "extramentalism," which holds that philosophical analyses are concerned with some aspect of reality that is not psychological, such as universals or natural kinds. Their own view is a version of "mentalism," which holds that philosophical analyses aim to elucidate concepts construed as psychological structures. The chapter closes with a consideration of how research on concepts by cognitive psychologists could assist philosophers engaged in the project of conceptual analysis.

Part III presents work by philosophers who are more supportive of traditional philosophical methods. This part begins, in chapter 12, with George Bealer directly addressing the relation between science and philosophy. He holds that philosophy, as traditionally practiced, is in principle autonomous and that it can even have authority over science. Bealer begins by providing a detailed account of the kind of intuition that figures centrally in philosophy, which turns out not to be a species of belief or judgment. Such intuitions are not infallible, according to Bealer, but he argues that they still enjoy a strong modal tie to the truth. Specifically, he claims that theoretical systematizations of intuitions arrived at in relevantly high quality cognitive conditions will be true. We may not approximate these conditions individually, but Bealer holds that working collectively over time we can approach them.

Richard Foley questions the proper extent of intellectual self-trust in chapter 13. His investigation is carried on from the first-person or egocentric perspective, and he is concerned in particular with how a person should proceed when his or her intellectual faculties or methods have been challenged, for example, by skeptical hypotheses or by psychological research. He argues that, in the relevant cases, there is no alternative to using the very faculties and methods that have been challenged to assess the challenge and determine how to respond. Moreover, in Foley's view there is nothing epistemically inappropriate about proceeding in this apparently circular way.

In chapter 14 Ernest Sosa defends the possibility of intuitive knowledge. He begins by presenting a minimal characterization of intuition. The core idea is that intuitive propositions are those abstract propositions a person would believe merely upon fully understanding the proposition. In order to respond to the critics of intuitive knowledge, he compares intuition so characterized with perception and introspection, arguing that they have failed to establish that the epistemic status of intuition is significantly inferior to these faculties, which are generally recognized as sources of knowledge.

Chapter 15 reprints a paper by George Graham and Terry Horgan, who are perhaps more sympathetic with the criticisms of traditional philosophy than the other authors represented in this part of the book. Graham and Horgan agree that a priori conceptual analysis is dead. However, they regard this as a metaphilosophical position—an account of what it is that philosophers are doing. For the most part they find no fault either with what philosophers traditionally have done, that is, inquire into significant human concepts, or with how they have gone about doing it, specifically, by employing the method, such as reflective equilibrium, that begins with "armchair obtainable" intuitive judgments. What they seek to do, therefore, is defend a new, "postanalytic" metaphilosophy that understands traditional philosophy as a kind of empirical inquiry.

The last chapter was neither presented at the conference nor previously published. In it, Michael DePaul attempts to defend the method of reflective equilibrium while granting that this method can offer no general guarantee of either truth or likelihood of truth. Instead, DePaul focuses on what, in essence, reflective equilibrium directs inquirers to do, and what, exactly, one would have to do to follow a real alternative method of philosophical inquiry. He claims that all such alternatives are irrational, and that inquirers who adopt them must give in to a profound pessimism about themselves as intellectual beings, submit to external authority, or accept what they themselves find unacceptable.

We hope this quick outline of the chapters is sufficient to demonstrate that fundamental issues are at stake here. The outline surely also indicates that few of the fundamental questions have been resolved to everyone's satisfaction. In particular, it is interesting to note that there are serious divisions even among philosophers who fall on the same side of the divide between defenders of more traditional philosophy and those who see the recent results from cognitive psychology as having more serious implications for philosophy. Among the fundamental questions that remain unanswered, the following are surely among those that are especially important:

- What is philosophy fundamentally concerned with—real things, like knowledge and virtue, or concepts, such as our concept of knowledge or the classical Greek concept of virtue, or is it concerned with properties or universals, or something else? And if philosophy is concerned with concepts, what is the status of concepts—are they a sort of mental or psychological entity, or should they be thought of as abstract entities?

- Is philosophy an a priori discipline or is it, or should it become, a sort of empirical inquiry?

- Is it appropriate to make use of intuitions in philosophical inquiry, either in the way specified by reflective equilibrium or in some other way, or must philosophy abandon the use of intuitions entirely and set off in some new direction?

- What exactly are intuitions, in particular, are they a kind of belief, inclination to believe, or judgment, or are they some other sort of intellectual seeming, or are they something else entirely?

- Do the recent results being obtained by cognitive psychologists have significant implications for traditional philosophical methods? Or are they irrelevant because, for example, they do not concern what philosophers mean by 'concepts' or 'intuitions', or not of fundamental importance because, for example, they only show that intuition is fallible, and philosophers have known this for a long time?

It might have been nice if either the conference or this volume had managed to resolve fully all these fundamental questions, but then it would have been naive to have expected so much. As we stated above, one of our primary goals was to initiate an examination of intuitive philosophical methods that is informed by recent empirical work being done by cognitive psychologists. What is important for this purpose is that the relevant psychological background has been filled in, the significant divisions have been marked, and some of the plausible initial positions nicely presented. We hope that with this good start toward answering these fundamental questions provided by our chapter authors, others will join in the effort to find their answers.

Since the majority of the chapters in this volume were originally presented at a conference, it is appropriate that we here acknowledge those who made it possible for us to hold the conference. We received generous financial support from the College of Arts and Letters, the Institute for Scholarship in the Liberal Arts, the Philosophy Department, and the Graduate School, all at the University of Notre Dame. The actual human beings making decisions for these entities who we should thank are Harold Attridge, Jennifer Warlick, Gary Gutting, and Nathan Hatch. We also received support from both of the John A. O'Brien Chairs in Philosophy, held by Philip Quinn and Alvin Plantinga, and the I. A. O'Shaughnessey Chair, held by Michael Loux. Harriet Baldwin at the Center for Continuing Education at Notre Dame, where the conference was held, handled many of the arrangements, providing us with a very comfortable setting for the conference. Other details were arranged by Ann Pouk and Coleen Hoover at the Philosophy Department. We may at times have driven them crazy with requests, but they preserved our sanity. There were a number of people who actively participated in the conference, for example, by chairing sessions, who have not contributed chapters to this volume. Their participation certainly enhanced the quality of the discussions at the conference, and thereby indirectly the quality of this volume, and so we take this opportunity to thank: Andrea Backscheider, Marian David, Stephen Downes, Brad Gibson, John Greco, Steve Horst, Andreas Kemmerling, Helen Longino, Bill Lycan, George Pappas, Roy Sorensen, Leopold Stubenberg, Peter Van Inwagen, and Barbara von Eckardt.

Finally, we should thank a few people associated with Rowman and Littlefield. Paul Moser, the general editor of the series, Studies in Epistemology and Cognitive Theory, in which this volume appears, Robin Adler, an associate editor, and Mary Bearden, our copy editor. Paul immediately agreed with us about the significance of this project and smoothed the way towards publication. Robin dealt with numerous small matters and was very patient and encouraging as we worked through a number of delays in delivery of the final manuscript. In addition to correcting the usual number of grammatical errors, Mary saved us from a couple of larger blunders that would have compromised the content of this volume.

Introduction

Chapter 1

"Rethinking Intuition": A Historical and Metaphilosophical Introduction

Gary Gutting

I want to begin by placing this volume's discussion of philosophical intuition into a broader historical context. My history (greatly indebted, as will be apparent, to Richard Rorty) will be absurdly sketchy, but I hope the effort will lead to a better understanding of the implications of the issues discussed here.[1]

For the ancients, philosophy was the "queen of the sciences," first, crowning and synthesizing the efforts of the special sciences and, second, providing a basis for the good human life. These two functions were closely connected because knowledge of nature—particularly of human nature—was regarded as the ground for knowledge of the good; our vision of the world and of our place in it was the basis for our knowledge of how to live. (The Middle Ages, of course, brought a significant modification of the role of philosophy, which, having been trumped by divine revelation, fell to the place of "handmaid" to the new queen, theology.) The modern period was initiated by the replacement of the ancient sciences (Aristotelian physics, biology, etc.), of which philosophy had been the culmination and queen, by the new modern sciences of Galileo, Newton, Dalton, and (eventually) Darwin.

The triumph of these new sciences was quickly seen by many intellectuals— Hobbes and Descartes, for example—as the destruction of the ancient system of philosophy, what had become the philosophy of the schools. This was fundamentally because the new science, taken realistically, undermined the metaphysical heart of scholastic philosophy. The new scientific world was one merely of inert matter and mechanistic forces; a world of, to use the old terminology, material and efficient but no formal or final causes. Then, as now, this new view was most plausible for the external, material world, less so for the phenomena that we have come to call mental. Descartes initiated the modern period's efforts to come to terms with this disparity by drawing in a new way the distinction between mind and body.

Before Descartes, philosophers had typically seen the mind/body distinction as one between reason and nonreason, thus including sense perception, for example, on the side of the body rather than the mind. Descartes, in an effort to make the entire bodily realm the domain of the new mechanistic science, needed a sense of the distinction that eliminated from our understanding of "body" anything that could not be explained by this science. This led him to assign to the

mind everything intentional and phenomenal (hence all "thoughts" in his maximally extended sense of all consciousness). Later modern philosophers often
enough rejected Descartes' dualism of two substances, mind and body; but they
accepted his fundamental way of understanding the division between the mental
and the physical as one between what was conscious and what was not. Even
those who denied one or the other term of the distinction (materialists and idealists) accepted this understanding of the categories.

Descartes is the "father of modern philosophy" in the sense that his sharp division between mind and body provided the basis for the distinctively modern
view of the mind as the object of philosophical inquiry. This was a particularly
attractive approach, since, as noted above, the new mechanistic sciences seemed
quite capable of an adequate account of matter but less capable of dealing with
the mind. However, the full development of this new conception of philosophy
was not achieved for more than a century, with Kant's critical philosophy.

The development began with Locke, who, following Descartes, took the
mind as the proper domain of philosophical investigation. Locke, however, did
not himself have a clear notion of philosophy as an independent discipline. He
was inclined to see his work as the development of a mechanistic account of the
mind, a moral philosophy paralleling Newton's natural philosophy. (Similarly,
Hume aspired to be "the Newton of the moral sciences.") But at the same time,
Locke was interested in questions about the justification of knowledge, the very
questions that later (with Kant) come to define the distinctively philosophical
discipline of epistemology. The central feature of Locke's work is his collapsing
of these two interests, in mechanistic explanation and in epistemological justification, into a single conception of knowledge. On this conception, to know
something is simply for the mind to have been affected in an appropriate way by
the object known. That is, the normative state of being justified in making a
given assertion is identified with the factual state of having been casually determined in a given way. To take an example from Wilfrid Sellars, Locke would
identify *knowing* a red triangle with *having a sense impression of* a red triangle,
that is, having an image of a red triangle produced in one's mind (cf. Sellars
1967).

Locke is led to this identification because, like Aristotle and his medieval
successors, he regards knowledge as fundamentally of an object rather than of a
proposition (knowing *a* rather than knowing that *a* is *B*). To know a proposition
is a matter of being *justified* in making various assertions, and knowledge in this
sense is not readily identified with being causally determined in a certain way.
Such an identification would seem to involve, as Sellars remarks, an epistemological version of the naturalistic fallacy (cf. Sellars 1963a). But to know an
object is presumably a matter of being somehow related to it, and it is natural to
regard this relation as a matter of some sort of causality. For Aristotle the
causality was formal; the mind "became" (assumed the intentional form of) the
object. But for Locke, who was trying to sustain a mechanistic picture of the
mind, the causality could be only efficient, a matter of the object somehow making an "impression" on the mind.

With Locke, then, the Cartesian mind emerges as the locus of the fledgling
discipline of epistemology, the philosophical study of knowledge. The mental

was the domain of certainty (indubitability), since we could, as Descartes pointed out, be entirely sure about the contents of our mind. Accordingly, these contents were the obvious starting point for the effort to build an entirely reliable body of knowledge, a project enjoined by the desire to overcome the skepticism about established truths encouraged by Renaissance humanists such as Montaigne and by the modern revolutions in science and religion. The great problem was to move from the mind's certainty about itself to knowledge of things outside it. Here, according to Rorty, epistemology is based on, first, Descartes' assumption that knowledge of the external world is a matter of having mental representations that accurately picture that world and on Locke's assumption that the accuracy of a representation depends on the manner of its causal production.

But these assumptions, at least as they were understood by the standard empiricist and rationalist accounts of knowledge that followed Locke, found no way of guaranteeing the accuracy of our mental representations of extra-mental reality and avoiding the skeptical conclusion that we are trapped behind a "veil of ideas." It was Kant's frustration with this failure that led to his Copernican Revolution. The two assumptions of truth as representation and of origin as guarantee of accurate representation continue in Kant's account, but in an inverted and transformed manner. Our ideas (of space, time, substance, causality) accurately represent the world not because they are causally produced by the world, but because they themselves are necessary conditions of the mind's noncausal production ("constitution") of the world as an object of knowledge. Knowledge of this constitution and its conditions is unproblematic in view of Descartes' assumption of the mind's privileged access to itself.

The key to Kant's approach is his distinction between two types of mental representations: concepts and intuitions. He saw his predecessors as either empiricists, who tried to reduce concepts (generalized ideas) to intuitions (immediate sense impressions) or rationalists, who tried to reduce intuitions to concepts. Both, he maintained, failed to realize that an experience of an object requires both conceptual and intuitive elements; the conceptual providing the framework of intelligibility without which the object could not be presented, and the intuitive providing the content without which the framework would be merely an empty scheme. The answer to the defining question of epistemology, How can our representations accurately represent objects?, was that the very meaning of "object" (at least in the crucial context of empirical knowledge) requires that an object be properly correlated with the mind's rules for forming representations of it.

Kant restored philosophy to an autonomous and privileged position in the domain of knowledge. Every other type of knowledge presupposed the conceptual (analytic or synthetic a priori) truths to which philosophy alone had access. Moreover, only the conceptual truths of philosophy could be known with the maximal certainty of direct intellectual insight. Philosophy is no longer, as in ancient times, the *culmination* of human knowing. But it is the *foundation* of human knowing, providing the ultimate justification of all epistemic claims and adjudicating conflicts between rival bodies of alleged knowledge.

Kant's Copernican Revolution did not provide a generally accepted solution to the problem of knowledge. But it did establish that problem as the defining issue of philosophy as a modern discipline in its own right. It did this by con-

vincing subsequent thinkers that an adequate account of knowledge required an irreducible distinction between general conceptual structures and specific experiential content. Such a distinction provided the basis for philosophy as an autonomous discipline; that is, a discipline with the task of delineating the mind's
general conceptual structures and explaining how they combined with experiential content to produce knowledge. The privileged status of philosophy was guaranteed by a sharp distinction between the a priori knowledge proper to it and the
a posteriori knowledge of empirical science. Philosophers after Kant frequently
rejected his conception of philosophy as the domain of transcendental truths necessary for any possible experience. But, in one way or another, they all preserved
a distinction of kinds of knowledge that provided philosophy with a privileged
access to a domain of foundational truth. Thus, idealists distinguished the necessary from the contingent, positivists the analytic from the synthetic. All modern
epistemologies are based on a division between knowledge in its formal, structural dimension and knowledge in its material, contentual dimension, with the
former always the domain of the philosopher.

Recent twentieth-century philosophy has severely challenged these epistemologies and, in so doing, has questioned every distinction supporting a distinctive domain and methodology for philosophical inquiry. Philosophers claiming
to have special access to a body of analytic truths have been confronted by
Quine's critique of the analytic-synthetic distinction; those proposing to logically construct knowledge from basic sensory givens have encountered Sellars's
critique of the theory-observation distinction; those hoping to make philosophy
an investigation of the a priori conceptual schemes through which we experience
the world have met Davidson's rejection of the scheme-content distinction. These
critiques have not decisively eliminated the possibility of a distinctive philosophical access to truth. But they have made most philosophers far more uneasy
and hesitant about the intellectual tools they have used and have led many
philosophers to see their discipline as much more closely tied (if not assimilable
to) empirical scientific inquiry.

As the chapters in this volume show, these issues can be very effectively
formulated in terms of the problem of philosophical intuition. The traditional
ideal, from Platonic noesis through Cartesian clear and distinct perception to
positivist sense data reports, has been to ground core philosophical truths in
some sort of self-justifying intuitive insight. Much of our contemporary lack of
philosophical confidence is the ultimate outcome of the scientific revolution,
from which we learned that our intuitions about nature (allegedly insights into
the essences of things) often told us more about ourselves than about the world,
and that genuine access to the natural world required methodical empirical testing
that frequently refuted our "insights." The subsequent history of philosophy was
a matter of our coming to see, both historically and analytically, that intuitions
about the nonphysical realm (introspection, conceptual analysis, etc.) were similarly questionable. Analytic philosophy had begun with a rejection of intuition
in the sense of special intellectual insights into reality. The positivists spoke
not of intuitions but of analytic truths about meanings or the incorrigible givens
of sense experience. But, in the wake of devastating critiques of analyticity and
of the myth of the given, analytic philosophers have begun to speak once again

of intuitions, now meaning simply the rock-bottom beliefs they find themselves forced to take as basic in their search for philosophical truth. This is apparent in the widespread acceptance of "reflective equilibrium" (explicitly formulated by Goodman and Rawls) as the method of analytic philosophy. This method simply codifies the fact that we have no alternative to beginning with our own de facto intuitions, even though they have no certification beyond our inability to get past them.[2]

In contemporary analytic discussions, as represented, for example, in this volume, "intuition" has become the name for whatever it is that might provide philosophy with a distinctive method and hence preserve it as a separate (in principle) intellectual domain. Our disagreement about the nature and epistemic authority of intuitions is at root a battle for the preservation of philosophy as an autonomous field of inquiry. In the following chapters, the lines of engagement have been drawn up under the banners of "Naturalism" and "Antinaturalism." Naturalists such as Kornblith and Cummins (and perhaps Horowitz), aided by cognitive psychologists such as Wisniewski, Gopnik, and Shafir argue that philosophical intuitions provide no distinctive access to reality, while antinaturalists such as Sosa and Bealer (and perhaps Foley), with somewhat ambivalent support from Goldman and Pust, maintain that philosophical intuitions support an essentially nonempirical domain of knowledge.

It is obvious that, whatever the ultimate strength of the antinaturalists' position, they have retreated significantly from that held by their classical modern predecessors. In the past, intuition was unabashedly presented as a form of direct knowledge, indeed, knowledge that provided its own cognitive authority and typically possessed the highest possible level of certainty. Our antinaturalists characterize intuitions as "propositional attitudes" (Bealer), "spontaneous judgments" (Goldman and Pust), "noninferential beliefs" (Sosa) that at best provide preliminary data in need of further scrutiny and testing to yield knowledge. Intuitions range from little more than hunches to at most expert opinions on disputed issues. Given this diminished conception of philosophical intuition, there is little talk of epistemic privilege or of philosophy as ground and judge for the claims of other disciplines. Even if the antinaturalists are able to vindicate philosophy as an autonomous discipline, it will be a philosophy much chastened and withdrawn from its traditional pretensions.

For their part, the naturalists in our volume are uncharacteristically coy about the meta-philosophical significance of their position. Kornblith concludes that "philosophy is continuous with the sciences" but assures us that it remains "an autonomous discipline." Cummins tells us that "philosophical intuition is epistemologically useless" but adds that "there is some hope for a philosophy without intuition." But on the naturalists' account, there are no philosophical topics that cannot be fruitfully investigated by the empirical sciences and no distinctive contribution that philosophy can bring to any such topic. This is no doubt consistent with the term "philosopher" continuing to denote a sociological class of the intelligentsia; it might, for example, be used to refer to people working at the very highest levels of abstract theorizing or people with a particular interest in interdisciplinary speculations. But it is not consistent with the survival of the search for philosophical truth in anything like the sense that the philosophers of the great tradition from Plato to Kant understood it.

To emphasize what is at stake in this naturalist/antinaturalist debate, let me return to some historical reflections. Our current arguments about intuition in many ways parallel arguments in the seventeenth century about the significance of Aristotelian natural philosophy in the face of the success of the new Galilean and Newtonian physics. Then, of course, the dispute was about our efforts to know the external material world. There were those who maintained that empirical science could not provide all our knowledge of this world and would have to be supplemented by philosophical insights into the essential natures of material bodies. There were also those who maintained that there was no room for any knowledge of nature other than that of the new empirical sciences. The latter won the argument, but the view of the former was revived for the domain of the mind by the emergence, sketched above, of classical modern philosophy. Now, with the increasing success of empirical psychology and social science, we are having a similar dispute, this time over the mental rather than the physical domain. The naturalists have taken the place of the proponents of Galilean science and the antinaturalists of the Aristotelian natural philosophers. The issue is, once again, the possibility of autonomous philosophical inquiry in a domain increasingly dominated by a new empirical science.

I draw this parallel not to suggest that the outcome will be the same this time, but to show just how high the stakes are in our current discussions of the nature and role of philosophical intuition. There is, indeed, at least one major disanalogy between our present situation and that of the seventeenth century. A major part of the eventual triumph of the new natural science was its astounding predictive and explanatory fruitfulness, which provided an overwhelming impetus for a realistic interpretation of its basic theoretical categories. The psychological and social sciences have shown no comparable theoretical power, a fact that may well hold us back from accepting the completeness of their descriptions. Moreover, we should recall that, even after philosophy's exclusion from our understanding of nature, it eventually discovered (or created), in the two hundred years from Descartes to Kant, a new domain where it could exercise hegemony. Even assuming a total triumph of the empirical sciences of the mind, philosophy might once again transform itself into a new, autonomous form—for example, as our only access to normative truths. But it might not. The discussions of this volume are at root about whether analytic philosophy will suffer the fate of Aristotelian natural philosophy.

This introduction is hardly the place for a definitive answer to so heady a question. But I would like to offer some positive suggestions about how we might defend the irreducible role of philosophical analysis of intuitions in intellectual culture.

As I see it, despite their admittedly questionable status, intuitions still have a fundamental place in philosophy—indeed, in any effort to understand ourselves and our world. They represent the inevitable starting point of any intellectual inquiry. Analytic philosophy, construed as the effort to attain maximum clarity regarding the content and basis of our intuitions, is essential not as a final determinant of truth but as a preliminary grasp of the precise nature of our starting point.[3] I want to insist on this essential role for analytic philosophy, while at the same time maintaining that our intuitions require not only analytic clarification but also evaluation in light of the historical processes that have produced them.

This last point can perhaps be made most effectively in terms of the "problems" that define the contemporary analytic project. Analytic philosophers accept as given a set of canonical philosophical problems (mind-body, free will/determinism, the existence of God, the nature of moral judgments, etc.), that they set out to solve (or dissolve) through a combination of conceptual analysis and logical argument. I would interrupt this project before it begins by suggesting that there may be nothing at all privileged about the problems from which analytic philosophers begin, that they may be just the residue of contingent turns of past thought. More specifically, I would suggest that some problems pose themselves only because we have unwittingly accepted assumptions (e.g., a certain picture of the mind, a conception of freedom, norms of rational acceptability) that are by no means inevitable but merely reflect a heritage from our philosophical past. Analytic philosophers may suggest that any questionable assumptions present at the beginning of their discussions will be unearthed in the process of analysis and argument. But without explicit reflection on historical origins, many assumptions are likely to go unnoticed. Moreover, even if unearthed by other means, many assumptions will still appear inevitable unless compared to alternatives provided by a historical sensibility.[4]

This historical sensibility requires a new conception of philosophical problems. According to this conception: (1) problems vary from period to period in the history of thought; (2) there is no privileged position for the problems and solutions central for contemporary philosophical inquiry; and (3) an understanding of the nature and significance of contemporary problems requires appreciating their historical origin. Analytic alternatives to this view either deny (1) or, if they accept it, maintain, contrary to (2), that contemporary problematics have superseded the halting formulations and pseudo-problems of the past. In either case, a denial of (3) follows immediately. Contemporary analytic philosophers typically take a Whiggish and heuristic view of the philosophical past. The Whig either accepts (1) but holds that contemporary formulations and solutions are clearly superior to those of earlier philosophers; or else denies both (1) and (2), holding that contemporary problematics best state the real philosophical issues, avoiding the murky formulations or out-and-out pseudo-problems of the past. The heuristic view allows that studying the past may sometimes suggest something worthwhile to our philosophical reflections, but that there is no special requirement that successful philosophical thought be based on an understanding of the history of philosophy.[5] What we in fact need is a history of philosophy that is neither Whiggish nor merely heuristic.

But limited or misleading as historical critique may show them to be, our intuitions remain an inevitable starting point for any intellectual inquiry. Accordingly, historical critiques cannot aim at eliminating intuitions, only at correcting them. Since the process of correction requires the best possible understanding of the intuitions to be corrected, we require their detailed articulation through analysis and argument. Thus, all inquiry requires a continuing process of philosophical analysis; but this process must itself be continuously monitored and evaluated by historical reflection. Philosophical achievement is the product of an enterprise defined by these two irreducible and ineliminable moments.[6]

We should, then, by no means reject the standard projects of analytic philosophy. We should recognize their legitimacy and, indeed, their essential place in the overall enterprise of human knowing. But, at the same time, we need to insist that ahistorical analysis cannot be the whole of philosophy. It must be complemented by historical reflection on the significance of analytic results. Ordinarily, we can distinguish a discipline from the history of the discipline. But philosophy, as Hegel emphasized, must include its own history.

The above endorsement of intuitions and of the analytic philosophy that clarifies them requires, however, detaching philosophy's clarificatory function from grandiose traditional projects of providing rigorous philosophical answers to deep questions about human existence. Such projects, originating with Plato, are misguided efforts to find a truth that goes beyond the contingent consensus of whatever intellectual conversations our history has led us to. This is not to say that we cannot responsibly formulate and defend views on the great Platonic question of how we should live. But it is wrongheaded to try to ground such ethical views in fundamental truths about human nature and its place in the cosmic scheme or to suggest that the lack of such a grounding would or should weaken our ethical commitment to our ideals. We can (and should) endorse and encourage analytic philosophy, as long as it does not claim any privileged access to truth and is willing to take its place with everyone else at the conversational roundtable. Once we have demystified the pretensions of philosophical privilege, we can recognize the distinctive though not dominating contribution of philosophy to our continuing conversation.

The project of analytic philosophy contrasts with that of "continental" thinkers, who are concerned more with creating new languages for describing the human condition than offering (analytic) explications of the entrenched languages.[7] This creative impulse is an essential counterpart to analytic philosophy. Whereas the baseline of analytic philosophy is the commonsense intuitions it subjects to conceptual and historical critique but ultimately accepts as normative, the project of continental philosophy looks for ways to move us beyond or beneath common sense. Continental creativity is based on a rejection of the analytic idea of philosophy as the discovery, elucidation, and correction of our fundamental intuitions.[8] As a result, continental philosophy is typically sexier than analytic, promising the excitement of novelty and iconoclasm. This very feature is also responsible for the continentalists' characteristic weakness of pretentious obscurity. When the effort to move creatively beyond old categories fails, as it usually does, the result may well be little more than self-important gibberish or, marginally better, an excruciating restatement of the obvious. Correspondingly, analytic philosophy's characteristic faults are the plodding clarity and misplaced rigor of someone who, in a glorious meadow that calls for exuberant roaming, crawls along as through a minefield.[9] The universalist aspirations of some philosophical souls will always lead them to the precarious enterprise of keeping a foot in both the continental and the analytic domains; and there is no doubt that both projects are important for our flourishing. But, at least as things stand for now, the two are best left to develop in their own terms, unimpeded by fruitless efforts of synthesis.

But let us return to the status of analytic philosophy as an autonomous intellectual enterprise. As noted above, contemporary challenges to the autonomy of philosophy have typically been mounted in terms of a thoroughgoing methodological naturalism—the view that philosophy has no cognitive resources beyond those of empirical science and should simply be regarded as a subdivision of science.[10] The most recent revival of this view began with Quine's heralding of a "naturalized epistemology" that is simply part of empirical psychology. He has been followed by many others, trained in philosophy Ph.D. programs, who see themselves as contributors to, say, quantum field theory, theoretical genetics, or cognitive science, more than philosophy as a distinct, autonomous discipline.

The view of philosophy I have been sketching suggests an effective response to methodological naturalism. To philosophize is to engage in the critique of intuitively given concepts and beliefs through analytic and/or historical reflection. Natural science has little use for either sort of reflection, first, because it has in most cases developed far beyond the intuitive common sense for which such reflection is a relevant critique and, second, because empirical testing provides a much more effective means of flushing out hidden defects in scientific conceptions.[11] Those with strong naturalist inclinations are free to give up thinking about issues that do not admit of rigorous empirical treatment. But doing so will not eliminate the body of traditionally philosophical issues that cannot be so treated, nor the general human need to engage such issues. Those of us unable or unwilling to suppress this need have no alternative but distinctively philosophical reflection.

A skeptical reader may ask why I would want to continue discussing issues that, by my own admission, we have no prospects of resolving. But my claim is not that there can be no significant progress on (or even perhaps relatively final solutions of) fundamental metaphysical, epistemological, and ethical questions.[12] My negative view of traditional philosophy concerns only claims—made by no means by all traditional philosophers—to have access to a special domain of truth and reality through distinctively philosophical modes of insight or argumentation. Such claims themselves are based on substantive metaphysical and epistemological assumptions about which we are properly skeptical. Analytic philosophers make a distinctive contribution to our grasp of fundamental human issues through the rigorous conceptual analysis and argument that elucidates the intuitive starting points of our thought. Continental philosophers provide creative alternatives to our standard modes of thought. Within both these groups, philosophy provides a unique self-reflective access to the history of past philosophical efforts as well as that distinctively philosophical synthetic vision of, in Sellars's famous phrase, "how things in the most general sense of the term, hang together, in the most general sense of the term." None of this places philosophers at the head of our intellectual table, but it does provide them with a distinctive and essential voice in the conversation.

Notes

1. Rorty 1979. For readers who are particularly sensitive historically, here is a brief defense of the high-flying Rortyan history I sketch. Rorty's approach (and my adaptation of it) does not fit neatly into either of the two standard categories of historical reconstruction or rational reconstruction. (For this distinction, see Rorty's essay in the volume cited below in note 4.) It is not, like rational reconstruction, an effort to scan the philosophical past for contributions relevant to contemporary problematics. For such an enterprise, the starting point is our own understanding of the relevant issues; and the great thinkers of the past are admitted to our discussions only to the extent that they say something we can appropriate for our own purposes. Rorty, by contrast, employs history to question the fundamental presuppositions of contemporary problematics. At the same time, Rorty is not involved in the historical reconstructionist's enterprise of seeking a faithful presentation of past philosophers' ideas in their own terms, responding out of their unique cultural context to the precise issues they saw as fundamental. Rorty's history tries rather to uncover just those aspects of the past (and our standard interpretations of it) that are relevant to understanding the nature and limits of current philosophizing. Its goal then is neither to understand what past philosophers thought in their own terms nor to discover timeless philosophical truths. The enterprise is rather a variety of what Foucault has called "history of the present": the illumination and critique of current views and practices by tracing relevant historical lines back to their origins. It is, therefore, not surprising that historians of modern philosophy have been highly critical of Rorty's account. But whatever its inadequacies as a rigorous historical reconstruction of individual thinkers, it is very plausible as an understanding and critique of the way many contemporary readers of modern philosophy have interpreted its overall thrust.

2. Saul Kripke holds an even stronger view: "Some philosophers think that something's having intuitive content is very inconclusive evidence in favor of it. I think it is very heavy evidence in favor of anything, myself. I really don't know, in a way, what more conclusive evidence one can have about anything, ultimately speaking" (Kripke 1972: 42).

3. The dangers of clarity are well-expressed by Proust's comment on his fictional author Bergotte: "his ideas seemed as often as not to be confused, for each of us sees clarity only in those ideas which have the same degree of confusion as his own" (Proust 1992: 171). But while clarity may not at all signal the truth, it is always necessary to show just where we may be going wrong. In the same vein, as Charles Larmore points out, without clarity, we close our ideas off from the criticism of others. See his excellent discussion of clarity in (Larmore 1996: 14-16).

4. There is no need to maintain anything more than the de facto usefulness of historical studies and the practical likelihood that, without them, we will continue to miss questionable assumptions in our philosophizing. Richard Rorty, Alasdair MacIntyre, and Charles Taylor have all tried to develop cases in principle for the necessity of historical reflection. Cf. their essays in Rorty, Schneewind, and Skinner 1984. To my mind, none of these cases are successful.

5. A currently less popular antihistoricist view is philosophical nostalgia (particularly associated with neo-scholasticism). This denies (1) and accepts (2); but it accepts (2) only because it holds that all major problems have already been

solved—or, at least, that a framework for the solution has been provided—by some great philosopher of the past.

6. We should, indeed, notice that we have arrived at this characterization by just such a historical reflection on the development of analytic philosophizing. Also, these two moments do not exhaust the philosophical enterprise, since it also includes the more creative efforts of continental philosophy, mentioned below.

7. Here I have in mind not the entire sweep of European philosophy during the twentieth century but only the radical form it eventually took in the late Heidegger and the French poststructuralists. Had this radical turn not occurred, the earlier continental/analytic division, between positivism and classical phenomenology, might well have been bridged, once positivists broadened their notion of experience and structuralism moved phenomenologists away from literary existentialism. The split became definitive only with the outright rejection by the poststructuralists of elucidation of commonsense intuitions in favor of the creation of new vocabularies. This rejection constitutes an unbridgeable gap between contemporary continental and analytic philosophizing.

8. Of course my comments here provide only an absurdly over-generalized account of recent continental philosophy. I think it is true of major figures such as Heidegger, Derrida, and Foucault, but hardly a complete characterization of their fundamental projects. In each case, my general account would have to be supplemented with the use the individual philosopher makes of his conceptual creations. In the case of Heidegger, for example, the goal seems to be to wean us away from the old categories of philosophical thought with the hope that this will prepare us for some as yet unconceived new way of thinking. For Derrida, the point seems rather to be the continual undermining of traditional categories to which, however, we have no hope of alternatives but can only keep playing against one another. Foucault, in quite a different vein, subordinates all of his creative philosophical constructions to specific enterprises of human liberation. There are, moreover, moments when all three of these philosophers appear to slip back into the old Platonic project. There is Heidegger's taking on the role of the vehicle of Being's speech, Derrida's hypostatization of différance, and Foucault's privileging of the vision of the mad. But in all such cases, critics rightly see such tendencies as relapses, inconsistent with the primary thrust of the philosopher's anti-Platonic thought.

9. There is, however, more room than what I have said so far might suggest for novelty and creativity in the analytic domain. Granted that the analyst by definition begins from a framework defined by some "obvious" intuitive givens, it is also true that, upon analysis, such givens may conflict with one another and require, for the sake of consistency, strikingly counterintuitive adjustments. (Thus Kripke is led to bizarre views on the existence of unicorns and David Lewis to amazing claims about possible worlds.) Analytic philosophy thus has its own form of creativity, even though it will always be less radical than that of continental thought.

10. I would prefer to call this view "methodological scientism," since it insists on reducing philosophy to empirical science. As I see it, the view of analytic philosophy I endorse more deserves the label "methodological naturalism." Unfortunately, the terminology of the discussion is already fixed.

11. Empirical testing is not, however, sovereign against every undetected flaw in a theory. There may, for example, be implicit assumptions that prevent us from undertaking relevant tests. In such cases, science itself may need something like philosophical reflection.

12. For more on the question of philosophical progress, see Gutting 1982.

Part I

Psychological Research on Intuitive Judgments

Chapter 2

Family Resemblances: Studies in the Internal Structure of Categories

Eleanor Rosch and Carolyn B. Mervis

As speakers of our language and members of our culture, we know that a chair is a more reasonable exemplar of the category *furniture* than a radio, and that some chairs fit our idea or image of a chair better than others. However, when describing categories analytically, most traditions of thought have treated category membership as a digital, all-or-none phenomenon. That is, much work in philosophy, psychology, linguistics, and anthropology assumes that categories are logical bounded entities, membership in which is defined by an item's possession of a simple set of criterial features, in which all instances possessing the criterial attributes have a full and equal degree of membership.

In contrast to such a view, it has been recently argued (see Lakoff 1972; Rosch 1973; Zadeh 1965) that some natural categories are analog and must be represented logically in a manner that reflects their analog structure. Rosch (1973, 1975b) has further characterized some natural analog categories as internally structured into a prototype (clearest cases, best examples of the category) and nonprototype members, with nonprototype members tending toward an order from better to poorer examples. While the domain for which such a claim has been demonstrated most unequivocally is that of color (Berlin and Kay 1969; Heider 1971, 1972; Mervis, Catlin, and Rosch 1975; Rosch, 1974, 1975a, 1977), there is also considerable evidence that natural superordinate semantic categories have a prototype structure. Subjects can reliably rate the extent to which a member of a category fits their idea or image of the meaning of the category name (Rosch 1973, 1975a), and such ratings predict performance in a number of tasks (Rips, Shoben, and Smith 1973; Rosch, 1973, 1975a, 1975b, 1977; Smith, Rips, and Shoben 1974; Smith, Shoben, and Rips 1974).

However, there has, as yet, been little attention given to the problem of how internal structure arises. That is, what principles govern the formation of category prototypes and gradients of category membership? For some categories that probably have a physiological basis, such as colors, forms, and facial expressions of basic human emotions, prototypes may be stimuli that are salient prior to formation of the category, whose salience, at the outset, determines the categorical structuring of those domains (Ekman 1971; McDaniel 1972; Rosch 1974, 1975b). For the artificial categories that have been used in prototype research—such as families of dot patterns (Posner 1973) and artificial faces (Reed

1972)—the categories have been intentionally structured and/or the prototypes have been defined so that the prototypes were central tendencies of the categories. For most domains, however, prototypes do not appear to precede the category (Rosch 1976) and must be formed through principles of learning and information processing from the items given in the category. The present research was not intended to provide a processing model of the learning of categories or formation of prototypes; rather, our intention was to examine the stimulus relations which underlie such learning. That is, the purpose of the present research was to explore one of the major *structural* principles which, we believe, may govern the formation of the prototype structure of semantic categories.

This principle was first suggested in philosophy; Wittgenstein (1953) argued that the referents of a word need not have common elements in order for the word to be understood and used in the normal functioning of language. He suggested that, rather, a family resemblance might be what linked the various referents of a word. A family resemblance relationship consists of a set of items of the form AB, BC, CD, DE. That is, each item has at least one, and probably several, elements in common with one or more other items, but no, or few, elements are common to all items. The existence of such relationships in actual natural language categories has not previously been investigated empirically.

In the present research, we viewed natural semantic categories as networks of overlapping attributes; the basic hypothesis was that members of a category come to be viewed as prototypical of the category as a whole in proportion to the extent to which they bear a family resemblance to (have attributes which overlap those of) other members of the category. Conversely, items viewed as most prototypical of one category will be those with least family resemblance to or membership in other categories. In natural categories of concrete objects, the two aspects of family resemblance should coincide rather than conflict since it is reasonable that categories tend to become organized in such a way that they reflect the correlational structure of the environment in a manner that renders them maximally discriminable from each other (Rosch 1976; Rosch et al. 1976).

The present structural hypothesis is closely related to a *cue validity* processing model of classification in which the validity of a cue is defined in terms of its total frequency within a category and its proportional frequency in that category relative to contrasting categories. Mathematically, cue validity has been defined as a conditional probability—specifically, the frequency of a cue being associated with the category in question divided by the total frequency of that cue over all relevant categories (Beach 1964; Reed 1972). Unfortunately, cue validity has been treated as a model in conflict with a prototype model of category processing where prototypes are operationally defined solely as attribute means (Reed 1972). If prototypes are defined more broadly—for example, as the abstract representation of a category, or as those category members to which subjects compare items when judging category membership, or as the internal structure of the category defined by the subjects' judgments of the degree to which members fit their "idea or image" of the category—then prototypes should coincide rather than conflict with cue validity. That is, if natural categories of concrete objects tend to become organized so as to render the categories maximally discriminable from one another, it follows that the maximum possible cue validity of items within each category will be attained (Rosch et al. 1976). The principle of family resemblance relationships can be restated in terms of cue validity since the attributes most distributed among members of a category and least distributed among members of contrasting categories are, by definition, the most valid cues to membership in the category in question. We use the term *family resemblance* rather than *cue validity* primarily to emphasize that we are dealing with a description of structural principles and not with a processing model. We believe that the principle of family resemblance relationships is a very general one and is applicable to categories regardless of whether they have features common to members of the category or formal criteria for category membership.

In all of the studies of the present research, family resemblances were defined in terms of discrete attributes such as *has legs, you drive it,* or *the letter B is a member.* These are the kinds of features of natural semantic categories that can be most readily reported and the features normally used in definitions of categories by means of lists of formal criteria. Insofar as the context in which an attribute occurs as part of a stimulus may always affect perception and understanding of the attribute, discrete attributes of this type may be an analytic myth. However, in one sense, the purpose of the present research was to show that it is not necessary to invoke attribute interactions or higher-order gestalt properties of stimuli (such as those used by Posner 1973; Reed 1972; Rosch, Simpson, and Miller 1976) in order to analyze the prototype structure of categories. That is, even at the level of analysis of the type of discrete attributes normally used in definitions of categories by means of criterial features, we believe there is a principle of the structure of stimulus sets, family resemblances, that can be shown to underlie category prototype structure.

The present chapter reports studies using three different types of category; superordinate semantic categories such as *furniture* and *vehicle*, basic level semantic categories such as *chair* and *car*, and artificial categories formed from sets of letter strings. For each type of stimulus, both aspects of the family resemblance hypothesis (that the most prototypical members of categories are those with most attributes in common with other members of that category and are those with least attributes in common with other categories) were tested.

Superordinate semantic categories are of particular interest because they are sufficiently abstract that they have few, if any, attributes common to all members (Rosch et al. 1976). Thus, such categories may consist almost entirely of items related to each other by means of family resemblances of overlapping attributes. In addition, superordinate categories have the advantage that their membership consists of a finite number of names of basic level categories that can be adequately sampled. Superordinate categories have the disadvantage that they do not have contrasting categories (operationally defined below); thus, the second half of the family resemblance hypothesis (that prototypical members of categories have least resemblance to other categories) had to be tested indirectly by measuring membership in, rather than attributes in common with, other superordinate categories.

Basic level semantic categories are of great interest because they are the level of abstraction at which the basic category cuts in the world may be made (Rosch 1976; Rosch et al. 1976). However, basic level categories present a sampling problem since their membership consists of an infinite number of objects. On the positive side, basic level categories do form contrast sets, thus, making possible a direct test of the second part of the family resemblance hypothesis.

Artificial categories were needed because they made possible the study of prototype formation with adequate controls. In natural language domains of any type, categories have long since evolved in culture and been learned by subjects. Both prototypes and the attribute structure of categories are independent variables; we can only measure their correlations. Artificial categories are of use because attribute structures can be varied in a controlled manner and the development of prototypes studied as a dependent variable.

Part I. Superordinate Semantic Categories

Experiment 1

Although it is always possible for an ingenious philosopher or psychologist to invent criterial attributes defining a category, earlier research has shown that actual subjects rate superordinate semantic categories as having few, if any, attributes common to all members (Rosch et al. 1976). Thus, if the "categorical" nature of these categories is to be explained, it appeared most likely to reside in family resemblances between members. Part of the purpose of the present experiment was to obtain portraits of the distribution of attributes of members of a number of superordinate natural language categories. Part of the hypothesis was that category members would prove to bear a family resemblance relationship to each other. The major purpose of the experiment, however, was to observe the relation between degree of relatedness between members of the category and the rated prototypicality of those members. The specific hypothesis was that a measure of the degree to which an item bore a family resemblance to other members of the category would prove significantly correlated with previously obtained prototypicality ratings of the members of the category.

Method

Subjects. Subjects were 400 students in introductory psychology classes who received this ten-minute task as part of their classroom work.

Stimuli. The categories used were the six most common categories of concrete nouns in English, determined by a measure of word frequency (Kucera and Francis 1967). All of the categories were ones for which norms for the prototypicality of items had already been obtained for fifty to sixty category members (Rosch 1975a). These norms were derived from subjects' ratings of the extent to which each item fit their "idea or image" of the meaning of the category name. (The rating task and instructions were very similar to those used in Experiment 3 of the present research. A complete account of the methods for deriving the six superordinate categories and complete norms for all items of the six categories are provided in Rosch 1975a.) The twenty items from each category used in the present experiment were chosen to represent the full range of goodness-of-example ranks. These items are listed, in their goodness-of-example order, in table 2.1.

Procedure. Each of the 120 items shown in table 2.1 was printed at the top of a page, and the pages assembled into packets consisting of six items, one from each superordinate category. Items were chosen randomly within a category such that each subject who received an item received it with different items from the other five categories and received the items representing each category in a different order. Each item was rated by twenty subjects. Each subject rated six items, one from each category.

Subjects were asked to list the attributes possessed by each item. Instructions were:

> This is a very simple experiment to find out the characteristics and attributes that people feel are common to and characteristic of different kinds of ordinary everyday objects. For example, for *bicycles* you might think of things they have in common like two wheels, pedals, handlebars, you ride on them, they don't use fuel, etc. For *dogs* you might think of things they have in common like having four legs, barking, having fur, etc.
>
> There are six pages following this one. At the top of each is listed the name of one common object. For each page, you'll have a minute and a half to write down all of the attributes of that object that you can think of. But try not to *just* free associate—for example, if bicycles just happen to remind you of your father, *don't* write down *father*.
>
> Okay—you'll have a minute and a half for each page. When I say turn to the next page, read the name of the object and write down the attributes or characteristics you think are characteristic of that object as fast as you can until you're told to turn the page again.

Measurement of family resemblance. To derive the basic measure of family resemblance, for each category, all attributes mentioned by subjects were listed and each item, for which an attribute had been listed, was credited with that attribute. Two judges reviewed the resulting table and indicated cases in which an attribute was clearly and obviously false. These attributes were deleted from the tabulation. The judges also indicated any attribute that had been listed for one or more items, but was clearly and obviously true of another item in the category for which it had not happened to be listed by any of the twenty subjects. These items were also credited with the relevant attribute. Judges were not permitted to list new attributes, and no item was credited with an attribute about which judges disagreed or about which either judge was uncertain. The total changes made by the judges were infrequent.

Each attribute received a score, ranging from 1 to 20, representing the number of items in the category that had been credited with that attribute. By this means, each attribute was weighted in accordance with the number of items in the category possessing it. The basic measure of degree of family resemblance for an item was the sum of the weighted scores of each of the attributes that had been listed for that item.

This basic measure of family resemblance possessed a source of potential distortion, however. In the measure, each additional item with which an attribute

Table 2.1

Superordinate categories and items used in Experiments 1 and 2.

Category

Item	Furniture	Vehicle	Fruit	Weapon	Vegetable	Clothing
1	Chair	Car	Orange	Gun	Peas	Pants
2	Sofa	Truck	Apple	Knife	Carrots	Shirt
3	Table	Bus	Banana	Sword	String beans	Dress
4	Dresser	Motorcycle	Peach	Bomb	Spinach	Skirt
5	Desk	Train	Pear	Hand grenade	Broccoli	Jacket
6	Bed	Trolley car	Apricot	Spear	Asparagus	Coat
7	Bookcase	Bicycle	Plum	Cannon	Corn	Sweater
8	Footstool	Airplane	Grapes	Bow and arrow	Cauliflower	Underpants
9	Lamp	Boat	Strawberry	Club	Brussel sprouts	Socks
10	Piano	Tractor	Grapefruit	Tank	Lettuce	Pajamas
11	Cushion	Cart	Pineapple	Teargas	Beets	Bathing suit
12	Mirror	Wheelchair	Blueberry	Whip	Tomato	Shoes
13	Rug	Tank	Lemon	Icepick	Lima beans	Vest
14	Radio	Raft	Watermelon	Fists	Eggplant	Tie
15	Stove	Sled	Honeydew	Rocket	Onion	Mittens
16	Clock	Horse	Pomegranate	Poison	Potato	Hat
17	Picture	Blimp	Date	Scissors	Yam	Apron
18	Closet	Skates	Coconut	Words	Mushroom	Purse
19	Vase	Wheelbarrow	Tomato	Foot	Pumpkin	Wristwatch
20	Telephone	Elevator	Olive	Screwdriver	Rice	Necklace

was credited added an equal increment of family resemblance. Thus, the measure depended upon the assumption that the numerical frequency of an attribute within a category was an interval measure of the underlying psychological weight of that attribute (e.g., the difference between an attribute that belonged to two items versus one item was equal to the difference between an attribute that belonged to nineteen versus eighteen items). Such an assumption is not necessarily reasonable; therefore, a second measure of family resemblance was also computed. To derive this measure, each attribute was weighted with the natural logarithm of the raw score representing the number of items in the category that had been credited with that attribute; the second measure, thus, consisted of the sum of the natural logarithms of the scores of each of the attributes that had been listed for an item.

Results and Discussion

The purpose of the study was both to provide a portrait of the structure of the categories and to test the correlation between family resemblance and prototypicality of items. In terms of structure, figure 2.1 shows the mean frequency distribution for the number of attributes applied to each number (1 to 20) of items/category. As had been previously found when subjects listed attributes for superordinate category names (Rosch et al. 1976), in the present study, few attributes were given that were true of all twenty members of the category—for four of the categories, there was only one such item; for two of the categories, none. Furthermore, the single attribute that did apply to all members, in three cases was true of many other items besides those within that superordinate (for example, "you eat it" for fruit). Thus, the salient attribute structure of these categories tended to reside, not in criterial features common to all members of the category that distinguished those members from all others, but in a large number of attributes true of some, but not all, category members.

Those attributes unique to a single member are not of primary interest for the present study since they do not contribute to the structure of the category per se. In actual fact, the number of unique attributes applicable to items was evenly distributed over members of the categories; for none of the six categories was the number of unique attributes significantly correlated with prototypicality. Of the attributes applicable to two or more members, figure 2.1 shows that the number of attributes decreases as the number of items to which the attribute is applicable increases. In summary: the majority of attributes listed for items in the six categories demonstrated a family resemblance relationship; that is, they were common to only some of the category members.

The major hypothesis of the experiment was that this family resemblance structure would prove significantly correlated with the prototypicality of items. Correlations were computed separately for each of the two measures of family resemblance and separately for each category. The measure of prototypicality was the mean rating on a seven-point scale of the extent to which items fit subjects' idea or image of the meaning of the category names (Rosch 1975a). The basic measure of degree of family resemblance for an item was the sum of the weighted raw scores of each of the attributes listed for the item. The logarithmic measure of family resemblance was the sum of the natural logarithms of the scores of each of the attributes that had been listed for an item. Items in each category were ranked 1 to 20 on the basis of prototypicality and were ranked 1 to 20 on the basis of each of the measures of family resemblance. Spearman rank-order correlations between the ranks of items on family resemblance and their ranks on prototypicality were performed separately for each of the measures of family resemblance and for each of the categories. These correlations, for the basic measure of family resemblance, were: furniture, 0.88; vehicle, 0.92; weapon, 0.94; fruit, 0.85; vegetable, 0.84; clothing, 0.91. These correlations for the logarithmic measure of family resemblance were: furniture, 0.84; vehicle, 0.90; weapon 0.93; fruit, 0.88; vegetable, 0.86; clothing, 0.88. All were significant ($p <$ .001).

Such results strongly confirm our hypothesis that the more an item has attributes in common with other members of the category, the more it will be considered a good and representative member of the category. Furthermore, the similarity in results obtained with the basic and the logarithmic measures of family resemblance argues that this relationship is not dependent upon the properties of the particular scale used in measurement. Specifically, items in a category tended to be credited with approximately equal numbers of attributes, but

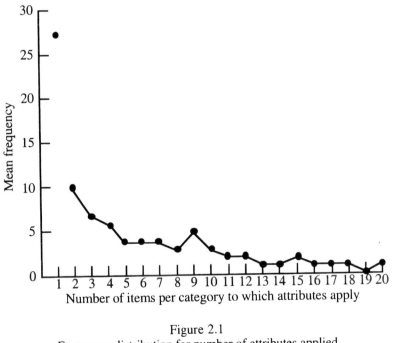

Figure 2.1
Frequency distribution for number of attributes applied
to each number of items/category.

the less prototypical the item, the fewer other items in the category tended to share each attribute. Thus, the ranks for the basic and logarithmic measures of family resemblance were almost identical, and the correlations between family resemblance and prototypicality were scarcely affected by the change in measure. The relationship between degree of family resemblance and prototypicality for these categories, thus, appears to be a robust one.

A corollary of this finding may account for one of the persistent illusions concerning superordinate categories. Subjects, upon receiving feedback from the experiment, and audiences, upon being told of it, generally argue that they feel positive that there are many attributes common to all members of the category even when they cannot think of any specific attributes for which there are not counterexamples. If the more prototypical members of a category are those that have the most attributes common to other members of the category, it is probable that they are most likely to have attributes in common with each other. To investigate this possibility, the number of attributes common to the five most and five least prototypical items in each category were compared. The number of attributes are shown in table 2.2. It is clear from this count that, while category members as a whole may not have items in common, the five most typical items of each category tend to have many items in common. Thus, if subjects think of the best examples of the category when hearing the category name (Rosch 1975a), the illusion of common elements is likely to arise and persist—an illusion that may be what makes definition of categories in terms of criterial attributes appear so reasonable.

A second corollary of the finding of a strong relationship between family resemblance and prototypicality concerns the structure of the semantic space in which items of a category are embedded. Previous studies of the nature of the semantic spaces of superordinate categories have focused on the dimensionality of the space (Henley 1969; Rips et al. 1973; Smith, Shoben, and Rips 1974). However, there are other properties of semantic spaces that can be of interest. For example, items that are perceived as closest to all members of a group of items should fall in the center of the space defined by means of proximity scaling of those items. For purposes of the present study, we can predict that items

Table 2.2
Number of attributes in common to five most and five least prototypical members of six categories.

Category	Most typical members	Least typical members
Furniture	13	2
Vehicle	36	2
Fruit	16	0
Weapon	9	0
Vegetable	3	0
Clothing	21	0

with the greatest family resemblance should fall in the center of the semantic space defined by proximity scaling of the items in a category; such an effect can be predicted regardless of the dimensionality or lack of dimensionality of the semantic space. If, in addition, items are perceived as similar to each other in proportion to the number of attributes they have in common, multidimensional scaling of the similarity judgments between all pairs of items in a category should result in a semantic space in which the distance of items from the origin of the space is determined by their degree of family resemblance.

A multidimensional scaling study of the categories *furniture, vehicle, weapon, fruit,* and *vegetable* was performed as part of a larger study.[1] Stimuli were the same twenty items in these categories shown in table 2.1 plus the superordinate category name. All possible pairs of the twenty-one items in each category were printed in a booklet and were rated on a nine-point scale for degree of similarity between the items. Fifteen subjects rated the items in each category. The similarity ratings were scaled by M-D scale (Shepard, 1962; Shepard, Romney, and Nerlove, Vol. I, 1972). Results showed that, while the dimensionality of the scaling solutions was generally difficult to interpret, in all cases the category name and the most prototypical items appeared to be the most central in the scaling solution regardless of the number of dimensions or the rotation used. To check this finding, Spearman rank-order correlations between degree of family resemblance and distance of an item from the origin in the three-dimensional scaling solution with minimum stress were performed for the five categories. These correlations were: furniture, 0.89; vehicle, 0.94; weapon, 0.95; fruit, 0.92; and vegetable, 0.90. All were significant ($p < .001$).

In the use of proximity scaling for items in semantic categories, it is customary to rely for interpretation on dimensions that characterize the space as a whole (see Shepard, Romney, and Nerlove, Vol. II, 1972). Such a trend is similar to the tradition of treating categories only in terms of logical defining features that are common to all members of the category. The present example of the use of scaling shows that, although family resemblance was defined in terms of discrete features, no one of which was common to all category members, and although the dimensionality of the categories was not obvious in the scaling solutions, the property of centrality of items in the semantic space was still interpretable; that is, degree of family resemblance was highly predictive of centrality in a semantic space defined by global similarity ratings of the items in the category.

In summary: The hypotheses of Experiment 1 were confirmed. For six superordinate categories, twenty members of the category were characterized by attributes that were common to some, but not all, members. The degree to which a given member possessed attributes in common with other members was highly correlated with the degree to which it was rated prototypical (representative) of the category name. In addition, degree of family resemblance predicted the centrality of items in the semantic space generated by multidimensional scaling of similarity ratings between items in the category.

Experiment 2

The initial hypothesis behind Experiment 2 was the direct converse of that of Experiment 1, namely that the most prototypical members of categories would not only have the greatest family resemblance to members of their category but would also be maximally distant from and, thus, have the least attributes in common with members of other categories at the same level of linguistic contrast. We found that this hypothesis could not be tested directly for superordinate categories.

The standard empirical method for deriving linguistic contrast sets from research participants is some variant of the question, "If X is not a Y, what is it (might it be)?" (Frake 1969). We pretested both the simple form of the question and the elaborated instructions used in Experiment 4. However, for the six superordinate categories of the present research, such instructions failed to produce consistent responses from subjects; those subjects who were able to respond at all tended to produce individual creative answers that were not considered reasonable by other subjects to whom they were shown. For superordinate categories, we, therefore, turned to an indirect test of the hypothesis by means of measurement of overlap in category membership. If the best examples of superordinate categories are those with least in common with other categories, they should be dominant members of few (or no) categories other than the superordinate in question. Thus, prototypicality should be correlated with a measure of the dominance of a category over its members (Loftus and Scheff 1971). Subjects could readily list superordinates for category members. The hypothesis of Experiment 2 was, thus, that the more prototypical a member of a superordinate category, the less dominant its membership would prove to be in categories other than the superordinate in question.

Method

Subjects. Subjects were 400 students in introductory and upper-division psychology classes, none of whom had participated in Experiment 1. They participated in the experiment as part of their classroom work.

Stimuli. Stimuli were the same members of five of the six most common superordinate categories of concrete nouns that had been used in Experiment 1 (*clothing* was erroneously omitted). The items were assembled in the same manner as described for Experiment 1. The only difference in format was that under each item, three lines labeled "1, 2, and 3" were printed on the page.

Procedure. Instructions were as follows:

> On each of the pages given you, you will see a noun and three lines. On each line, we want you to write a category to which the noun belongs. For example, if the noun were "collie," you might write *dog*, *animal*, or *pet* (etc.).
>
> Note that all of the words you see are to be interpreted as concrete nouns, not as verbs. For example, if you saw the word "dress," interpret it as the ar-

ticle of clothing "dress" and not the action of getting dressed.

Be sure to write three categories to which the noun belongs for each noun.

Computation of category membership score. Categories listed in first, second, and third place were weighted accordingly: three for first place mention, two for second place mention, one for third place mention. Since our hypothesis concerned single versus multiple category memberships and salient category memberships in any category other than the designated superordinate, we required a measure of the degree of dominance of the designated superordinate over the other most frequently mentioned superordinates. For each item, this was the following weighted measure: (designated superordinate minus most frequently mentioned other superordinate) plus (designated superordinate minus second most frequently measured other superordinate). This produced a single measure of category dominance for each item.

Results and Discussion

Category dominance of each item was scored as described above; the items within each category were ranked in accordance with their relative degree of category dominance. A Spearman rank-order correlation was performed for each category between category dominance and prototypicality. These correlations were: fruit, 0.71; furniture, 0.83; vegetable, 0.67; vehicle, 0.82; weapon, 0.77. All were significant ($p < .001$).

Our hypothesis was that the more prototypical an item in a given category, the less it would bear a family resemblance to items in other categories, and, thus, the less likely it would be to have salient membership in those other categories. Membership in other categories was the variable that it proved possible to measure. The strong positive correlations between prototypicality and dominance of membership in the category for which prototypicality had been measured confirms this hypothesis.

Part II. Basic Level Categories

It has been previously argued (Rosch 1976; Rosch et al. 1976) that there is a basic level of abstraction at which the concrete objects of the world are most naturally divided into categories. A working assumption has been that, in the domains of both man-made and biological objects, there occur information-rich bundles of attributes that form natural discontinuities. These bundles are both perceptual and functional. It is proposed that basic cuts are made at this level. Basic objects (for example, *chair, car*) are the most inclusive level of abstraction at which categories can mirror the correlational structure (Garner 1974) of the environment and the most inclusive level at which there can be many attributes common to all or most members of these categories. The more abstract combinations of basic level objects (e.g., categories such as *furniture* and *vehicle* used in Experiments 1 and 2) are superordinates that share only a few attributes; the common attributes are rather abstract ones. Categories below the basic level are subordinates (e.g., *kitchen chair, sports car*). Subordinates are also bundles of predictable attributes and functions, but contain little more information than the basic level object to which they are subordinate. Basic categories are, thus, the categories for which the cue validity of attributes within categories is maximized: Superordinate categories have lower cue validity than basic because they have fewer common attributes within the category; subordinate categories have lower cue validity than basic because they share attributes with contrasting subordinate categories (e.g., *kitchen chair* shares most of its attributes with *living room chair*).

In a converging series of experiments (Rosch et al. 1976), it was confirmed that basic objects are the most inclusive categories in which clusters of attributes occur which subjects agree are possessed by members of the category; sets of common motor movements are made when using or interacting with objects of that type; commonalities in the shape, and, thus, the overall look, of objects occur; it is possible to recognize an averaged shape of an object of that class; and it is possible to form a representation of a typical member of the class that is sufficiently concrete to aid in detection of the object in visual noise. In addition, basic objects were shown to be the first categorizations made by young children, and basic object names the level of abstraction at which objects are first named by children and usually named by adults.

The present research concerned the question of whether the family resemblances of items in basic level categories were related to prototypicality in the way in which it had proved to be in the superordinate categories studied in Experiments 1 and 2. Do subjects agree concerning which members of basic object categories are the more prototypical—do they agree, for example, about which cars more closely fit their idea or image of the meaning of *car*? And, if agreement in prototypicality ratings is obtained, does it hold, as it did in the case of superordinate categories, that the more prototypical category members are those with most resemblance to members of that category and least resemblance to other categories? In Experiment 3, the hypothesis was tested that prototypicality ratings and degree of family resemblance were positively correlated. Experiment 4 tested the converse hypothesis that prototypicality ratings were negatively correlated with the degree to which an item possessed attributes that were also possessed by members of contrasting categories.

Experiment 3

Method

Subjects. Subjects were 182 paid undergraduate volunteers who participated as a part of a fundraising for a student organization. None had participated in the superordinate category experiments. Thirty-two subjects rated the stimuli for goodness-of-example; 150 listed attributes.

Stimuli. Superordinate categories have a finite number of members designable by words, with norms available for the frequency with which the members are listed by subjects (Battig and Montague 1969). The members of basic level categories, however, are actual objects, an essentially infinite population. Six categories were chosen for the present experiment, which had been shown to be at the basic level of abstraction by the convergent techniques used in Rosch et al. (1976). The categories were: car, truck, airplane, chair, table, and lamp. Each of these was a category for which pictures of many objects could be readily obtained and a category that had the property that the attributes of the object most listed by subjects (Rosch et al. 1976) could be seen in pictures of the object. Pictures to be used in the present research were selected from a large sample of pictures (described in Rosch et al. 1976); two judges chose fifteen pictures by the following method—for each category, they first found the picture they felt most prototypical of the category, then the picture they felt was the worst example of the category (but still clearly called a *car*, *chair*, etc.). They then selected thirteen other pictures that they agreed spanned the distance between the two extreme pictures in as equal subjective steps as possible given the available pool of pictures. The ninety pictures, fifteen in each category, chosen in this manner served as stimuli in the experiment.

Procedure

1. Prototypicality ratings. Subjects were given essentially the same instructions as had been given subjects who rated the prototypicality of members of superordinate categories. Basically, subjects were asked to rate, on a seven-point scale, the extent to which an instance represented their idea or image of the meaning of the category name. Precise instructions were:

> This study has to do with what we have in mind when we use words which refer to categories. Let's take the word *red* as an example. Close your eyes and imagine a true red. Now imagine an orangish red . . . imagine a purple-red. Although you might still name the orange-red or the purple-red with the term *red*, they are not as good examples of red (as clear cases of what *red* refers to) as the clear "true" red. In short, some reds are redder than others. The same is true for other kinds of categories. Think of dogs. You all have some notion of what a "real dog," a "doggy dog" is. To me a Retriever or a German Shepherd is a very doggy dog while a Pekinese is a less doggy dog. Notice that this kind of judgment has nothing to do with how well you like the thing; you can like a purple-red better than a true red but still recognize that the color you like is not a true red. You may prefer to own a Pekinese without thinking that it is the breed that best represents what people mean by dogginess.
>
> In this study you are asked to judge how good an example of a category various instances of the category are. The members of the category are pictures; you will be told the name of the category and shown fifteen pictures of items in the category. On your answer sheet are six columns of fifteen numbers, After each number is a blank. You are to rate how good an example of the category each picture is on a seven-point scale. A 1 means that you feel the picture is a very good example of your idea or image of what the category is; a 7 means you feel the picture fits very poorly with your idea or image of the category (or is not a member of it at all). A 4 means you feel the picture fits moderately well. Use the other numbers of the seven-point scale to indicate intermediate judgments.

Don't worry about why you feel that something is or isn't a good example of the category. And don't worry about whether it's just you or people
in general who feel that way. Just mark it the way you see it.

Slides of the fifteen pictures in a category were shown the subjects once
through rapidly in random order; then, each slide was shown the group for thirty
seconds while subjects made their ratings. Means of the ratings of the thirty-two
subjects in the experiment formed the basis for ranking the items.

2. *Attribute listing.* Subjects were given the same instructions for listing attributes as the subjects in Experiment 1, with the exception that they were told
they would be seeing pictures and were asked to list the attributes of the item in
each picture. Each subject listed attributes for six pictures, one from each of the
basic level categories. Sets of pictures were assembled by the same principles as
the sets of words had been in testing superordinate categories. Ten subjects listed
attributes for each picture. Subjects were allowed 1.5 min to list attributes for
each slide.

Results and Discussion

Methods used for computing family resemblance and for computing the correlation between family resemblance of attributes and prototypicality ratings were
the same methods as had been used in Experiment 1. As expected (Rosch et al.
1976), basic level categories differed from the subordinates in that many more attributes were common to all members of the basic level categories. However,
there were also many attributes listed that were not common to all members.
These attributes were used in the correlation between family resemblance and
prototypicality. The Spearman rank-order correlations between the basic measure
of family resemblance and prototypicality were: car, 0.94; truck, 0.84; airplane,
0.88; chair, 0.81; table, 0.88; and lamp, 0.69. The correlations between the logarithmic measure of family resemblance and prototypicality were: car, 0.86;
truck, 0.88; airplane, 0.88; chair 0.79; table, 0.85; and lamp, 0.64. All were
significant ($p < .01$). Thus, we have verified for pictures of basic level objects,
as well as for names of members of superordinate categories, the more prototypical items are those that have the most attributes in common with other members
of the category. As in the case of superordinate categories, this relationship was
not dependent on the particular scale used to measure family resemblance.

Experiment 4

The purpose of both Experiments 2 and 4 was to provide data complementary to
that of Experiments 1 and 3. The basic hypothesis of both experiments was that
categories tend to become organized in such a way that they are maximally discriminable from other categories at the same level of contrast; hence, the most
prototypical members of a category are those with least resemblance to, or
membership in, other categories. For superordinate categories, it had not been
possible to obtain contrast sets and, thus, not possible to measure commonality
of attributes between contrasting categories directly; instead, the hypothesis had
been tested indirectly by means of an item's membership in multiple categories.

For members of basic level categories, the hypothesis proved testable directly.

The basic design of the experiment was: (a) to determine which categories were seen in direct contrast to a sample of the basic level categories for which we had obtained prototypicality ratings and attribute lists in Experiment 2, (b) to obtain lists of attributes for pictures representing items in the contrasting categories, and (c) to correlate the number of attributes that items shared with contrasting categories with prototypicality ratings for the items; a negative correlation was predicted.

Method

Subjects. Subjects were forty-four students in psychology classes who performed the task as part of their classroom work; twenty-four of the subjects served in the contrast set portion of the experiment; twenty subjects listed attributes.

Stimuli and procedure. The first part of the experimental procedure required obtaining contrast sets of the basic level categories to be used. Subjects were read the following instructions:

Suppose that you are participating in a communication task experiment. Another person is describing "items" to you, and you have to figure out what kind of "item" he is describing. The person tells you about each item's *physical attributes* (what it looks like, what parts it has, etc.), and about its *functions* (what people do with it), and about its *actions* (what it does). Suppose, also, that you have guessed once for each item, and you have been told that your answer was not correct, but was very close to the correct one. Assume that each word I read was your first answer to one item. After I read each item, write down what your second answer would be. Remember that your first guess was very close to being correct. Think of something that has physical attributes, functions, and actions very similar to the ones your "first answer" had.

Subjects were then given the six names of basic level items used in Experiment 2 and asked to write their first guess as to what the item might be. Thirty seconds per item were allowed.

Subjects' responses were tallied. From the six basic level categories, two were selected for which the most consistent responses had been given. These two, *chair* and *car*, were used for the second part of the experiment.

Stimuli for the attribute listing consisted of pictures of two examples of each of the three most frequently given contrast items for *chair* and *car*. These were: for chair—sofa, stool, and cushion; for car—truck, bus, and motorcycle. The pictures were chosen randomly from the pool of available pictures of these items, with the restriction that all of the pictures chosen had been rated (by two judges) as good examples of their category.

Attribute lists had already been obtained for the chair and car pictures in Experiment 3. Attributes for the six contrast categories were obtained by the same procedures as used in Experiment 3; subjects were read the same instructions as in Experiment 3, were shown slides of the pictures in the contrast categories in random order, and were given 1.5 min to list attributes for each picture. Each subject saw six pictures, one of each contrast item. Each picture was seen by ten subjects.

Results and Discussion

For each of the fifteen chair and fifteen car pictures, a tally was made of the number of attributes listed for that picture, which had also been listed for at least one of the pictures of one of the three contrast categories. This tally was used as the measure of amount of overlap between the attributes of a given item and the attributes of items in the closest contrasting categories. A Spearman rank-order correlation was performed between the prototypicality and attribute overlap ranks of the fifteen chair and fifteen car pictures. Results were: chairs $r = -.67$; cars, $r = -.86$. Both were significant ($p < .01$). In short, it was clearly confirmed for two basic level categories that the more prototypical of the category a picture had been rated, the fewer attributes it shared with categories in direct contrast with that category.

Part III. Artificial Categories

In the four preceding experiments, it was shown for a sample of naturally occurring categories that items rated more prototypical of the category were more closely related to other members of the category and less closely related to members of other categories than were items rated less prototypical of a category. Categories designated by the words of natural languages have the advantage for study that they have evolved and occur in actual human usage; however, they have the disadvantage that the variables of interest occur in uncontrolled and, thus, unanalyzable conjunction with each other and with other extraneous factors. In the previous experiments, the object was to determine the structure of preexisting categories. In the following two experiments, artificial categories were constructed in which items differed only in the degree of family resemblance within categories or amount of overlap of attributes between categories. In these experiments, the structure was provided as an independent variable; our hypothesis was that this structure would affect rate of learning of category items; reaction time in judging category membership once the categories were learned; and ratings of prototypicality of items.

In Experiment 5, only the family resemblance of items within categories was varied; the categories that subjects learned to discriminate contained no elements in common and, thus, no overlap. In Experiment 6, categories that had previously been learned in Experiment 5, where there was no overlap, were taught in conjunction with categories whose attributes overlapped some items. Thus, changes in learning, reaction time, and judgments of prototypicality created by the difference in contrast sets could be observed.

Experiment 5

Method

Subjects. Subjects were thirty students in introductory psychology classes who received course credit for participation.

Stimuli. All of the stimuli were constructed out of strings of letters. The digits 1 to 9 were mixed with the letters when more symbols were needed. Vowels were used only in one stimulus type and only at the ends of strings so that pronounceability was not a factor.

Three types of family resemblance structures were used. Table 2.3 shows one example of each structure with the items ordered so that the nature of the structure can be seen. After each letter string, the family resemblance score of that string is shown. This score is computed as described for the basic family resemblance measure in Experiments 1 and 3. Each letter received a weight (1 to 5) representing the number of strings in the category in which it occurred; the weights of each letter in a string were summed to generate the family resemblance score of that string. (A letter could not receive a weight of 6 because no letter occurred in all six items in a category.)

In the control group structure, all members of the category overlapped other members (possessed letters in common with other members) to an equal degree; thus, the family resemblance scores of each item were the same. The structure of the control group categories was generated in an ad hoc manner in order to achieve equal family resemblance scores for all items. (To understand better the derivation of the family resemblance score, the reader might wish to count the number of strings in the category in which each letter occurred and then sum the weights of the letters in a given string.)

Two experimental groups were used in which members of categories possessed letters in common with other members to an unequal degree and, hence, possessed differing degrees of family resemblance. One of these groups was constructed with a symmetric structure. Each string differed systematically by one letter from the preceding string, resulting in two "central" strings that were maximally overlapped with the other strings in the category. The nature of the symmetric category structures should be apparent from the items shown in table 2.3. The two central, two intermediate, and two peripheral items of the symmetric categories possessed the same degrees of family resemblance. The other experimental group was constructed with an asymmetric structure. These categories were generated so that one letter only occurred in five strings, another letter in four strings, another letter in three strings, three letters occurred in two strings, and all other letters occurred only once. This structure yielded differences in degree of family resemblance between all six of the strings of the asymmetric categories. Specifically, the strings of the asymmetric categories possessed the following letter weights: string 1 = 5, 4, 3, 2, 2; string 2 = 5, 4, 3, 2, 1; string 3 = 5, 4, 3, 1, 1; string 4 = 5, 4, 1, 1, 1; string 5 = 5, 2, 1, 1, 1; string 6 = 2, 2, 1, 1, 1. The reader can verify these letter weights by counting the number of strings in which each letter occurs. For each string, the letter weights are summed to produce the family resemblance scores shown in table 2.3.

There were six items (six letter strings) within each category. Each letter

Table 2.3
Artificial category structures used in Experiments 5 and 6.

| | | Type of category structure | | | | | | | |
| | | Control set | | | Symmetric experimental set | | | Asymmetric experimental set | |
Use of the category	Item in category	Letter string	Family resemblance score	Overlap score	Letter string	Family resemblance score	Overlap score	Letter string	Family resemblance score
Basic category structure	1	HPNWD	12	0	JXPHM	15	0	DLT83	16
	2	HPNSJ	12	2	XPHMQ	19	1	DLT8A	15
	3	GKNTJ	12	4	PHMQB	21	2	DLTPM	14
	4	4KCTG	12	5	HMQBL	21	3	DLGKI	12
	5	4KC6D	12	3	MQBLF	19	4	D9H60	10
	6	HPC6B	12	1	QBLFS	15	5	3YH7V	7
Nonoverlap contrast category (Experiment 5)	1	R7QUM	12		CTRVG	15		SXB25	16
	2	R7QXV	12		TRVGZ	19		SXB2Q	15
	3	Z5Q2V	12		RVGZK	21		SXBRE	14
	4	L5F27	12		VGZKW	21		SXVFW	12
	5	L5F1M	12		GZKDW	19		S4Z1&	10
	6	R7F19	12		ZKDWN	15		5JZCN	7
Overlapped contrast category[a] (Experiment 6)	1	8SJKT		4[b]	GVRTC				
	2	8SJ3G		3	VRTCS				
	3	9UJCG		3	RTCSF				
	4	4UZC9		2	TCSFL				
	5	4UZRT		3	CSFLB				
	6	MSZR5		3	SFLBQ				

[a] Overlap is with the basic category structure not the nonoverlap contrast category.

[b] Contrast strings in control do not have same structure as initial category strings and were not analyzed in Experiment 6.

string was typed horizontally in capital letters in the center of a 12.70 x 20.32 cm white card. Ten different sets of letter combinations were used for each category type, all of which possessed a structure identical to the set of that type shown in table 2.3. Each subject received a different set. The letters in a string were not presented to the subject in their "structural" order as shown in table 2.3, but were randomly ordered within each string. An item appeared in the same order throughout the task for a given subject.

Procedure. The letter strings were displayed in a Harvard two-field tachistoscope. Subjects were told that they were to learn to distinguish two categories, *1s* and *2s*. They pressed a telegraph key with the forefinger of the dominant hand to indicate a *1* and another key with the forefinger of the other hand to indicate a *2*. They were first shown the strings that made up each category. First the *1s* and then the *2s* were displayed in random order, four seconds per item, with an approximate inter stimulus interval of ten seconds. The twelve strings that composed the two categories were then displayed in random order. Subjects responded by pressing one of the keys to indicate their judgment of the category to which the item belonged. They received verbal feedback of *correct* and *wrong* from the experimenter until they had achieved two errorless runs. At that point, the experimenter told the subject that he had learned the categories, but would continue seeing the items and that he was to respond with the category designation as quickly as possible without making errors. The subject continued for fifteen additional trials. At the conclusion, the subject was given the six cards in each category, read the instructions for rating prototypicality, and asked to rank order the six cards in terms of the degree to which each fit the idea or image that he had developed of the category.

Results and Discussion

There were three dependent variables of interest: rate of learning, reaction time, and rankings of prototypicality. Rate of learning was measured by the total number of errors subjects made in classifying an item; reaction time was the time a subject took to respond to an item in his last run; and rankings of prototypicality were the subjects' rankings of the prototypicality of the items.

The two structural types of experimental stimuli were each divided into three parts: the two stimuli with greatest family resemblance, the two with middle degree of family resemblance, and the two with least family resemblance. (For the symmetric group, the two items within each of the three parts possessed an equal degree of family resemblance.) For the control set, no such division was possible, and the six items of the set were analyzed separately. Table 2.4 shows the means for all three experimental variables for the three types of category structures.

A one-way analysis of variance (ANOVA) for correlated scores was performed on the high, medium, and low family resemblance items for the two experimental sets and on all six of the items for the control set. For the control group, results were not significant for any of the three variables. For both experimental groups, however, the results were significant for all three variables: Symmetric categories—rate of learning, $F(2,9) = 7.09$, $p < .05$; reaction time, $F(2,9) = 6.41$, $p < .05$; prototypicality rating, $F(2,9) = 11.35$, $p < .01$; Asymmetric categories—rate of learning, $F(2,9) = 9.48$, $p < .01$; reaction time, $F(2,9) = 7.91$, $p < .05$; prototypicality rating, $F(2,9) = 14.66$, $p < .01$. Thus, the predicted results were obtained. In artificial family resemblance sets, when no single attribute is common to all members of the set, even when contrast sets have no elements in common with each other, items that have greater degree of family resemblance with the members of their own set are learned more rapidly, identified more rapidly even after practice, and judged as more prototypical members of the category than are items with a lesser degree of family resemblance.

Experiment 6

For the natural categories in the first four experiments, we found that the more prototypical items had less resemblance to contrasting categories than the less prototypical items. In natural categories, greater family resemblance within a category and less resemblance to contrasting categories are inseparable if categories are assumed to form in accordance with the natural contingency structure of an environment in which attributes occur in correlated clusters (Rosch et al. 1976). In artificial categories. however, it is possible to separate those two principles. Experiment 5 showed prototype formation to be a function of greater family resemblance when there was no influence of overlapping attributes from contrasting categories. The hypothesis of Experiment 6 is that items are considered more prototypical of a category to the extent that they do not overlap with contrasting categories.

The experiment was performed for two sets of stimuli. For the control stimuli of Experiment 5, no item had greater family resemblance with any other item, and no differences in learning, reaction time, or prototypicality ratings were found. For categories with this structure, the hypothesis is that prototypicality can be induced purely as a function of extent of overlap with a contrasting

Table 2.4
Effect of degree of family resemblance on response measures.

Stimulus type	Response measures								
	Number of Errors			Reaction time (msec)			Prototypicality Rating		
	Hi[a]	Med	Lo	Hi	Med	Lo	Hi	Med	Lo
Symmetric experimental	2.8	4.4	5.5	560	617	692	5.0	3.4	2.
Asymmetric experimental	2.4	6.8	9.5	532	619	765	5.5	3.5	1.6
Control	6.5	6.4	6.7	670	651	644	3.7	3.4	3.4

[a] Hi, Med and Lo refer to family resemplance scores.

category. For the experimental groups of Experiment 5, the hypothesis is that extent of overlap and family resemblance within the category will combine to produce prototypicality under conditions of overlap. Only the symmetrically structured group was used. (The asymmetrical structures proved impossible to learn in the hour of subject time available when the items with greatest family resemblance within the category overlapped a contrast category.)

Method

Subjects. Subjects were twenty students in introductory psychology who had not participated in the previous experiment. They received course credit for their participation.

Stimuli and procedure. Stimuli were constructed as described for Experiment 5. The contrast sets used were the overlapping contrast sets shown in table 2.3. Scores for the amount of overlap with the contrast category were computed by the same methods as described in Experiment 4; each letter that occurred at least once in the contrast category received a weight of "1." These weights were summed to give the overlap score of a string. The overlap score, thus, represents simply the number of letters in a string that occur in the contrast category. The contrast categories for the categories that had been controls in Experiment 5 were constructed in an ad hoc manner in order to provide overlap scores 0 to 5 for the strings of the initial category. These contrast category strings did not possess the same structure or same overlap scores as the initial category strings. Contrast categories for the symmetrical groups were constructed with the same symmetric structure and same degree of overlap as the initial categories. The overlap scores for each string in the initial category and the overlap contrast category are shown in table 2.3. (To understand better the derivation of the overlap score, the reader might wish to count the number of letters in a string that occur in at least one string of the contrast category and sum the number of such letters.)

Procedures were identical to those of Experiment 5.

Results and Discussion

The control and experimental sets of Experiment 5 had different structures. For the control set, the items had shown no difference in learning, reaction time, or prototypicality ratings when learned in conjunction with nonoverlapping contrast sets. By the method of measuring amount of overlap described under *Method* above, the contrast sets in the present experiment changed this set into one in which items ranged from zero attributes of overlap to all five attributes overlapped (only the initial category and not the contrast category itself was analyzed for this set—see table 2.3).

Table 2.5 shows learning, reaction time, and prototypicality scores for the greatest, middle range, and least overlapped items. A one-way ANOVA for correlated scores was performed for these measures for the three dependent variables. All three were significant: rate of learning, $F(2,9) = 8.36$, $p < .01$; reaction time, $F(2,9) = 10.75$, $p < .01$; prototypicality, $F(2,9) = 11.19$, $p < .01$.

For the symmetric experimental set, overlap is in conflict with the family resemblance structure internal to the category. There are two hypotheses that we wished to test with the analysis: The first was that, with internal family resemblance held constant by the analysis, extent of overlap with the contrast category would show a significant effect on learning, reaction time, and prototypicality. The second was that internal family resemblance would still have an effect and would tend to counter the effect of degree of overlap for the three items in which these two principles were opposed.

In terms of internal family resemblance, the symmetric category can be divided into two halves (items 1, 2, and 3 versus items 4, 5, and 6) that are structurally identical. In relation to the present contrast set, however, items 1, 2, and 3 had, respectively, 0, 1, and 2 overlapped attributes; while items 4, 5, and 6 had, respectively, 3, 4, and 5 overlapped attributes. Our prediction was that, while in the tasks of Experiment 5, the two halves showed no significant differences, such differences would be apparent in the present experiment. T-tests were performed separately for each dependent variable for the means of items in the two halves for the data from Experiment 5 and for those means in the present experiment. None of these tests was significant for the Experiment 5 data. However, all were significant for the data from the present experiment: rate of learning, $t(9) = 5.57$, $p < .001$; reaction time, $t(9) = 6.08$, $p < .001$; prototypicality, $t(9) = 9.38$, $p < .001$. Thus, degree of overlap with the contrasting category clearly influenced performance even in a set that had an internal family resemblance structure.

The second part of the hypothesis was that the internal family resemblance structure would also influence performance. In three of the items (items 1, 2, and 3 in table 2.3), internal family resemblance structure and degree of overlap were contradictory. (For the Experiment 5 data, in which only family resemblance within the category varied, results had been significant for all the variables: learning, $F(2,9) = 4.56$, $p < .05$; reaction time, $F(2,9) = 5.16$, $p < .05$; prototypicality, $F(2,9) = 9.24$, $p < .01$.) For the data from the present experiment, neither the learning rate nor the prototypicality results were significant. The one significant variable, reaction time—$F(2,9) = 5.29$, $p < .05$—showed shorter reaction times for items with less overlap, although these items also had less family resemblance within the category. Thus, internal family resemblance, when in conflict with overlap, serves to mitigate the effect of overlap.

In sum, the results of the present experiment have demonstrated that extent of

Table 2.5
Effect of degree of overlap on response measures for control set.

Response measure	Degree of overlap		
	Low	Medium	High
Number of errors	7.1	9.4	12.6
Reaction time (msec)	909	986	1125
Prototypicality rating	5.3	3.4	1.8

overlap with a contrast category serves to structure categories in which items did not previously differ in degree of family resemblance and to influence the structure of categories in which items did previously differ in degree of family resemblance.

General Discussion

The results of the present study confirmed the hypothesis that the most prototypical members of common superordinate, basic level, and artificial categories are those that bear the greatest family resemblance to other members of their own category and have the least overlap with other categories. In probabilistic language, prototypicality was shown to be a function of the cue validity of the attributes of items. In the particular studies in this chapter, we defined and measured family resemblance in terms of discrete attributes; however, previous studies indicate that the principle can be applied, to some extent, to other types of categories, such as dot patterns distorted around a prototype and categories consisting of items composed of continuous attributes that have a metric (Posner 1973; Reed 1972; Rosch, Simpson, and Miller 1976). In such categories, the prototype dot pattern and the pattern with attributes at mean values have more in common with (are more like) the other items in the category than are items further from the prototype or the mean. Family resemblances (even broadly defined) are undoubtedly not the only principle of prototype formation—for example, the frequency of items and the salience of particular attributes or particular members of the categories (perceptual, social, or memorial salience) as well as the as yet undefined gestalt properties of stimuli and stimulus combinations, undoubtedly contribute to prototype formation (Rosch 1975b)—however, the results of the present study indicate that family resemblance is a major factor.

Such a finding is important in six ways: (a) It suggests a structural basis for the formation of prototypes of categories, (b) It argues that in modeling natural categories, prototypes and cue validity are not conflicting accounts, but, rather, must be incorporated into a single model, (c) It indicates a structural rationale for the use of proximity scaling in the study of categories, even in the absence of definable category dimensionality, (d) It offers a principle by which prototype formation can be understood as part of the general processes through which categories themselves may be formed, (e) It provides a new link between adult and children's modes of categorization, and (f) It offers a concrete alternative to criterial attributes in understanding the logic of categorical structure.

Family resemblance as a structural basis for prototype formation. The origin of prototypes of categories is an issue because, as outlined in the introduction, there is now considerable evidence that the extent to which members are conceived typical of a category appears to be an important variable in the cognitive processing of categories (Rosch 1975a, 1975b, 1975c, 1976, 1977). From that previous work alone, it could be argued that ratings of prototypicality are only measures of the associative linkage between an item and the category name and that it is such associative strength that determines the effects of typicality on processing tasks such as those used in semantic memory. While in a processing model, associative strength may, by definition, be directly related to typicality effects, associative strength need not be conceived only as the result of the frequency of (arbitrary or accidental) pairings of the item with the category name. The present experiments have attempted to provide a structural principle for the formation of prototypes; family resemblance relationships are not in contradiction to, but, rather, themselves offer a possible structural reason behind associative strength.

The principle of family resemblance is similar but not identical to two recent accounts of prototype effects: the attribute frequency model (Neumann 1974) and an element tag model (Reitman and Bower 1973). Both of these models were designed to account, without recourse to an "abstraction process," for the findings of several specific previous experiments—primarily those of Bransford and Franks (1971) and Franks and Bransford (1971). Both models predict memory (particularly the mistaken memory for prototype items that were not actually presented) from the frequency with which elements appear in a learning set.

A family resemblance account of prototypes is of greater generality than these models. In the first place, it accounts for prototypes in terms of distributions of attributes rather than in terms of the simple frequency of attributes (a factor that also distinguishes family resemblances from a narrow definition of cue validity). In the second place, it includes an account of the distribution of attributes over contrasting categories rather than focusing only on the category in question. That it is distribution rather than simple frequency of attributes that is most relevant to prototypes in natural categories is argued by two facts: (a) The measure of distribution used in the present study was highly correlated with ratings of prototypicality for superordinate categories, whereas, a measure of the frequency of items (that is necessarily correlated with frequency of attributes) in the category is not correlated with prototypicality (Mervis, Rosch, and Catlin 1975), and (b) The overlap of attributes with contrasting categories is itself a distributional property not a property of simple frequency. (In the artificial categories of Experiment 5 as given in this chapter, distributional and simple frequency were equivalent; however, in the other experiments, they were not—clarification of the relations between distribution and frequency of attributes is an issue that requires further research.) That the distribution of attributes over contrasting categories is as important a principle of prototype formation as distribution of attributes within a category is argued by the results of Experiments 2, 4, and 6.

At this point, it should be reiterated that the principle of family resemblance, as defined in this chapter's research, is a descriptive, not a processing principle. Family resemblances are related to process models in two ways: (a) Any account of the processes by which humans convert stimulus attributes into mental or behavioral prototypes (such as an attribute tag model) should be able to account for the family resemblance attribute structure of categories outlined in the present chapter's research, and (b) Classification by computation of cue validity and classification by matching to a prototype have been treated as alternative process models that are in conflict; however, the principle of family resemblance suggests that, for natural categories, both should be aspects of the same processing model.

Family resemblance as an argument for the compatibility of cue validity and prototype models. Probability models, such as cue validity, and distance models, such as matching to a prototype, have been treated as two fundamentally different forms of categorization model whose conflicting validities must be tested by empirical research (Reed 1972). However, the present chapter has shown that empirically defined prototypes of natural categories are just those items with highest cue validity. Such a structure of categories would, in fact, appear to provide the means for maximally efficient processing of categories. Computation and summation of the validities of individual cues is a laborious cognitive process. However, since cue validity appears to be the basis of categories (Rosch et al. 1976), it is ecologically essential that cue validities be taken into account, in some manner, in categorization. If prototypes function cognitively as representatives of the category, and if prototypes are items with the highest cue validities, humans can use the efficient processing mechanism of matching to a prototype without sacrificing attention to the validity of cues. (Note that such an account is similar to the compromise model that ultimately proved the most predictive for Reed's 1972 categories of schematic faces—a prototype matching model in which the importance of each feature in the prototype was weighted in accordance with its cue validity.) In short, humans probably incorporate probabilistic analysis of cues and computation of distance from a representation of the category into the same process of categorization; future research on categorization would do well to attempt to model the ways in which that incorporation can occur rather than to treat cue validity and prototypes as conflicting models.

Family resemblance as a basis for proximity scaling. Just as it has been customary to treat categories in terms of logical defining features that were assumed to be common to all members of the category, it is also not uncommon to treat proximity scaling of items in categories only as a means of determining the general dimensions along which items of the category are seen to differ. However, the results of the multidimensional scaling of the items of the superordinate categories in Experiment 1 (performed with Smith, Shoben, and Rips 1974) indicated that family resemblance was predictive of centrality of items in the derived similarity space regardless of interpretability of dimensions or of item clusters. It should, in general, be the case that the more that items have in common with other items in a class (the closer the items are to all other items irrespective of the basis of closeness), the more central those items will be in a space derived from proximity measures. The demonstration of the importance of family resemblances (and of prototypicality) in classification provided by the present research suggests that the dimension of centrality may itself be an important aspect and deserve to be a focus of attention in the analysis of proximity spaces.

Family resemblance as a part of the general process of category formation. The concept of family resemblances is also of general use because it characterizes prototype formation as part of the general process by which categories themselves are formed. It has been argued by Rosch et al. (1976) that division of the world into categories is not arbitrary. The basic category cuts in the world are those that separate the information-rich bundles of attributes that form natural discontinuities. Basic categories have, in fact, been shown to be the most inclusive categories in which all items in the category possess significant numbers of attributes in common, and, thereby, are used by means of similar sequences of motor movements and are like each other in overall appearance. Basic categories are the categories for which the cue validity of attributes within categories is maximized since superordinate categories have fewer common attributes within the category than do basic categories and subordinate categories share more attributes with contrasting categories than do basic categories. Basic categories are, thus, the categories that mirror the correlational structure of the environment.

The present study has shown that formation of prototypes of categories appears to be likewise nonarbitrary. The more prototypical a category member, the more attributes it has in common with other members of the category and the less attributes in common with contrasting categories. Thus, prototypes appear to be just those members of the category that most reflect the redundancy structure of the category as a whole. That is, categories form to maximize the information-rich clusters of attributes in the environment and, thus, the cue validity of the attributes of categories; when prototypes of categories form by means of the principle of family resemblance, they maximize such clusters and such cue validity still further within categories.

Family resemblance as a link with children's classifications. The principle of family resemblances in adult categories casts a new perspective on children's classifications. Young children have been shown to classify objects or pictures by means of *complexive classes*, that is, classes in which items are related to each other by attributes not shared by all members of the class (Bruner, Olver, and Greenfield 1966; Vygotsky 1962). For example, Vygotsky speaks of the child in the "phase of thinking in complexes" starting with a small yellow triangle, putting with it a red triangle, then a red circle—in each case matching the new item to one attribute of the old. Bruner et al. describe the young child's tendency to classify by means of "complexive structures," for example, "banana and peach are yellow, peach and potato round. . . ." Such complexive classes have been considered logically more primitive than the adult-preferred method of grouping taxonomically by "what a thing is"—that is, grouping by superordinate classes and justifying groups by their superordinate names. However, the present research has shown that family resemblances, a form of complexive grouping, appears to be one of the structural principles in the composition of the superordinate classes themselves, and, thus, one of the structural principles in adult classification. Since adult taxonomic classes such as *furniture* or *chair* themselves consist of complexive groupings of attributes, it would appear appropriate to study the development of the integration of complexive into taxonomic categories rather than the replacement of the former by the latter.

Family resemblance as a logical alternative to criterial attributes. There is a tenacious tradition of thought in philosophy and psychology that assumes that items can bear a categorical relationship to each other only by means of the possession of common criterial attributes. The present chapter is an empirical confirmation of Wittgenstein's (1953) argument that formal criteria are neither a logical nor psychological necessity; the categorical relationship in categories that do not appear to possess criterial attributes, such as those used in the present study, can be understood in terms of the principle of family resemblance.

Notes

An earlier version of this chapter appeared in *Cognitive Psychology* 8 (1975): 382-439. Reprinted with permission from Academic Press and Eleanor Rosch and Carolyn Mervis.

This research was supported by grants to the first author (under her former name Eleanor Rosch Heider) by the National Science Foundation (GB-38245X), by the Grant Foundation, and by the National Institutes of Mental Health (1 R01 MH24316-01). We wish to thank David Johnson, Joseph Romeo, Ross Quigley, R. Scott Miller, Steve Frank, Alina Furnow, and Louise Jones for help with testing and analysis of the data. We also wish to thank Ed Smith, Ed Shoben, and Lance Rips for permission to refer to the multidimensional scaling study of superordinate categories, which was performed jointly with them. Carolyn Mervis is now at Cornell University. She was supported by an NSF Predoctorol Fellowship during the research.

1. The larger study was performed in collaboration with E. E. Smith, E. J. Shoben and L. J. Rips of Stanford University. Half of the subjects were tested at the University of California, Berkeley, half at Stanford University. The multidimensional scaling was performed entirely at Stanford.

Chapter 3

The Psychology of Intuition

Edward J. Wisniewski

What role should intuition play in attempting to understand how humans think and behave in the world? In this chapter, I argue that intuition should play a rather limited role in achieving this goal. Based on research from cognitive and social psychology and observations about evolution, I describe the dangers of appealing to intuition as the sole methodology for obtaining knowledge. I begin by describing several salient examples of fairly basic intuitions that seem obviously true, but that are contradicted by the results of psychological studies. Such examples are not rare and the fact that strong intuitions sometimes turn out to be wrong should make one very cautious about trusting any intuition (see Dawes 1988; Gilovich 1991; Kahneman, Slovic, and Tversky 1982; Nisbett and Ross 1980; and Stanovich 1996 for many examples and extensive discussion).

Importantly, I then suggest that intuition, uninformed by psychological research, is inherently limited as a method that researchers can use to understand how people think and behave. Specifically, people do not always have conscious access to their thought processes, and they are sometimes unaware of factors that influence their thoughts and behavior. However, intuition is fundamentally a *conscious* enterprise. Therefore, it is not possible to form intuitions about some aspects of thought and behavior by directly and consciously observing the processes and factors that give rise to them. Therefore, the lay person, as well as the researcher who relies solely on intuitions (the *intuition researcher*), is deprived of an important source of information for developing accurate intuitions about thought and behavior. Consistent with these observations, I present psychological research showing that lay people and intuition researchers can have poor intuitions about thought and behavior.

To develop accurate explanations of thought and behavior, standard methods of psychological research are necessary in order to indirectly infer that which is consciously unobservable. Furthermore, I will suggest that researchers who study behavior and thought within an experimental framework develop *better* intuitions about these phenomena than those of intuition researchers or lay people who do not study these phenomena within such a framework. The intuitions are better in the sense that they are more likely to be correct when subjected to experimental testing. Before I begin, let me very briefly explain the experimental approach that is used by psychologists to study thought and behavior. Unknown to many lay people, this approach has been applied to virtually every question asked about human thought and behavior. It also characterizes all of the experiments that I discuss in this chapter.

The Experimental Approach

Consider a hypothetical situation in which there are two people who are *identical*—they are both named Marcella, they are identical-looking, they have identical kidneys, they think, perceive, and feel in an identical manner, they have identical experiences that happen in identical places and at identical times, and so on. Suppose that you are interested in whether a chemical compound causes people to be happier than they otherwise would be. You could design an experiment to test your hypothesis: the first Marcella takes pills that contain the compound and the second Marcella takes placebos—pills that do not contain the compound but that are otherwise identical. Assume that neither of the Marcellas can tell the difference between these pills nor knows about the hypothesis.

The Marcellas take their pills (at identical times and places and in identical ways) and a week later you notice a marked change in the behavior and feelings of the first Marcella—she smiles and reports feeling happier than the second Marcella, and so on. Furthermore, you have accurately perceived the behavior of each Marcella and acted identically toward each Marcella during the test. Also assume that smiling and reports of feeling happy accurately describe what happiness is all about. Then, it is logically the case that your chemical compound causes an increase in happiness. In this experiment, there are two conditions that are identical in every aspect but one—the variable of interest (i.e., the presence versus absence of a chemical compound). Thus, the chemical compound must have caused the difference in behavior between the two Marcellas.

Clearly, it is impossible to conduct an experiment like the one described above, as no two people are identical. However, in psychology one is able to conduct experiments in which it is likely that the only *systematic* difference between conditions is the variable of interest. To illustrate, consider how the psychologist would go about testing the hypothesis described above. The psychologist would randomly and independently assign subjects to either a condition in which they took pills that contained the compound or a condition in which they took the placebos. Of course, a subject in one group will not be identical to a subject in the other group, and they will vary along many dimensions—some of which are related to happiness (e.g., perhaps self-esteem, job security, level of stress, sex life, and so on). However, because a subject is equally likely to be assigned to one or the other condition, it is equally likely that the various values of these happiness variables will be assigned to one or the other condition. Therefore, before the pills are taken, it is unlikely that there will be a systematic difference between the two groups in terms of happiness. Thus, if the experimenter subsequently finds that the group that takes the pills containing the compound is happier than the placebo group, then the experimenter can conclude that it is likely (though not logically the case) that the compound causes happiness. This simple but powerful technique of random assignment does not equate the groups on every happiness variable but rather minimizes the likelihood that there initially will be a systematic difference between the groups in terms of happiness. Other techniques are employed that do equate variables that can influence the results. For example, a single experimenter might be employed rather than separate experimenters for each condition to avoid the possibility that differences between happiness in the groups was due to differences in how different experimenters treated the groups.

Of course, this sketch of experimental methodology provides a very simple picture of the process. There are many other concerns that must be faced in designing and conducting a good experiment and in evaluating its results. For example, a finding might be due simply to chance, a result obtained from studying college sophomores may or may not generalize to other subject populations, subjects may think that they have figured out the experimenter's hypothesis and intentionally act in way that supports (or undermines) the hypothesis, an experimenter may interpret data in a biased fashion, a variable may not truly measure what it purports to measure (e.g., is "number of times that children touch toy guns" an accurate measure of violence?), and so on. Furthermore, because of ethical reasons, it is either difficult to study some things by using the experimental approach (e.g., causes of violence) or not possible to directly investigate them (e.g., whether cigarette smoking causes cancer in people). These concerns (and many others) are legitimate but by and large, they are wrinkles that are often ironed out (for discussion on how the wrinkles are ironed out see Mitchell and Jolley 1992; Underwood 1966). I now turn to some counterintuitive findings that have been uncovered by this experimental approach.

Strong but Wrong Intuitions

Consider the following statements that are meant to describe the typical human being who has normal cognitive functioning:

1. Given a choice, most people prefer less pain to more pain.

2. A person first comprehends an idea and then decides whether or not it is true.

3. Given two options (call them A and B), if a person *prefers* option A over option B, then that person should also *reject* option B in favor of option A.

I assume (although it is only a strong intuition on my part) that virtually everyone would confidently endorse these statements (including philosophers and psychologists). It also seems fairly easy to envision each statement acting as a basic premise in a philosophical analysis. For example, one might find statement 1 in a discussion of ethics, statement 2 in a discussion of language, and statement 3 in a discussion of folk psychology. As alluring as these statements may be, they are contradicted by a number of findings from psychological experiments.

Pain

Recently, Kahneman and his colleagues have investigated how people evaluate past episodes of pain. In one study, Kahneman, Fredrickson, Schreiber, and Redelneir (1993) exposed subjects to aversive experiences involving the immersion of their hands into cold water. On one trial of the experiment, subjects placed a hand into a tub of cold water ($14.1°$ C [$57.4°$ F]) for 60 seconds (the short trial). On another trial, these subjects placed their other hand into the same tub of cold water for 90 seconds (the long trial). In this case, the cold water remained at $14.1°$ C for 60 seconds (as in the first trial) but was then gradually increased from $14.1°$ C to $15.2°$ C ($59.4°$ F) over the additional 30 seconds. (The order of the short and long trials and their assignment to the dominant or nondominant hand were counterbalanced across subjects.) During a trial, subjects used their other hand to adjust a potentiometer, which recorded their subjective sense of discomfort on a scale from 0 to 14. The average discomfort rating was almost identical for the short trial and the first 60 seconds of the long trial (a rating a little over 8). For the additional 30 seconds of the long trial, the gradual increase in water temperature caused a drop in discomfort, but the average rating (5.7) still indicated that subjects were experiencing a fair amount of discomfort.

Interestingly, after completing the trials, subjects were asked to pick which of the two cold-water trials they would repeat—69 percent of the subjects chose the *longer* trial—thus preferring more pain to less pain. Kahneman et al. (1993) explain the finding by providing evidence that memory for a painful event is based on its worst and final moments and is relatively unaffected by duration. Even though the longer trial involved more pain, discomfort was less at the end of this trial than the shorter trial (with the peak levels of discomfort being the same in the two trials). Kahneman et al. (1993) also cite studies showing that this characterization of memory for pain is true for a number of other situations as well—including exposure to loud drilling noises and highly aversive films involving amputations and colonoscopies.

Comprehension and Truth Assessment

Gilbert and his colleagues have addressed the relationship between people's understanding of an idea and their judgments of the truth of that idea. Gilbert (1991) describes contrasting views of this relationship by two early philosophers. According to Descartes, people first comprehend an idea and then are free to judge or assess its truthfulness. Thus, there is a clear distinction between comprehension and assessment. Gilbert (1991) also suggests that among philosophers and psychologists the Cartesian view is the consensus view of how people understand ideas. In contrast, Spinoza suggested that comprehension and assessment were part of the same psychological act, and that in order to comprehend an idea people initially *had* to accept it. Of course, they were free to unaccept that idea, but unacceptance was a secondary, deliberate revision of an initially accepted belief.

Gilbert, Krull, and Malone (1990) tested Spinoza's intuition in several studies. For example, in one experiment they had subjects learn some facts about an imaginary animal called a glark. They were then shown a series of propositions about glarks (e.g., Glarks have white fur) and were asked either to judge whether a proposition was true or false (based on what they had learned) or on a few occasions, to *just read and comprehend* a proposition (and thus not assess its veracity). More specifically, after learning facts about glarks, a proposition was presented on a computer screen either preceded by the question, "Is the following sentence TRUE?" or by the command, "Speed read the following sentence."

The sentences were presented in such a way that subjects assessed the veracity of a proposition under one of three conditions: (a) after having recently assessed the veracity of that same proposition (the assessment-then-assessment condition), (b) after having recently read (comprehended) that proposition (the comprehension-then-assessment condition), or (c) after not having recently seen that proposition (the assessment only condition).

Interestingly, after comprehending a proposition (that happened to be true), subjects were more likely to assess that proposition as true compared to the case in which they had previously not seen that proposition. Even more striking, after comprehending a proposition (that happened to be false), subjects were also more likely to assess that proposition as true compared to the situation in which they had not previously seen that proposition. In other words, subjects were more likely to consider a proposition as true if they had just recently read the proposition than if they if they had not.

As a side note, the astute reader might argue that in the comprehension-then-assessment condition, subjects' greater tendency to assess a proposition as true may have simply been due to prior exposure of that proposition rather than the involuntary acceptance of that proposition as true. That is, mere exposure to any proposition increases one's tendency to judge it as true (whether or not it is). However, other findings undermine this alternative explanation. Recall that in one condition, subjects had prior exposure to true and false propositions that they were asked to assess (rather than just comprehend). In these cases, subjects should also be more likely to judge a previously seen proposition as true (whether or not it is). However, subjects were *less likely* to assess a false proposition as true compared to the situation in which they had not previously seen that proposition.

Gilbert et al. (1990) explain their results (and those from further studies that they conducted) by suggesting that the understanding of an idea is inextricably bound to initially accepting that idea as true. When subjects are asked to just comprehend a proposition they cannot help but initially assume that the proposition is true. In cognitive psychology, such a process would be called automatic (Shiffrin and Schneider 1977). Thus, when subsequently asked to explicitly assess the truth of that proposition, subjects will be more accurate at assessing the propositions that are true but less accurate at assessing those that are false.

Gilbert (1991) cites a number of other studies from social, developmental, and cognitive psychology whose results converge on this view.

Preferring versus Rejecting

In a series of studies, Shafir (1993) examined people's choices between options that were framed either in terms of preferring or rejecting. In one study, subjects were presented with a description about Parent A and one about Parent B. They were asked to imagine that they were serving on the jury for an only-child sole-custody case following a fairly messy divorce. Half of the subjects were asked which parent they would *prefer* to award sole custody of the child. The other half were asked which parent they would deny (i.e., *reject*) sole custody of the child. Parent A had the following characteristics: average income, average health, average working hours, reasonable rapport with the child, and a relatively stable social life. Parent B was described as having above-average income, a very close relationship with the child, an extremely active social life, lots of work-related travel, and minor health problems.

Interestingly, the subjects who were asked which parent they preferred to award sole custody *and* the subjects who were asked which parent they would deny sole custody more often chose Parent B. That is, subjects were both more willing to award and deny sole custody of the child to the same parent. Shafir (1993) explains this result (and those of further studies that he conducted) by noting that options sometimes contain both highly positive and negative features. Framing a choice in terms of preference causes people to more heavily weight highly positive features, whereas framing a choice in terms of rejection causes them to more heavily weight highly negative features. Thus, it is possible to both prefer and reject the same option. In the descriptions of the parents above, note that Parent B has both highly desirable and undesirable features with respect to child raising, whereas Parent A has no striking positive or negative features.

There are many other studies that show such inconsistencies in choice. For example, in choosing between gambling options, people sometimes select a bet A over a bet B but are willing to sell bet B for more than bet A (Lichtenstein and Slovic 1973). As another example, the extent to which physicians (and patients) prefer one kind of cancer treatment versus another depends on whether the treatment options are framed in terms of lives lost versus lives saved (McNeil et al. 1986). These results, like those of Shafir's, are quite counterintuitive.

To summarize, I have described some examples of strong intuitions about thought and behavior that are actually wrong. Strong but wrong intuitions are not rare. An interesting question is why people do not have the right intuitions about these examples. Perhaps people entertain both the right and wrong intuitions but believe that the "wrong" intuitions are much more plausible. However, another possibility is that people never even consider the right intuitions in the first place. The intuitions are not considered because they involve influences of which people are not consciously aware. For example, when people make judgments about pain they may simply be unaware that sometimes they are affected by the peak and final moments of pain but not affected by its duration.

Thus, it is difficult for a person to have an intuition about which of these factors affect their recollections of pain.

Unconscious Processes

There has been a long history of debate about unconscious processing in psychology. In modern psychology, the importance of the unconscious was championed by Freud, then largely banished from psychology by the behaviorists only to re-emerge as a basic tenet in cognitive psychology, where it was taken as self-evident that much of thinking was unconscious. Certainly, many basic cognitive processes are largely unconscious (e.g., object recognition, depth perception, understanding a sentence, motor tasks, and so on). These processes often happen extremely fast. In fact, our corresponding phenomenological experience is a sense that there are no processes operating at all. For example, when I look into my living room, I almost instantaneously see objects laid out in depth—chairs, a table in front of a wall and windows, and so forth.

Language understanding and production are paradigmatic cases of basic cognitive processes that are largely unconscious. In producing and understanding linguistic expressions, people largely rely on tacit knowledge that is unconsciously available to them. That speakers possess such knowledge is evidenced by their command of the language—but they are not aware of using it and are rarely able to articulate it. For example, in the sentence "The pain that Marcella feels is unpleasant" the complementizer "that" is optional but in the sentence, "The dog that bit Marcella ran away," it is not. Any native speaker of English knows these distinctions but cannot explain why they know them.

Importantly, because such knowledge is not consciously accessible, one cannot rely solely on intuition to determine how people understand and produce language. To illustrate the difficulties of (just) using intuitions to draw conclusions about language understanding and use, consider some views from philosophy on the comprehension of nonliteral (i.e., figurative) speech and the use of count and mass syntax. In a paper that has greatly influenced psycholinguistic research, Grice (1975) argued that language use is a cooperative enterprise between a speaker and a listener in which the speaker adheres to certain conversational maxims in communicating ideas to the listener. For example, speakers typically do not say what they believe to be false or that for which they lack adequate evidence (the maxim of quality, Grice 1975: 46). Importantly, on this account, speakers sometimes deliberately violate these maxims and listeners recognize the violations so as to infer that the speaker intended something else. For example, suppose that you and Marcella are sitting in the kitchen on a summer day, a turkey broiling away in the oven, and the windows closed. Both of you are sweating. If Marcella were to say, "I'm hot" you would probably get up and open a window. According to Grice, Marcella's statement violates the conversational maxim of being informative since it is obvious to both you and Marcella that it is hot. You recognize the violation and assume that Marcella is making a request (or indirect speech act).

This intuitively compelling view of language use and understanding provides a straightforward account of how people comprehend nonliteral speech, often called the *standard pragmatic view*. When a speaker produces an utterance, the listener derives its literal meaning and determines whether it makes sense in the present context. If not, the listener assumes that the speaker has deliberately violated a conversational maxim and attempts to determine a nonliteral interpretation of the utterance. For example, upon hearing the nominal metaphor "that dinner was a roller coaster" the listener determines that it does not make sense literally and that the speaker intended to violate a conversational maxim (e.g., quality). The listener then derives a nonliteral interpretation such as "that dinner involved a series of courses which alternated between tasting awful and tasting delicious." The philosopher Searle (1993) details just such an account of nonliteral language understanding, but it also has been proposed by psycholinguists (Clark and Lucy 1975) and cognitive psychologists (Gagne and Shoben, 1997).

However, although conversational maxims are an important aspect of language use, there is much evidence against the standard pragmatic account of how people understand figurative language (e.g., see Gibbs 1989, 1994; Glucksberg, Gildea, and Bookin 1982; Glucksberg 1991; Keysar 1989; Rumelhart 1993; Wisniewski and Love, forthcoming). For example, the standard pragmatic view predicts that people should be slower to interpret figurative than nonfigurative language. However, given an appropriate discourse context, people do not take longer to understand figurative utterances, such as "billboards are warts on the landscape" or "the ham sandwich left without paying" (see Gibbs 1994 for a review). As another example, the standard pragmatic view implies that people seek nonliteral meanings if and only if the literal meaning makes no sense in context (Glucksberg 1991). However, Keysar (1989) found that the time to judge the truth of a statement that literally made sense in a particular context was facilitated or inhibited by whether the context *also implied* that its metaphorical meaning was true or false (see Glucksberg et al. 1982 for a related finding).

To summarize, although the standard pragmatic account of how people understand figurative language is intuitively appealing, it is not correct. (Just exactly how people understand figurative language is not resolved, but see, e.g., Glucksberg and Keysar 1990 and Gentner 1989 for some proposals.) Of course, the work of Searle and Grice does show that conscious introspection about how we think can suggest plausible accounts of the processes that are involved. However, such intuitions were not based on consciously inspecting these processes.

As a second example of intuitions about language use, consider the distinction between count and mass nouns made in many languages. A number of syntactic constructions apply to count nouns but not (usually) to mass nouns, and vice versa. For example, count nouns in English typically can follow determiners such as "a" and "another" in their singular form (e.g., "a pig" but not "a water") and numerals in their plural form (e.g., "three pigs" but not "three waters"). On the other hand, singular mass nouns typically can follow determiners that pick out an indeterminate quantity of what the noun refers to (e.g., "too much beer" but not "too much computer").

In English, count/mass usage is quite varied and flexible. The distinction is made across many different kinds of nouns, including object and substance terms (e.g., "a dog" but not "a soap"), superordinates that refer to broad categories of perceptually diverse things (e.g., "an animal" but not "a furniture"), and abstract nouns (e.g., "an idea" but not "an evidence"). Also, many nouns can have a role as either a count or a mass noun (e.g., "a candy" as well as "too much candy"). In addition, similar aspects of reality are nevertheless distinguished with count/mass usage. For example, Gleason (1969) notes that beans is a count noun whereas rice is a mass noun and that this grammatical distinction is present even though the nouns appear to name things that seem similar (i.e., small, edible things that almost always co-occur). Also, some pairs of count/mass nouns appear coreferential, such as fuzz versus cops, clothing versus garments, snow versus snowflakes (see Ware 1979 for discussion). That is, there is a count/mass distinction between some pairs of nouns even though intuitively they refer to similar things.

As a result of these observations, a number of linguists (e.g., Bloomfield 1933; Gleason 1969; McCawley 1975) and philosophers (e.g., Quine 1989; Ware 1979) have struggled with their intuitions to find some compelling reason that explains why this distinction is made across such diverse domains that have little in common and why both count and mass terms are apparently used to refer to the same aspects of reality. Unable to find such a reason, they have questioned whether there is a systematic relationship between count/mass grammar and conceptualization, suggesting that the relationship is arbitrary, unprincipled, or idiosyncratic.

However, other researchers argue that count/mass syntax marks a general distinction between cognitively individuated and unindividuated entities (e.g., Bloom 1994a, 1994b; Imai and Gentner 1994; Jackendoff 1991; Langacker 1987; Wierzbicka 1988; Wisniewski, Imai, and Casey 1996). According to this principle, speakers conceptualize the referents of count nouns as distinct, countable, individuated things and those of mass nouns as nondistinct, uncountable, unindividuated things.

Importantly, research suggests that there are a variety of factors that either enhance or compromise individuality that depend on the type of entity involved. Thus, the relationship between count/mass syntax and conceptualization is not arbitrary, unprincipled, or idiosyncratic. For example, whether people use mass or count syntax to refer to a set of objects depends on the degree to which they are spatially contiguous. In several unpublished studies, Lyman Casey and I presented subjects with pairs of object sets. In one set, the objects were very close together but in the other set they were farther apart. Subjects were then presented with a fictitious phrase such as "Here is some chorb" (mass syntax) or "Here are some chorbs" (count syntax) and asked to select the set that is best characterized by the phrase. Subjects typically selected the mass syntax phrases for sets of objects that are close together and the count syntax phrases for sets of objects that are farther apart. Whereas spatial contiguity often affects whether *objects* are individuated, temporal contiguity affects whether *sounds* are individuated. Bloom (1994b) showed that people preferred a plural count noun to label a sound occurring over discrete intervals, implying that they construed the sound as a number of distinct, temporally bounded, and separate individuals. However, people preferred a mass noun to label a sound occurring over a long, continuous period of time, implying that they construed the sound as a temporally unbounded, unindividuated entity.

Note that in both of these examples, subjects were most likely unaware of why they preferred to label one stimulus with count syntax and another with mass syntax. However, by carefully manipulating certain variables hypothesized to affect such choices (and preventing others from systematically varying), the experimenters determined which aspects of the world map onto the count/mass distinction.

In psychology, there is a growing appreciation of the ubiquity of unconscious influences across all aspects of cognition. Below I briefly describe unconscious influences on two other aspects of cognition—explanations for one's own behavior and beliefs about whether one's memory is of an event that actually happened.

Explaining Behavior and Feelings

A number of studies in social psychology suggest that people sometimes explain their behavior or feelings by using their intuitions to decide which factors of the situation caused their behavior. If their intuitions do not suggest plausible causes, then people believe that the reason for their behavior was random or arbitrary. As a result, people sometimes erroneously attribute their behavior to intuitively plausible causes that nevertheless did not influence their behavior, or they ignore intuitively implausible factors that nevertheless did influence their behavior. Thus, people sometimes fail to understand why they do things or feel a particular way. Of course, this view makes sense given that people do not always have conscious access to their thought processes.

To illustrate this phenomenon, consider several studies from social psychology. Nisbett and Wilson (1977) had subjects view a brief documentary on the plight of the Jewish poor in large cities. In one condition, subjects viewed the film while a power saw made noises in the hall outside. In another condition, subjects viewed the film without distraction. Then, subjects rated the film along several dimensions: how interesting they thought the film was, how much they thought other people would be affected by it, and how sympathetic they found the main character to be. After making the ratings the experimenter apologized to those who saw the film under the noisy condition and asked the subjects to indicate whether any of their ratings were affected by the noise. The presence of the noise did not affect subjects' ratings compared to the group who viewed the film without the noise. However, a majority of subjects in the noise condition erroneously reported that the noise had lowered at least one of their ratings.

As another example, Lewicki (1985) conducted a study that typifies the nonconscious influences of recently activated but irrelevant information on judgments. Subjects participating in an experiment entered a room where they were briefly interviewed by an experimenter before proceeding to the main part of the experiment. The experimenter asked the subject three questions, the last one being "What is your birth order?" The subjects, aged 18-19, typically did not understand the question and asked the experimenter exactly what she meant. In the slightly irritated condition, the experimenter replied in a slightly irritated way: "Don't you really know the meaning of birth order?!" The experimenter then explained the meaning and took down the subject's birth order. In the neutral condition, the experimenter explained the meaning of birth order after being asked and took down the subjects' birth order, leaving out the irritated reply. Half of the subjects were randomly assigned to each of these conditions.

After finishing this short interview, each subject went to another room where the main part of the experiment was to take place. In the other room there were two new experimenters sitting at separate tables: one looked somewhat similar to the first experimenter who had done the short interview (she had short hair and glasses like the first experimenter) and the other was dissimilar (she had long hair and did not wear glasses). The subject was to approach an experimenter who currently was not busy in order to start the experiment. However, both experimenters were busy writing things so a subject had to make a choice on some other basis. Subjects in the slightly irritated condition were four times as likely to choose the new experimenter who did not look like the first experimenter. After performing a task that involved choosing the most interesting irregular polygons, subjects filled out a questionnaire concerning their feelings during the experiment ostensibly designed to help the experimenters better understand the subjects in general and to make them more comfortable during the experiments. There were many questions that involved rank ordering numerous possibilities pertaining to all the phases and details of the experiment. Located toward the end of the questionnaire was a question that asked subjects why they chose the experimenter that they did. Most subjects ranked "my choice was completely random" as their first choice. Subjects also rated how much they liked the first experimenter—subjects in the slightly irritated condition did not rate the first experimenter any less likable than did subjects in the neutral condition.

The results of these studies suggest that people did not explain their thoughts, feelings, or behavior by consciously examining the cognitive processes that produced them. Rather, they evaluated the context in which the thoughts, behavior, or feelings occurred and attempted to construct an explanation that implicated factors that were intuitively plausible causes. In the Nisbett and Wilson (1977) study, subjects recalled that they viewed the film under a noisy condition and assumed quite plausibly that it affected their ratings of the film (although it did not actually affect their ratings). In the Lewicki (1985) study, there was no plausible, compelling factor that should affect a subject's choice of one or the other experimenter. Thus, a subject plausibly assumed that they had arbitrarily selected one of the experimenters.

Although people's intuitions about the causes of their thoughts and behavior can be accurate (Nisbett and Wilson 1977; Smith and Miller 1978), many studies suggest that a person's intuitions either fail to implicate the correct cause or implicate an erroneous cause (see Nisbett and Wilson 1977; Wilson and Stone 1985; Wilson and Brekke 1994 for reviews). Thus, by itself, intuition is a poor tool for understanding how people think and behave.

The Origin of Memories

Another interesting issue that has received much attention concerns intuitive judgments about the source or origin of memories and beliefs (see Johnson, Hashtroudi, and Lindsay 1993 for a review). For example, it is often crucial to distinguish whether your memory of an event is something that actually happened in the past or something that you imagined in the past. That is, is the source of this memory a real or imagined event? This question is particularly relevant with respect to evaluating the validity of claims about repressed childhood memories (Loftus 1993). As another example, which is especially relevant in academics, it is often important to know whether you were the one who originally thought of the bright idea or whether the source was a colleague who told you that bright idea.

Baddeley (1990) describes a particularly notable example of confusing the source of a memory, which involved the psychologist Donald Thomson. As told by Baddeley, Thomson had conducted studies showing that eyewitness identification is likely to be strongly influenced by the clothes that the criminal was wearing at the time of the crime. He found that innocent people are likely to be picked out of a line-up if they are wearing clothes that resemble those worn by the criminal. Thomson appeared on a television program that discussed this issue. A few weeks later he was picked up by the police and subsequently picked out of a line-up by a woman who claimed that she had been raped by him. By coincidence, Thomson's appearance on the television program coincided with the time of the rape and the woman happened to be watching the show. She was correct in recognizing Thomson's face but had confused the source of the memory.

A fair amount of research suggests that the source of a memory or belief is not explicitly stored with that memory. Instead, people examine their memories and use certain processes to decide the source of that memory. Sometimes the decisions about the source are based on deliberative conscious processes, such as attributing a statement that you remember to your friend Marcella because she would be the only who would say that sort of thing, so she must have said it. In these cases, people might have *good* intuitions about how they determine a source of a memory.

However, this research also suggests that the accuracy of identifying the source depends on many factors of which people are largely unaware. One factor is the amount of perceptual and contextual information associated with the memory. Real events generally contain more of such information than imagined events, and people use this cue in remembering a past event as real or imagined. A second factor has to do with the cognitive operations associated with encoding the memory. Confusions between real and imagined events are related to the degree of cognitive processing involved in the event. For example, in a study by Finke, Johnson, and Shyi (1988), people were asked to rate the complexity of geometric forms, which included half forms. Whenever they saw a half form they were asked to "mentally complete" the figure in order to rate its complexity. From previous research, it is known that objects that are symmetrical along the vertical axis are easier to mentally complete than those symmetrical about the horizontal axis. After doing this task, subjects were shown examples of all the completed geometric forms, and they were asked to distinguish those figures they had actually seen completed from those they had imagined as completed. Subjects were more likely to say that they had imagined as completed the half forms that were symmetrical about the horizontal axis. The implication of this finding is that when something is easily imagined it will be harder to remember at a later time whether it was imagined or actually occurred, and that people use this cue to determine whether they experienced something real or imagined.

Yet another factor that influences the identity of a source is whether the attributes associated with the source are uniquely characteristic of that source. For example, Johnson et al. (1993) describe a study in which subjects imagined themselves saying some words and heard the experimenter saying other words. Under this condition, they were relatively good at distinguishing whether they had imagined saying a word or whether they had heard the experimenter say the word. However, in another condition, subjects imagined themselves saying the words in the experimenter's voice. Later, they had much more difficulty deciding whether they imagined saying a word or whether the experimenter said it. Interestingly, there are also developmental differences in identifying the source of a memory. A child six years of age has trouble remembering whether she actually touched her nose or whether she only imagined touching her nose, although she can distinguish whether she touched her nose or whether another person touched his nose.

Evolution

At some level of explanation, a theory of mind and thinking must take seriously the evolutionary history of the human brain. Our current mind is grounded in mechanisms that developed over the course of evolution and that were built by refining or adding to existing mechanisms instead of optimally designing a new mechanism from scratch that perfectly solved a problem. That is, mind design was a compromise between preserving what was there and developing what was needed. Furthermore, the mechanisms of our current mind are largely beneficial to surviving in a past world that perhaps does not resemble our current world in at least some important respects. The mechanisms that were useful in that past world are useful in the current world, but the extent of their usefulness may vary if for no other reason than that the current world is different from the world in which those mechanisms emerged.

These observations have very important implications for the use of intuition in studying thought and behavior. People's intuitions are products of the world as we know it today and not of the world in which our minds evolved. In this light, it is useful to revisit Gilbert's findings that comprehension of an idea is intertwined with an initial assumption that the idea is true. Gilbert (1991) speculates that cognition is an evolutionary outgrowth of perception. The idea is that for the most part, our percepts accurately reflect aspects of reality. Because our percepts usually mirror reality, the perceptual system unconsciously and automatically assumes that they are true and often for good reason. In earlier times, a person contemplating the veracity of their percepts might be eaten by an approaching tiger.

Gilbert's claim then is that the evolution of thought resulted in a brain that is built upon existing mechanisms that served us quite well. More specifically, our belief mechanism has a comprehension and assessment component that is analogous to perceptual processes. In Gilbert's own words, "people believe in the ideas they comprehend as quickly and automatically as they believe in the objects they see." At the same time our belief system has mechanisms that allow for subsequent unacceptance of ideas. Within an evolutionary framework, Gilbert's claims and supporting findings make sense. However, outside of this framework they may seem counterintuitive.

An Important Moral

It is clear that researchers must be very careful about relying on their intuitions in formulating theories of thought and behavior. Experimental methods are absolutely essential for determining the validity of such intuitions. Perhaps less obvious is that familiarity and direct experience with psychological research may lead to better intuitions about thinking and behavior. Cognitive and social psychologists, like other scientists, attempt to develop theories that explain a wide range of phenomena and that predict new phenomena. Consider a psychologist who has developed a theory that explains a number of surprising and counterintuitive findings. The psychologist will use the theory to make predictions about new phenomena that will be intuitive to the psychologist (because they follow from the theory) but that are likely to be surprising and counterintuitive to researchers and lay people who do not know about the theory. To the extent that the theory is a good one (by the usual scientific criteria), the psychologist's intuitions are more likely to turn out right than those of people who are not familiar with the theory and the phenomena it explains.

Chapter 4

Philosophical Intuitions and Cognitive Mechanisms

Eldar Shafir

Intuition occupies a central role in philosophical theorizing. Some of the most poignant and memorable passages in philosophical writings have relied on examples whose appeal to intuition can make compelling a theory that until then seemed obscure. The appeal to intuition can be observed in domains ranging from metaphysics and epistemology, to ethics and the philosophy of mind. In what follows, I shall be unabashedly descriptive in my treatment of intuitions. I shall focus on systematic and well-documented aspects of the psychology that underlies people's intuitions; I shall ignore questions such as whether there are moral facts, or facts about rationality, and whether we may have intuitive, perceptual, or other privileged access to such facts. This chapter will consider the systematic ways in which intuitions shift as a result of supposedly inconsequential manipulations, and the implications this might have for the stability and significance of philosophical theorizing.

A descriptive account of the psychology that underlies people's attitudes and intuitions should be given serious consideration, even by scholars mostly concerned with normative or prescriptive theory. The compelling nature of normative theory notwithstanding, most scholars of human behavior tend to endorse theories that they consider psychologically feasible. Even those who suppose an exceedingly high degree of rationality or morality on the part of individuals have typically regarded their assumptions to be plausible, if somewhat idealized. Unwilling to deny the relevance of human nature, these theorists adopt a naive account of mental life that, if approximately correct, could yield behaviors largely consistent with those dictated by normative theory. Requirements of deductive closure or unbounded memory, for example, are obviously unrealistic about us and thus not part of the assumptions that most people make. Likewise, moral principles are taken seriously to the extent that the creatures to which they are applied are assumed to be able to follow them. Many errors of reasoning, inconsistencies in choice, failures of self-control, and moral transgressions, to name a few, are considered interesting, if not embarrassing, precisely because there is the feeling that one could, and should, have done better.

The descriptive approach is based on empirical observation and experimental studies of behavior. The evidence indicates that people's sentiments and preferences exhibit patterns that are often at odds with intuitive assumptions, and empirical generalizations emerge that help explain the nonintuitive patterns. In what follows, I review selected findings and discuss some psychological principles that underlie preference and evaluation. In particular, I focus on a systematic discrepancy that is observed between evaluations that are conducted in isolation, when one alternative is considered at a time, and choices that are observed in comparative settings, when two or more alternatives are considered simultaneously. Typically, isolated evaluations are obtained in a "between-subject" design, where some people evaluate one scenario and others evaluate another, or when the same person evaluates different scenarios sequentially, at different points in time, so as to render direct comparison difficult. Simultaneous evaluations are observed in a "within-subject" design, when a person is presented with two or more scenarios concurrently. The systematic discrepancy observed between the two modes of evaluation has profound implications for the role of philosophical intuition. Whereas most life experiences take place in what can be thought of as a between-subject design (you encounter one scenario; someone else may encounter another), philosophical intuitions typically are the introspective result of a within-subject evaluation (a philosopher contemplates a scenario and its alternatives). The implications of this tension are explored in what follows (see also Kahneman 1996). In the next two sections, alternative elicitation methods are shown to give rise to differential weighting of dimensions and, consequently, to inconsistent decisions. Related phenomena are then reviewed in the realm of counterfactual evaluation and in contexts that explore people's feelings of sympathy, urgency, and indignation. Section IV contrasts the phenomenology of uncertainty with compelling intuitions about reasoning in uncertain situations. Concluding remarks occupy the last section.

Compatibility and Preference Reversals

Elicitation of Preference

Preferences can be elicited through different methods. People can indicate which option they prefer; alternatively, they can be asked to price each option by stating the amount of money that is as valuable to them as the option. A standard assumption, known as *procedure invariance,* requires that logically equivalent elicitation procedures give rise to the same preference order. Thus, if one option is chosen over another, it is also expected to be priced higher. Procedure invariance is essential for the interpretation of both psychological and physical measurement. The ordering of physical objects with respect to mass, for example, can be established either by placing each object separately on a scale, or by placing both objects on two sides of a pan balance. Procedure invariance requires that the two methods yield the same ordering, within the limit of measurement error. Analogously, the rational theory of choice assumes that an individual has a well-defined preference order that can be elicited either by choice or by pricing, giving rise to the same ordering of preferences.

Compatibility Effects

Despite its appeal as an abstract principle, people systematically violate procedure invariance. For example, people often choose one bet over another, but price the second bet above the first. In one study, subjects were presented with two prospects of similar expected value. One prospect, the H bet, offered a high probability to win a relatively small payoff (e.g., 8 chances in 9 to win $4) whereas the other prospect, the L bet, offered a low probability to win a larger payoff (e.g., a 1 in 9 chance to win $40). When asked to choose between these prospects, most subjects chose the H bet over the L bet. Subjects were also asked, on another occasion, to price each prospect by indicating the smallest amount of money for which they would be willing to sell this prospect. Here, most subjects assigned a higher price to the L bet than to the H bet. One recent study that used this particular pair of bets observed that 71 percent of the subjects chose the H bet, while 67 percent priced L above H (Tversky, Slovic, and Kahneman 1990). This phenomenon, called "preference reversal," has been replicated in experiments using a variety of prospects and incentive schemes; it has been observed in a study involving professional gamblers in a Las Vegas casino (Lichtenstein and Slovic 1973; Slovic and Lichtenstein 1983), and in a study conducted in the Peoples' Republic of China for real payoffs equal to several months' worth of the subjects' salary (Kachelmeier and Shehata 1992).

What is the cause of preference reversal? Why do people assign a higher monetary value to the low probability bet, but choose the high probability bet more often? It appears that the major cause of preference reversal is a differential weighting of probabilities and payoffs in choice and pricing, induced by the type of response. In line with the general notion of compatibility, which has long been recognized by students of perception and motor control, experimental evidence indicates that an attribute of an option is given more weight when it is compatible with the response format than when it is not (Tversky, Sattath, and Slovic 1988; for review, see Shafir 1995). Because the price that the subject assigns to a bet is expressed in dollars, the payoffs of the bet, which are also expressed in dollars, are weighted more heavily in pricing than in choice. As a consequence, the L bet (which has the higher payoff) is evaluated more favorably in pricing than in choice, which can give rise to preference reversals. (The foregoing account is further supported by the observation that the incidence of preference reversals is greatly reduced for bets involving nonmonetary outcomes, such as a free dinner at a local restaurant, where outcomes and prices are no longer expressed in the same units and are therefore less compatible; see Slovic, Griffin, and Tversky 1990.)

The compatibility hypothesis does not depend on the presence of risk. It predicts a similar discrepancy between choice and pricing in the context of riskless options that have a monetary component. Consider a long-term prospect L, which pays $2,500 five years from now, and a short-term prospect S, which pays $1,600 in one and a half years. Subjects were invited to choose between L and S and to price both prospects by stating the smallest immediate cash payment for which they would be willing to exchange each prospect (Tversky, Slovic, and Kahneman 1990). Because the payoffs and the prices again are expressed in the same units, compatibility suggests that the long-term prospect (offering the higher payoff) will be overvalued in pricing relative to choice. In accord with this hypothesis, subjects chose the short-term prospect 74 percent of the time but priced the long-term prospect above the short-term prospect 75 percent of the time. These observations indicate that different methods of elicitation, such as choice and pricing, can induce different weightings of attributes, which, in turn, can give rise to different preferences.

Note that the pricing of an option involves independent evaluation and could be used to assign worth in isolation. Choice, on the other hand, is an inherently comparative process, that requires concurrent presentation. When options are encountered one at a time, they can be priced or assigned other measures of attractiveness, but direct comparison is not feasible. The weights that enter into our evaluations when conducted in isolation are thus expected to differ from those that characterize concurrent evaluation, when both options are before the attention. When a philosopher introspects about how people will, or even ought to, evaluate different options when these are presumably encountered in isolation, the philosopher will be confined to a concurrent evaluation, with the various alternatives before his or her attention. To the extent that the two forms of evaluation—concurrent and in isolation—lead to differential weightings, there will be a systematic tendency for people to experience events in isolation that will remain beyond the scope of within-subject intuition. In everyday life, we tend to experience and evaluate scenarios one at a time, whereas intuitions about relative worth often arise from introspectively comparative evaluations. As a result, the weighting of dimensions that goes into the making of common intuition can differ systematically from the weights that are assigned in actual experience.

The Prominence Hypothesis and Reversals in Perceived Importance

People often feel that one attribute (e.g., safety) is more important than another (e.g., cost). Although the interpretation of such claims is not entirely clear, there is evidence that the attribute that is judged more important looms larger in choice than in independent evaluation, such as pricing (Slovic 1975; Tversky, Sattath, and Slovic 1988). This is known as the prominence hypothesis and can lead to systematic violations of invariance.

Consider, for example, the following study concerning people's responses to environmental problems (Kahneman and Ritov 1994). Several pairs of issues where selected, where one issue addresses human health or safety and the other concerns protection of the environment. Each issue included a brief statement of a problem, along with a suggested form of intervention, as illustrated below.

> *Problem*: Skin cancer from sun exposure is common among farm workers.
> *Intervention*: Support free medical checkups for threatened groups.

Problem: Several Australian mammal species are nearly wiped out by hunters.
Intervention: Contribute to a fund to provide safe breeding areas for these species.

One group of respondents was asked to choose which of the two interventions they would rather support; a second group was presented with one issue at a time and asked to determine the largest amount they would be willing to pay for the respective intervention. Because the treatment of cancer in humans is generally viewed as more important than the protection of Australian mammals, the prominence hypothesis predicts that the former will receive greater support in direct choice than in independent evaluation. This prediction was confirmed. When asked to evaluate each intervention separately, respondents, who might have been moved by these animals' plight, were willing to pay more, on average, for safe breeding of Australian mammals than for free checkups for skin cancer. However, when faced with a direct choice between these options, most subjects favored free checkups for humans over safe breeding for the mammals. As expected, the issue that is considered more important acquired a greater prominence in the choice condition, which allows for a direct comparison between issues, than in separate presentation, where each issue is evaluated in accord with its own generated emotions. Irwin, Slovic, Lichtenstein, and McClelland (1993) report related findings in settings where improvements in air quality were compared with improvements in consumer commodities. In general, people may evaluate one alternative more positively than another when these are evaluated independently, but then reverse their evaluation in direct comparisons that accentuate the prominent attribute.

A similar pattern may occur in cases where an attribute is particularly difficult to gauge in isolation. Hsee (1996), for example, presented subjects with two alternative second-hand music dictionaries; one with 20,000 entries but a slightly torn cover, the other with 10,000 entries and a cover like new. Subjects had little notion of how many entries to expect in a music dictionary. Consequently, under separate evaluation, they expressed a willingness to pay more for the dictionary with the new cover than for the one with a slightly torn cover. When the two dictionaries were evaluated concurrently, however, most subjects obviously preferred the dictionary with twice as many entries, despite its inferior cover.

Intuitions about importance, worth, gravity, as well as ethical propriety are often obtained in comparative settings; we ask ourselves which issue, A or B, is more grave, or more worthy of our attention; which act, A or B, constitutes a greater ethical violation. In life, we often encounter the relevant scenarios one at a time; we might encounter scenario A today, and somebody else, or we, at another time, might encounter scenario B. To the extent that our encounters with these scenarios trigger sentiments and reactions that partly depend on their being experienced in isolation, some critical (and perhaps normatively appropriate) aspects of our response are likely to be missed by intuitions that arise from concurrent, within-subject introspection.

Affect and Principles

In a study ostensibly intended to establish the amounts of compensation payment that the public considers reasonable, Miller and McFarland (1986) presented respondents with brief descriptions of victims who had applied for compensation and asked them to decide upon a monetary payment. Two such descriptions concerned a male victim who was described as having lost the use of his right arm as a result of a gunshot wound suffered during a robbery at a convenience store. Some respondents were told that the robbery happened at the victim's regular store. Others were told that the victim was shot at a store he rarely frequented, that he went to because his usual store was temporarily closed. It was hypothesized that subjects would assign higher compensation to a person whose victimization was preceded by an abnormal event. This is because abnormal events strongly evoke a counterfactual undoing, which tends to raise the perceived poignancy of outcomes and the sympathy for their victims. (For more on the psychology of counterfactual thinking, see Kahneman and Miller 1986; Roese and Olson 1995.) Indeed, the victim who was shot at a store he rarely visited was assigned significantly greater compensation than the victim who was shot at his regular store. The difference in poignancy created by the normal-versus-abnormal manipulation translated into a $100,000 difference in compensation judged appropriate for the two cases.

The affective impact of events is often influenced by the ease with which an alternative event can be imagined. The death of a soldier on the last day of the war seems more poignant than the death of his comrade six months earlier. The fate of a plane crash victim who switched to the fatal flight only minutes before take-off is seen as more tragic than that of a fellow passenger who had been booked on that flight for months. Whereas the affective impact of such distinctions is predictable and often strong, do people actually consider these distinctions relevant? Consider the earlier study about compensation to victims. Recall that the two versions of the robbery scenario—at the regular versus the unusual stores—were presented to separate group of subjects. Their affective responses— stronger for the unusual than for the regular scenario—were thus obtained in isolation. On the other hand, when respondents were presented with both versions concurrently, the great majority (90 percent) thought that the victims in the two cases should not be awarded different compensations (Kahneman 1996). Evidently, despite the large difference in awards observed above, most subjects consider the difference between the two scenarios irrelevant to compensation. In a within-subject design that allows direct comparison, rules about what is relevant are easy to apply: we can decide, for example, that the victim's past frequency of visits to the store is immaterial. Between subjects, on the other hand, the application of rules remains elusive: there is no way to assure that the affective reactions that guide our response in isolation conform to the rules that would be endorsed upon concurrent evaluation. Using data from the 1992 Summer Olympics, Medvec, Madey, and Gilovich (1995) showed that athletes who had won silver medals tended to be less satisfied than those who won bronze. Apparently, the silver medalists compare themselves to those who had won the gold, whereas for the bronze medalists a natural counterfactual is not having won any medals. Of course, if they had to choose all these athletes would presumably prefer the silver over the bronze. Thus, the feelings of relief or disappointment that loom large in the separate experiences are clearly overwhelmed by preference for a better placement upon concurrent evaluation.

The intensity of satisfaction, empathy, or indignation that we feel can be affected by nuanced factors. Principles of decision intended to transcend some of these factors can be compelling in direct comparisons, but difficult to apply in isolated evaluations. This tension presents interesting philosophical questions. In one study (Tversky and Griffin 1991), respondents were presented with two hypothetical job possibilities, one offering a higher yearly salary in a company where others with similar training earn more (You: $35,000; Others: $38,000), and the other offering a lower salary in a company where others with similar training earn less (You: $33,000; Others: $30,000). Most of us tend to abide by a simple principle according to which we ought to prefer outcomes that improve our lot more over outcomes that improve it less. In fact, a majority of respondents chose the job with the higher absolute salary, despite the lower relative position. This simple principle, however, does not apply with equal force when we contemplate each of the job offers separately: in this condition, without the other offer serving as a comparison, earning a salary lower than comparable others can highlight sentiments that reduce our feelings of satisfaction. Indeed, contrary to the preference observed above, the majority of respondents who evaluated each of the job offers separately anticipated higher satisfaction in the job with the higher relative position and lower salary. A variant of this study was replicated with second-year MBA students, who were presented with two alternative job offers. In one, they would be paid $75,000, the same as other starting MBAs; in the other, they would be paid $85,000 while some other graduating MBAs would receive $95,000. As predicted, the students proved more willing to accept the former job offer when these were evaluated in isolation, but chose the latter offer when the two were evaluated concurrently (Bazerman et al. 1994; see also Bazerman, White, and Loewenstein 1995, for related discussion).

It is interesting to note in this context that consequentialist or utilitarian considerations appear to loom larger in concurrent than in isolated evaluations. In line with related observations regarding the malleability of utility estimation in decision making, it seems that the utilitarian worth of outcomes, which is often hard to gauge out of context, plays a greater role in direct comparisons than in isolated settings. Hsee (1997), for example, presented subjects with pictures of two servings of Hägen-Dazs ice cream. One serving contained more ice cream that failed to fill a larger cup; the other contained less ice cream that overfilled a smaller container. When the two were evaluated jointly, subjects were willing to pay more for what was clearly a larger serving. In separate evaluation, however, when the precise amount of ice cream was hard to gauge, subjects tended to pay more for the overfilled cup than for the one that seems partly empty.

Simple principles of merit, entitlement, worth, or maximization, which can play a decisive role in comparative settings, often prove difficult to apply in isolated situations. The compensation a victim is entitled to, the attractiveness of a job offer, or the value of a serving of ice cream can be hard to gauge when these occur in isolation. In fact, other considerations, such as the emotional impact of the victim's plight, the sense of fairness produced by a co-worker's salary, or the amount of ice cream relative to the size of the container, can strongly influence our evaluations when these occur in isolation. To the extent that our experiences with such matters generate sentiments and reactions that partly depend on their being evaluated in isolation, these important aspects of our affective responses are likely to be missed by intuitions that arise from well-defined principles that are sometimes only possible to apply in concurrent, within-subject evaluations.

Uncertainty and the Sure-Thing Principle

Many decisions are made in the presence of some uncertainty about their consequences. A critical feature of thinking under uncertainty is the need to consider possible states of the world and their potential consequences for our beliefs and actions. A fundamental principle which underlies most analyses of rational choice was described by Savage (1954: 21), who captured the intuition in the following passage:

> A businessman contemplates buying a certain piece of property. He considers the outcome of the next presidential election relevant to the attractiveness of the purchase. So, to clarify the matter for himself, he asks whether he would buy if he knew that the Republican candidate were going to win, and decides that he would do so. Similarly, he considers whether he would buy if he knew that the Democratic candidate were going to win, and again finds that he would do so. Seeing that he would buy in either event, he decides that he should buy, even though he does not know which event obtains. . . . It is all too seldom that a decision can be arrived at on the basis of the principle used by this businessman, but, except possibly for the assumption of simple ordering, I know of no other extralogical principle governing decisions that finds such ready acceptance.

Savage went on to define this principle formally: If x is preferred to y knowing that event A obtained, and if x is preferred to y knowing that event A did not obtain, then x should be preferred to y even when it is not known whether A obtained. As Savage points out, this principle, which he called the *sure-thing principle* (henceforth, STP), has a great deal of both normative and descriptive appeal. It is one of the simplest and least controversial principles of rational behavior and is implied by "consequentialist" accounts of decision making, in that it captures a fundamental intuition about what it means for a decision to be determined by the anticipated consequences.[1] It is a cornerstone of Expected Utility Theory, and it holds in other models of choice that impose less stringent criteria of rationality. It is intuitively very compelling. Nonetheless, people's decisions do not always abide by STP.

The Disjunction Effect

Consider the following problem that occurs in one of two versions, as indicated in brackets.

Imagine that you have just played a game of chance that gave you a 50 percent chance to win $200 and a 50 percent chance to lose $100. The coin was tossed and you have [won $200 / lost $100]. You are now offered a second, identical gamble: 50 percent chance to win $200 and 50 percent chance to lose $100. Would you:

	Won	Lost
a) Accept the second gamble	69%	59%
b) Reject the second gamble	31%	41%

Tversky and Shafir (1992) presented subjects (ninety-eight Stanford undergraduates) with the Won version of the problem above, followed a week later by the Lost version, and ten days after that by the following version that is a disjunction of the previous two:

Imagine that you have just played a game of chance that gave you a 50 percent chance to win $200 and a 50 percent chance to lose $100. Imagine that the coin has already been tossed, but that you will not know whether you have won $200 or lost $100 until you make your decision concerning a second, identical gamble: 50 percent chance to win $200 and 50 percent chance to lose $100. Would you:

a) Accept the second gamble	36%
b) Reject the second gamble	64%

These problems were embedded among several others and temporally separated so the relation among the three versions was not transparent. To the right of each option is the percentage of subjects who chose it. The data show that the majority of subjects accepted the second gamble after having won the first gamble, and the majority accepted the second gamble after having lost the first gamble. However, contrary to STP, the majority of subjects rejected the second gamble when the outcome of the first was not known. Among those subjects who accepted the second gamble, both after a gain and after a loss on the first, 65 percent rejected the second gamble in the disjunctive condition, when the outcome of the first gamble was uncertain. In fact, this particular pattern—accept when won, accept when lost, but reject when do not know—was the single most frequent pattern exhibited by these subjects (see Tversky and Shafir 1992; Shafir and Tversky 1992, for more data and discussion). We call this pattern a *disjunction effect*. A disjunction effect occurs when a person prefers x over y when she knows that event A obtains, and she also prefers x over y when she knows that event A does not obtain, but she prefers y over x when it is unknown whether or not A obtains. The disjunction effect amounts to a violation of STP, and hence of consequentialism.

When confronted with the disjunctive scenario above, our subjects appear not to evaluate the attractiveness of the second gamble from the two alternative positions, one assuming a gain and one assuming a loss, as implied by STP. Instead, the presence of uncertainty induces its own phenomenology, in which the unresolved outcome looms large and unknown. The first gamble has a positive expected value, but it also involves the risk of a nontrivial loss. In the Won condition, the decisionmaker is already up $200, so regardless of the outcome of the second gamble, he is assured to remain ahead overall, which makes the gamble quite attractive. In the Lost condition, the decisionmaker is down $100: since most people hate a sure loss, the second gamble offers an attractive chance to "get out of the red." In the disjunctive condition, however, neither motive is entirely compelling. The decisionmaker experiences neither the reassurance that comes with knowing that he can no longer lose, nor the compulsion to recover recent losses; instead, a prevalent attitude is one of caution, a reluctance to rush into further action when previous ones have not yet been resolved. (For related analyses in terms of reasons in choice, see Shafir, Simonson, and Tversky 1993.)

We have replicated the above effect in a between-subject design. Three different groups of subjects were presented with the Won version, the Loss version, and the disjunctive version. As with the previous study, a majority accepted the gamble in the Won and in the Loss conditions (69 percent and 57 percent, respectively), but only 38 percent accepted it in the disjunctive condition. The fact that the distribution of choices was nearly identical in the two studies suggests that the respondents in the original study evaluated each version independently, with no detectable effects of one version on another. In fact, although technically a "within-subject" design, the original study obtained clearly independent evaluations, thus rendering it comparable to a between-subject manipulation.

A Theoretical Analysis

The above disjunction effect may be interpreted in terms of the value function from Kahneman and Tversky's (1979) Prospect Theory. The function, shown in figure 4.1, represents the subjective value of modest gains and losses and has been generally supported by numerous empirical studies. In accord with the principle of diminishing sensitivity, the function incorporates a concave segment to the right of the origin, namely, in the domain of gains, and a convex segment to the left, in the domain of losses. Furthermore, the function is steeper for losses than for gains, in accord with the principle of loss aversion.[2] The function in figure 4.1 represents a typical decisionmaker who is indifferent between a 50 percent chance of winning $100 and a sure gain of roughly $35, and, similarly, is indifferent between a 50 percent chance of losing $100 and a sure loss of roughly $40. Such a pattern of preferences can be captured by a power function with an exponent of .65 for gains and .75 for losses.

Consider, then, a person P whose values for gains and losses are captured by the function of figure 4.1. Suppose that P is presented with the gamble problem above and is told that he has won the first toss. He now needs to decide whether to accept or reject the second. P needs to decide, in other words, whether to maintain a sure gain of $200 or, instead, opt for an equal chance at either a $100 or a $400 gain. Given P's value function, his choice is between two options whose expected values are as follows:

Accept the second gamble: $.50 * 400^{(.65)} + .50 * 100^{(.65)}$

Reject the second gamble: $1.0 * 200^{(.65)}$

Because the value of the first alternative is greater than that of the second, P is predicted to accept the second gamble. Similarly, when P is told that he has lost the first gamble and needs to decide whether to accept or reject the second, P faces the following options:

Accept the second gamble: $.50 * -[200^{(.75)}] + .50 * 100^{(.65)}$

Reject the second gamble: $1.0 * -[100^{(.75)}]$

Again, because the first quantity is larger than the second, P accepts the second gamble.

Thus, once the outcome of the first gamble is known, the function in figure

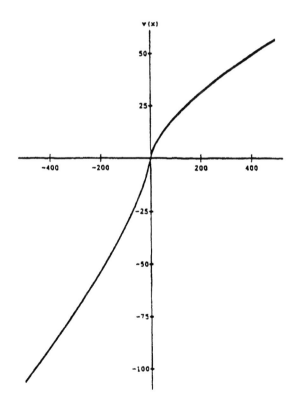

Figure 4.1

The value function $v(x) = x^{.65}$ for $x \geq 0$ and $v(x) = -(-x)^{.75}$ for $x \leq 0$.

4.1 predicts that person P will accept the second gamble whether he has won or lost the first. But as long as the outcome of the first gamble is not known, P might proceed as if for the moment no change has transpired. Not knowing whether he has won or lost, P assumes that he is still where he began, at the status quo, at the origin of his value function. When faced with the decision to accept or reject the second gamble, P evaluates it from his original position, without aggregating the outcome of the first gamble, which remains unknown. Thus, P is deciding to accept or to reject a gamble that offers an equal chance to win $200 or lose $100:

Accept the second gamble: $.50 * -[100^{(.75)}] + .50 * 200^{(.65)}$

Reject the second gamble: 0

Because the expected value of accepting is just below 0, P decides to reject the second gamble in this condition.

In situations of uncertainty, different outcomes often do trigger different actions. It can be reasonable in such cases to suspend judgment until there is further resolution. When confronted with the disjunctive scenario above, people do not evaluate the attractiveness of the second gamble from two alternative positions, one assuming a gain and one assuming a loss, as implied by STP. Instead, not knowing whether they have won or lost the first, people segregate the two gambles and evaluate the second from their current position, as if for the moment no change has occurred. Uncertain about the previous outcome, people evaluate the situation as if no outcome had obtained. This interpretation is further supported by the observation that a similar percentage of people accept the gamble in the disjunctive condition as in a simple condition in which no prior gamble had been played (36 percent and 33 percent, respectively).

The Disjunction Effect and Intuition

The above analysis offers a positive as well as a negative account. The positive account suggests that disjunctive situations bring about a different psychological state from when outcomes are certain. Having won the first gamble assures the person of a no-loss situation, and having lost compels her to try to recover the losses. Uncertainty, on the other hand, brings about a state that is not a disjunction of the former two, but an independent tendency to be cautious and avoid further losses. Implicit in this is a negative account, namely, that subjects do not see through the otherwise compelling logic that characterizes this situation. In fact, as is the case with other normative rules of decision, once the applicability of STP is detected, for example in a transparent within-subject design, people typically find it compelling to the point of being irresistible. But as long as the applicability of a compelling principle has not been made salient, mental life abides by rules of its own, often in direct contradiction to the patterns that are endorsed by contemplative, within-subject intuition.

Recall that in the original study we presented subjects with the Won, Lost, and disjunctive versions each a week apart, so that the logical relation among the versions was not detected. In another study, subjects were presented with all three versions concurrently, on the same page, thus rendering the applicability of the sure-thing principle transparent. The percentages of subjects who accepted the second gamble in the Won condition (71 percent) and in the Loss condition (56 percent), when these were presented concurrently, were almost identical to those observed originally, when the versions were presented a week apart. On the other hand, the tendency to accept the second gamble in the disjunctive condition rose from 36 percent in the original, separated presentation, to 84 percent in the concurrent presentation. In fact, the proportion of subjects in the concurrent presentation who exhibited the pattern "accept when won, accept when lost, but reject when do not know" declined by more than 80 percent relative to the separated presentation. Once people realize that they would accept the second gamble regardless of the outcome of the first, they are compelled to accept it in the disjunctive condition.

Violations of STP are likely to be observed only when people have not considered the implications of the possible outcomes, and are likely to disappear in transparent, within-subject presentation. Indeed, numerous studies have shown that, contrary to Savage's businessman, subjects often refrain from partitioning a scenario or a category into their constituent events or subcategories. In the face of uncertainty, various intellectual, emotional, and motivational factors can influence perception, often quite independently of how the situation is perceived once the uncertainty is resolved. This can lead to violations of STP when the uncertain condition is considered in isolation, as typically occurs in a between-subject design. On the other hand, a within-subject design, in which people consider their preference and observe that it remains unchanged throughout, renders salient the compelling intuition underlying STP. But then how could Savage, having just contemplated the relevant outcomes in his example, intuit the potential STP violation? In fact, with the alternative versions of the problem immediately before his attention, Savage is experiencing precisely the concurrent presentation condition described above, and in that condition the logic of STP proves inescapable. Philosophical intuitions such as those articulated by Savage involve the philosopher serving as subject in what amounts to a within-subject introspection. People's experiences, on the other hand, typically occur in between-subject conditions. Those aspects of behavior that are confined to a between-subject analysis are likely to go undetected by within-subject intuitions.

Concluding Remarks

A number of psychological factors were considered that occasionally contribute to inconsistent sentiments, judgments, and preferences in isolated versus concurrent evaluations. First, different methods of elicitation, such as choice versus pricing, were seen to induce divergent weightings of attributes and thus give rise to inconsistent preferences. Next, dimensions that were considered more important, or harder to evaluate, were seen to acquire greater prominence in concurrent presentations, which allow for direct contrast, than in isolated presentation. Similarly, rules of decision that favor some factors over others were seen to play a decisive role in direct comparisons, but proved difficult to apply in isolated evaluations. Finally, a phenomenology of uncertainty that was observed in isolated presentation was hard to capture in concurrent, within-subject, introspection. This collection of instances, it was suggested, mirrors a discrepancy between the nature of people's everyday experiences and the conditions that yield philosophical intuitions. In life, people typically experience and evaluate things one at a time, as in a between-subject design, whereas many of the relevant intuitions result from concurrent, within-subject introspection.

Intuition need not always arise from a purely concurrent mode of evaluation. In fact, a person may attempt to evaluate one alternative "in isolation" and then proceed to evaluate the second. However, this attempt at a sequential evaluation of isolated events is likely to prove difficult and of limited success, particularly when—as in Savage's STP—the desired intuition depends on the interaction, or comparison, of the disparate evaluations. Furthermore, even if one were successful at intuiting reactions to events in isolation, that would not resolve the conflict with intuitions that emerge under a concurrent evaluation.

Within-subject introspection, it turns out, provides a better account of people's intuitions than of their actual behavior. Many principles of ethics and rationality are compelling because they originate from strong intuitions that most of us share. When confronted with judgments or preferences that violate normative principles, people often wish to modify their behavior to conform with the principles. Evidently, people's behavior is often at variance with their own normative intuitions. In this sense, both normative and descriptive accounts capture important aspects of human competence: the first addresses reflective deliberation, whereas the second focuses on actual behavior. The two analyses, of course, are interrelated but they do not coincide. Often, people prefer to adhere to normative principles, but these sometimes conflict in nontrivial ways with tendencies that arise in specific situations. Thus, people generally agree that one should contribute to worthy causes and ought to refrain from lying, despite the fact they do not always do so. Similarly, people tend to accept the normative force of invariance, despite the fact that it is often violated in their actual choices. The distinction between normative and descriptive accounts is easier to intuit when it stems from notions such as self-interest or lack of self-control; it proves less intuitive when the violation of normative principles stems from the nature of cognitive operations.

Because intuitions can be very compelling, counterintuitive findings often need to be demonstrated in between-subject designs. Only in such contexts can we discover certain facts about our mental life that cannot be accessed by intuition. This has obvious implications for the study of philosophical problems (see also Goldman 1993a, for further discussion). Consider, for example, the intuitive distinction most of us feel between acts of omission and acts of commission. Or between intentional versus nonintentional acts. Or between different forms of allocation, distribution, and justice. In most of these cases, our intuitions arise from direct comparison and concurrent evaluation. It seems important to know to what extent these sentiments are maintained in a between-subject context, when evaluated in isolation. In light of the findings above, we should expect some systematic differences to emerge, and these could have nontrivial policy implications. Imagine that some distinctions our intuition tells us are important disappear in between-subject evaluations, and that distinctions we did not previously entertain suddenly prove important. What should we do then? Should we strive for arrangements that improve things according to intuitions that emerge from concurrent evaluation, or should we instead, contrary to our intuitions, strive to create a world that ameliorates experiences in between-subject conditions? You can entertain both these possibilities or, perhaps, you should consider one and I the other.

Notes

This work was supported by U.S. Public Health Service Grant No. 1-R29-MH46885 from the National Institute of Mental Health, and has benefited from discussions with Daniel Kahneman.

1. The notion of consequentialism appears in the philosophical and decision theoretic literature in a number of different senses. See, e.g., Hammond 1988; Levi 1991; and Bacharach and Hurley 1991, for technical discussion. See McClennen 1983, for a critique. See also Shafir and Tversky 1992, for a discussion of nonconsequential decision making.

2. For more on Prospect Theory, see Kahneman and Tversky 1979; Tversky and Kahneman 1986. For recent extensions of Prospect Theory, see Tversky and Kahneman 1992. For more on loss aversion, see Tversky and Kahneman 1991. Prospect theory also incorporates a weighting function that replaces stated probabilities by some nonadditive measure. In the present treatment the weights coincide with stated probabilities. This is for the sake of simplification: it is not essential to the analysis.

Chapter 5

Whose Concepts Are They, Anyway? The Role of Philosophical Intuition in Empirical Psychology

Alison Gopnik and Eric Schwitzgebel

A Dialogue in the Sandbox

Over the past ten years, interest among developmental psychologists in how young children conceive of the mind has grown dramatically. A very generally, though not universally, accepted hypothesis is that there is a radical conceptual change in children's understanding of belief between about three and five years of age. Three-year-olds seem to believe that all beliefs are true, and if they know that the world is a particular way, they seem to think that no one else could believe otherwise. Four-year-olds, in contrast, seem to have a view more like the adult view. They know that beliefs can be false, can differ between people, and can change over time, even while the reality behind the beliefs remains constant. The prevailing view suggests that this development happens in part as a result of children's experience of the behavior of others. Behavior that seems inexplicable without the assumption of a false belief on the part of the agent, for example, can serve as counterevidence to the three-year-old's understanding of belief.

One day the first author of this chapter spent all morning in the daycare center talking to three-year-olds about belief and then all afternoon talking to a distinguished visiting philosopher about the same subject. That night she had a strange dream, a dream composed, as dreams often are, of an odd reshuffling of the day's events. In the dream, she happened to overhear the conversation of two three-year-olds in the daycare center sandbox. We will call them Phil and Psyche.

Psyche: You know, Phil, something's been bothering me. You know how beliefs are always true? Well, an odd thing happened the other day. My big brother saw my mom put a piece of chocolate in the cupboard and then left to play Nintendo, and while he was away my mom took the chocolate out of the cupboard and put it in the drawer. When my brother came back, he went straight to the cupboard and said loudly, several times, that he was sure the chocolate was in there. But of course, it was really in the drawer. So I have this idea: Could it be that he had a belief that was just like ordinary beliefs, except false?

Phil: My dear Psyche, as I have so often pointed out to you before, your con-
          fusion is due to a category mistake. You are treating the truth of beliefs
          as if it were an empirical matter. Actually, it is simply a conceptual
          fact about beliefs that they are always true. Indeed, we might say that it
          is criterial for a belief to be a belief that it be true. Look, consult your
          intuitions, consult the intuitions of anyone else in the sandbox. All of
          us agree, immediately, intuitively, without inference or theory, that all
          beliefs are true. Ask yourself what a belief is. What else could it be but
          a true representation of events?

Psyche: But couldn't we all be wrong? Couldn't there be an alternative way of
          conceiving of belief that none of us happen to subscribe to now?

Phil: Another category mistake. When I say that beliefs are necessarily true,
          this isn't a mere contingent psychological fact about the concepts of all
          us three-year-olds. It's an eternal, platonic, *philosophical* fact about the
          nature of belief and truth.

Psyche: Well, what about my brother?

Phil: He is probably participating in an alternative form of life. I always
          thought he was kind of weird.

Psyche: But you see, it isn't just him. It even seems to be me. Since the choco-
          late incident, wherever I look, I see evidence that beliefs may be false.
          Why just yesterday, a woman came into the daycare center with a candy
          box and I said "Candy!" and then she opened the box and there were
          pencils inside. I know intuitively that I must have thought there were
          pencils in the box all along, and of course that's what I told her when
          she asked me. But then why did I say "Candy!"? Am I turning into a
          madwoman?

Phil: (gravely) I fear you may have a worse affliction. I fear you are turning
          into a cognitive psychologist. As I was saying just the other day, "It
          would be dangerous to deny from a philosophical armchair that cogni-
          tive psychology is an intellectually respectable discipline, provided, of
          course, it stays within proper bounds."[1] This is what happens when
          those bounds are breached.

Psyche: But surely there must be some explanation?

Phil: Philosophy does not provide explanations, only diagnoses. (Intones) Of
          that we cannot speak, thereof we must be silent. . . .

At this point the dreamer woke up suddenly, if not quite screaming, at least
gravely shaken. She was temporarily comforted by the thought that in the sandbox kids like Phil get thwacked over the head with a bucket and the cognitive
development of three-year-olds as a group proceeds unchecked. But in spite of
appearances, we do not want to thwack our philosophical readers over the head
with a bucket. Instead, what we would like to do is suggest some ways of making the dialogue between philosophers and psychologists more productive than it
was in the dream. We would also like to point out some arenas where that kind
of productive dialogue is already taking place. Philosophical work has a real contribution to make to the enterprise of understanding the nature of the mind, a
contribution that is sometimes under appreciated by cognitive psychologists. At

the same time, we want to suggest that some empirical results in psychology, particularly developmental psychology, may have important implications for philosophical research, and we want to explain in some detail the rather common philosophical error of which we think Phil is guilty.

The core of Phil's argument is his appeal to the intuitions of the children in the sandbox. This chapter will explore both the benefits for empirical psychology of such philosophical appeals to intuition—the intuitions not of children but of educated adults—and the limitations of such appeals. We will examine several ways in which philosophical attention to intuition can contribute to empirical scientific psychology. We will then discuss Phil's error and describe some areas in contemporary philosophy where we think similar errors are being made. Finally, we will provide developmental evidence for the mutability and fallibility of our everyday intuitions about the mind, evidence that undermines arguments, like Phil's, that depend on taking such intuitions as a final authority for substantive claims about what the mind is like.

The Nature of Intuition

It will be helpful to begin by making clear what exactly we mean by the word 'intuition'. We will call any judgment an *intuitive judgment*, or more briefly an *intuition*, just in case that judgment is not made on the basis of some kind of explicit reasoning process that a person can consciously observe. Intuitions are judgments that grow, rather, out of an underground process, of whatever kind, that cannot be directly observed. So, for example, we make intuitive judgments about such things as the grammaticality of sentences, the morality of actions, the applicability of a certain term to a certain situation, Bob's likely reaction to an insult, the relative sizes of two distant objects, and so forth. In each of these cases, the judgments flow spontaneously from the situations that engender them, rather than from any process of explicit reasoning.

The content of these intuitive judgments may vary. In particular, we may have intuitions about aspects of the physical world, for example, we may intuit that objects cannot be in the same place at the same time, or that an object that is moving will end up in a different location than where it started, or that causes must precede effects. We may also have intuitions about the psychological world, we may intuit that pain always involves an element of displeasure, or that mental states like belief refer to the outside world.

Much philosophical work consists of articulating and elaborating these intuitive judgments. Sometimes philosophers elaborate on our ordinary intuitions about the physical world. John Mackie (1974), for example, has explored and criticized our intuitive view of causation, including such ideas as that a cause must be something without which the effect would not have occurred and that a cause cannot come after its effect. John Campbell (1995) elaborates on our ordinary conception of space and time. More often, philosophers elaborate on intuitions about the psychological world. Daniel Dennett (1978), for example, has explored some of the consequences and difficulties of the intuitive view that pain, by its nature, has an element of displeasure. John Searle (1983) presents an elaborate intuitive taxonomy of our mental states. The views these philosophers describe are intuitive in the sense that ordinary people (or at least ordinary English speakers) frequently make intuitive judgments that agree with the views and would, on reflection, generally assent to those views, even if they could not support their assent by any explicit argument.

Intuitions, are, surprisingly, not always obvious. Philosophers may go to some length to ferret out our intuitions on a particular topic. Hilary Putnam (1975), for example, constructs an elaborate scenario involving Earth and a planet, "Twin Earth," identical to Earth in every respect except that on Twin Earth there is no water, only "twater," identical to water in every respect observable to the inhabitants of Earth and Twin Earth, but composed of chemicals other than H_2O. If Wayne on Earth and Dwayne on Twin Earth are molecule-for-molecule identical to each other (except that Dwayne is 70 percent twater), it is intuitive to claim that they, nonetheless, mean different things when they utter the word 'water'. This intuition is generally taken to support the surprising thesis that the meaning of words depends not wholly on what takes place in one's head but also on one's environment.

The Contribution of Philosophical Intuition

We suggest that there are several quite different ways in which philosophically-informed intuition can contribute to empirical psychology. It may be that other applications will occur to the reader—we do not mean to suggest that our three applications exhaust the possibilities.

Intuitions as Hypotheses

Perhaps the most obvious application of intuitions to the empirical sciences in general, and of philosophical intuitions to psychology, in particular, comes when we use our intuitions as a source of empirical hypotheses. We might think of intuitive judgments as particularly plausible initial hypotheses about the nature of the world. Thus, our intuitions that pain has an element of displeasure and that causes cannot come after effects, lead to the hypotheses that, in reality, pain has an element of displeasure, and that causes cannot come after effects.

Like all such hypotheses, our intuitions are accurate as a guide to the world to different degrees, depending on both the person who has those intuitions and the subject area to which those intuitions apply. Twentieth-century physics, for example, has notoriously shown the inaccuracy of our everyday intuitions as hypotheses about the nature of space and time, light, and the microscopic world. The well-cultivated intuitions of a theoretical physicist may be more accurate in this regard, to the extent her physical theories work their way underground into her intuitive judgments. In contrast, our commonsense intuitions about the behavior of mid-sized objects, as we interact with them in everyday life, are generally rather good, though there are notorious exceptions. For example, many adults intuit that objects that are thrown in a curve will continue moving on a curved trajectory until they complete a circle. As another example, consider that many of us have essentially no intuitions about the quality of different chess moves—we can only evaluate moves by reasoning about their likely outcomes—while Gary Kasparov surely has quite accurate intuitions in this regard. Our intuitions can develop substantially as our expertise grows.

We are all experts, in a pragmatic sort of way, in everyday psychology, and for this reason our everyday psychological intuitions can be taken as plausible initial hypotheses about how the mind really works. Empirical psychology can then use these everyday intuitions as a starting point for its research. The work of philosophers of mind like John Searle who articulate the everyday intuitive view of the mind can therefore aid empirical psychology by making explicit what the intuitive starting point is, and by providing a set of hypotheses from which to begin. Similarly, philosophical work that clarifies our intuitive views of semantics or epistemology can be employed as a starting point for empirical work in semantics and in understanding human knowledge. In order for philosophical work of this sort to be helpful, it should be noticed, it is not necessary that philosophers have better intuitions about the mind, or semantics, or knowledge than the rest of us do. It is simply necessary that philosophers be skilled at spelling out the intuitions they (and we) do have.

The intuitions articulated by philosophers, then, in so far as they are treated as initial hypotheses about the way the world really is, can guide empirical research, especially in those domains in which human beings have particular expertise. Indeed, it is probably impossible to start a science from scratch with hypotheses and assumptions that are entirely based on observation or experiment. One must begin with intuition and correct it with experiment. As sciences mature, however, they typically revise, alter, and sometimes entirely reject, these initial hypotheses. In Galileo's day, it was permissible for physicists in defending one view or another to appeal to what we would now call our "folk physical" intuitions about what would happen in various circumstances. In contemporary physics, such appeals would be ruled out.

Similarly, as psychological science has matured, we have become more confident in leaving intuitions behind when they conflict with well-supported empirical findings, as for example in the cases of blindsight (Weiskrantz 1986) and attribution error (Nisbett and Ross 1980). Our initial hypotheses may be, indeed often are, moderated or defeated by later evidence. So although we may justifiably take reflective psychological intuition as a good preliminary guide, we no longer take it as the final authority about the mind.

Intuitions as Evidence

We can also use intuitions in a quite different way. Sometimes we treat intuitions as evidence about the nature of the mind of the person who generates those intuitions, not as hypotheses about the external world. In these cases we think of intuitions as data that need to be explained by a psychological theory. Grammatical theories, for instance, generally regard our linguistic intuitions about the grammaticality or ungrammaticality of sentences as a crucial part—even, perhaps, the whole—of their explanatory domain, just as celestial mechanics takes the movement of the stars and planets as a crucial part of its explanatory domain.

The intuition that the sentence "Jamie of gave" is ungrammatical is a piece of data for grammatical theories in roughly the same way that the observation that Venus was at such-and-such a location at such-and-such a time is a piece of data for celestial mechanics. Both the linguistic intuition and the astronomical observation can serve as evidence in support of or against particular linguistic and astronomical theories.

Yet the use of intuition in these cases should be differentiated from the use of intuition to provide plausible hypotheses. These intuitions are not first passes at a psychological theory, instead they are the very data that a psychological theory seeks to explain. Consequently, a theory that deviates from these intuitions must be able to provide some principled explanation of why the deviation should not be regarded as fatal to the theory; and a theory that deviates too much from the data it seeks to explain is doomed. When we consider them as evidence, intuitions have some of the same quality of indefeasibility that evidence always has. Parallel lines may, or may not, meet, and we may, or may not, have first-person access to our mental states, but it is indubitably true that we believe that parallel lines will not meet and that we have first-person access to our own mental states. A psychological theory has to explain why we have these intuitive beliefs even if, indeed especially if, the beliefs are quite false. The psychologist cannot simply reject the beliefs if she is treating them as evidence about the mind of the person who has them.

On the other hand, nothing stands in the way of the complete overthrow of intuitions if they are construed as psychological hypotheses. We might think of the contrast thus: Gary Kasparov's intuitions about chess can be taken as prima facie support for one or another theory of the quality of chess moves, that is, they can be taken as hypotheses about chess, or they can be treated evidentially as a topic of study in themselves. In the former case, it may turn out that those intuitions must largely be repudiated, since the intuitions may not capture the facts about the quality of chess moves very well. Perhaps Kasparov's hypotheses about chess moves are really not very good, say, if Kasparov has won by incredible luck, or only because everyone else is even worse at evaluating chess moves. But if we are trying to understand not chess, but Kasparov, the case is quite different. In that case, the question of the accuracy of the intuitions is only of secondary importance, since the piece of the world that the theory seeks to explain is not chess itself but Kasparov's intuitions about chess.

Psychology frequently treats intuitive judgments as evidence in the construction of psychological theories. Perceptual psychology, for example, seeks to explain, among other things, our intuitive judgments about size, color, distance, shape, and so forth. Psychologists interested in science education have attempted to describe and explain our naive intuitions about physics. Developmental psychologists have attempted to characterize and explain children's intuitions on a variety of subjects throughout childhood. Intuitive judgments are an important part of our mental lives; psychological theory, therefore, aims to explain the nature and origin of those intuitions.

Philosophical work that articulates our everyday intuitions on a particular topic can be useful for those parts of empirical psychology that take intuitions about that topic as their subject matter. Developmental psychology in particular has greatly benefited from the philosophical articulation of our intuitions about a variety of subjects. In the literature on the development of the child's understanding of mind, the debt is often quite explicit. Developmental psychologists have mined intuitive characterizations of the mind by philosophers for material on which to test children: When do children understand that belief is "representational" in Fred Dretske's (1988) sense? When do they understand the relation between intention and action in roughly the way it has been articulated by philosophers of action? (Interestingly, it has been more typical for developmental psychologists to turn to philosophers for their characterizations of the adult conception of the mind than for them to turn to empirical research on the same topic.) Similarly, developmental psychologists studying the child's understanding of "natural kinds" have explicitly made reference to philosophical work on the topic (see e.g., Keil 1989; Gelman and Wellman 1991).

Theoretical Applications of Intuition

A third way in which intuitions articulated by philosophers can be applied to aid empirical psychology is in the elaboration of psychological theories and theoretical possibilities and in drawing out the consequences of these theories and possibilities. Used in this way, we will say that the intuitions are being employed *theoretically*.

Psychological theories, like all theories, are formulated in a language that relies on some mix of technical and ordinary terms. When the meanings and extensions of these terms are clear and univocal, the theories that employ them can be understood more precisely, and their empirical implications are more readily discerned. In the very best cases the concepts in the theories may be specified in very precise mathematical terms and the relations between them may be very clearly specified. Even in these cases, however, it may be difficult to tell if a mathematical concept is being applied appropriately. More frequently, however, the theoretical terms and concepts are not specified this precisely. When the meanings and extensions are left hazy, the theories become difficult to assess. Unless we really know what is meant by the term 'representation', for example, how can we fully evaluate a psychological theory that postulates the manipulation of representations in a certain functional subsystem of the brain?

Philosophical work that clarifies such central terms and concepts in psychology as 'representation', 'drive', and 'memory'—whether that work is done by philosophers attuned to psychology or whether it is done by psychologists with a philosophical knack—is plainly of great use to psychologists. When the terms and concepts in question are meant to be understood simply in their nontechnical, everyday sense, the articulation of intuitions about those terms should suffice to provide a profitably clear understanding of those terms for psychological purposes. Philosophers have long excelled at the sometimes difficult task of spelling out such intuitions. Intuitions develop quickly, also, among people using technical terms or appropriating everyday terms to technical uses, so that similar philosophical work can be done about the proper application of terms such as 'supervenience' or 'nominalist' in philosophy, or psychological terms such as those mentioned at the beginning of this paragraph. To arrive at a useful understanding of such technical or quasi-technical terms requires a scientifically informed balance of intuitive considerations with historical, stipulative, and pragmatic elements. One might fantasize that the meanings of technical terms could simply be stipulated afresh each time they were employed, but of course in reality it is impossible fully to shed historical and intuitive associations. Regardless, any stipulative definition of a word must be provided in terms of other words, and it is difficult to imagine that the meanings of each of these words could be entirely stipulated, all the way down to the ground floor. Even in the case of highly mathematical and precise theories there is some point at which the theorist will have to rely on an intuitive judgment that, for example, a particular conclusion follows from certain premises, as in Lewis Carroll's paradox of Achilles and the Tortoise.

Philosophical work on the "theory theory" in developmental psychology can serve as a case in point. According to the theory theory of cognitive development, children operate somewhat as scientists do, collecting evidence about the world, evaluating that evidence, and constructing theories to explain what they have observed. Cognitive change occurs when enough counterevidence has built up against an existing theory that an alternative theory becomes more attractive to the child. To spell out the full implications of saying that young children literally have *theories* about the world requires both conceptual inquiry into what can, and should, be meant by 'theory' in this context, as well as a factual inquiry into the nature of theories and theoretical change. The factual inquiry may be partly empirical, grounded in observations about theories and theoretical change that have been revealed by the history of science, for example, and it may be partly based on intuitions about the nature of theories. With broad factual knowledge about theories, coupled with conceptual work on how the term 'theory' ought to be employed for the purposes at hand, the claims of the theory theory can be evaluated much more clearly. For example, we might argue that, intuitively, if children's beliefs are theoretical they should also be revisable in the light of new evidence, and we might then look for evidence of such revisability.

A particularly common theoretical use of intuitions in science involves a kind of analogical reasoning. Science often proceeds by the use of analogy. Electric current is likened to the flow of water through pipes, the atom is likened to the solar system, the transmission of light is likened to the movement of a wave through water. In each of these cases, there is, to use Mary Hesse's (1966) terminology, both a "positive analogy"—respects in which the two systems are thought to be similar—and a "negative analogy"—respects in which the two systems are thought to differ. The use of analogies in these cases both helps us to understand an unfamiliar phenomenon in terms of a more familiar one and suggests areas for testing and research, to see how far the positive analogy can be pushed. If light is really like a wave, then it should do such-and-such in such-and-such circumstances that we have not yet tested. The results of such tests occasionally are stunningly successful. Fresnel's wave model of light predicted the appearance of a bright spot in the center of the shadow of a small circular disk when a narrow beam of light was shone upon the disk, and much to the surprise of many scientists at that time, when the experiment was conducted the bright spot was found. Of course in the twentieth century, the wave analogy for light has produced some equally stunning predictive failures.

To return to the example of the "theory theory," the more we know about theories, and the more precisely we can articulate our concept of a theory, the better sense we can make of the use of the term 'theory' in empirical psychology, whether that use is meant literally or analogically. The use of 'theory' in the theory theory is, in fact, a good example of a case where literal and analogical uses shade into each other. Should the theory theory be seen as regarding children as *literally* possessed of theories, or should it see their cognitive changes simply as *analogous* to scientific theory change? A theory theorist's answer to this question may be largely a matter of taste.

Some of the most significant advances in cognitive psychology and cognitive science have taken intuitive, commonsense, or "folk" psychology as their base and used it analogically, modifying and expanding it to apply to new kinds of phenomena, much as our language and knowledge about waves was expanded to apply to the domain of optics. The best functionalist cognitive psychology, in this vein, takes folk psychological notions like "inferring" or "reasoning" or "following a rule" or "believing" or "desiring" and applies them in cases where no folk psychologist ever would. Cognitive psychologists have used the vocabulary of belief, inference, rule-following, and achieving goals to explain phenomena like perceiving the moon on the horizon, uttering a grammatical sentence, or automatically and unconsciously reaching for a close object. Indeed, it might be argued that the very idea of computation, the centerpiece of cognitive science, is itself derived from folk psychology. Alan Turing (1950) begins his classical discussion of computation, after all, with an account of what it is like to do a particular kind of conscious problem solving, an account that would accord with anyone's folk psychological intuitions.

Rather than assimilating the folk psychological notions wholly without modification, however, Turing, Chomsky, and other modern theorists of cognitive science expanded, modified, and formalized these notions, applied them to new domains, and tested them with new kinds of evidence. These extensions have notoriously violated the intuitions of folk psychology itself. Indeed, it is precisely this fact that makes the extensions and applications interesting. Claiming that we compute when we add a column of numbers or follow rules when we play Monopoly is uninformative at best. Claiming that we compute when we perceive or follow rules when we talk has, in contrast, been very scientifically productive. Analogical uses like this have a way, if they are successful, of becoming literalized over time. We came to say, literally, that light was a kind of wave (though twentieth-century science presented some complications here). We now say that, literally, electrons have orbits. At some point—perhaps now—we may also want to say, literally, that the visual system computes.

One Prevalent Misuse of Intuition

Because the cognitive sciences have employed our intuitions in the diverse ways we have described above, they have profited enormously from the philosophical work of articulating intuitions and drawing out the implications of our intuitive views. What is it, then, that leads to the sort of dialogue with which we started this essay? What is wrong with Phil? Our answer, only partly ironic, is that the poor kid is the victim of a category mistake. Within philosophy of mind, there has been a tradition of either accidentally confusing different uses of intuition, or deliberately treating them as identical, and consequently drawing inappropriate conclusions. An unspoken assumption of much argumentation in the philosophy of mind has been that to articulate our folk psychological intuitions, our ordinary concepts of belief, truth, meaning, and so forth, is itself sufficient to give a theoretical account of what belief, truth, meaning, and so forth, actually are. We believe that this assumption rests on an inadequate understanding of the nature of intuition and its appropriate applications, and that it results in errors of the sort that the case of Phil dramatically illustrates. The error is more vivid in Phil's case only because the intuitions to which he appeals are so clearly (to us) out of step with the world.

We will briefly discuss three notable examples of what we take to be this sort of misuse of intuition in philosophy. We will focus, in particular, on cases in which developmental psychology provides relevant evidence. The first example occurs in the long and fevered debate about externalism in semantics, prompted by Hilary Putnam's (1975) and Saul Kripke's (1972) philosophical work. These authors articulate in an interesting and perceptive way an unexpected and surprising intuition we ordinarily have about meaning (at least many philosophers seem to have found this intuition surprising). The intuition is that meaning is, in Putnam's words, not in the head. We have the intuition that what a word means, for a person, depends not only on what is going on internally with that person, but also on facts about the world external to the person. This is the point of Putnam's Twin Earth example, described above. That we have this intuition turns out to be an important and interesting fact about us, one that a scientific psychology would want to explain. The intuitions described by Putnam, Kripke, and others after them are not just exotic philosophical intuitions—Frank Keil (1989) and Susan Gelman (Gelman and Wellman 1991) have shown that they may be shared even by fairly young children, and cognitive psychologists like Murphy and Medin (1985) and Rips (1989) have shown that they are shared by ordinary adults and play an important role in adult action and judgment. This intuition is an important piece of data for empirical psychology; Keil and the rest are treating the Twin Earth intuitions evidentially.

Moreover, Putnam's and Kripke's arguments alert us to the fact that our standard internalist psychological theories of meaning do not exhaust the theoretical possibilities. We might apply them to generate new hypotheses about the nature of meaning. Psychologists interested in the internal structure of the individual's mind may naturally be drawn toward an internalist account of meaning that sees the meanings of a subject's words as dependent solely on the internal states of that subject. However, science has often profited enormously from relational, supra-individual concepts that ascribe properties to individuals not solely on the basis of facts internal to that individual. Explanatory notions like "fitness" in biology are inherently relational and supra-individual in this way. Perhaps it will turn out that the notion of semantics we need to do explanatory work in scientific psychology will be similarly relational. So, in addition to being an interesting piece of psychological data, this intuition provides an interesting hypothesis about the nature of meaning.

We should not confuse these two applications of the Twin Earth intuitions however. These intuitive hypotheses about meaning need not be scientifically viable in the long run. That is, the fact that our ordinary understanding of the mind presupposes an externalist, supra-individual semantics says very little about whether an externalist semantics is the best choice for a theory of meaning. It may be the case that a relational, supra-individual conception of meaning does the best job in explaining meaning. But then again, it may not be. The fact that the ordinary conception of meaning within our daily experience has this character provides only rudimentary evidence about what notion of meaning will work best for psychologists and others who wish to talk about meaning in a scientifically informed way—just as our ordinary intuitions about physics provide only a rudimentary starting point for the creation of physical laws. These intuitions may have played a crucial initial role for Galileo, but most of them did not survive in the end.

Empirical evidence about the nature of belief is irrelevant to Phil's observation that his three-year-old concept of a belief is a concept of something that cannot be false. Psyche's observations cannot undermine this claim of Phil's, and to the extent that Phil is only articulating his current concept of the mind, he is safe from cognitive science. Indeed those intuitions will be an important source of data for developmental psychologists. However, when Phil goes on to infer that his intuitions about the mind, treated as hypotheses about human cognition, are similarly untouchable by empirical observation, he has committed an error. Any philosopher who claims that our intuitions about Twin Earth reveal some scientifically unassailable fact about the human ability to mean things by words—rather than simply revealing something about what we *mean* by 'meaning'—makes an error similar to Phil's.

A second example of the error is in John Searle's critique of cognitive science (Searle 1990, 1992). Searle observes that in our ordinary intuitive understanding, states with intrinsic propositional or intentional content like desire and belief are bound up with conscious experience, or phenomenology, in a particular way. Indeed, in our everyday experience mental states and conscious states almost always co-occur: The creatures or systems that occupy states whose causal, functional roles are the same as those of belief, desire, and other states with intrinsic intentional content have always been the same systems that had conscious phenomenology. Consequently, the intuitive conception we have of intrinsic intentional states presupposes the co-existence of these two factors. Now, suppose it turns out, as it seems it might, that there are systems that, behaviorally speaking, occupy the causal roles associated with intrinsic intentional states—they act as though they have, for example, beliefs—but do not have conscious phenomenology. In that case the intuition is foiled, at least if it is construed as a hypothesis about the necessary relation between certain causal, functional facts and phenomenology. Searle acknowledges the possibility of such systems, but he insists that such systems cannot be said *really* to have intrinsic intentionality.

Now, in fact, cognitive scientists have done a lot of interesting work on the

mind that depends on ascribing states with intrinsic intentional content to sub-
systems of the mind that generate no phenomenology, or at least no phenomenology of the sort that is intuitively associated with the intentions that are
being ascribed. Noam Chomsky's work on grammar (Chomsky 1980) and David
Marr's work on vision (Marr 1982) are two prominent examples. In general,
computational theories of the mind depend on describing the mind as engaged in
all kinds of computational processes (with intrinsic intentional content) uncon-
nected or only remotely connected to conscious phenomenology.

So what is a scientist to do? If we can better understand, explain, and predict
scientifically what is going on in such systems when we treat them as though
they had intrinsic intentional content, then it would be a mistake to forbid doing
so, as Searle seems to want. Everyday intuition does not and should not have authority over how terms and concepts are to be applied and extended in the sciences; if science benefits from declaring that intentional states "really" need have
no phenomenal accompaniment, philosophy ought not prevent such a conceptual
change. This is not to say that Searle or any other philosophical skeptic about
this aspect of cognitive science has no recourse: He can argue that science does
not benefit from such an analogical extension of our intuition, and he can caution against certain inferences that may depend upon aspects of the old conception that have been cast aside. But it is illegitimate to put an analysis of our intuitive concepts to work as a block to the movement of science in one direction
or another, as though it revealed some independent truth that science was power-
less to overthrow. A potential compromise position would allow cognitive scientists to employ the vocabulary of intrinsic intentionality, all the while insisting that the use is analogical (or in Searle's terminology, "as-if"). In fact, some
cognitive scientists may have something like this in mind—although it would
certainly be understandable were they to tire of insisting that the use is analogical and decide to broaden the literal meaning of these terms to cover the cases at
hand.

If the intuitions about intentionality to which Searle is appealing are simply
treated as data, then we can vest some level of confidence in the truths *about our
concepts* that we so discover, but if we treat our intuitions about intentionality
as hypotheses about how the world really is independent of our concepts—that
is, if we treat them as hypotheses about the mind—then they have at best a
rudimentary, preliminary, and prima facie warrant. One way, though perhaps not
the only way, of interpreting what we take to be Searle's error in his treatment
of cognitive science, is that he employs his folk psychological intuitions hypo-
thetically to reveal something about the world beyond our concepts, but he sees
them as having a degree of warrant that is justified only when they are employed
to reveal the content of our present concepts. A similar error is made by those
who would, in an argument that is in some ways the mirror image of Searle's,
take the connection between functional role and phenomenology in ordinary intuition as some kind of proof that conscious phenomenology will necessarily
emerge if ever we create a robot with the right functional relations between its
inputs and its behavioral outputs.

A third example, which has been discussed at greater length in Gopnik
(1993), is the question of the nature of first-person authority about our mental

states, our conviction about the accuracy of our own reports of our beliefs, desires, moods, and so forth. A wide variety of philosophers have defended first-person authority by pointing to the intuitive links between first-person authority and other deeply embedded aspects of our commonsense psychology. Thus, Davidson (1987), for example, suggests that first-person authority is intimately bound up with and presupposed by certain facts about the interpretation of language, while Shoemaker (1988) more simply, suggests that first-person authority is bound up with our very concept of belief. Even if these philosophers are entirely correct in the ways they have spelled out our concepts and our intuitions about the mind—even if it is impossible for us to conceive of belief without conceiving of it as known to us first-person, or to conceive of ourselves as responsible or interpretable agents without first-person authority, this does not settle the question of whether we actually do have first-person authority. The fact that we are so convinced that we do have first-person authority is an interesting and important fact for psychological theory to explain. And perhaps psychological research will in fact demonstrate that our intuitions of first-person authority are not in error—there may be links, for example, between being in a certain brain or functional state and having certain subjective experiences, such that having those experiences provides one with a special warrant for claiming that one is in those states (see Goldman 1993b for such an argument). But the mere fact that our everyday folk psychological intuitions are congruent with such a picture does not imply that that picture is correct as a deeper theoretical account of our psychological structure.

Why is this kind of confusion about the appropriate application and warrant of intuitive judgments so widespread in philosophy of mind? To sound like Phil, here is a diagnosis and a suggested therapy. The diagnosis is that the confusion is the result of the relatively close relation, at this stage of the game, between the structure of our folk psychological everyday conceptions of the mind and our scientific conceptions, and the very fertility of our scientific borrowing of folk notions. Our scientific accounts, quite properly and productively, take off from the folk account. Our ordinary psychological intuitions are the first and best source of hypotheses about how the mind works. As long as the concepts and structures of the two accounts are relatively similar, they are easily confused.

If (or when) psychological theories are formulated in terms that are incongruent with intuitive psychology, the independence of the two becomes clearer. For example, we know that much of our low-level visual perception can be explained as a system that performs a Fourier analysis of information in the retina. We could imagine making a Searlean objection that perception does not feel like Fourier analysis. That objection, though, would seem patently to miss the point. The reason is that there is nothing that we intuitively think Fourier analysis feels like. The concept plays no role at all in our intuitive psychology. In contrast, when we say that perception involves inference, an elision is much more likely between this theoretical, analogical extension of our folk psychological concept and its application in folk psychology itself.

It is interesting to note that, historically, philosophy has abandoned the project of articulating our physical intuitions about the world or using those intuitions as evidence about the underlying structure of the world. Perhaps the last great effort in this direction was made by Kant and his followers in the eighteenth and nineteenth centuries. Kant (at least as he is often interpreted) supposed that an examination of the necessary presuppositions of our physical intuitions would reveal something about the structure of the physical world, just as contemporary philosophers of mind suppose that an examination of the necessary presuppositions of our psychological intuitions will reveal something about the structure of the mind.

The abandonment of the Kantian project was the direct result of the great conceptual and empirical progress in physics over the last two hundred years. The advances of physics and its eventual deep departure from our ordinary physical intuition made the distinction between the conceptual structure of our "folk physics" and the conceptual structure of theories in scientific physics painfully clear. The devastating effect of progress in physics on the Kantian project was so absolute that it is difficult even to understand the appeal of the project now. There is no contemporary philosophy of body or of space and time that does not begin with an intimate knowledge of empirically justified scientific research.

Similar progress in psychology might well lead to a similar result and to similar changes in what are seen as appropriate enterprises for philosophy. This argument has, of course, been made at some length by Paul Churchland (1981) and Stephen Stich (1983) among others. But, it may be countered, this is unfairly eschatological. We have no way of knowing, now, that a scientific psychology will in fact have the success of a scientific physics or depart from ordinary intuition in the same way. It seems unconvincing to counter claims that intuition is a genuine guide to psychological fact by making reference to a possible future psychology that will consign those intuitions to the dustbin of history. Psychology is different from physics, and perhaps indeed the nature of those differences is such that no scientific psychology that is widely different from folk psychology will ever be possible.

Fortunately, we need not wait for a psychological Einstein to be convinced of the contingency and instability of even our deep-seated intuitive psychological beliefs and experience. We have no crystal ball that lets us view the future of our psychology, but we do know quite a lot about its past. By looking at development, an almost completely neglected source in philosophy of mind, we can make much the same point as Churchland and Stich without the eschatology. We can be confident that our currently constituted folk intuitions are not the last word about the mind because they were not the first word. The best therapy for the confusions outlined in this section, we would argue, as indeed for many other adult ills, is to spend more time with children.

What Children Tell Us About Intuition

In some respects the project of cognitive developmental psychology is more like the philosophical project of elaborating and articulating commonsense intuitions than it is like standard, grown-up cognitive psychology. Just as one aim of philosophy is to articulate certain sorts of adult intuition, one aim of developmental psychologists is to characterize the intuitive beliefs of children. Unlike philosophers, however, the developmentalists need to use more systematic means than introspection to accomplish this end, hence their laboratories, research budgets, and mastery of ANOVAs. In using experimental techniques to discover how minds intuitively construe the world, development joins hands with such diverse aspects of psychology as clinical cognitive neuroscience, ethology, and cognitive anthropology. By looking at the intuitions of these diverse populations, we can evaluate and understand the nature of the intuitions, provided by philosophy, of healthy, adult, Western, human beings.

The developmental data suggest that children's intuitions about quite standard psychological (and physical) matters are often quite different from those of adults. There is by now an extensive literature in cognitive development and theory of mind that charts these differences. We will briefly mention three examples that parallel the three examples of the philosophical misuse of intuition described above.

First, we now have extensive studies of children's understanding of "natural kinds" in their folk semantics and ontology (Keil 1989; Gelman and Wellman 1991; Carey 1985). The studies suggest that children's semantic intuitions are both similar to and different from the intuitions of adults in systematic ways. Even very young children, as young as two-and-a-half or three, seem sometimes to assume that words refer to the underlying causal powers of objects rather than to their superficial perceptual features (Gelman and Wellman 1991). On the other hand, children seem to be less sensitive to the constancy of causal powers over superficial transformations. Keil, for example, asked children a series of "Putnamesque" questions about the fate of a cat that was perceptually transformed to look like a skunk (it was painted black with a white stripe, it had a smelly bag added, etc.). Children seven or eight years old showed a pattern of intuitions like the Putnam intuitions—they said the cat would still be a cat and should still be called 'cat'. Equally significant, however, children five or six years old did not show this pattern of intuitions. Their intuitions told them that the cat would indeed become a skunk and be called 'skunk' under these conditions. Using another Putnamesque intuition pump yielded still another pattern. Children eight or nine years old said that if scientists discovered that skunks had the same internal structure as cats, they would be cats and should be called cats, but the younger children who showed "natural kind" intuitions about transformations did not have similar intuitions about scientific discovery, although they understood the nature of the scientists' work. In short, some aspects of the Putnam intuitions, such as attention to underlying causal powers, seem to be in place very early, while other intuitions emerge gradually with increasing knowledge and experience.

A second example concerns children's intuitions about the relations between intentional states and conscious phenomenology. In a long and elegant series of studies, John Flavell and his colleagues (Flavell, Green, and Flavell 1995) have explored children's intuitions about conscious experience. Children, like adults, gave every evidence of knowing and recognizing what conscious experience was. Earlier studies (for example, Estes, Wellman, and Woolley 1989) found that even three-year-old children could discriminate with some sophistication between the thought or image of a hot dog and an actual hot dog. They reported, for example, that the thought was internal, private, and subject to change by the will alone, while the real hot dog was not. However, in Flavell's studies, children seemed intuitively to associate conscious phenomenology with a different set of stimulae and behavioral patterns than adults did. For example, children reported that someone who was wide awake but was simply looking at a blank wall would have no conscious phenomenology, no stream of thoughts, impressions, images, and so forth. More strikingly, they reported that they themselves had no conscious phenomenology in similar conditions, despite the availability of a wide range of words with which to report such experience. In one experiment, Flavell et al. rang a bell at regular one-minute intervals. On the last trial, the bell only rang after two minutes. When they asked the children about their conscious phenomenology in the delay period, children said that they had not been thinking about or expecting the bell, and that no thoughts of the bell had entered their heads. In contrast, children sometimes ascribed phenomenology in conditions that adults would not. They reported that people did have conscious phenomenology in dreamless sleep and that therefore one could, for example, decide to turn in bed while deeply asleep. Again, even relatively old children, in this case five- or six-year-olds, seemed to have quite different intuitions about the relation between phenomenology and function than adults do. They certainly had different intuitions than John Searle does.

The last example comes from the first author of this chapter's work on children's reports of their own past mental states and the mental states of others (Gopnik and Astington 1988; Gopnik and Slaughter 1991). As we outlined at the beginning of this chapter, three-year-old children appear to think that beliefs, their own beliefs and those of others, are necessarily true, and they misreport their own immediately past beliefs. In contrast, these three-year-old children seem to have much the same intuitions as adults about simple perceptions. They report that their current perceptions may differ from those they had in the past and may differ from those of other people. Three-year-olds are also better at reporting changes in desires or in the appearances of objects than they are in reporting beliefs. Moreover, recent evidence from our lab suggests that even younger children, twenty-four to thirty-six-month-olds, do not make the same predictions about perception that adults and three-year-olds do. In short, there seems to be a gradually developing sequence of folk psychological intuitions in children, just as there is a gradually developing sequence of folk semantic intuitions in the work of Keil and Gelman, and a gradually developing sequence of intuitions about the occasions of phenomenal experience in Flavell's work. As these folk psychological intuitions develop, children become more reliable sources in reporting their own mental states, including their present and recently past phenomenology and their present and recently past beliefs and desires.

It is important, but difficult, to remember that when we talk about "children" we are talking about our past selves. Hilary Putnam, John Searle, Sydney Shoemaker, and the rest of us once, not so long ago, had very different intuitions about the nature of meaning, phenomenology, and belief than we do now. Our intuitions are not constant; they have changed quite radically in the past.

There are two possible explanations for these differences and changes. One possibility is that the underlying psychological structure of children, even seven-

or eight-year-old children, is radically different from our own, and so their intuitions are correct about three-year-old minds but not adult minds. This, in spite of the fact that three-year-olds talk, behave, interact, and function in very many ways just as we do. Were it not for the research of developmental psychologists we would not, in fact, have any idea that these children had different intuitions than we do. In order to preserve the idea that intuition is an accurate guide to underlying psychological structure, we would be forced to this radical and unpalatable conclusion.

The alternative and more plausible explanation, the one favored in developmental psychology, is that children have quite similar underlying psychological structures to our own, and that a theory of their semantics, consciousness, and belief would be similar to a theory of adult semantics, consciousness, and belief. However, their conception of that psychological structure, their knowledge about it, their folk psychology, is quite different from our own. The most likely explanation of this difference is quite straightforward: Children know less about the mind than adults do, and they learn more as they grow older. And, quite naturally, as they learn more about the mind, their conceptions about the mind, and so their intuitions, change.

But then, of course, the eschatological possibility described by Churchland and Stich becomes not only possible but likely. If our intuitions about the mind were mistaken in the past, and the error of these intuitions was revealed as our knowledge about the mind grew, then surely our intuitions about the mind now, as imperfect adults, can be mistaken in ways that will be revealed as our knowledge about the mind grows. This may already be happening, as twentieth-century adult intuition changes to accommodate newly popular concepts, like that of the unconscious. The four-year-old Phil looking back on his earlier self would, we hope, be struck by the folly of his earlier errors. Perhaps also he would be preserved from making similar errors in the future.

Notes

The preparation of this paper was supported by NSF grant DBS9213959 to the first author. We are grateful to John Campbell, Clark Glymour, and Pauline Price for helpful discussion and comments, and to the organizers and participants in the Notre Dame conference.

1. Apparently McDowell (1994) had found its way on to the picturebook shelf.

Part II

Rethinking Intuition and Philosophical Method

Chapter 6

Reflective Equilibrium, Analytic Epistemology and the Problem of Cognitive Diversity

Stephen Stich

This chapter is about different ways of thinking—or cognitive diversity, as I shall sometimes say—and the problem of choosing among them. In the pages to follow I will defend a pair of claims. The first is that one influential proposal for solving the problem of cognitive diversity, a proposal that invokes the notion of reflective equilibrium, will not work. The second is much more radical. What I propose to argue is that although some of the objections to the reflective equilibrium solution turn on details of that idea, the most serious objection generalizes into an argument against an entire epistemological tradition—the tradition that I shall call "analytic epistemology." Before attending to either of these claims, however, I will have to say something about how I conceive of cognition and cognitive diversity.

Cognition and Cognitive Diversity

Let me begin with a simplifying assumption that I hope you will not find wildly implausible. I shall assume that in humans and other higher animals there is a distinct category of mental states whose function it is to store information about the world. When the organisms in question are normal, adult humans in a culture not too remote from our own, folk psychology labels these states *beliefs*. Whether or not this folk label can be used appropriately for the belief-like states of animals, automata, young children and exotic folk is a question of considerable controversy. (See Davidson 1982; Routley 1981; Stich 1979, 1983: 89-106, 1984.) For present purposes, however, it is a controversy best avoided. Thus, I propose to adopt the term "cognitive state" as a broad cover term whose extension includes not only beliefs properly so-called, but also the belief-like information-storing mental states of animals, young children, and those adult humans, if any there be, whose cognitive lives differ substantially from our own.

Our beliefs, and the cognitive states of other creatures, are in a constant state of flux. New ones are added and old ones removed as the result of perception, and as a result of various processes in which cognitive states interact with each other. In familiar cases, folk psychology provides us with labels like "thinking" and "reasoning" for these processes, though once again the propriety of these labels becomes controversial when the cognitive states being modified are those of children, animals, or exotic folk. So I will use the term "cognitive processes" as a cover term whose extension includes our own reasoning processes, the updating of our beliefs as the result of perception, and the more or less similar processes that occur in other organisms.

Cognitive processes are biological processes; they are something that brains do. And, like other biological processes, they have been shaped by natural selection. Thus, it is to be expected that our genes exert an important influence on the sorts of cognitive processes we have. It is also to be expected that the cognitive processes of other species with other needs and other natural environments will be in varying degrees different from those to be found among humans. But from the fact that genes inevitably exert a major influence on cognitive processes it does not follow that all of our cognitive processes are innate, or, indeed, that any of them are.

To see the point, we need only reflect on the case of language. My ability to speak English is a biological ability; processing English is something my brain does. Moreover, my genes are surely heavily implicated in the explanation of how I came to have a brain that could process English. Still, English is not innate. The ability to process English is an ability I acquired, and had I been raised in a different environment I might have acquired instead the ability to speak Korean or Lapp. This is not to deny that *something* relevant to language is innate. All normal human children have the ability to acquire the language spoken around them. And that is a very special ability. There is no serious evidence indicating that members of any other species can acquire human languages or anything much like them.

Now the point I want to stress is that, as far as we know, human cognitive processes may be like human language processing abilities. They may be acquired in ways that are deeply dependent on environmental variables, and they may differ quite radically from one individual or culture to another. Of course, it is also possible that human cognitive processes are much less plastic and much less under the influence of environmental variables. It is possible that cognition is more similar to digestion than to language. To make matters a bit messier, there is no reason a priori for all cognitive processes to be at the same point on this continuum. It may be that some of our cognitive processes are shared by all normal humans, while others are a part of our cultural heritage.[1] I am inclined to think that this last possibility is the most plausible one in the light of available evidence, and for the remainder of this chapter I will take it for granted. But it must be admitted that the evidence is both fragmentary and very difficult to interpret. (See Cole and Scribner 1974; Cole and Means 1981.)

If we suppose that there is a fair amount of acquired diversity in human cognitive processes, and that patterns of reasoning or cognitive processing are to some substantial degree molded by cultural influences, it adds a certain urgency to one of the more venerable questions of epistemology. For if there are lots of different ways in which the human mind/brain can go about ordering and reordering its cognitive states, if different cultures could or do go about the business of reasoning in very different ways, *which of these ways should we use?* Which cognitive processes are the *good* ones? It is just here that the analogy with language breaks down in an illuminating way. Most of us are inclined to think that, at least to a first approximation, one language is as good as another. The one you should use is the one spoken and understood by the people around you.[2] By contrast, most of us are *not* inclined to accept this sort of thorough-going relativism about cognitive processes. If primitive tribesmen or premodern scientists or our own descendants think in ways that are quite different from the ways we think, few of us would be inclined to suggest that all of these ways are equally good. Some ways of going about the business of belief revision are better than others. But just what is it that makes one system of cognitive processes better than another, and how are we to tell which system of reasoning is best? In the remaining sections of this chapter I want to consider one influential answer to this question. I shall argue that both the answer itself and the philosophical tradition it grows out of should be rejected.

Reflective Equilibrium as a Criterion for Assessing Cognitive Processes

The answer I will disparage was first suggested about three decades ago when, in one of the more influential passages of twentieth-century philosophy, Nelson Goodman (1965) described a process of bringing judgments about particular inferences and about general principles of inference into accord with one another. In the accord thus achieved, Goodman maintained, lay all the justification needed, and all the justification possible for the inferential principles that emerged. Other writers, most notably John Rawls, have adopted a modified version of Goodman's process as a procedure for justifying moral principles and moral judgments. To Rawls, too, we owe the term 'reflective equilibrium,' which has been widely used to characterize a system of principles and judgments that have been brought into coherence with one another in the way that Goodman describes (Rawls 1971: 20ff).

It is hard to imagine the notion of reflective equilibrium explained more eloquently than Goodman himself explains it.

> How do we justify a *de*duction? Plainly by showing that it conforms with the general rules of deductive inference. An argument that so conforms is justified or valid, even if its conclusion happens to be false. An argument that violates a rule is fallacious even if its conclusion happens to be true. . . . Analogously, the basic task in justifying an inductive inference is to show that it conforms to the general rules of *in*duction. . . .
>
> Yet, of course, the rules themselves must ultimately be justified. The validity of a deduction depends not upon conformity to any purely arbitrary rules we may contrive, but upon conformity with valid rules. When we speak of *the* rules of inference we mean the valid rules—or better, *some* valid rules, since there may be alternative sets of equally valid rules. But how is the validity of rules to be determined? Here . . . we encounter

philosophers who insist that these rules follow from some self-evident axiom, and others who try to show that the rules are grounded in the very nature of the human mind. I think the answer lies much nearer to the surface.
Principles of deductive inference are justified by their conformity with accepted deductive practice. Their validity depends upon accordance with the
particular deductive inferences we actually make and sanction. If a rule yields
unacceptable inferences, we drop it as invalid. Justification of general rules
thus derives from judgments rejecting or accepting particular deductive inferences.

   This looks flagrantly circular. I have said that deductive inferences are
justified by their conformity to valid general rules, and that general rules are
justified by their conformity to valid inferences. But this circle is a virtuous
one. *A rule is amended if it yields an inference we are unwilling to accept;
an inference is rejected if it violates a rule we are unwilling to amend.* The
process of justification is the delicate one of making mutual adjustments between rules and accepted inferences; and in the agreement thus achieved lies
the only justification needed for either.

   All this applies equally well to induction. An inductive inference, too, is
justified by conformity to general rules, and a general rule by conformity to
accepted inductive inferences. (Goodman 1965: 66-67; emphasis is
Goodman's.)

There are three points in this passage that demand a bit of interpretation. First,
Goodman claims to be explaining what justifies deductive and inductive inferences. However, it is not clear that, as he uses the term, *inference* is a cognitive
process. It is possible to read Goodman as offering an account of the justification
of principles of logic and of steps in logical derivations. Read in this way,
Goodman's account of justification would be of no help in dealing with the
problem of cognitive diversity unless it was supplemented with a suitable theory
about the relation between logic and good reasoning. But as several authors have
lately noted, that relation is much less obvious than one might suppose
(Cherniak 1986: chap. 4; Harman 1986: chap. 2; Goldman 1986: section 5.1). It
is also possible to read Goodman as speaking directly to the question of how we
should go about the business of reasoning[3] and offering a solution to the problem of cognitive diversity. This is the reading I propose to adopt.

   A second point that needs some elaboration is just what status Goodman
would claim for the reflective equilibrium test he describes. It is clear Goodman
thinks we can conclude that a system of inferential rules is justified if it passes
the reflective equilibrium test. But it is not clear *why* we can conclude this. Two
different sorts of answers are possible. According to one answer, the reflective
equilibrium test is *constitutive* of justification or validity. For a system of inferential rules to be justified just *is* for them to be in reflective equilibrium. Another sort of answer is that if a set of inferential principles passes the reflective
equilibrium test, this counts as good *evidence* for them being valid or justified.
But, on this second view, being in reflective equilibrium and being justified are
quite different. One is not to be identified with the other. I am inclined to think
that it is the former, constitutive, view that best captures Goodman's intentions.

But since my concern is to criticize a view and not an author, I do not propose to argue the point. Rather, I will simply stipulate that the constitutive reading is the one I am stalking.[4]

The third point of interpretation concerns the status of the claim that reflective equilibrium is constitutive of justification. On this point, there are at least three views worth mentioning. The first is that the claim is a *conceptual truth*— that it follows from the meaning of 'justification' or from the analysis of the concept of justification. Like other conceptual truths, it is both necessarily true and knowable a priori. If we adopt this view, the status of the claim that reflective equilibrium is constitutive of justification would be akin to the status of the claim that being a closed, three-sided plane figure is constitutive of being a triangle, though the claim about justification is, of course, a much less obvious conceptual truth. A second view is that the claim is a nonconceptual necessary truth that is knowable only a posteriori. This would accord it much the same status that some philosophers accord to the claim that water is H_2O. Finally, it might be urged that the claim is being offered as a stipulative proposal. It is not telling us what our preexisting concept of justification amounts to, nor what is essential to the referent of that concept. Rather, in a revisionary spirit, it is proposing a new notion of justification. Actually, the divide between the first and the last of these alternatives is not all that sharp, for one might start with an analysis of our ordinary notion and go on to propose modifications in an effort to tidy the notion up a bit here and there. As the changes proposed get bigger and bigger, this sort of "explication" gradually shades into pure stipulation. So long as the changes an explication urges in a preexisting concept are motivated by considerations of simplicity and do not result in any radical departures from the ordinary concept, I will count them as a kind of conceptual analysis. I think a good case can be made that Goodman took himself to be providing just such a conservative explication. But again, since it is a view rather than an author that I hope to refute, I will simply stipulate that the conceptual analysis or conservative explication interpretation is the one to be adopted here.

Does the Reflective Equilibrium Account Capture our Notion of Justification?

Goodman, as I propose to read him, offers us an account of what our concept of justified inference comes to. How can we determine whether his analysis is correct? One obvious strategy is to ask just what systems of inferential rules result from the process of mutual adjustment that Goodman advocates. If the inferential systems generated by the reflective equilibrium process strike us as systems that a rational person ought to invoke, this will count in favor of Goodman's analysis. If, on the other hand, the reflective equilibrium process generates what we take to be irrational or unjustified inferential rules or practices, this will cast doubt on Goodman's claim to have captured our concept of justification. Since we are viewing conceptual explication as a kind of analysis, we should not insist that Goodman's account coincide perfectly with our intuitive judgments. But if there are lots of cases in which Goodman's account entails that a system of inferential rules is justified and intuition decrees that it is not, this is a symptom that the analysis is in serious trouble.

In an earlier paper, Nisbett and I exploited the strategy just described to argue that the reflective equilibrium account does not capture anything much like our ordinary notion of justification (Stich and Nisbett 1980). On the basis of both controlled studies and anecdotal evidence, we argued that patently unacceptable rules of inference would pass the reflective equilibrium test for many people. For example, it appears likely that many people infer in accordance with some version of the gambler's fallacy when dealing with games of chance. These people infer that the likelihood of throwing a seven in a game of craps increases each time a nonseven is thrown. What is more, there is every reason to think that the principle underlying their inference is in reflective equilibrium for them. When the principle is articulated and the subjects have had a chance to reflect upon it and upon their own inferential practice, they accept both. Indeed, one can even find some nineteenth-century logic texts in which versions of the gambler's fallacy are explicitly endorsed. (In a delightful irony, one of these books was written by a man who held the same chair Goodman held when he wrote *Fact, Fiction and Forecast*.)[5] It can also be shown that many people systematically ignore the importance of base rates in their probabilistic reasoning, that many find the principle of regression to the mean to be highly counterintuitive, that many judge the probability of certain sequences of events to be higher than the probability of components in the sequence, and so forth.[6] In each of these cases, and in many more that might be cited, it is very likely that, for some people at least, the principles that capture their inferential practice would pass the reflective equilibrium test. If this is right, it indicates there is something very wrong with the Goodmanian analysis of justification. For on that analysis, to be justified is to pass the reflective equilibrium test. But few of us are prepared to say that if the gambler's fallacy is in reflective equilibrium for a person, then his inferences that accord with that principle are justified.

Of course, each example of the infelicitous inferential principle that allegedly would pass the reflective equilibrium test is open to challenge. Whether or not the dubious principles that appear to guide many people's inferential practice would stand up to the reflective scrutiny Goodman's test demands is an empirical question. And for any given rule, a Goodmanian might protest that the empirical case has just not been made adequately. I am inclined to think that the Goodmanian who builds his defenses here is bound to be routed by a growing onslaught of empirical findings. But the issue need not turn on whether this empirical hunch is correct. For even the *possibility* that the facts will turn out as I suspect they will poses a serious problem for the Goodmanian story. It is surely not an a priori fact that strange inferential principles will always fail the reflective equilibrium test for all subjects. And if it is granted, as surely it must be, that the gambler's fallacy (or any of the other inferential oddities that have attracted the attention of psychologists in recent years) could possibly pass the reflective equilibrium test for some group of subjects, this is enough to cast doubt on the view that reflective equilibrium is constitutive of justification as that notion is ordinarily used. For surely we are not at all inclined to say that a person is justified in using any inferential principle—no matter how bizarre it may be—

simply because it accords with his reflective inferential practice.

Faced with this argument the friends of reflective equilibrium may offer a variety of responses. The one I have the hardest time understanding is simply to dig in one's heels and insist that if the gambler's fallacy (or some other curious principle) is in reflective equilibrium for a given person or group, then that principle is indeed justified for them. Although I have heard people advocate this line in conversation, I know of no one who has been bold enough to urge the view in print. Since no one else seems willing to take the view seriously, neither will I.

A very different sort of response is to urge that the notion of reflective equilibrium is itself in need of patching—that some bells and whistles must he added to the justificatory process Goodman describes. One idea along these lines is to shift from narrow Goodmanian reflective equilibrium to some analog of Rawls's "wide reflective equilibrium" (Rawls 1974). Roughly, the idea here is to broaden the scope of the judgments and convictions that are to be brought into coherence with one another. Instead of attending only to our assessments of inferential principles, wide reflective equilibrium also requires that our system of inferential rules is to cohere with our semantic, epistemological, metaphysical, or psychological views. Just how various philosophical or psychological convictions are supposed to constrain a person's inferential principles and practice has not been spelled out in much detail, though Norman Daniels, whose papers on wide reflective equilibrium are among the best around, gives us a hint when he suggests, by way of example, that Dummett's views on logic are constrained by his semantic views (Daniels 1979, 1980a, 1980b). It would also be plausible to suppose that the classical intuitionists in logic rejected certain inferential principles on epistemological grounds.

A rather different way of attempting to preserve a reflective equilibrium account of justification is to restrict the class of people whose reflective equilibrium is to count in assessing the justification of inferential principles. For example, Nisbett and I proposed that in saying an inferential principle is justified, what we are saying is that it would pass the (narrow) reflective equilibrium test for those people whom we regard as experts in the relevant inferential domain (Stich and Nisbett 1980).

A dubious virtue of both the wide reflective equilibrium and the expert reflective equilibrium accounts is that they make clear-cut counterexamples harder to generate. That is, they make it harder to produce actual examples of inferential rules, which the analysis counts as justified and intuition does not. In the case of wide reflective equilibrium, counterexamples are hard to come by just because it is so hard to show that anything is in wide reflective equilibrium for anyone. ("Would she continue to accept that rule if she thought through her epistemological and metaphysical views and came to some stable equilibrium view?" Well, God knows.) In the case of the expert reflective equilibrium account, the dubious but reflectively self-endorsed inferential practice of the experimental subject or the Las Vegas sucker just do not count as counterexamples, since these people do not count as experts.

But though clear-cut cases involving actual people may be harder to find, each of these elaborations of the reflective equilibrium story falls victim to the argument from possible cases offered earlier. Consider wide reflective equilibrium first. No matter how the details of the wide reflective equilibrium test are spelled out, it is surely not going to turn out to be impossible for a person to reach wide reflective equilibrium on a set of principles and convictions that includes some quite daffy inferential rule. Indeed, one suspects that by allowing people's philosophical convictions to play a role in filtering their inferential principles, one is inviting such daffy principles, since many people are deeply attached to outlandish philosophical views. The expert reflective equilibrium move fares no better. For unless experts are picked out in a question-begging way (e.g., those people whose inferential practices are in fact justified), it seems entirely possible for the expert community, under the influence of ideology, recreational chemistry, or evil demons, to end up endorsing some quite nutty set of rules.[7]

A "Neo-Goodmanian" Project

At this point, if the friend of reflective equilibrium is as impressed by these arguments as I think he should be, he might head off to his study to work on some further variations on the reflective equilibrium theme that will do better at capturing our concept of justification. Despite a string of failures, he might be encouraged to pursue this project by a line of thought that runs something like the following. I will call it the *neo-Goodmanian* line.

> It can hardly be denied that we do *something* to assess whether or not an inferential practice is justified. Our decisions on these matters are certainly not made at random. Moreover, if there is some established procedure that we invoke in assessing justification, then it must surely be possible to describe this procedure. When we have succeeded at this we will have an account of what it is for an inferential practice to be justified. For, as Goodman has urged, to be justified just *is* to pass the tests we invoke in assessing an inferential practice. Our procedures for assessing an inferential practice are constitutive of justification. Granted, neither Goodman's narrow reflective equilibrium story nor the more elaborate stories told by others has succeeded in capturing the procedure we actually use in assessing justification. But that just shows we must work harder. The rewards promise to repay our efforts, since once we have succeeded in describing our assessment procedure, we will have taken a giant step forward in epistemology. We will have explained what it is for a cognitive process to be justified. In so doing we will have at least begun to resolve the problem posed by cognitive diversity. For once we have a clear specification of what justification amounts to, we can go on to ask whether our own cognitive processes are justified or whether, perhaps, those of some other culture come closer to the mark.

There is no doubt that this neo-Goodmanian line can be very appealing. I was myself under its sway for some years. However, I am now persuaded that the research program it proposes for epistemology is a thoroughly wrong-headed one. In the pages that follow I will try to say why. My case against the neo-

Goodmanian project divides into two parts. First I shall raise some objections that are targeted more or less specifically on the details of the neo-Goodmanian program. Central to each of these objections is the fact that the neo-Goodmanian is helping himself to a healthy serving of empirical assumptions about the conceptual structures underlying our commonsense judgments of cognitive assessment, and each of these assumptions stands in some serious risk of turning out to be false. If one or more of them is false, then the project loses much of its initial attractiveness. In the following section I will set out a brief catalog of these dubious assumptions. The second part of my critique is much more general and I will be after much bigger game. What I propose to argue is that neither the neo-Goodmanian program nor any alternative program that proposes to analyze or explicate our presystematic notion of justification will be of any help at all in resolving the problem posed by cognitive diversity. But here I am getting ahead of myself. Let me get back to the neo-Goodmanian and his dubious empirical presuppositions.

Some Questionable Presuppositions of the Neo-Goodmanian Project

Let me begin with a fairly obvious point. The neo-Goodmanian, as I have portrayed him, retains his allegiance to the idea of reflective equilibrium. We last saw him heading back to his study to seek a more adequate elaboration of this notion. But nothing the neo-Goodmanian has said encourages us to expect that reflective equilibrium or anything much like it plays a role in our procedure for assessing the justification of a cognitive process. So even if it is granted that we have good reason to work hard at characterizing our justification-assessing procedure, we may find that the notion of reflective equilibrium is simply a nonstarter. Confronted with this objection, I think the only move open to the neo-Goodmanian is to grant the point and concede that in trying to patch the notion of reflective equilibrium he is simply playing a hunch. Perhaps it will turn out that something like reflective equilibrium plays a central role in our assessments of justification. But until we have an accurate characterization of the assessment process, there can be no guarantees.

Two further assumptions of the neo-Goodmanian program are that we ordinarily invoke only *one* notion of justification for inferential processes, and that this is a *coherent* notion for which a set of necessary and sufficient conditions can be given. But once again these are not matters that can be known in advance. It might be that different people mean different things when they call a cognitive process 'justified' because there are different notions of justification in circulation. These different meanings might cluster around a central core. But then again they might not. There are lots of normatively loaded terms that seem to be used in very different ways by different individuals or groups in society. I would not be at all surprised to learn that what I mean by terms like 'morally right' and 'freedom' is very different from what the followers of the Rev. Falwell or admirers of Col. Khadafi mean. And I would not be much more surprised if terms of epistemic evaluation turned out to manifest similar interpersonal ambiguities.

Even discounting the possibility of systematic interpersonal differences, it might be that in assessing the justification of a cognitive process we use different procedures on different occasions, and that these procedures have different outcomes. Perhaps, for example, our intuitive notion of justification is tied to a number of prototypical exemplars, and that in deciding new cases we focus in some context sensitive way on one or another of these exemplars, making our decision about justification on the basis of how similar the case at hand is to the exemplar on which we are focusing. This is hardly a fanciful idea, since recent work on the psychological mechanisms underlying categorization suggests that in *lots* of cases our judgment works in just this way.[8] If it turns out that our judgments about the justification of cognitive processes are prototype- or exemplar-based, then it will be a mistake to look for a property or characteristic that all justified cognitive processes have. It will not be the case that there is any single test passed by all the cognitive processes we judge to be justified. I am partial to a reading of the later Wittgenstein on which this is just what he would urge about our commonsense notion of justification, and I am inclined to suspect that this Wittgensteinian story is right. But I do not pretend to have enough evidence to make a convincing case. For present purposes it will have to suffice to note that this *might* be how our commonsense concept of justification works. If it is, then the neo-Goodmanian program is in for some rough sledding.

A final difficulty with the neo-Goodmanian program is that it assumes, without any evidence, that the test or procedure we use for assessing the justification of cognitive processes exhausts our concept of inferential justification, and thus that we will have characterized the concept when we have described the test. But this is hardly a claim that can be assumed without argument. It might be the case that our procrustean concept of justification is an amalgam composed in part of folk epistemological theory specifying certain properties or characteristics that are essential to justification, and in part of a test or cluster of tests that folk wisdom holds to be indicative of those properties. Moreover, the tests proposed might not always (or ever) be reliable indicators of the properties.[9] I do not have any compelling reason to believe that our commonsense notion of justification will turn out like this. But I would not be much surprised. Though our understanding of the mechanisms underlying commonsense concepts and judgments is still *very* primitive, as I read the literature it points to two important morals. First, the mental representation of concepts is likely to turn out to be a very messy business. Second, it is no easy job to separate commonsense concepts from the folk theories in which they are enmeshed. All of this bodes ill for the neo-Goodmanian who hopes that the analysis or explication of our concept of justification will yield some relatively straightforward elaboration of the reflective equilibrium test.

Against Analytic Epistemology

The problems posed in the previous section shared a pair of properties. They all turned on empirical assumptions about the nature of our ordinary concept of justification, and they were all targeted fairly specifically at the neo-Goodmanian project.[10] In the current section I want to set out a very different sort of argument, an argument, which if successful, will undermine not only reflective equilibrium theories but also the whole family of epistemological theories to which they belong.

To give some idea of the range of theories that are in the intended scope of my critique, it will be helpful to sketch a bit of the framework for epistemological theorizing suggested by Alvin Goldman in his book, *Epistemology and Cognition* (Goldman 1986). Goldman notes that one of the major projects of both classical and contemporary epistemology has been to develop a theory of epistemic justification. The ultimate job of such a theory is to say which cognitive states are epistemically justified and which are not. Thus, a fundamental step in constructing a theory of justification will be to articulate a system of rules evaluating the justificatory status of beliefs and other cognitive states. These rules (Goldman calls them *justificational rules* or *J-rules*) will specify permissible ways in which a cognitive agent may go about the business of forming or updating his cognitive states. They "permit or prohibit beliefs, directly or indirectly, as a function of some states, relations, or processes of the cognizer" (Goldman 1986: 60).[11]

Of course, different theorists may have different views on which beliefs are justified or which cognitive processes yield justified beliefs, and thus, they may urge different and incompatible sets of J-rules. It may be that there is more than one right system of justificational rules, but it is surely not the case that all systems are correct. So in order to decide whether a proposed system of J-rules is right, we must appeal to a higher criterion, which Goldman calls a "criterion of rightness." This criterion will specify a "set of conditions that are necessary and sufficient for a set of J-rules to be right" (Goldman 1986: 64).

But now the theoretical disputes emerge at a higher level, for different theorists have suggested very different criteria of rightness. Indeed, as Goldman notes, an illuminating taxonomy of epistemological theories can be generated by classifying theories or theorists on the basis of the sort of criterion of rightness they endorse. Coherence theories, for example, take the rightness of a system of J-rules to turn on whether conformity with the rules would lead to a coherent set of beliefs. Truth linked or reliability theories take the rightness of a set of J-rules to turn in one way or another on the truth of the set of beliefs that would result from conformity with the rules. Reflective equilibrium theories judge J-rules by how well they do on their favored version of the reflective equilibrium test. And so on. How are we to go about deciding among these various criteria of rightness? Or, to ask an even more basic question, just what does the correctness of a criterion of rightness come to; what makes a criterion right or wrong? On this point Goldman is not as explicit as one might wish. However, much of what he says suggests that, on his view, *conceptual analysis* or *conceptual explication* is the proper way to decide among competing criteria of rightness. The correct criterion of rightness is the one that comports with the conception of justifiedness that is "embraced by everyday thought or language" (Goldman 1986: 58). To test a criterion we explore the judgments it would entail about specific cases, and we test these judgments against our "pretheoretic intuition." "A criterion is supported to the extent that implied judgments accord with such intuitions, and weakened to the extent that they do not" (Goldman 1986: 66). Goldman is careful to note that there may be a certain amount of vagueness in our commonsense notion of justifiedness, and thus there may be no unique best criterion of rightness. But despite the vagueness, "there seems to be a common core idea of justifiedness" embedded in everyday thought and language, and it is this common core idea that Goldman tells us he is trying to capture in his own epistemological theorizing (Goldman 1986: 58-59).

The view I am attributing to Goldman on what it is for a criterion of rightness to itself be right is hardly an idiosyncratic or unfamiliar one. We saw earlier that a very natural reading of Goodman would have him offering the reflective equilibrium story as an explication or conceptual analysis of the ordinary notion of justification. And many other philosophers have explicitly or implicitly adopted much the same view. I propose to use the term *analytic epistemology* to denote any epistemological project that takes the choice between competing justificational rules or competing criteria of rightness to turn on conceptual or linguistic analysis. There can be little doubt that a very substantial fraction of the epistemological writing published in English in the last quarter of a century has been analytic epistemology.[12] However, it is my contention that if an analytic epistemological theory is taken to be part of the serious normative inquiry whose goal is to tell people which cognitive processes are good ones, or which ones they should use, then for most people it will prove to be an irrelevant failure.

I think the most intuitive way to see this point is to begin by recalling how the specter of culturally based cognitive diversity lends a certain urgency to the question of which cognitive processes we should use. If patterns of inference are acquired from the surrounding culture, much as language or fashions or manners are, and if we can learn to use cognitive processes quite different from the ones we have inherited from our culture, then the question of whether our culturally inherited cognitive processes are good ones is of more than theoretical interest. If we *can* go about the business of cognition differently, and if others actually *do*, it is natural to ask whether there is any reason why we should continue to do it our way. Even if we cannot change our cognitive processes once we have acquired them, it is natural to wonder whether those processes are good ones. Moreover, for many people the absence of a convincing affirmative answer can be seriously disquieting. For if we cannot say why our cognitive processes are any better than those prevailing elsewhere, it suggests that it is ultimately no more than an historical accident that we use the cognitive processes we do, or that we hold the beliefs that those processes generate, just as it is an historical accident that we speak English rather than Spanish and wear trousers rather than togas.

Consider now how the analytic epistemologist would address the problem that cognitive diversity presents. To determine whether our cognitive processes are good ones, he would urge, we must first *analyze* our concept of justification (or perhaps some other commonsense epistemic notion like rationality). If our commonsense epistemic notion is not too vague or ambiguous, the analysis will give us a criterion of rightness for J-rules (or perhaps a cluster of closely related criteria). Our next step is to investigate which sets of J-rules fit the criterion.

Having made some progress there, we can take a look at our own cognitive processes and ask whether they do in fact accord with some right set of J-rules. If they do, we have found a reason to continue using those processes; we have shown that they are good ones because the beliefs they lead to are justified. If it turns out that our cognitive processes do not accord with a right set of J-rules, we can try to discover some alternative processes that do a better job, and set about training ourselves to use them.

It is my contention that something has gone very wrong here. For the analytic epistemologist's effort is designed to determine whether our cognitive states and processes accord with our commonsense notion of justification (or some other commonsense concept of epistemic evaluation). Yet surely the evaluative epistemic concepts embedded in everyday thought and language are every bit as likely as the cognitive processes they evaluate to be culturally acquired and to vary from culture to culture.[13] Moreover, the analytic epistemologist offers us no reason whatever to think that the notions of evaluation prevailing in our own language and culture are any better than the alternative evaluative notions that might or do prevail in other cultures. But in the absence of any reason to think that the locally prevailing notions of epistemic evaluation are superior to the alternatives, why should we care one whit whether the cognitive processes we use are sanctioned by those evaluative concepts? How can the fact that our cognitive processes are approved by the evaluative notions embraced in our culture alleviate the worry that our cognitive processes are no better than those of exotic folk, if we have no reason to believe that our evaluative notions are any better than alternative evaluative notions?

To put the point a bit more vividly, imagine that we have located some exotic culture that does in fact exploit cognitive processes very different from our own, and that the notions of epistemic evaluation embedded in their language also differ from ours. Suppose further that the cognitive processes prevailing in that culture accord quite well with *their* evaluative notions, while the cognitive processes prevailing in our culture accord quite well with ours. Would any of this be of any help at all in deciding which cognitive processes we should use? Without some reason to think that one set of evaluative notions was preferable to the other, it seems clear that it would be of no help at all.

In the philosophical literature there is a tradition, perhaps traceable to Wittgenstein, that would reject the suggestion that our evaluative notions should themselves be evaluated. Justifications, this tradition insists, must come to an end. And once we have shown that our practice accords with our evaluative concepts, there is nothing more to show. Our language game (or form of life) does not provide us with any way to go about evaluating our evaluative notions. There is no logical space in which questions like "Should we hold justified beliefs?" or "Should we invoke rational cognitive processes?" can be asked seriously. If a person did not recognize that the answers to these questions had to be affirmative, it would simply indicate that he did not understand the logical grammar of words like 'should' and 'justified' and 'rational'.

I am inclined to think that there is at least a kernel of truth in this "Wittgensteinian" stand. Justifications do ultimately come to an end. However, it is, I think, a disastrous mistake to think that they come to an end here. For there are lots of values that are both widely shared and directly relevant to our cognitive lives, though they are quite distinct from the "epistemic values" that lie behind our ordinary use of terms like 'justified' and 'rational'. It is against the background of these nonepistemic values that our socially shared system of epistemic evaluation can itself be evaluated. Thus, for example, many people attach high value to cognitive states that foster happiness (their own or everyone's), and many people value cognitive states that afford them the power to predict and control nature. Some people share Mother Nature's concern that our cognitive lives should foster reproductive success. And, on a rather different dimension, many people care deeply that their beliefs be true.[14] Each of these values, along with many others that might be mentioned, affords a perspective from which epistemic values like justification and rationality can be evaluated. We can ask whether the cognitive states and processes endorsed by our notions of epistemic value foster happiness, or power, or accurate prediction, or reproductive success, or truth. More interestingly, we can ask whether the cognitive states and processes we actually have or use foster happiness, power, or the rest. And if they do not, we can explore alternatives that may do a better job, though there is of course no guarantee that all of these values can be maximized together.[15]

At this point, it might be protested that the values I am proposing to use in evaluating our socially shared notions of epistemic evaluation are themselves lacking any deeper justification. If someone can accept *these* as ultimate values, why could not someone do the same for justification or rationality? My reply is that of course someone could, but this is no objection to the view I am urging. There are many things that people might and do find ultimately or intrinsically valuable. Some of these values might be rooted more or less directly in our biological nature, and these we can expect to be widely shared. Other values, including intrinsic, life-shaping values, might be socially transmitted, and vary from society to society. Still others might be quite idiosyncratic. It is entirely possible for someone in our society to attach enormous value to having justified beliefs or to using rational inferential strategies—that is, to having beliefs or inferential processes that fall within the extension of 'justified' or 'rational' as they are used in our language. Similarly, it is entirely possible for someone in another society to attach enormous value to having cognitive states that fall within the extension of the terms of cognitive evaluation current in that society. In each case the evaluation may be either instrumental or intrinsic. A person in our culture may value the states and processes that fall within the extension of 'rational' or 'justified' because he thinks they are likely to be true, to lead to happiness, and so forth, or he may value them for no further reason at all. And a person in another culture may have either sort of attitude in valuing what falls within the extension of his language's terms of cognitive evaluation. Where the value attached is instrumental, there is plenty of room for productive inquiry and dialogue. We can try to find out whether rational or justified cognitive processes do lead to happiness or power or truth, and if they do we can try to understand why. But where the value accorded to one or another epistemic virtue is intrinsic, there is little room for debate. If you value rationality for its own sake, and the native of another culture values some rather different cognitive characteristic ("shmashinality" as Hilary Putnam might put it) for its own sake, there is not much you can say to each other. Moreover, there is not much I can say to either of you, since on my view the fact that a cognitive process is sanctioned by the venerable standards embedded in our language of epistemic evaluation, or theirs, is of no more interest than the fact that it is sanctioned by the venerable standards of a religious tradition or an ancient text—unless, of course, it can be shown that those standards correlate with something more generally valued.[16] But I do not pretend to have any arguments that will move the true epistemic xenophobe. If a person really does attach deep intrinsic value to the epistemic virtues favored by folk epistemology, then dialogue has come to an end.

Finally, let me say how all of this relates to analytic epistemology. The analytic epistemologist proposes to arbitrate between competing criteria of rightness by seeing which one accords best with the evaluative notions "embraced by everyday thought and language." However, it is my contention that this project is of no help whatever in confronting the problem of cognitive diversity unless one is an epistemic xenophobe. The program of analytic epistemology views conceptual analysis or explication as a stopping place in disputes about how we should go about the business of cognition. When we know that a certain cognitive process falls within the extension of our ordinary terms of epistemic evaluation—whatever the analysis of those terms may turn out to be—we know all that can be known that is relevant to the questions of how we should go about the business of reasoning. But as I see it, the only people who should take this information to be at all relevant to the question are the profoundly conservative people who find intrinsic value in having their cognitive processes sanctioned by culturally inherited standards, whatever those standards may be. Many of us care very much whether our cognitive processes lead to beliefs that are true, or give us power over nature, or lead to happiness. But only those with a deep and free-floating conservatism in matters epistemic will care whether their cognitive processes are sanctioned by the evaluative standards that happen to be woven into our language.

Notes

A previous version of this chapter appeared in *Synthese* 74 (1988): 391-413. Reprinted with kind permission from Kluwer Academic Publishers and Stephen Stich.

This paper has been evolving for a long time. Earlier versions were presented in my seminars at the University of Sydney, the University of Maryland, and the University of California, San Diego, and in colloquia at the University of Adelaide, La Trobe University, the Australian National University, the University of Illinois at Chicago, the University of Vermont, Tulane University, the University of Southern California and the University of Colorado. Suggestions and criticism from these varied audiences have led to more changes than I can remember or acknowledge. My thanks to all who helped, or tried. Special thanks are due to Philip Kitcher, David Stove, and Joseph Tolliver.

1. Nor are these the only alternatives. There are lots of characteristics that are innate (not part of our cultural heritage) though they differ substantially from one group to another. Sex, hair color, and blood type are three obvious examples.

2. Actually, the issue is not so straightforward if we compare languages at very different stages of development, or languages involving different theoretical assumptions. It is only when the choice is between languages that are more or less intertranslatable with our own that we are inclined to judge that one is as good as another. Thanks to Paul Churchland for reminding me of this point.

3. L. J. Cohen (1981) seems to read Goodman this way since he exploits Goodman's notion of reflective equilibrium in giving an account of good reasoning.

4. Well, I will argue it a little. Note first that according to Goodman the only justification needed for either rules or inferences "lies in" the agreement achieved by the reflective equilibrium process. This talk of justification *lying in* the agreement strongly suggests the constitutive reading. Moreover, on the nonconstitutive reading, Goodman's doctrine would be an oddly incomplete one. It would present us with a test for justification without telling us why it was a test or giving us any account of what it is that is being tested for. On the constitutive reading, by contrast, no such problem arises. We have in one tidy package both an analysis of the notion of justification and an unproblematic explanation of the relation between justification and the process Goodman describes.

5. The writer was Henry Coppee (1874). Here is a brief quote:

Thus, in throwing dice, we cannot be sure that any single face or combination of faces will appear; but if, in very many throws, some particular face has not appeared, the chances of its coming up are stronger and stronger, until they approach very near to certainty. It must come; and as each throw is made and it fails to appear, the certainty of its coming draws nearer and nearer. (162)

6. For an excellent survey of the literature in this area see Nisbett and Ross (1980); a number of important studies are collected in Kahneman, Slovic, and Tversky (1982).

7. As Conee and Feldman (1983) point out, the situation is actually a bit worse for the version of the expert reflective equilibrium analysis that Nisbett and I offered. On that account, different groups may recognize different people as experts. And it is surely at least possible for a group of people to accept as an expert some guru who is as bonkers as he is charismatic. But we certainly do not want to say that the followers of such a guru would be rational to invoke whatever wild inferential principle might be in reflective equilibrium for their leader.

8. For a good review of the literature, see Smith and Medin (1981).

9. For some insightful observations on the potential complexity of commonsense concepts and the ways in which intuitive tests can fail to capture the extension of concepts, see Rey (1983).

10. Actually, the last three of my four objections might, with a bit of reworking, be generalized so as to apply to all of analytic epistemology, as it is defined below. But I do not propose to pursue them since, as we shall see, analytic epistemology has more pressing problems.

11. For the reader who wants a more hands-on feel for Goldman's notion of a J-rule, the quote continues as follows:

For example, J-rules might permit a cognizer to form a given belief because of some appropriate antecedent or current state. Thus, someone being 'appeared to' in a certain way at t might be permitted to believe p at t. But someone else not in such a state would not be so permitted. Alternatively, the rules might focus on mental operations. Thus, if S's believing p at t is the result of a certain operation, or sequence of operations, then his belief is justified if the system of J-rules permits that operation or sequence of operations.

12. For an extended review of part of this literature see Shope (1983). As Shope notes, relatively few of the philosophers who have tried their hands at constructing an "analysis" of knowledge (or of some other epistemic notion) have been explicit about their objectives (see pp. 34-44). However, absent indications to the contrary, I am inclined to think that if a philosophical project proceeds by offering definitions or "truth conditions," and testing them against our intuitions about real or imaginary cases, then the project should be viewed as an attempt at conceptual analysis or explication. Unless one has some pretty strange views about intuitions, it is hard to see what we could hope to gain from capturing them apart from some insight into the concepts that underlie them.

13. Evidence on this point, like evidence about crosscultural differences in cognitive processes, is hard to come by and hard to interpret. But there are some intriguing hints in the literature. Hallen and Sodipo (1986) studied the terms of epistemic evaluation exploited by the Yoruba, a west African people. It is their contention that the Yoruba do not have a distinction corresponding to our distinction between knowledge and (mere) true belief. They do, however, divide beliefs into two other categories: those for which a person has immediate, eyewitness evidence, and those for which he does not. In the standard Yoruba-English dictionaries, the Yoruba term for the former sort of belief, 'mo', is translated as 'knowledge' while the term for the latter sort, 'gbagbo', is translated as 'belief'. However, Hallen and Sodipo argue that these translations are mistaken, since 'mo' has a much narrower extension than 'knowledge'. Most of what we would classify as scientific knowledge, for example, would not count as 'mo' for the Yoruba, because it is based on inference and second-hand report. Since the Yoruba do not draw the distinction between knowledge and (mere) true belief, they have no use for our notion of epistemic justification, which earns its keep in helping to draw that distinction. Instead, the Yoruba presumably have another notion that they exploit in distinguishing 'mo' from 'gbagbo'. Hallen and Sodipo do not indicate whether the Yoruba have a single word for this notion, but if they do, it would be a mistake to translate the word as '(epistemic) justification'. Clearly, if Hallen and Sodipo are right, the Yoruba categories of epistemic evaluation are significantly different from our own.

14. I should note, in passing, that I think it is a mistake to include truth on the list of intrinsically valuable features of one's cognitive life. But that is a topic for another paper (see Stich in preparation), and I will ignore the point here.

15. The point I am making here is really just a generalization of a point made long ago by Salmon (1957), Skyrms (1975), and a number of other authors. Strawson (1952) argued that the rationality or reasonableness of inductive reasoning was easy to demonstrate, since being supported by inductive inference is part of what we *mean* when we say that an empirical belief is *reasonable*. To which Salmon replied that if Strawson is right about the meaning of 'reasonable' it is not at all clear why anyone should want to be reasonable. What most of us do care about, Salmon notes, is that our inferential methods are those that are "best suited to the attainment of our ends" (Salmon 1957: 41). "If we regard beliefs as reasonable simply because they are arrived at inductively and we hold that reasonable beliefs are valuable for their own sake, it appears that we have elevated inductive method to the place of an intrinsic good" (Salmon 1957: 42). The analytic epistemologist elevates being within the extension of our ordinary terms of epistemic evaluation to the place of an intrinsic good. In so doing, the analytic epistemologist embraces a system of value that few of us are willing to share.

16. Let me try to head off a possible misunderstanding. Some analytic epistemologists claim that our ordinary notions of epistemic evaluation are conceptually linked to truth. On Goldman's account, for example, the rightness of a set of J-rules is

a function of how well the processes sanctioned by those rules do at producing truths. If this is right, then a person who attached intrinsic value to having true beliefs would, of course, have reason to be interested in whether his cognitive states and processes were sanctioned by the standards embedded in our language. But here it is the appeal to truth that is doing the work, not the appeal to traditional standards. For if Goldman is wrong in his conceptual analysis and '(epistemic) justification' is not conceptually tied to truth, the person who values truth will stay just as interested in whether his cognitive processes reliably lead to truth, though he may have no interest whatever in how traditional notions of epistemic evaluation judge his cognitive processes. Thanks to Steven Luper-Foy for the query that prompted this note.

Chapter 7

Reflection on Reflective Equilibrium

Robert Cummins

Reflective Equilibrium and Scientific Method

As a procedure, reflective equilibrium (RE) is simply a familiar kind of standard scientific method with a new name. (For descriptions of reflective equilibrium, see Daniels 1979, 1980b, 1984; Goodman 1965; Rawls 1971.) A theory is constructed to account for a set of observations. Recalcitrant data may be rejected as noise or explained away as the effects of interference of some sort. Recalcitrant data that cannot be plausibly dismissed force emendations in theory. What counts as a plausible dismissal depends, among other things, on the going theory, as well as on background theory and on knowledge that may be relevant to understanding the experimental design that is generating the observations, including knowledge of the apparatus and observation conditions. This sort of mutual adjustment between theory and data is a familiar feature of scientific practice. Whatever authority RE seems to have comes, I think, from a tacit or explicit recognition that it has the same form as this familiar sort of scientific inference.

One way to see the rationale underlying this procedure in science is to focus on prediction. Think of prediction as a matter of projecting what is known onto uncharted territory. To do this, you need a vehicle—a theory—that captures some invariant or pattern in what is known so that you can project it onto the unknown. How convincing the projection is depends on two factors: (i) how sure one is of the observational base, and (ii) how sure one is that the theory gets the invariants right. The two factors are not independent, of course. One's confidence in the observational base will be affected by how persuasively the theory identifies and dismisses noise; one's confidence in the theory, on the other hand, will depend on one's confidence in the observations it takes seriously. Prediction is important as a test of theory precisely because verified predictions seem to show that the theory has correctly captured the general in the particular, that it has got the drift of the observational evidence in which our confidence is ultimately grounded. Falsified prediction seems to show that it has not. We are justified in accepting a theory to the extent that we are justified in thinking it properly transfers our confidence concerning observed cases to those that have not been observed. Theory is certainly more than a vehicle for sophisticated inductive inference, but it needs to be at least that if it is to count as more than mere speculation.

Because RE has the same form as standard theory construction, it seems reasonable to ask whether it has the same rationale. RE, one might reasonably suppose, is epistemologically normative just in case it too can be seen as a sophisticated case of inductive inference. To explore this idea, imagine the application of a set of principles in RE to a case in which intuition is silent. For the result to be authoritative, we must take the principles to constitute a theory of the property P that is the target of the intuitions, a theory that captures whatever it is that makes something a P. In such a case, the theory constitutes a bridge that transfers our relative certainty about the clear cases to an unclear case. In principle, this could be a simple matter of enumerative induction, but in practice, a theory is required because the intuitions do not typically constitute a set of observations over which we can execute a simple enumerative induction. Imagine, for example, a set of judgments about solutions to various distribution problems in which the proposed solutions are judged fair or unfair.

Experiment one:
Several children are playing on the beach, and they uncover a box of pennies: (i) each child receives the same number of pennies; (ii) they are divided according to the relative sizes of the children, with the largest getting most, and so on; (iii) one child divides the pennies into groups, and the others choose in an order determined by drawing lots; (iv) they are divided according to wealth, with the poorest receiving most, and the richest receiving least.

Experiment two:
Several children are playing on the beach, and they uncover a box of mixed jewels: (i) each child receives the same number of jewels; (ii) they are divided according to the sizes of the children; (iii) one child divides them into groups, and the others pick in an order determined by lot; (iv) they are divided according to wealth, with the poorest receiving most, and the richest receiving least.

A set of "fair" or "unfair" judgments cannot be mechanically generalized in the way you can generalize from a sample of swans to the color of all swans (or to the next swan to be observed). But the underlying epistemological goal is the same: to find a bridge that projects what is known onto uncharted territory.

A theory in RE certainly makes predictions about cases on which intuition is silent or unstable. But how is one to tell if these predictions are successful? They cannot be checked against intuition, for, by hypothesis, intuition is silent or unstable on the cases in question.[1]

But perhaps this gets the analogy wrong. We do not test scientific theory on cases in which observation is impossible or unstable. We rather make predictions about cases in which the relevant observations have not been made, or were not part of the observational base from which the theory was generated. So perhaps we should think of our intuitively based philosophical theories as making predictions about cases on which intuition has not yet been consulted, or on cases that were not part of the intuitive base from which the theory was generated. This seems a pretty fair representation of philosophical practice. Theory is tested against intuitions about cases dreamed up or brought to attention by the opposition, and we can count on these not being cases involved in the generation of the theory. Fair enough: theories in RE are subject to predictive test just as their scientific look-alikes are. If we want to criticize RE, then, we are squarely reduced to asking what authority the intuitions themselves have; to asking, that is, whether intuition can play the role observation plays in science.[2]

Intuition and Observation

We can dismiss out of hand the idea that philosophical intuition is a case of perception, since it is elicited by linguistic specifications of actual and hypothetical cases. In comparing philosophical intuition to observation, then, I am using 'observation' as this term is used in texts on experimental design and statistics, to mean a data point. Understood this way, it makes sense to ask whether philosophical intuitions stand to philosophical theories as observations stand to scientific theories.[3]

We can get this question in clearer focus by asking what should happen when we are faced with incompatible intuitions. Incompatible scientific observations must be dealt with in one of two ways. Either one or both of the observations must be plausibly dismissed as error or artifact, or both must be discounted. To a good first approximation, observations are admissible scientific evidence only if they are intersubjective. Observations that can, in principle, be made by only one party to a dispute do not count as evidence. Of course, anyone can have an intuition about a given case. But this is not what the intersubjectivity of observation requires. It requires rather that when we make the same observations, we get the same results. If I see a clockwise rotation of the constellations when I look at the night stars, but you see a counterclockwise rotation, we must either explain away one or both observations, or we will have to discard both. We cannot, in this instance, agree to disagree, because we cannot maintain the objectivity of science while tolerating a fundamental subjectivity in the observational evidence. Correspondingly, if one of two conflicting intuitions cannot be explained away, both must be discarded as evidence if RE is to yield theories with any intersubjective force. One might reasonably take the view, then, that a theory is not in RE until conflicts of intuition have been resolved. Taking this line concedes that a theory in RE has no power to settle the dispute, for we have ruled that it is not in RE until the dispute is settled. But this should come as no surprise: Genuine disputes about the data cannot be settled by a theory those data are supposed to test. The data can, occasionally, settle disputes about theory, but the theory cannot settle disputes about the data. Perhaps I cannot help what I intuit any more than I can help what I see, but when conflicts cannot be explained away, I must make no evidential appeal to observations or intuitions in conflict with others.

I belabor this point because I think it is little honored in practice. Philosophers do labor to explain away the conflicting intuitions of others, but it is most assuredly not standard practice to put disputed intuitions in escrow, as it were, pending resolution. Theorists regularly claim support from disputed intuitions when there is no resolution in sight. Indeed, disputed intuitions are often the linchpin on which everything turns. Consider the role of Twin-Earth cases in current theories of content. It is commonplace for researchers in the Theory of Content to proceed as if the relevant intuitions were undisputed (Fodor 1990, 1994). Nor is the reason for this practice far to seek. The Putnamian take (Putnam 1975) on these cases is widely enough shared to allow for a range of thriving intramural sports among believers. Those who do not share the intuition are simply not invited to the games. This kind of selection allows things to move forward, but it has its price. Since most nonphilosophers do not share the intuition, the resulting theories of content have little weight with them, and this is surely a drawback for a theory that is supposed to form an essential part of the foundations of cognitive psychology. Making a Putnamian conscience an entrance requirement for the theory of content threatens to make it irrelevant. We must take care that such agreement about the intuitions as there is is not merely a selection effect. This is easier said than done, since it is all too easy for insiders to suppose that dissenters just do not understand the case. If we are honest with ourselves, I think we will have to confront the fact that selection effects like this are likely to be pretty widespread in contemporary philosophy.

The role of Twin-Earth examples in the theory of content is just an example, but it is significant because there are deep reasons why serious effort is seldom devoted to explaining away divergent philosophical intuitions, and relying instead on social pressures to maintain enough uniformity to keep the game going. For, at bottom, *all* philosophical intuition can be explained away. To get to this bottom line, we will need to go a little indirectly. I propose first to explain why philosophical intuition, unlike scientific observation, is never calibrated, though it certainly could be. This discussion will set the stage for an argument designed to show that all philosophical intuitions are likely to be artifacts.

Calibration

Observations are explained away as errors or artifacts. Errors range from such gross mistakes as pointing the telescope in the wrong direction, to subtle matters of accuracy. An artifact is an observation that carries information about the observational apparatus or process rather than about the target. An example is the apparent curvature of objects in peripheral vision introduced by astigmatism or reading glasses.

Every scientific subdiscipline spends a good deal of effort identifying and correcting errors and artifacts. What is important for present purposes is that an observational technique is deemed acceptable just to the extent that it can be relied upon to produce accurate representations or indicators of its targets. This is why observational procedures in general, and instruments in particular, have to be calibrated. When Galileo pointed his newly devised telescope at the moon and saw mountains—earthlike blemishes on what should have been a perfect celestial object—it was legitimate for the opposition to inquire whether the apparent mountains were artifacts. The proper response was to point the telescope at something of known size, shape, distance, color, and so on to determine what distortions it introduced; to calibrate it, in short.

The details of calibration can be subtle and vary considerably from case to case. An invariable requirement, however, is that there be, in at least some cases, access to the target that is independent of the instrument or procedure to be calibrated. That access need not itself be observational, but it does need to be independent in the sense that it cannot rely on either the instrument or procedure being tested, nor on the theory the newly generated observations are recruited to support. Galileo could not legitimately argue, for example, that the mountains were unlikely to be artifacts on the grounds that the Copernican hypothesis he was concerned to support abolishes the distinction between terrestrial and celestial objects that makes lunar mountains an embarrassment.

Unlike genuine observational techniques, no one ever attempts to calibrate philosophical intuition. To see why, consider again the fairness example. Suppose we want to calibrate someone's fairness intuitor. What we need is a list of representative distributions, together with a test key, that is, something that tells us which distributions on the list are fair and which unfair, or, perhaps, a ranking. We then let our subject take the test and see how well he does. Trouble is, where do we get the key? We might try to use only uncontroversial cases—that is, cases everyone agrees on in advance. But if we know that everyone, including our subject, agrees on the test items, there is no point in administering the test. If the subject gives a "wrong" answer, that just shows that the item did not belong on the test. Of course, we could simply be looking to see if the subject is like everyone else we have tested so far. This might be interesting. Perhaps, pursuing this strategy, we might find that everyone, or nearly everyone, or nearly everyone in a certain culture, or economic class, or what have you, shares certain fairness judgments. That would be worth knowing, but it would not count as calibrating our subject's fairness intuition.

We could, perhaps, get a key by consulting the experts. This is unobjectionable, provided the experts do not simply consult their fairness intuitions, for, of course, they have not yet been calibrated. Fortunately, what the experts are certain to do is to apply the best theory of fairness they have to the cases on the test. Of course, if there is a lot of controversy about the best theory of fairness, our experts are liable to disagree. If that happens, we will just have to wait until more is known. And even if the experts agree, they might still be wrong. So we would have to qualify our conclusion: "On the assumption that current theories of distributive justice are on the right track," we might report, "the subject appears to have reliable intuitions about fairness." Not definitive, perhaps, but no worse than the sort of conclusions we can draw about electron microscopes. A final and crucial proviso is that the experts do not base their theories on intuition, for this would evidently launch us on a regress.[4]

So philosophical intuition could be calibrated, but only on the assumption that there is some nonintuitive access to its targets. Personally, I am inclined to think there are, at least in some cases, nonintuitive routes to the targets of philosophical intuition. We can give up on intuitions about the nature of space and time and ask instead what sort of beasts space and time must be if current physical theory is to be true and explanatory. We can give up on intuitions about representational content and ask instead what representation must be if current cognitive theory is to be true and explanatory. But even if philosophical intuition *can* be calibrated, it never *is* calibrated, because philosophers could have no possible use for intuition in a context in which the relevant theory was well enough settled to form the basis of a credible calibration test. Philosophical theory in such good shape is ready to bid the Socratic midwife farewell and strike out on its own in some other department. Philosophical intuition, therefore, is epistemologically useless, since it can be calibrated only when it is not needed. Once we are in a position to identify artifacts and errors in intuition, philosophy no longer has any use for it. But if we are *not* in a position to do this, philosophy should not have any faith in it.

The Probable Sources of Philosophical Intuition

In spite of what I have just argued, I think we can be pretty confident that philosophical intuitions *are* artifacts. *Consider the source*, as we old folks used to say when doubting press releases from the U.S. military in VietNam. Given the current state of knowledge, I think there are just the following possible sources of philosophical intuitions.

1. *Explicit Theory.* Philosophical intuitions are the result of applying some more or less explicit theory.

2. *Ordinary Beliefs.* Philosophical intuitions are, or are obvious consequences of, things people simply happen to believe as the result of education, socialization, and the like.

3. *Language.* Philosophical intuitions are, or are generated by, the knowledge base one acquires in acquiring one's language.

4. *Concepts.* Philosophical intuitions are generated by concepts.

5. *Tacit Theory.* Philosophical intuitions are the result of applying some tacit theory.

I propose to look at each of these in turn. Some will quickly reduce to others, so the survey will be more manageable than one might suppose.

Explicit Theory

Imagine two cannon balls of exactly the same size—one solid, one hollow—dropped simultaneously from a height of 100 feet. Which will hit the ground first? My "considered judgment" is that they will land at the same time. Some people think the solid ball will land first. No one thinks the hollow ball will land first.

There is no question about the origin of my considered judgment: I can remember when I learned the relevant theory and its application to this case in high school physics. I remember the name of my teacher, how he looked, and how the classroom looked. I remember all this, because this particular application of the theory made a profound impression on me. It had this effect because, prior to that time, I would certainly have said that the solid ball would land first, a belief I picked up partly from my own experience and partly from the implications of things others said.

There is, of course, nothing whatever wrong with "considered judgments" that are applications of an explicit theory. Indeed, it is one of the important functions of an explicit theory to generate such judgments. But the judgments, or intuitions, as we have been calling them, cannot be cited as evidence for the theories that generate them. Those "intuitions" might, of course, be cited as evidence for some other theory, but their epistemological status then evidently reduces to that of the theory that generates them. They have no epistemological weight of their own. In general, intuitive judgment generated by explicit theory inherits whatever epistemological weight belongs to its parent. I can evidently dismiss the alleged observational status of the intuitions that figure in your RE if I can show that they are generated by some explicit theory you hold.

Ordinary Belief

We all collect a lot of beliefs as we go through life being socialized and educated, conversing with friends and strangers, reading books and articles, watching TV, and so on. Many of these beliefs, perhaps even most of them, are true, particularly if we have had a pretty good education and have learned to tell the wheat from the chaff. I am inclined to think a lot of our so-called intuitions about fairness are beliefs of exactly this kind. In the current jargon, they are a part of the "values" we picked up in our families, schools and play groups, our reading and TV watching. It would take a really mad kind of chauvinist, however, to suppose that these have the sort of special epistemological status required to ground a philosophical theory of distributive justice. If I can show that your reflective equilibrium depends on intuitions with this source, I can dismiss it out of hand.

Language

The idea here is that philosophical intuitions are essentially linguistic intuitions about whether, for example, something should be called *fair* or a belief *about* H_2O. One might hold that they are semantic intuitions on a par with grammatical intuitions, judgments more or less on all fours with judgments about which version of the following sentences are correct:

> We are digging a trench to insure/ensure that the spring rains do not wash out the road.

> The professor's contemptuous sneer inferred/implied that the student's answer was naive.

More loosely, one might hold that the intuitions in question are part of, or are generated by, the knowledge base one acquires in learning the language.

I have sometimes heard the following argument: "I am a competent speaker of English. A competent speaker of a language is, among other things, someone who can apply its terms correctly. Since 'fair' is a term of English, it follows that I can apply it correctly." If this argument really worked, it would show that every North American child of six could tell beeches from elms. But a competence to use the language correctly is not, more's the pity, an ability to apply its terms truly. One can be a competent speaker of a language and yet regularly misapply many of its terms, especially what we might call its theoretical terms. Holding a might-makes-right theory of fairness will impugn my morals, not my linguistic competence vis-à-vis the word 'fair'. If a child, asked to use 'fair' in a sentence, says, "It isn't fair for girls to get as much as boys," we should suspect the child's politics, not his language.[5]

To harken back to a point made earlier, we can get 'elm' and 'beech' right by deferring to the experts. But we have already seen that the competence this confers cannot be used to shore up RE. Still, I think there is little question that linguistic knowledge is implicated in the generation of philosophical intuitions, and so it is worth asking what kind of linguistic knowledge might be relevant to philosophical intuition.

An account that originated with Davidson (1967) and is championed by Fodor (1975) holds that knowing a language requires knowing satisfaction conditions for its semantically primitive terms. We might store a mentalese sentence equivalent to the following:

'fair' applies to x iff x is fair

Evidently, however, this provides no help in applying 'fair' unless the mentalese equivalent of 'fair', which appears on the right hand side of this biconditional, is either the output of a detector or a pointer to a theory of fairness. Actually, we are going to need a theory either way, since it is pretty obvious that the only way of building a fairness detector is to incorporate a theory of fairness. That theory might be procedural or declarative, or it might be a point in weight space, but the detection of fairness has got to be theoretically mediated. Moreover, the point generalizes: no property that is the target of philosophical intuition is going to be detectable without the mediation of a theory of that property.[6] Any theory of language understanding, then, that involves mapping natural language words onto mentalese equivalents or paraphrases is going to have to assume that applying the natural language term involves accessing a theory of the property the term designates. That theory might be explicit, as it is when we apply a technical scientific term, or it might be tacit, as orthodox cognitive science supposes is the case when we apply ordinary terms to distal stimuli. I have already dealt with explicit theory as the source of philosophical intuition. I will deal with tacit theory below.

A rather less explicit, hence more popular, account of the linguistic knowledge relevant to philosophical intuition is that acquisition of a language involves acquisition of concepts corresponding to the semantic primitives of the language. This version of the idea that linguistic knowledge or competence underlies philosophical intuition, then, reduces to the idea that it is concepts that underlie philosophical intuition. Let us turn, then, to concepts.

Concepts

There is not a lot of consensus about what concepts are.[7] I think three general approaches can be distinguished, however, all of which lead us to other ground in the context of this discussion.

> *Mental Representations.* If we suppose that the concept of fairness is simply a symbol of mentalese meaning *fairness*, then a concept of fairness could generate philosophical intuitions only by functioning as a pointer to something else: an explicit or tacit theory, and hence this idea leads us into no new territory.

> *Recognition or Detection Procedures.* This appears to be the core of empiricist accounts of concepts. Since, as we have already seen, detection of the properties targeted by philosophical intuition is bound to be mediated by some tacit or explicit theory, this approach to concepts leads to the same ground we have already mapped out.

> *Theories.* The majority view, I think, is that concepts are theories, either explicit, as in the case of technical scientific or legal concepts, or tacit, as in the case of "ordinary" concepts. As emphasized above, for the purposes of the present discussion, I want to construe this option broadly to cover any account that takes the functions of concepts to be mediated by knowledge about the property (or whatever) the concept is a concept *of.*

My own view, for what it is worth, is that my concept of an elevator is just everything I know about elevators, different bits of which are activated or accessed on different occasions, depending on cues and previous activations, plus some quick and dirty recognition procedures that account for prototype effects. All that matters for present purposes is that thinking of concepts as the origin of philosophical intuition requires supposing that having the relevant concepts involves having some tacit or explicit theory of the target properties. We can gloss over almost all of the interesting psychological questions here, for these mostly concern what *form* our concepts take. All that matters for my argument is that concepts cannot be what generates philosophical intuitions unless they have a certain *content:* they must be, or provide pointers to, explicit or tacit theories of the target properties.

Tacit Theories

Every remotely plausible story about the origin of philosophical intuitions, then, leads us to the view that they are generated by explicit or tacit theories of the target properties. I have already dealt with the idea that intuitions are generated by explicit theories: There is nothing whatever wrong with judgments of fairness or aboutness being made by the application of an explicit theory. Indeed, I think that is the only respectable way of generating such judgments. But since you cannot suppose that intuitions support the very theories that generate them, this account of the origin of philosophical intuitions undermines RE as a justificatory methodology in philosophy.

Here is the state of play: Philosophical intuitions are generated either by explicit or tacit theory. If the former, they are, perhaps, legitimate, but cannot play the epistemological role required of them by RE. The defender of RE, then, is reduced to the view that philosophical intuition is generated by tacit theory. The picture, then, is this:

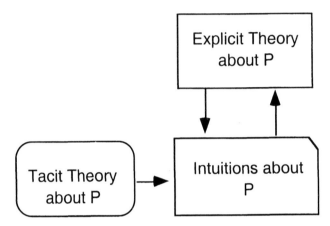

It takes no great insight to see that the intuitions, and hence the explicit theories based on them, are only as good as the tacit theory that generates those intuitions. So the viability of RE reduces to the question of the reliability of tacit theories generally, and, in particular, to the question of the reliability of tacit theories of the properties targeted by philosophical intuition. Since the prospects for such theories are very poor, I think we must conclude that RE is not a viable methodology.

What reasons might we have for trusting tacit theories? Descartes argued, in effect, that they are innate, and that what is innate, being from God, cannot be mistaken, since God is no deceiver. I do not think Cartesian theists are a large enough subset of the defenders of RE to worry about. I suspect, however, that some contemporary theorists are tempted to replace God by evolution, arguing that innate theories must be adaptive, since they have survived. I find myself more than a little tempted by the hypothesis that various moral concepts are innate, just as I am tempted by the hypothesis that various mathematical and physical concepts are innate. But Descartes was wrong about innateness being a guarantee of truth. Even the most panglossian reading of evolution will yield at most that innate theories are adaptive, not that they are true. You would have to be either extremely cynical about morals, or extremely naive about social interactions among primates and other social species, to suppose that adaptive moral concepts are accurate. More generally, adaptive theories are *effective* theories, and the effectiveness of a theory is not a simple function of its accuracy. It is also a function of its tractability, and of the kinds of problems it is typically called upon to solve.

We are finite creatures with a fixed cognitive design. Whether a theory is good for us depends a good deal on our design and on the problems we face. How important it is to avoid errors, and which errors to avoid, depends on task and environment. False negatives in food recognition are of little concern when food is plentiful, and they may be a fair price to pay to avoid false positives when there are also lots of poisons around. Conversely false positives in predator recognition are a good price to pay to achieve speed and avoid false negatives. Since accuracy is almost always expensive in terms of time or space or both, cognitive systems often trade accuracy for time and space in cases in which the inaccuracies, though perhaps large, are not serious. Relatively tractable inaccuracy is always better than relatively intractable accuracy provided the inaccuracies are not fatal.

No doubt there is some innate theory. It is pretty likely that we are endowed with some innate physics (Baillargeon, Spelke, and Wasserman 1985; Baillargeon 1987; Spelke 1991). It looks like there might be an innate module responsible for at least some moral reasoning (Cummins 1996a, 1996b). I do not find it at all implausible to suppose that we are endowed with some innate philosophy, especially moral and social philosophy. But when you come to think of what these theories are for, there is no more reason to think that innate philosophy is a good basis for philosophy than that innate physics is a good basis for physics. We have cultural institutions like science and philosophy largely to *overcome* the limitations of our innate endowment. There is, then, no good reason to think that the innate tacit theories that might underlie philosophical intuition are true, and some compelling general reasons for thinking that they are likely to be pretty inaccurate.

Acquired tacit theory fares no better when scrutinized. Undisciplined learning of the sort that produces tacit as opposed to explicit theory is bound, like evolution, to be more guided by effectiveness than by accuracy. Indeed, all learning is guided by effectiveness. It is just that, in explicit educational settings, we take special care that inaccurate theories will not be effective. That is what examinations are all about. We can hardly expect tacit theory to be molded by any such artificial mechanisms, however. Moreover, tacit theory acquisition is bound to exhibit what I call the MCI effect: the verbally and behaviorally expressed views of family and friends are going to loom large in the outcome. They are, in short, going to be biased.

Not only are tacit theories, whether acquired or innate, likely to be inaccurate, they are likely to generate inconsistent intuitions over time. This is partly because one's tacit knowledge can be expected to change over time, but also because which bits of one's tacit knowledge are in fact accessible will vary from occasion to occasion, depending on cues and prior activations. As a consequence, we should expect both order effects and context effects in the intuitions they generate. Perhaps a carefully formulated organon for RE could compensate for such effects, but no one is likely to bother. No one is likely to bother, because, once it is clear what tacit theories are, we are bound to see the intuitions they generate as very likely to be artifacts or errors. And since, as argued in the previous section, we cannot calibrate philosophical intuition unless we are possessed of the sort of theory that would render it idle, there is never going to be any point to compensating for order or context effects in the elicitation of philosophical intuition from tacit theory. If you know enough to start fixing problems with philosophical intuition, you already know enough to get along without it.

Capturing the Intuitions

Objection: It is beside the point to argue that philosophical intuitions have no justificatory force, for the point of the enterprise is just to construct a theory that accounts for the intuitions, not to use the intuitions as evidence for that theory.

Of course, there is some interest in knowing what tacit theories we in fact hold, and I suppose something like RE might be a way of at least generating hypotheses about these matters: a theory in RE with intuition might be a reasonable candidate specification of a tacit theory. But, of course, this is simply armchair psychology, and no substitute for empirically disciplined research by people trained to do the job right.

Moreover, achieving RE in some domain is no guarantee that there *is* a tacit theory at work. The intuitions might be the result of an explicit theory, the results of the RE process itself, seeded, as it were, by some initial tacit or explicit beliefs one happens to have picked up. More seriously, even if there is a tacit theory at work, it is not going to have much psychological interest unless it is pretty universal at some developmental stage or other. Otherwise, it tells us nothing about the architecture of the mind, but simply reflects tacit effects of more or less idiosyncratic experience and indoctrination. Psychology must be careful to distinguish MCI effects from effects of the mind's structure and development. From the point of view of scientific psychology, the fact that some people have internalized a causal theory of reference or a utilitarian theory of distributive justice is of no more interest than the fact that some people have internalized creationism or a Buddhist theory of reincarnation. People get ideas. Unless they are ideas that they always get, irrespective of variations in their environment, psychology may safely leave them to the pages of the *National Enquirer*.

And anyway, the point of RE is not to "capture the intuitions"; the point is to construct and justify a theory of fairness, or aboutness, or some other property of philosophical interest. Knowing what my intuitions about *aboutness* are, and how they are best systematized, is a matter of biographical interest at best. This is often disguised by speaking as if what has been achieved is a systemization of "our" intuitions, the implication being that everyone has them. But, in academic philosophy, at least, this is mainly an illusion created by only allowing fellow travelers to participate in the game. More importantly, even if it were true that everyone shared the intuitions in question, this would have, as we have seen, no tendency to show that those intuitions are accurate.

Coherence

There is, of course, a way of promoting any belief you happen to have into evidence, and that is to embrace some naive form of coherentism. (See Tersman 1993, for just such a defense of RE in ethics.) But just as a plausible coherentism must account for the special role of observation in science, so it must also reveal the disanalogies I have been pressing between intuition and observation. If coherentism cannot tell the epistemological difference between philosophical intuition generators and telescopes, then it will fail as an epistemology. For the point of epistemology is to help us to understand such things as the importance of calibration. Trying to save philosophical intuition by adopting coherentism is putting the cart before the horse.

Of course, no coherentism worth its salt requires one to accept one's intuitions, any more than it requires one to accept any other beliefs one happens to have. Hume said that belief is involuntary, that one cannot, for the most part, simply choose what to believe (Hume 1777). You cannot simply decide to believe that you have seven fingers on your right hand. It is a feat completely beyond your powers. I am not sure that all belief is like this, but some certainly is. As far as I can see, there are only two ways a coherence theory can respond to involuntary beliefs. One is to simply allow them their share in determining over-all coherence. The other is to introduce some mechanism for "bracketing" involuntary beliefs that, as it were, one does not want to accept. The first strategy is unattractive because it makes involuntary beliefs tyrannical. Indeed, they will act like foundational beliefs in foundationalist theories, but without anything to ground their special epistemological status beyond their involuntariness. It is not surprising, then, that coherence theorists generally adopt some form of the second strategy (Lehrer 1983, 1991). Once a bracketing mechanism is at hand, however, a coherence theorist is free to dismiss RE and philosophical intuition on the grounds that it is, as I have argued, either unnecessary or uncalibratable, and hence does not cohere well with entrenched cannons of scientific inference.

Conclusion

Philosophical intuition is epistemologically useless, since it can be calibrated only when it is not needed. Once we are in a position to identify artifacts and errors in intuition, philosophy no longer has any use for it. Moreover, the most plausible account of the origins of philosophical intuitions is that they derive from tacit theories that are very likely to be inaccurate. There is a sense, then, in which philosophical intuitions can always be "explained away": when a dispute arises, I can always, with some plausibility, suppose your intuitions are the artifacts of bad tacit theory. This is a game everyone can play, and I think we should all play it. We should, that is, dismiss philosophical intuition as epistemologically valueless.

To many, this will appear as an unemployment opportunity. But I think there is some hope for a philosophy without intuition. In my field, which is the theory of mental representation, we can, as I mentioned earlier, stop asking whether 'water' refers to H$_2$O on Earth but to XYZ on Twin Earth, and start asking what explanatory role representation plays in the theories that appeal to it. This puts the philosophy of psychology on a par with the philosophy of physics. Philosophers of physics interested in space and time do not consult their intuitions any more, they ask how we must understand space and time if the physical theories that appeal to them are to be true and explanatory. I do not know if something analogous will replace intuition in every branch of philosophy, but *something* had better replace it. It cannot support any conclusion worth drawing.

Let me conclude with something about where I think the burden of proof lies. Philosophers, especially those interested in ethics and mathematics, are inclined to argue as follows: "You are no skeptic about ethics and mathematics, so you have to accept the epistemological value of intuition. What else, after all, could ground moral or mathematical knowledge?" I do not know. For that matter, I do not think we have a satisfactory account of perceptual knowledge, either. But "what else" arguments just do not cut it in epistemology. I have just been at pains to show that philosophical theory cannot be grounded in intuition.[8] If, in a given case, we cannot say what it *should* be grounded in, that is no reason for reinstating intuition. It is rather a reason to think harder about the methodology and questions of one's own discipline. I have given up on Twin Earth in the theory of content. Maybe moral philosophers should give up on Trolleys.

Notes

1. It might be, of course, that the process of achieving RE generates a stable intuition where before there was none, but then the generated intuition has no power to confer an independent check on the theory.

2. This oversimplifies matters a bit. It is not always observations that are the object of scientific prediction. In a sense, any bit of knowledge, whether general or particular, that is not involved in the generation of the theory will do as predictive target. I will return to this point below when it becomes relevant.

3. Could we have perceptions of, say, fairness or aboutness against which philosophical intuition could be tested? If this were possible, RE would not be so central and pervasive. RE looms large in philosophy precisely because no one thinks theories of justice or theories of reference can be perceptually tested.

4. Long regresses, I suspect, will eventually join big circles as examples of vicious structures that are said to become benign if only they are of sufficient magnitude.

5. The phrase 'linguistic competence' is a technical term of East Pole (Dennett 1986) linguistics. There, competence is opposed to performance, not to incompetence. The competence-performance distinction in linguistics is not an epistemological distinction, it is an expression of the idea that linguistic behavior is best understood via a strategy of idealization. The idea is just that actual linguistic performance does not accurately mirror the underlying grammar, because actual performance is distorted by factors ranging from resource constraints to motivation. Just as we can understand the behavior of a pendulum as the behavior of an "ideal" pendulum—a pendulum in which period depends only on length and gravity—whose behavior is modified

by friction and air resistance, so, it is alleged, we can understand the linguistic behavior as the behavior of an ideal speaker—a speaker whose behavior depends only on the underlying grammar—modified by the effects of resource constraints, variable motivation, and the like. Competence in this sense is not the ability to apply terms truly.

6. This is not saying much. Probably no distal property can be detected without the mediation of a certain amount of contingent background knowledge. You might be able to build a pretty good P-detector without incorporating any very substantive knowledge of P if there are a range of reliable indicators of P that can be detected already. For example, as Putnam points out (1975), one way to detect beeches and to distinguish them from elms is to ask an expert. So, if you can detect the relevant experts, and you can get them to say whether the target is a beech, you can detect beeches even though you do not have anything approaching the theory that allows the expert to do the trick. Less trivially, you might detect beeches by leaf shape, yet still know relatively little about beeches, and so be at a loss in the winter. I am going to ignore this complication, because all the subsequent argument requires is that the detection of the sort of property that is the target of philosophical intuition must be mediated by some background knowledge.

7. 'Concept' is ambiguous. Generally, a concept is a psychological structure of some sort, but sometimes concepts are taken to be abstract objects that stand to terms as propositions stand to sentences. In the following discussion, concepts are psychological structures.

8. I have heard the following *tu quoque*: "Your arguments against appeal to intuition in philosophy are themselves grounded in intuition." I do not think so; I think they are grounded in psychology and successful scientific practice. But here is a *tu quoque* back: If you believe in intuition, and think my premises and logic are intuitive, you should accept my conclusion. If you do that, you have a *reduction* against intuition on your hands.

Chapter 8

The Role of Intuition in Philosophical Inquiry: An Account with No Unnatural Ingredients

Hilary Kornblith

George Bealer does it. Roderick Chisholm does it a lot. Most philosophers do it openly and unapologetically, and the rest arguably do it too, although some of them would deny it. What they all do is appeal to intuitions in constructing, shaping, and refining their philosophical views. In this chapter, I examine the role of intuitions in philosophical theory construction, with special emphasis on their source and their epistemic status.

For some philosophers, the status of appeals to intuition is easily explained. Our intuitions are a priori justified. They are a product of conceptual analysis, and little more needs to be said. As a naturalist, however, I find this explanation unacceptable, rejecting, as I do, both the a priori and the very idea of conceptual analysis, as they are traditionally conceived. This would raise no difficulties for me were it not for the fact that I too have appealed to my intuitions in the course of theory construction, and this is a part of my philosophical practice that I do not believe I can eliminate. The difficulty arises in explaining how to square my own philosophical practice with my naturalistic philosophical convictions.

My difficulty here is not idiosyncratic. As George Bealer has argued in a series of papers,[1] and as others have urged as well, this is a problem for naturalists generally. A priorists are not the only philosophers around who appeal to their intuitions. Naturalists do it too, Bealer argues, while simultaneously proclaiming allegiance to a theory that leaves no room for such a practice. So much the worse for naturalism, concludes Bealer. The very practice of philosophy is incompatible with a naturalistic epistemology.

Precisely what intuitions are is, of course, controversial, but there is, without doubt, a phenomenon of appealing to intuitions, which is widespread among philosophers, and Bealer is right, I believe, in thinking that naturalists do it too. I want to examine this phenomenon, this bit of philosophical practice, from a naturalistic perspective. There is room for a naturalistic account of the practice, an account that does not make naturalism self-defeating. Bealer and I disagree about proper philosophical method and about the proper description and significance of the practice of appealing to intuitions. But there should be no disagree-

ment, I argue, about whether there is room within a naturalistic epistemology
for the very practice in which naturalistic philosophers are engaged.

Appeals to Intuition

First, let us get clear about the phenomenon. Although any characterization of
the phenomenon will be highly contentious, there is no difficulty in giving examples of the practice at issue. We will thus do best to pin down the practice by
way of examples, examples of what we hereby dub 'appeals to intuition'; later
we may address the question of what it is these examples are examples of.

There are substantial bodies of literature in philosophy that are driven in large
part by frankly acknowledged appeals to intuition and are motivated by a desire
to formulate accounts that square with those intuitions. Thus, in epistemology,
there is the literature on the analyses of knowledge and justification, and especially would-be solutions to the Gettier problem. Imaginary cases are described,
involving Brown and his travels in Spain, Nogot, Havit and their vehicles, Tom
Grabit and his kleptomaniacal proclivities at the library, gypsy lawyers, Norman
the clairvoyant, barn facades in the countryside, and a host of others. In each of
the cases described, there is a good deal of agreement about whether, under the
described conditions, a subject knows, or is justified in believing, something to
be the case. Intuitions about these cases are then used to clarify the conditions
under which various epistemic notions rightly apply. No empirical investigation
is called for, it seems. Each of us can just tell, immediately, whether the case described involves knowledge, or justified belief, or neither.

But epistemologists are not the only ones to use this method. In philosophy
of language, there is the literature on the Gricean account of meaning, replete
with subjects and their self-referential intentions, including the American soldier
who hopes to convince his Italian captors that he is German by uttering the one
German sentence he knows, "Kennst du das Land wo die Zitronen blühen?," not
to mention a character who intends to clear a room with his rendition of "Moon
Over Miami," at least in part, of course, in virtue of his audience recognizing
that very intention. Here we have quite clear intuitions about when it is that a
subject means something by an utterance, and when a subject merely means to
achieve a certain affect without meaning anything by the utterance at all. There
is also the literature on the causal or historical theory of reference, with the cases
of Gödel, Schmidt, and the goings-on on Twin Earth.

There is the literature on personal identity, with its cases of brain transplanta-
tion, memory loss and duplication. And there is the literature in moral philosophy involving children who amuse themselves by pouring gasoline on cats and
igniting them, the woman who wakes up one morning to find herself an essential part of the life support system for an ailing violinist, and a very large number of people unaccountably loitering on trolley tracks.

This method of appeal to intuitions about cases has been used in every area of
philosophy, and it has often been used with subtlety and sophistication. There
are those—and I count myself among them—who believe that there are substantial limitations to this method, and who believe that some of these bodies of lit-

erature have diverted attention from more important issues. Even we, however, must acknowledge that the method of appeal to intuitions not only plays an important role in actual philosophical practice, but that the method has been used to achieve some substantial insights in a wide range of fields. We need an account of how it is that this method may achieve such results.

Bealer's Antinaturalistic Account of the Appeal to Intuition

Now George Bealer offers us precisely such an account, and he uses this account to argue that naturalism[2] is self-defeating. In order to see how Bealer's argument proceeds, we must begin with his characterization of the phenomenon.

Bealer describes what he calls "the standard justificatory procedure" [164-167]. As Bealer notes, "we standardly use various items—for example, experiences, observations, testimony—as *prima facie* evidence for things, such as beliefs and theories" [164]. After describing a typical Gettier example, Bealer notes that intuitions as well count as prima facie evidence. But what are intuitions? According to Bealer, "When we speak of intuition, we mean *a priori* intuition" [165].

Although use of the term 'intuition' varies widely among philosophers, Bealer is careful to make his use of the term clear. "Intuition," Bealer tells us, "must . . . be distinguished from common sense. . . . common sense is an amalgamation of various widely shared, more or less useful empirical beliefs, practical wisdom, *a priori* intuitions, and physical intuitions. Common sense certainly cannot be *identified* with *a priori* intuition" [167]. This distinction, Bealer tells us, is "obvious once [it] is pointed out" [167].

Once this account of the standard justificatory procedure is in place, with its reliance on intuition in Bealer's sense, the route to an indictment of naturalism is clear. Naturalists subscribe to a principle of empiricism: "A person's experiences and/or observations comprise the person's *prima facie* evidence" [163]. This rules out intuition as a legitimate source of evidence, and thus flies in the face of the standard justificatory procedure. Naturalists themselves make use of intuitions; they too subscribe, in practice, to the standard justificatory procedure. So naturalistic theory is belied by naturalistic practice. Indeed, if consistently followed in practice, Bealer argues, naturalistic theory would not only rule out philosophy generally as illegitimate, but, given the role intuition plays in "following rules and procedures—for example, rules of inference," [167] a consistent naturalist would have little room left for legitimate belief of any sort at all.[3]

Bealer argues that some naturalists face an additional problem as well. Those who wish to make use of, rather than eliminate, epistemic terminology will find, Bealer argues, that their theory is at odds with their practice in yet another way. What Bealer calls "the principle of naturalism" holds that "the natural sciences . . . constitute the simplest comprehensive theory that explains all, or most, of a person's experiences and/or observations" [163]. Naturalists also endorse what Bealer calls "the principle of holism": "A theory is justified . . . for a person if and only if it is, or belongs to, the simplest comprehensive theory that explains all, or most, of the person's *prima facie* evidence" [163]. When these two principles are added to the principle of empiricism, which limits our source of prima facie evidence to observation, naturalists are forced to eschew all epistemic terminology, because "the familiar terms 'justified,' 'simplest,' 'theory,' 'explain,' and *'prima facie* evidence' . . . do not belong to the primitive vocabulary of the simplest regimented formulation of the natural sciences" [180]. Not only is naturalistic theory at odds with naturalistic practice, but the very terms in which naturalistic theory is formulated, Bealer argues, are disallowed as illegitimate by that very theory. Naturalism is thus found to be self-defeating twice over.

Naturalism is more resourceful, I believe, than Bealer allows. There is room within a naturalistic epistemology for the practice of appeals to intuition and also for the use of epistemic terminology. What I wish to do is explain how the naturalist may accommodate these phenomena. Much of what I say will be familiar; the story I have to tell, I believe, is at least implicit in the work of a number of investigators working within the naturalistic tradition.[4] But the clarity and focus of Bealer's attack, and the extent to which others have made similar arguments (see especially BonJour 1994), demand a reply. I thus hope to make clear that this kind of attack on naturalism cannot, in the end, succeed.

A Naturalistic Account of the Appeal to Intuition

Naturalists and those who are opposed to naturalism have divergent views about how philosophy ought to be practiced. At the same time, however, there is a great deal more agreement in actual practice than there is in theory about that practice. I do not believe that these differences are insignificant, and later in this chapter I will want to say something about what those differences are and why they matter. But for now, I want to focus on the areas of agreement in practice between naturalists and antinaturalists, and I will assume that the characterization Bealer gives of the standard justificatory procedure accurately characterizes that common practice. That is, I will assume, with Bealer, that philosophers of all sorts assign prima facie weight to experience, observation, testimony *and intuition*, although I will not assume, with Bealer, that intuition here comes down to "a priori intuition." Instead, I will take intuition to be pinned down by the paradigmatic examples of it given earlier.

How should naturalists regard the standard justificatory procedure? The first thing to say about the intuitions to which philosophers appeal is that they are not idiosyncratic; they are widely shared, and—to a first approximation—must be so, if they are to do any philosophical work. Some philosophers will say, "I'm just trying to figure out what *I* should believe; I'm just trying to get my own intuitions into reflective equilibrium." But even philosophers who say this sort of thing must recognize that wholly idiosyncratic intuitions should play no role even in figuring out what they themselves ought to believe. If I attempt to offer a philosophical account of knowledge by drawing on my intuitions, and it should turn out that crucial intuitions upon which my account relies are had by no one but me, then this will not only dramatically reduce the interest of my account for others; it ought, as well, reduce the interest of my account for me. If my intuitions are wildly idiosyncratic, then most likely the project of accommodating them is no longer one that is engaged with the phenomenon others are attempting to characterize. Unless I can show that others have been somehow misled, what I ought to conclude is that I am probably the one who has been misled, and I ought to focus my attention on correcting my own errors, rather than taking my intuitive judgments at face value. The intuitions of the majority are not definitive, but they do carry substantial epistemic weight, at least in comparison with the intuitions of any single individual, even oneself.

Why is it that the intuitions of the majority carry such weight? It is not, of course, that we merely wish to be engaged in the project, whatever it may be, that other philosophers are engaged in. This would make philosophy into a shallow enterprise, a kind of intellectual imitation game in which the participants seek to engage one another in what they are doing, without concern for what that might be. Instead, we must be assuming that disagreement with the majority is some evidence of error, and now the question is how that error should be characterized.

Now it is at this point that many philosophers will be tempted to bring in talk of concepts and conceptual analysis: in appealing to our intuitions, it will be said, we come to understand the boundaries of our shared concepts. But I do not think this way of seeing things is illuminating. As I see it, epistemologists ought to be concerned with the nature of knowledge, not the concept of knowledge; the proper subject matter of ethics is the right and the good, not the concepts of the right and the good; and so on. I will focus here on examples from epistemology, simply because that is the field I know best; but what I say about epistemology should apply equally to other fields within philosophy.

Epistemologists are trying to understand what knowledge is. There is a robust phenomenon of human knowledge, and a presupposition of the field of epistemology is that cases of knowledge have a good deal of theoretical unity to them; they are not merely some gerrymandered kind, united by nothing more than our willingness to regard them as a kind. More than this, if epistemology is to be as worthy of our attention as most epistemologists believe, and if knowledge is to be as worthy of our pursuit, then certain deflationary accounts of knowledge had better turn out to be mistaken. What I have in mind here are those social constructivist accounts that, while granting a substantial theoretical unity to cases of knowledge, see that unity as residing in the social role that knowledge plays. Knowledge, on this view, is merely a vehicle of power. Knowledge may well play some such social role, but its ability to play such a role, if I am right, is explained by a deeper fact, and it is this deeper fact about knowledge that gives it its theoretical unity.[5]

Now one of the jobs of epistemology, as I see it, is to come to an understanding of this natural phenomenon, human knowledge. Understanding what knowledge is, if the project turns out as I expect it will, will also, simultaneously, help to explain why knowledge is worthy of pursuit. When we appeal to our intuitions about knowledge, we make salient certain instances of the phenomenon that need to be accounted for, and that these are genuine instances of knowledge is simply obvious, at least if our examples are well chosen. What we are doing, as I see it, is much like the rock collector who gathers samples of some interesting kind of stone for the purpose of figuring out what it is that the samples have in common. We begin, often enough, with obvious cases, even if we do not yet understand what it is that provides the theoretical unity to the kind we wish to examine. Understanding what that theoretical unity is is the object of our study, and it is to be found by careful examination of the phenomenon, that is, something outside of us, not our concept of the phenomenon, something inside of us. In short, I see the investigation of knowledge, and philosophical investigation generally, on the model of investigations of natural kinds.

When viewed this way, the method of appeal to intuitions is, I believe, easily accommodated within a naturalistic framework. The examples that prompt our intuitions are merely obvious cases of the phenomenon under study. That they are obvious, and thus uncontroversial, is shown by the wide agreement these examples command. This may give the resulting judgments the appearance of a priority, especially in light of the hypothetical manner in which the examples are typically presented. But on the account I favor, these judgments are no more a priori than the rock collector's judgment that if he were to find a rock meeting certain conditions, it would (or would not) count as a sample of a given kind. All such judgments, however obvious, are a posteriori, and we may view the appeal to intuition in philosophical cases in a similar manner.[6]

What should we say about the rock collector's judgments at early stages of investigation, that is, prior to any deep theoretical understanding of the features that make his samples samples of a given kind? Such judgments are, of course, corrigible, and will change with the progress of theory. What seemed to be a clear case of a given kind in the absence of theoretical understanding may come to be a paradigm case of some different kind once the phenomena are better understood. At the same time, it would be a mistake to see these initial naive judgments as wholly independent of background theory. Our rock collector is naive, but he is not a tabula rasa. Background knowledge will play a substantial role in determining a first-pass categorization of samples. Judgments about which features of the rocks are even deemed relevant in classification—hardness, for example, but not size perhaps—are themselves theory-mediated, although the operation of theory here is unself-conscious and is better revealed by patterns of salience than it is by overt appeal to principle. The extent to which naive investigators agree in their classifications is not evidence that these judgments somehow bypass background empirical belief, but rather that background theory may be widely shared.

So too, I want to say, with appeals to intuition in philosophy. These judgments are corrigible and theory-mediated. The extent of agreement among subjects on intuitive judgments is to be explained by common knowledge, or at least common belief, and the ways in which such background belief will inevitably influence intuitive judgment, although unavailable to introspection, are nonetheless quite real.

Indeed, I want to push this analogy considerably further. The judgments of rock collectors at early stages of investigation are substantially inferior, epistemically speaking, to those at later stages, when theoretical understanding is further advanced. We should not say that initial judgments are of no evidential value, for were this the case, progress in theory would be impossible. Our untutored judgment must have some purchase on the phenomenon under investigation; but, that said, it must also be acknowledged that judgment guided by accurate background theory is far superior to the intuitions of the naive. Intuition must be taken seriously in the absence of substantial theoretical understanding, but once such theoretical understanding begins to take shape, prior intuitive judgments carry little weight unless they have been endorsed by the progress of theory. The greater one's theoretical understanding, the less weight one may assign to untutored judgment.

All of this applies equally well to the case of appeals to intuition in philosophy. We sometimes hear philosophers speak of some intuitions as "merely" driven by theory, and thus to be ignored. While it is certainly true that judgments driven by bad theories are not to be taken seriously, the solution is not to try to return to some pure state of theory-independent judgment, before the fall, as it were; rather the solution is to get a better theory. Intuition in the absence of theory does not count for nothing, especially if no credible theory is available. But this is not to award high marks to intuitive judgment before the arrival of successful theory, let alone after, when the initially low value of such judgment drops still lower.

Now if this account is correct, why do philosophers spend so much time scrutinizing their intuitions, that is, looking inward, if, on my view, what they are really interested in is external phenomena? I have two things to say about this. First, if I am asked a question about rocks, for example, one way to answer the question is to ask myself what I believe the answer is. Although I am asked a question about rocks, I answer it by inquiring into what I believe. This is a perfectly reasonable thing to do if I have good reason to think that my current beliefs are accurate, or if I do not have access to a better source of information. By looking inward, I answer a question about an external phenomenon. This, to my mind, is what we do when we consult our intuitions.

At the same time, however, I do not think that this can be the whole story here, and this is where the difference between the practice of naturalists and that of antinaturalists comes into play. If my account is correct, then what we ought to be doing is not just consulting the beliefs we already have, but more directly examining the external phenomena; only then would appeals to intuition be given what, on my view, is their proper weight. Thus, appeal to intuition early on in philosophical investigation should give way to more straightforwardly empirical investigations of external phenomena. This is, to my mind, just what we see in the practice of naturalistically minded philosophers. Just a few decades ago, the philosophical practice of naturalistically minded epistemologists, for example, was almost indistinguishable from that of their more traditionally minded colleagues. Examples and counterexamples were used to motivate various accounts of knowledge and justification, and the progress of these accounts was shepherded along by a succession of appeals to intuition. This was, by my lights, a good thing to do at that stage of the investigation. Important insights were gained, which, given the absence of available explicitly articulated theory, could not have been gained by any other means. But now, as theory has progressed, more straightforwardly empirical investigation should be called upon;

and this, of course, is just what we see. There is work on the psychology of inference, concept formation, cognitive development, and so on. Similarly, at the social level there is work on the distribution of cognitive effort, and, more generally, the social structures of science that underwrite and make scientific knowledge possible. As theory has advanced here, raw appeals to intuition have declined. Just look at the difference between early papers by Fred Dretske and Alvin Goldman, for example, and their more recent work. Similar results may be found by looking at naturalistically minded work in philosophy of mind, and even in ethics, where work in cognitive science and anthropology have been shaping the work of contemporary naturalists. The difference in methodology between naturalists and their more traditional colleagues has, to my mind, been paying substantial dividends for those willing to draw on empirical work. But even those who disagree with me here will have to agree that naturalistic methodology is now importantly different from that of other philosophers, even if not very long ago it would have been difficult to separate the naturalists from the nonnaturalists by looking at their methods.

From a naturalistic perspective, there are substantial advantages to looking outward at the phenomena under investigation rather than inward at our intuitions about them. Most obviously, since it is some external phenomenon we are interested in, we should approach it by the most direct means possible, rather than the more indirect approach of looking at what we currently believe about it. Aside from being indirect, the approach of examining our intuitions clearly robs us of the best available source of correctives for current mistake. Moreover, the appeal to imaginable cases and what we are inclined to say about them is both overly narrow and overly broad in its focus. It is overly narrow because serious empirical investigation of a phenomenon will often reveal possibilities that we would not, and sometimes could not, have imagined before. It is overly broad because many imaginable cases are not genuine possibilities and need not be accounted for by our theories. We might be able to imagine a rock with a certain combination of color, hardness, malleability, and so on, and such a rock, were it to exist, might be difficult or impossible to fit in to our current taxonomy. But this raises no problem at all for our taxonomic principles if the imagined combination of properties is nomologically impossible. On the naturalistic view, the same may be said for testing our philosophical views against merely imaginable cases.

I do not mean to suggest that on the naturalistic view we will ever be able wholly to avoid appealing to our intuitions. I do think that appeals to intuition will continue to play a role in the development of philosophical views, even as theory progresses. I noted earlier that the actual practice of naturalistically minded philosophers has changed with the progress of theory so that now there is a good deal more empirical examination of various phenomena rather than an exclusive reliance on appeals to intuition. But this does not mean that appeals to intuition simply drop out of the picture. Thus, for example, in philosophy of mind not so many years ago there was a good deal of discussion about whether creatures who failed to exhibit certain sorts of characteristic behavior might nevertheless be in pain. These discussions did not involve much of a look at the empirical literature on pain; instead, they relied exclusively on appeals to intuition. Now, although work in philosophy of mind involves a great deal of examination of the empirical literature, we still see appeals to intuition playing a role, although the intuitions are about more esoteric matters. For example, there is discussion of what magnetosomes represent, whether it be the presence of certain sorts of magnetic fields or, instead, the presence of anaerobic conditions.

The intuitions that naturalists currently appeal to, intuitions about matters far more esoteric than what is known about Brown in Barcelona, present clear cases of theory-mediated judgment, judgment that is rightly influenced by a large body of background belief. At the same time, these judgments are phenomenologically basic; their inferential heritage is not introspectively available. More than this, these judgments are typically far less well integrated with our best available theories, and thus not nearly so well justified,[7] as our more explicitly theory-guided judgments. As the scope of our theories expands, the use of such weakly founded judgments is a necessary stepping-stone to better theory. The use of intuitive judgment does not disappear at any stage of theorizing. Instead, old intuitions give way to well-integrated theoretical judgments, and, in addition, to new intuitions about matters not yet fully captured in explicit theory.

We may thus respond to the first of Bealer's objections to naturalism by pointing out that appeals to intuition do not require some nonnatural faculty or a priori judgment of any sort. Bealer's argument gets off on the wrong foot by assuming that intuitions are a priori; more than this, Bealer says, the distinction between commonsense empirical judgment and intuition is "obvious" [165]. Obvious it may be to those opposed to naturalism, but the appeal to a priority is, of course, contentious in this context. Bealer is right to think that naturalists owe us an explanation of their practice of appealing to intuition, especially in light of their rejection of the a priori. At the same time, I hope I have shown that this explanation is one that naturalists may easily provide. The practice of appealing to intuition has no nonnatural ingredients.

A Naturalistic Account of Following Rules of Inference

Bealer argued that naturalists are not only unable to account for their own philosophical practice, but that naturalistic scruples leave little room for legitimate belief about any subject, since "following rules and procedures—for example, rules of inference" [167] requires an acknowledgment of the force of a priori intuition. But naturalists do not see the following of rules and procedures, in particular, the role of rules of inference, in the way in which Bealer does.

Naturalists, of course, make inferences, and they need to account for the legitimacy of this practice, at least to the extent that it is legitimate. The legitimacy of an inference, on the naturalist view, is dependent upon its reliability: reliable inferential practices are epistemically legitimate; those that are unreliable are not. We must thus engage in a project of self-examination, in which we scrutinize our own epistemic practice. We wish to examine the inferential rules that underlie our practice of belief acquisition, and to the extent that we find unreliable inference patterns at work, we need to reexamine and modify our own practice. The empirical work involved in understanding our inferential habits is well under way, as is the assessment of its epistemological importance.

Reliability is the naturalist's standard here. Meeting a priori standards is simply irrelevant. Rules of inference that tend to produce true beliefs in the kinds of environments that human beings occupy may fail to live up to a priori standards of cogency, but they are none the worse for that. By the same token, rules of inference that do meet a priori standards may be unworkable in practice or hopelessly mired in problems of computational complexity. These kinds of problems are not in any way ameliorated if the rules do meet a priori standards of cogency. A priori standards thus drop out of the picture entirely as simply irrelevant to proper epistemic practice. They fail to bear on the conduct of inquiry.[8]

A naturalistic account of proper belief acquisition thus does not need to appeal to a priori intuition of appropriate principles of inference. Recognition of appropriate inferential patterns is an empirical affair for the naturalist. More than this, justified belief, on at least one widely held naturalistic account, is a matter of reliable belief production and does not itself require recognition of that reliability. Naturalistic scruples about appropriate belief production thus leave room for a great deal of knowledge.

A Naturalistic Account of Epistemic Terminology

Let me turn then to the last of Bealer's charges against naturalism, that in eschewing a priori intuition, naturalism leaves no room for epistemic terminology. This charge too, I believe, falls short of its mark. While the account naturalists give of epistemic terminology is anything but uncontroversial, it should not be controversial that naturalists have an account of that terminology that satisfies their own epistemic standards. The suggestion that naturalism is self-defeating is thus turned aside.

Epistemology, according to naturalism, investigates a certain natural phenomenon, namely, knowledge, and the term 'knowledge' and other epistemic idioms gain their reference in much the same way that natural kind terms do. Now supposing that terms like 'knowledge' gain their reference in this way is not without its presuppositions, as I pointed out earlier. The phenomenon we call knowledge must have a certain degree of theoretical unity if reference is to be secured. Were we to discover that there is no more theoretical unity to the various items we call knowledge than there is to the set consisting of ships and shoes and sealing wax, then a presupposition of the introduction of the term would be undermined, and the view that there is no such thing as knowledge would be sustained. But naturalists, and indeed, most nonnaturalists, do not think that such a possibility is at all likely.[9] Indeed, almost all epistemologists believe that there is a great deal of unity to the phenomenon of human knowledge. If there is indeed such a unity, one goal of epistemology is to say what it consists in. And of course if it should turn out there is no such unity, then one goal of epistemology would be to make that fact plain.

The investigation of the phenomenon of knowledge, on the naturalist's view, is an empirical investigation, and the legitimacy of epistemic terminology depends on its properly latching on to a genuine, theoretically unified kind. That is all that naturalistic scruples require. Because epistemology thus conceived is a wholly empirical investigation, naturalists have nothing here to apologize for. Their terminology earns its keep in just the way that chemical or biological or physical terminology earns its keep: it must be part of a successful empirical theory. The fact that terms like 'knowledge' are not part of physics or chemistry does not show that they are not naturalistically acceptable. Rather, the question for naturalists is whether knowledge turns out to be a theoretically unified phenomenon, and this gives every appearance of being a legitimate empirical question.

Some will say that this enterprise, because it is descriptive, fails to engage the normative dimension of epistemological theorizing. They will argue that it is only by removing knowledge from the empirical realm, and making it the object of a priori investigation, that its normative character may emerge. I do not believe this is correct. The empirical investigation of knowledge may well reveal a phenomenon worthy of our pursuit. Surely such a suggestion does not require a degree of optimism ungrounded in fact. But this is all the normativity that our epistemic notions require. We should not suppose that the investigation of knowledge must be nonempirical if we are to be able to explain why knowledge is worth having.

Epistemic terminology, and, indeed, philosophical terminology in general, must be grounded in the world if it is to be naturalistically legitimate. This does not require that such terminology appears in our physical theories, for naturalists need not accept any sort of reductionism. Once we regard epistemology as the investigation of a certain natural phenomenon, we clear the way for distinctively epistemic terminology. Naturalism would only threaten to eliminate epistemic terminology as illegitimate if there were no prospect of discovering theoretically unified epistemic phenomena. But there is little reason, I believe, to think that this is currently a genuine possibility. Moreover, if there were reason to worry on this account, it would spell the demise not only of naturalistic epistemology, but epistemology generally. Bealer's final objection, that naturalists are not entitled to the very epistemic terminology they make use of, thus ultimately fails.

Against the Autonomy of Philosophy

I want to close by addressing one further issue, a concern that, I believe, motivates Bealer's attack on naturalism, and this has to do with the autonomy of philosophy. In a lengthy attack on the kind of scientific essentialism I favor, Bealer (1987) begins by suggesting that naturalism raises the possibility that science will somehow "eclipse" philosophy, a prospect that, I believe, is invigorating for some and threatening for others. Naturalism threatens the autonomy of philosophical inquiry, Bealer argues, and it is thus only by rejecting naturalism that we may make room for a distinctively philosophical enterprise. To put the point somewhat less cautiously, if naturalism is right, we should all give up doing philosophy and take up science instead.

Now I myself have a high regard for philosophy, and, although I am a naturalist, my career plans do not include a move to one of the natural science departments at my university. Naturalists do not regard philosophy as illegitimate, nor do they see it as in any way threatened by the progress of science. At the same time, we do not wish to grant philosophy the degree of autonomy that Bealer, and other opponents of naturalism, would favor. There are important issues here, and it is worth making clear just where naturalism stands on them.

Questions about knowledge and justification, questions about theory and evidence, are, to my mind, legitimate questions, and they are ones in which philosophy has a special stake. The questions philosophers wish to ask about these topics are different from those addressed by historians, sociologists, and psychologists, but no less important or intellectually respectable. If the autonomy of a discipline consists in its dealing with a distinctive set of questions, or in approaching certain phenomena with a distinctive set of concerns, then philosophy is surely an autonomous discipline. There is no danger that these questions and concerns will somehow be co-opted by other disciplines.

When Bealer raises the issue of philosophy's autonomy, however, he has in mind something quite different from this. For Bealer, the autonomy of philosophy is identified with the claim that philosophical knowledge is a priori, entirely independent of anything the empirical sciences have to offer. Now this, of course, is a claim any naturalist will want to reject. On the naturalist's view, philosophical questions are continuous with the empirical sciences. Work in the empirical sciences is deeply relevant to philosophical questions, and our philosophical theories are constrained and guided by results in other disciplines. It is worth noting that the special sciences are not autonomous in anything like Bealer's sense, that is, they are not wholly independent of work in other disciplines. Work in biology is not wholly independent of chemistry; sociology is not wholly independent of psychology; and so on. But the loss of this sort of autonomy does not rob these disciplines of their legitimacy, nor does it threaten the special sciences with the loss of their distinctive subject matter. Biologists need not fear that their field will be taken away from them by chemists once it is recognized that chemistry is relevant to biological concerns.

So too with philosophy. In recognizing that philosophy is continuous with the sciences, we need not fear that philosophy will thereby be "eclipsed" by science. The constraints science presents for philosophical theorizing should be welcomed, for philosophical theorizing unconstrained by empirical fact loses its connection with the very phenomena we, as philosophers, seek to understand. Philosophy is an autonomous discipline, in the sense that it addresses a distinctive set of questions and concerns, and in this respect it is no more nor less autonomous than physics or chemistry or biology. This is surely all the autonomy we should want. It is, in any case, all the autonomy we may have.

I thus conclude that Bealer's multicount indictment of naturalism is not supported by the facts. On every count, naturalists plead not guilty. When it comes to appealing to intuitions, naturalists may keep doing it.

Notes

I have received helpful comments from David Christensen, Derk Pereboom, and David Shatz, as well as conference participants at Notre Dame, especially George Bealer.

1. Bealer (1987, 1993). Page numbers in brackets within the text refer to Bealer (1993).

2. Bealer has argued against a number of different targets, including naturalism, scientific essentialism, and empiricism. There are, of course, numerous versions of each of these views, and one may consistently subscribe to more than one of them. Indeed, the view I favor, and which I defend here, may rightly be described as falling under each of these three headings. It is for this reason that I feel called upon to answer Bealer's attacks on all of these positions.

3. A similar argument is made by Laurence BonJour (1994). Mark Kaplan argues that naturalists cannot account for the notion of "cogent arguments," and cannot account for their own practice of attempting to provide such arguments (see Kaplan 1994).

4. For example, Michael Devitt remarks, "The naturalist does not deny 'armchair' intuitions a role in philosophy but denies that their role has to be seen as a priori: the intuitions reflect an empirically based expertise at identification" (1994: 564, fn. 27). Devitt refers here to Bealer's work. The present chapter may be seen as an attempt to expand on this remark of Devitt's. After completing a draft of this chapter, my attention was drawn to work of Terry Horgan's, which has many points of contact with the views expressed here. See Horgan (1993a) and Horgan and Graham (1994). Finally, see also Richard Boyd (1988), esp. pages 192-193.

5. I have discussed this point at greater length in Kornblith (1994, 1995).

6. Here I simply take for granted a causal or historical account of the reference of natural kind terms.

7. I do not mean to be diverging here from a reliabilist account of justification. Instead, I mean only to be pointing out that allowing one's judgments to be influenced by accurate theory tends to be a source of increased reliability.

8. I discuss this point in greater detail in Kornblith (manuscript).

9. But see Williams (1996).

Chapter 9

Philosophical Intuitions and Psychological Theory

Tamara Horowitz

Introduction

Some philosophers, particularly ethicists and epistemologists, see as one of their tasks the discovery of norms, ethical or epistemological, that we more or less live by. Reflection on naturally occurring moral or epistemological dilemmas will reveal these norms to some extent just as observation of the physical world will reveal the laws of physics to some extent. But just as physicists must perform controlled experiments to decide among rival hypotheses that they cannot distinguish by observing naturally occurring events, philosophers must perform thought experiments to illuminate norms that naturally occurring dilemmas do not reveal. This is not to say that ethics is like physics in other respects. Physicists see themselves as discovering physical laws, whereas philosophers often take themselves to be exploring the structure of our concepts, or, in the case of ethicists, uncovering moral norms.

It is an open question to what extent philosophical thought experiments can reveal norms. Only case studies can answer the question, or at least answer it in part. This chapter is such a case study.

The Doctrine of Doing and Allowing

Warren Quinn relies on thought experiments in his discussion of what he calls the Doctrine of Doing and Allowing. He says:

> Sometimes we cannot benefit one person without harming, or failing to help, another; and where the cost to the other would be serious—where, for example, he would die—a substantial moral question is raised: would the benefit justify the harm? Some moralists would answer this question by balancing the good against the evil. But others deny that consequences are the only things of moral relevance. To them it matters whether the harm comes from action, for example from killing someone, or from inaction, for example from not saving someone. They hold that for some good ends we may properly allow some evil to befall someone, even though we could not

actively bring that evil about. (Quinn 1993: 149)

The proposition expressed by the last sentence of this passage is the Doctrine of Doing and Allowing. Quinn appeals to philosophical thought experiments for three distinct, though related, reasons. First, he tries to refine the Doctrine of Doing and Allowing by testing various formulations of it against intuitions that naturally arise when one performs various thought experiments. Second, he appeals to the intuitions one has while performing certain thought experiments as grounds for accepting the Doctrine of Doing and Allowing. Third, he argues that these intuitions show that the ethical norms at work in these cases should not be given a consequentialist analysis. The following thought experiment is typical; in fact this is the only one of Quinn's thought experiments I shall consider in this chapter. I believe there will be no loss of generality.

The thought experiment:[1]

Choose the appropriate action in each of the following two cases:

Rescue Dilemma 1: *We can either save five people in danger of drowning in one place or a single person in danger of drowning somewhere else. We cannot save all six.*

Rescue Dilemma 2: *We can save the five only by driving over and thereby killing someone who (for an unspecified reason) is trapped on the road. If we do not undertake the rescue the trapped person can later be freed.*

Quinn's intuition is that in Rescue Dilemma 1 we are perfectly *justified* in saving the group of five people even though we thereby fail to save the solitary person, whereas in Rescue Dilemma 2 it is "far from obvious how we *may* proceed." In his discussion he reports that the intuitions of some other philosophers match his own. And he seems to think it likely that the reader will have intuitions that match his own. For the purposes of this chapter I shall assume that Quinn is right about this widespread similarity of intuitions.

Quinn appears to assume that anyone who responds to these cases as he does has moral intuitions, which like his, conform to the Doctrine of Doing and Allowing. After trying several formulations of this doctrine he says, "Perhaps we have found the basic form of the doctrine and the natural qualifications that, when combined with other plausible moral principles, accurately map our moral intuitions" (Quinn 1993: 167). Quinn then goes on to develop a philosophical defense of the doctrine. I am not concerned here whether or not there is a philosophical defense of the Doctrine of Doing and Allowing. I am concerned instead with Quinn's assumption that people who share his intuitions in the case of Rescue Dilemma 1 and Rescue Dilemma 2 do so because they accept, however inexplicitly, the Doctrine of Doing and Allowing. Indeed I am concerned with Quinn's assumption that *he himself* has these intuitions because he (antecedently) accepts the Doctrine of Doing and Allowing. The ground for my concern is that it might be the case, rather, that Quinn has these intuitions as a result of covert reasoning of the kind posited by Prospect Theory. If this is the best explanation, then Quinn is wrong to think of these intuitions as the product of a very different pattern of reasoning involving a distinction between doing and allowing.

Prospect Theory

Daniel Kahneman and Amos Tversky (1979) developed Prospect Theory to be a descriptive theory of human decision making that would match the decisions people actually make better than classical Expected Utility Theory.[2] For instance Prospect Theory predicts the following experimental results whereas classical Expected Utility Theory does not.

The subjects in one group were given the following decision problem:

Assume yourself richer by $300 than you are today. You have to choose between:
1. a sure gain of $100
2. a 50 percent chance of gaining $200 and a 50 percent chance of gaining nothing

The subjects in a second group were given this decision problem:

Assume yourself richer by $500 than you are today. You have to choose between
1. a sure loss of $100
2. a 50 percent chance of losing nothing and a 50 percentchance of losing $200

In problem 1 a majority of people chose the option that offers a sure gain rather than the risky option. In problem 2 a majority of people chose the risky option rather than the sure loss. So most people are risk averse in problem 1 and risk seeking in problem 2 despite the fact that in each case the decision maker faces a choice between gaining $400 for sure and an even chance of gaining $500 or gaining $300.[3] If people always acted so as to maximize expected utility they would not exhibit this pattern of choices.[4]

In a second experiment, Kahneman and Tversky presented one group of subjects with this decision problem:

Imagine that the United States is preparing for an outbreak of an unusual Asian disease that is expected to kill 600 people. Two alternative programs to fight the disease, A and B, have been proposed. Assume that the exact scientific estimates of the consequences of the programs are as follows:

If program A is adopted, 200 people will be saved.
If program B is adopted, there is a 1/3 probability that 600 people will be saved, and a 2/3 probability that no people will be saved.
Which program would you choose?

The subjects in a second group were given the same cover story with the following description of two different alternative programs, C and D:

> *If program C is adopted 400 people will die.*
> *If program D is adopted there is a 1/3 probability that nobody will die and a 2/3 probability that 600 will die.*

Once again the subjects were asked which program they would choose. Programs A and C are equivalent from the point of view of expected survival as are programs B and D. Nevertheless, a majority of the first group of subjects chose program A over program B, while a majority of the second group of subjects chose program D over program C. So when the outcomes were stated in positive terms, "lives saved," subjects tended to be risk averse whereas when the outcomes were stated in negative terms, "lives lost," subjects tended to be risk seeking.

Prospect Theory is designed to explain these and many similar experimental results, as well as a range of structurally distinct experimental results apparently in conflict with Expected Utility Theory. The theory distinguishes two phases in the choice process, the first of which is "editing." During this phase the options are reformulated so as to simplify the second phase of the choice process, the evaluation of the prospects. The editing phase consists of a number of different operations, only one of which need concern us here: "framing."[5] In the framing process the agent chooses one possible outcome of her actions as the "neutral" outcome. And she classifies the other possible outcomes as either "gains" or "losses" relative to this neutral outcome; that is, she classifies outcomes as either "positive" or "negative" deviations from the neutral outcome.

In the evaluation phase of the choice process the agent rates each of the contemplated alternative actions. As is common in Expected Utility Theory, possible alternative actions are conceived of as distributions of probability over outcomes. The idea is that for any given contemplated action, the agent expects various outcomes to follow upon her performing the action, where these levels of expectation can be expressed as a probability. During the evaluation phase the agent encodes her judgments of desirability differences with a value function, v. The function v takes the value 0 for the neutral outcome and takes positive or negative real values for other outcomes in such a way as to reflect the positive or negative deviations in desirability of those outcomes from the neutral outcome. It is an open question what factors determine an agent's selection of a neutral outcome, although it often seems to correspond to the *status quo*. What is most important for our purposes, though, is that different formulations of a decision problem can lead an agent to make different choices of the neutral outcome. How this can happen will become clear when we turn to the Prospect Theoretic analysis of the first experiment. But first let us complete our sketch of the theory.

In deciding which actions are preferable to which other actions, agents do not simply multiply the value of outcomes by the probability of those outcomes. Some probabilities are factored in at more than their face value, while other probabilities are factored in at less than their face value. Or so a large body of experimental research seems to suggest. To reflect this fact, Prospect Theory attributes to the agent a weighting function, $w(p)$, which associates with each probability a "decision weight."

Suppose the possible actions available to an agent are very simple in form. Each of them can be represented by a probability distribution $(x,p; y,q)$. A possible action, or "prospect," of the form $(x,p; y,q)$ is a possible action regarded by the agent as leading to outcome x with probability p and outcome y with probability q, and leading to the neutral outcome with probability $1 - p - q$. For the moment, assume that outcomes are monetary amounts. Prospects can be strictly positive, strictly negative, or regular. A prospect $(x,p; y,q)$ is strictly positive if $x > y > 0$ and $p + q = 1$, strictly negative if $x < 0$ and $y < 0$, and regular otherwise. The all-in value of the action $(x,p; y,q)$, in the eyes of this agent, is denoted in Prospect Theory by $D(x,p; y,q)$. If $(x,p; y,q)$ is a regular prospect, Prospect Theory proposes that $D(x,p; y,q)$ is equal to $w(p)v(x) + w(q)v(y)$, where $v(0) = 0$, $w(0) = 0$, and $w(1) = 1$. Clearly, D and v will coincide for sure prospects since $D(x,1.0) = v(x)$. Prospect Theory suggests a different rule for evaluating positive and negative prospects but that need not concern us here since the prospects we will be considering are all regular.[6] The generalization to the case of an action with some finite number of possible outcomes greater than 2 follows the same pattern.

Many studies have confirmed that value functions over possible outcomes generally conform to the following pattern: they are concave for gains, convex for losses, and steeper for losses than for gains. People tend to be risk averse when it comes to gains, risk seeking when it comes to losses, and their response to losses tends to be more extreme than their response to gains (Kahneman and Tversky 1979: 279). In the first experiment, for example, Prospect Theory explains why people tend to prefer the sure gain to the risky alternative and disprefer the sure loss to the risky alternative, although the sure gain and the sure loss are equivalent in terms of expected monetary value, as are the two risky options.

The explanation goes like this: In the first part of the experiment a typical subject picks the *status quo* plus $300 as the neutral outcome. The subject regards a further gain of $100 as a positive deviation from this neutral reference point, and she regards a further gain of $200 as an even greater positive deviation from the reference point. But she does not evaluate a gain of $200 as having twice the value of a gain of $100. This reflects the concavity of her v function for gains. (See figure 9.1.)

We assume that the decision weight of a 50 percent chance is 0.5. Then if the all-in value D of a sure gain of $100 is given by $D = v = k$, the subject will assign an all-in value less than k to the risky prospect, since she evaluates a gain of $200 at less than double a gain of $100.

In the second part of the experiment, a typical subject settles on the *status quo* plus $500 as the neutral reference point. She evaluates a loss of $100 and a loss of $200 as negative deviations from this reference point, but the value of her v function for a loss of $200 is not twice as large negative as the value of her v function for a loss of $100. This reflects the convexity of v for losses. (See figure 9.2.) As a result, the subject's all-in evaluation of a 50 percent chance of losing nothing and a 50 percent chance of losing $200 is greater than the subject's all-in evaluation of a sure loss of $100.

In this experiment Prospect Theory yields a different prediction from Expected Utility Theory for a combination of two reasons. First, differing instructions given to the subjects in the two parts of the experiment are assumed to result in differing choices of neutral reference point. Second, the valuation function for positive deviations from a reference point is assumed to be concave whereas the valuation function for negative deviations from a reference point is assumed to be convex.

The Prospect Theoretic analysis of the "Asian disease" experiment has exactly the same structure. The chief difference in this case is that it is assumed that subjects shift reference points because of the overall phrasing of the decision problem, not because some preliminary instruction of the form "assume you are x dollars richer than you are now" induces a choice of neutral outcome. In the first part of the experiment, for example, the results of disease-fighting programs are formulated in terms of "people saved. " So one can hypothesize that subjects choose the outcome in which 600 people are dead as the neutral outcome. But in the second part of the experiment, programs are described in terms of "people dying." So it is reasonable to assume that subjects choose the outcome in which 600 people live as the neutral reference point. As in the first experiment, this shift in neutral reference point presumably forces the subjects to evaluate disease fighting programs as leading to positive deviations in one case but negative de-

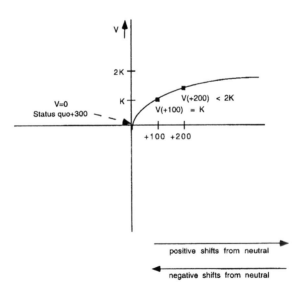

Figure 9.1
Concavity of *v* function for gains.

viations in the other, with a corresponding shift from concave to convex v functions. (See figures 9.3 and 9.4.)

We must remember that Prospect Theory, as we have formulated it, hypothesizes that a certain psychological law characterizes these decision-making events, and that the form of the law differs according to whether or not the possible actions involved are what are called "regular prospects." The definition of a regular prospect presupposes that we are dealing with outcomes that have some natural numerical representation. This was plausible when the outcomes were monetary gains and losses. Perhaps it is equally plausible when the outcomes are human lives saved or human lives lost. Here our assumption has been that the natural numerical representation of such outcomes goes by simply counting individual lives. But this is a substantive hypothesis about how people measure the value of human life, and we have a right to wonder whether further empirical research would confirm the psychological reality of this simple numerical measure. It is worth noticing, for instance, that some legislatures have decided to treat double murder as deserving the death penalty when the murder of a single person, in the absence of other aggravating circumstances, deserves only life imprisonment. I only mean that remark to be suggestive. Perhaps in some cases we think of two deaths as *much* worse than one death. Nevertheless, for the remainder of this chapter I will assume that it is psychologically realistic to suppose that people evaluate multiple death simply by body count.

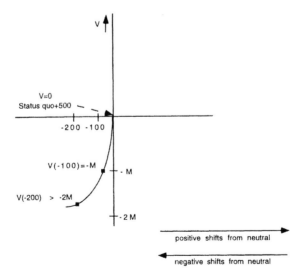

Figure 9.2
Convexity of v function for losses.

The Argument for the Doctrine of
Doing and Allowing Reconsidered

Now let us return to Quinn's thought experiment. Quinn assumes that he, and others who share his intuitions, respond differently to the first and second decision problems because they are sensitive to a difference between doing and allowing. But if we combine some of the basic insights of Prospect Theory with a few additional plausible assumptions we can construct an alternative possible explanation for these same responses. Of course, in order to demonstrate that Prospect Theory offers a possible alternative explanation, these additional assumptions will have to be tested experimentally.

In the first rescue problem Quinn expresses a preference for Option 1 over Option 2:

Option 1.
(a) Save a group of five people in danger of drowning
and
(b) Fail to save one person in danger of drowning.

Option 2.
(c) Save one person in danger of drowning
and
(d) Fail to save the group of five people in danger of drowning.

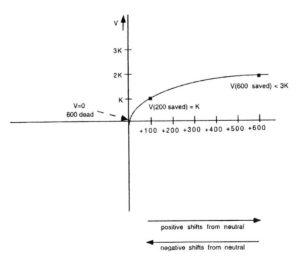

Figure 9.3
Disease fighting program seen as positive deviation.

In considering the second rescue problem, however, Quinn is not sure how to rank Option 3 relative to Option 4:

Option 3.
(e) Save a group of five people in danger of drowning
and
(f) Kill one person who would otherwise live.

Option 4.
(g) Fail to save the group of five people in danger of drowning
and
(h) Refrain from killing one person.

The Prospect Theoretic explanation of Quinn's intuitively clear ranking of Options 1 and 2 versus his uncertainty in the case of Options 3 and 4 can be developed in the following way. First, it is implicit in Quinn's discussion that

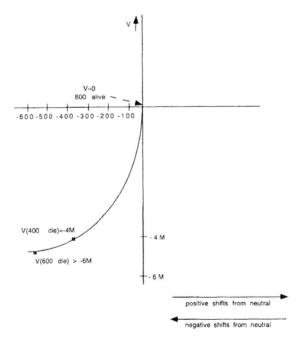

Figure 9.4
Disease fighting program seen as negative deviation.

choosing Option 1 certainly will result in saving five lives and losing one life, choosing Option 2 certainly will result in saving one life and losing five lives, and similarly for the other options. Thus the decision value **D** assigned by the decisionmaker to these possible actions will be the outcome value v she has assigned to the outcome that has probability 1, as we saw above.

Our problem is to decide what outcome values Quinn is likely to be assigning to the various outcomes at issue in Options 1 through 4. These outcomes are: (a) and (b), (c) and (d) in the one case, (e) and (f), and (g) and (h) in the other.

The best way to approach this problem is to consider a simpler example. You must decide what to do in each of two different decision problems. In the first problem you must decide whether to kill someone who would otherwise be safe. In the second problem you must decide whether to let someone die even though you could save the person at no risk or cost to yourself. When you analyze these two problems it may seem to you worse to kill than to let die. That is, it may seem to you that in the first problem the reason you have to spare the person's life is *more compelling* than the reason you have to save the person in the second problem. This way of putting the matter presupposes that an agent can compare the force of the reasons for doing one thing or another *across several distinct decision problems*. Prospect Theory does not contain this assumption, and it is problematic. It implies that an agent has evaluated the relevant out-

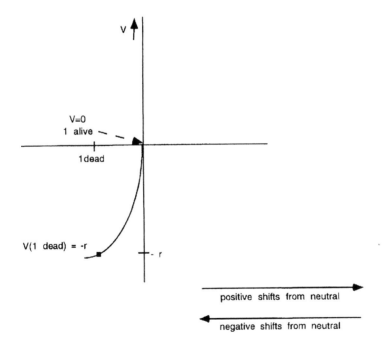

Figure 9.5
One person alive seen as neutral, killing as a negative deviation.

comes in several different decision problems *on the same scale*. I doubt that this is true in general. But it may be true in some special circumstances, for example when an agent is considering several decision problems that are very similar in structure and subject matter and when the agent is considering these problems at roughly the same time. That agents do compare the force of reasons in this way is an empirical hypothesis, and should be tested. In the remainder of this chapter I will assume that it is true.[7]

With this assumption in place we can turn to Prospect Theory for an account of the differing intuitive responses between the two decision problems in this simple case. There is a shift in choice of neutral outcome. In deciding whether to kill the person or leave the person alone one thinks of the person's being alive as the *status quo* and chooses this as the neutral outcome. Killing the person is regarded as a negative deviation, and its value is found in a correspondingly steep part of the *v*-curve. But in deciding whether to save a person who would otherwise die, the person being dead is the *status quo* and is selected as the neutral outcome. So saving the person is a positive deviation, with a correspondingly less steep *v*-curve. Notice that here it is the comparative steepness of *v*-curve for positive versus negative deviations that does the explanatory work not the concavity of one versus the convexity of the other. (See figures 9.5 and 9.6.)

In the problem involving killing the person or letting the person live, the ab-

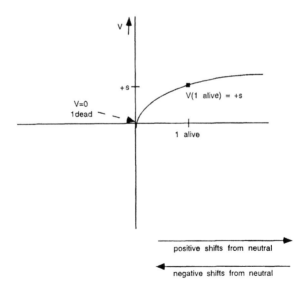

Figure 9.6
One person dead seen as neutral, saving as positive deviation.

solute value of v for the killing option is larger than the absolute value of v for the saving option in the problem involving saving or letting die. Or so we may assume if it is legitimate to make this cross-problem comparison. So in the problem involving killing or letting live, the absolute value of D for the killing option is greater than the absolute value of D for the saving option in the problem involving saving or letting die. Our conjecture is that this difference in absolute value of D is perceived as a difference in the force of one's reasons in the two cases.

If this is right, then one's intuition that there is this difference in the force of the reasons should not be explained in terms of a perceived difference between action and inaction, but rather in terms of differing responses to gains and to losses. The advantage of this explanation is that it rests on a psychological theory that predicts fairly well in a wide variety of decision-making situations. It is not clear that a theory can be formulated, turning on perceived differences between action and inaction, that has comparable empirical authority. Certainly none with comparable generality.

In order to go on to develop a Prospect Theoretic account of the conjunctive acts in Quinn's original example another assumption is needed. Quinn's Rescue Dilemma 1 and Rescue Dilemma 2 each involves a comparison of conjunctive actions; that is, actions that lead with certainty to a conjunction of two outcomes. In Rescue Dilemma 1, the comparison is between actions of the form *do M and do X* and *do N and do Y*. In Rescue Dilemma 2, the comparison is between actions of the form *do M and do F* and *do N and do G*. The comparison of doing M with doing N is present in both problems.

The simplest assumption I can think of to deal with the valuation of actions with conjunctive outcomes is this: The agent separates the conjunctive outcome of each conjunctive action into its conjuncts, assigns a value of v to each conjunct, and adds these values of v to get a value of v for the conjunction of outcomes. In the cases we are considering Prospect Theory would predict a value of D equal to the value of v for each conjunctive action. Now consider Rescue Dilemma 1. According to our assumption the subject evaluates Option 1, the conjunction of (a) and (b), by adding the values of (a) and (b) taken separately. Likewise the subject evaluates Option 2 by adding the values of (c) and (d) taken separately. The subject proceeds in the same way with Rescue Dilemma 2. It is clear that the absolute value of the difference in v for Option 1 and Option 2 will be larger than the absolute value of the difference in v for Option 3 and Option 4. This is because in this case, just as in the simplified pair of decision problems we considered earlier, the gap in v between killing and sparing is larger than the gap in v between letting die and saving. Then applying our first assumption, the subject perceives her reason for choosing Option 1 over Option 2 to be more compelling than her reason for choosing Option 3 over Option 4.

My simple assumption about the evaluation of conjunctions almost certainly is not generally valid. One would expect the conjuncts to interact to some degree, sometimes more and sometimes less. In the case of Quinn's Rescue Dilemmas, however, the interaction, if it exists, may be rather similar as between Option 1 and Option 3, and as between Option 2 and Option 4. If this is so, our extension of Prospect Theory to this case should be approximately correct. Obviously this is an empirical hypothesis that must be tested. But with this assumption, as with our earlier assumption about crossproblem comparisons, we know what hypotheses about human psychology need to be tested in order for our philosophical analysis to succeed. With Quinn's proposal that the differences lie in differing evaluations of action and inaction, we do not know even this much.

Let us take stock of the epistemology of the situation. Quinn's intuitions can be explained fairly well by Prospect Theory. Prospect Theory also explains subjects' intuitions in many other kinds of choice situations. Therefore it has some claim to capturing a piece of "psychological reality." To the best of my knowledge, no similarly broad and plausible psychological theory, based on the idea that people intuit a distinction between doing and allowing, is available to explain Quinn's intuitions. What we have from Quinn is introspective testimony that this is the right explanation, combined with a few anecdotal claims that other people have come to the same opinion. If a reader of Quinn's paper also comes to this opinion, that will still be no more than one additional piece of introspective evidence. By the ordinary epistemic standards of decision psychology, the Prospect Theoretic explanation is the one we should accept.

As I mentioned earlier, the example I have chosen to discuss is not the only example in the philosophical literature purporting to exhibit an intuitive moral difference between doing and allowing. Someone might argue that unless Prospect Theory explains all, or at least most, of the intuitions people have when they consider these other examples, it is implausible to claim that it accounts for Quinn's intuitions. I disagree. The requirement that Prospect Theory account for all of these cases would be question-begging. To require of a psychological theory that it explain all of the intuitions in some class of examples described as "cases where people respond to a distinction between doing and allowing" is to assume that we know antecedently that the intuitions in all these cases are *due to* a distinction between doing and allowing. It may be, in fact, that several different unnoticed psychological mechanisms account for the responses of subjects in these cases, and that the distinction between doing and allowing is a superficial characterization without psychological reality.[8]

I have *not* made the claim that Prospect Theory provides a distinction among Quinn's Rescue cases *that is morally significant.* I do not see why anyone would think the distinction is morally significant but perhaps there is some argument I have not thought of. If the distinction is *not* morally significant, then Quinn's thought experiments cannot play the role in his argument he intends them to play. It is crucial for Quinn that the intuitions he elicits be moral intuitions, since he wants to argue that our moral intuitions both support the Doctrine of Doing and Allowing and conflict with consequentialism. Further, he wants the doctrine of rights that he develops in his paper to explain these very moral intuitions. But to the extent that the intuitions elicited by Quinn's thought experiments are explained by Prospect Theory, they are not moral intuitions at all.

To put the same point differently, suppose someone argues that even if the Prospect Theoretic account of the differing responses to the Rescue Dilemmas is not morally significant, these differing responses to the Rescue Dilemmas can still play a role in ethical argumentation if the argumentative method being used is one of reflective equilibrium.[9] The suggestion is that if we appeal to our intuitions about the Rescue Dilemmas in the course of constructing a moral theory by getting our intuitions into reflective equilibrium with our theory, then the fact that our intuitions have their origins in Prospect Theory would not matter any more than it would matter that our intuitions had their origin in religious training. But when we engage in reflective equilibrium reasoning we are, to paraphrase Rawls, looking to see if the principles we formulate match our considered ethical convictions. The principles we formulate, then, must be brought into reflective equilibrium with moral judgments (whatever the origin of these). My contention is that when Quinn, or anyone else, judges that there is a difference in what it is permissible to do in the two Rescue Dilemmas, they are mistaken in thinking that they are making a moral judgment at all.

Is the Process Posited by Prospect Theory Reasoning?

Philosophers who have a certain conception of psychological theory together with a certain conception of the nature of reasoning might argue that the suggestion I have made completely misses the mark.[10] Quinn is trying to articulate some pattern of reasoning shared by everyone whose intuitions about the Rescue Dilemmas are similar to his own. His suggestion is that there is such a pattern of reasoning, and it involves making a distinction between doing and allowing. I have argued that Prospect Theory provides us with a different and conflicting account of the pattern of reasoning common to those who share Quinn's intuitions about the Rescue Dilemmas. But my suggestion obviously presupposes that Prospect Theory should be understood as positing that in certain circumstances people engage in processes of reasoning of which they are unaware, and perhaps processes of reasoning to which they cannot gain conscious access even with careful introspection. The objector I have in mind points to this unconscious aspect of the mechanism posited by Prospect Theory and concludes that this mechanism should not be regarded as a process of reasoning at all. Rather, we should think of Prospect Theory as providing us with a causal law of psychological nature, according to which certain factors cause, or incline, a subject to form certain preferences. To the extent that this causal law is expressed in language appropriate to processes of reasoning in the ordinary sense of the term 'reasoning', the language is misleading. And, says this objector, the language appears to have misled me in this chapter.

Someone might base this objection on either of two related arguments. The first argument goes like this: In order for a process of thought to be reasoning it must be subject to norms or standards of correctness. There must be a distinction between correct and incorrect reasoning, between reasoning that is performed as it ought to be and reasoning that is not performed as it ought to be. A philosopher will be inclined to believe this to the extent that she sees the concept of a process of reasoning as closely connected to the concept of having reasons for a belief or an action. If one has a reason for a belief or an action, it will be a more or less good reason or a more or less bad reason. It will be subject to evaluation. A sequence of psychological states occurring in a person should be called a "process of reasoning" only if it constitutes the person coming to "have a reason." On this conception of the meaning of the expression 'process of reasoning', any sequence of psychological states that deserves to be called a process of reasoning must be subject to evaluation just as the having of a reason is subject to evaluation. Someone else might deny this close conceptual tie between the concept of a process of reasoning and the concept of having a reason. The philosopher I have in mind accepts the tie.

The argument continues along the following lines: There can be no standards of correctness for reasoning that are in principle hidden from view. If reasoning is hidden from view, how could standards of correctness ever develop, and how could they ever be applied?

The second argument starts with the premise that according to Prospect Theory some aspects of the so-called "reasoning" it posits are not under the control of the subject. For instance, the language used to formulate a decision problem can result in a subject choosing one or another neutral outcome to serve as a reference point for the evaluation of other outcomes. It appears that subjects often have little if any control over this choice of neutral outcome. But "ought" implies "can." If a subject ought to reason in a certain way, then it must be up to the subject to voluntarily choose to reason in that way. So the concepts of what the subject ought and ought not to do cannot be applied coherently to these thought processes. Therefore, they are not processes subject to norms or standards of correctness, and thus are not processes one should call "reasoning."

This second argument clearly is off the mark as it stands. Some very simple instances of logically valid arguments are so compelling that it may be impossible for most people to accept the premises while rejecting the conclusion. Probably an argument of the form "A, B, therefore A and B" would compel the acceptance of most adults. So it will not do to claim that genuine reasoning always is under the control of an agent to accept or reject.

But the second argument nevertheless is getting at a legitimate worry. The thought processes posited by Prospect Theory are not outside the voluntary control of the subject because they compel assent, but because they are hidden from view and not open to critical appraisal at all. So the second argument really is a special case of the first. The question, then, is whether we should accept the first argument.

I am granting for the sake of argument that a thought process must be subject to standards of correctness in order to qualify as reasoning. Some psychological theories posit unnoticed processes that fail to meet this criterion, even though psychologists sometimes call such processes "reasoning." For instance, a theory in the psychology of vision might explain the seeing of illusory contours by positing a gap-filling process that obeys a certain law. The law might be expressible as a differential equation, or by some other mathematical relationship. Presumably subjects are not aware that their vision is governed by this law.

When one of these gap-filling processes occurs in a person, the process itself does not constitute the person's "having a reason," for believing contours exist where in fact there are no physical contours. As a result of the gap-filling process, it may "look to the person as though there are contours." *This* fact would be a reason for the person to believe there really are contours. But it is plausible to think that this fact is a *result* of the gap-filling process, and is not strictly identical to it. Even if the gap-filling process *is* strictly identical to the fact of "it looking as though there are contours," we should not conclude that the gap-filling process constitutes a reason, since the seemingly relational predicate 'is a reason for' is nonextensional at both ends.[11]

No standards of correctness apply to these posited gap-filling processes. So on the assumption I am making for purposes of argument, these processes are not instances of reasoning.

The question is whether every psychological theory positing unnoticed "thought" processes share this feature. The answer, clearly, is no; and Prospect Theory is a good example with which to illustrate the difference. Prospect Theory posits various thought processes that are unnoticed by the subject in whom they occur. Therefore those very thought processes are not open to criticism in ordinary circumstances. But many of these thought processes are processes of a *kind* that can occur in people consciously and voluntarily. And when they do, they are instances of reasoning in any ordinary sense of the term, subject to standards of correctness and readily criticizable by the subject and by others who become aware of them. The unnoticed thought processes posited by Prospect Theory are subject to standards of correctness because other thought processes *of the same form* are routinely subjected to standards of correctness. What it is for an instance of reasoning to be subject to a standard of correctness is for it to be an instance of a form that is thus criticizable. This is an old idea, and a very good one.

For example, suppose a board of directors is dutifully making its annual performance evaluation of the CEO. Some members of the board claim that the CEO had a poor year, since the company suffered a net loss for the year. Other members of the board disagree. They argue that the CEO had a good year since the beginning of the year projections were that every company in the industry would suffer much greater losses than this company eventually suffered and all the other companies did, in fact, suffer much greater losses. The CEO did a better job of weathering the general downturn than any of her competitors. In order to finally decide how to evaluate the CEO, members of the board must decide which reference point to use. Should they choose the point where there are no gains or losses for the year, or should they choose a point defined by the projected losses for companies in the industry as a whole? The issue of which reference point to choose is likely to be a matter of debate. Standards of correctness and incorrectness could be brought to bear on the choice of a reference point, and eventually such standards would have to be brought to bear.

The formal analogy between what the board of directors must do and what, according to Prospect Theory, individual decisionmakers often do is obvious. Of course Prospect Theory posits many other kinds of thought processes in addition to choosing reference points, but for many of these other processes there are equally familiar analogues engaged in by people consciously, publicly, and in a way that is subject to standards of correctness.

I conclude that the objections I have raised to my earlier suggestion both fail. It is therefore possible that Prospect Theory, augmented by the empirical hypotheses I described earlier, provides the correct account of the reasoning engaged in by people who come to have Quinn's intuitions concerning his Rescue Dilemmas. If this is so, then Quinn's philosophical thought experiments do not provide us with an argument for his philosophical conclusions. What this shows, I believe, is that the extraction of philosophical conclusions from philosophical thought experiments is at least sometimes an *a posteriori*, not an *a priori* matter. The question naturally arises whether it ever is an *a priori* matter. I suspect the answer is no.

Should we conclude that the important philosophical method of thought experimentation is valueless if it is not *a priori*? I think the jury is still out. It may be that philosophers are capable of making fairly accurate judgments concerning their processes of reasoning most of the time. Quinn's thought experiments may be an unusually unfavorable case. Or it may be that misjudgments are the rule. For example, philosophers with a developed set of philosophical views may be just as susceptible to experimenter effects as are linguists who have developed views. (See Labov 1975 and Spencer 1973, cited in Labov.) The matter must be empirically studied.[12]

Notes

An earlier version of this chapter appeared in *Ethics* 108, No 2, (January 1998): 367-385. Reprinted with permission from Tamara Horowitz and the University of Chicago Press.

I am indebted to Joseph Camp, Robyn Dawes, Joel Pust, Alexander Rosenberg, Eldar Shafir, Michael Thompson, Mark Wilson, two editors of *Ethics*, and audiences at the University of Pittsburgh, Carnegie Mellon University, and the "Rethinking Intuition" conference held at the University of Notre Dame in April 1996, for their helpful criticisms and suggestions.

1. The Doctrine of Doing and Allowing and this thought experiment are originally due to Professor P. Foote. See Foote (1984): 178-185.

2. For an account of Prospect Theory see Kahneman and Tversky (1979). By "classical Expected Utility Theory" I mean to refer to either the theories found in VonNeumann and Morgenstern (1972) or in Savage (1972).

3. Problem 2 is obtained from problem 1 by increasing the original amount by $200 and subtracting this amount from both options.

4. An expected utility maximizer would not exhibit this pattern since any person who is maximizing expected utility would choose the first option in each problem or the second option in each problem.

5. The other operations include combining probabilities associated with identical outcomes, segregating risky from riskless components of prospects, discarding components that are shared by all of the available prospects, rounding off probabilities or outcomes, and rejecting dominated alternatives. For a full discussion of these processes see Kahneman and Tversky (1979): 274.

6. Positive and negative prospects are evaluated in the following way: First, in the editing phase they are segregated into two components, a riskless component that is the minimum loss or gain certain to be received, and a risky component comprised of the additional gain or loss at stake. These prospects are then evaluated in the

following way: If p + q = 1 and either x > y > 0 or x < y < 0, then $D(x,p; y,q) = v(y) + w(p)[v(x) - v(y)]$. This value equals the value of the riskless component, plus the difference between the two outcomes multiplied by the weight associated with the outcome with the greater absolute value. See Kahneman and Tversky (1979): 276.

7. Notice that no such hypothesis is needed for the analysis of the experiments reported by Kahneman and Tversky. They are concerned to explain the *order* in which subjects prefer certain possible actions in different decision problems. To do this, they must hypothesize that in each decision problem a subject arrives at a **D** value for various alternative actions, but they are never required to hypothesize that these **D** values can be compared from one decision problem to the other.

8. Nevertheless, I suspect Prospect Theory does explain most of these intuitions, though I will not try to survey them here.

9. This is a version of an objection offered by one of the editors of *Ethics*.

10. I am especially indebted to Joe Camp for many helpful discussions of the issues treated in this section.

11. Assume that I am at a gym, wearing my glasses. A thief to my left steals my pocketbook off a chair. Fortunately there is a police officer in uniform to my right. Then (A): *the thief to my left stealing my pocketbook* is a reason for (B): *my calling to the police officer to my right*. If my glasses are off, I will not be so lucky because (C): *the dark figure to my left holding a dark object* is not a reason for (D): *my calling to the dark figure to my right*. One can argue that (A) and (C) are strictly identical states, and that (B) and (D) are strictly identical states. 'Is a reason for' resembles 'implies' in its logic.

12. It was called to my attention after this chapter was done that Robert Nozick points to the "strong similarity" between the doing and allowing distinction and framing effects in Nozick (1995): 60.

Chapter 10

Prototypes and Conceptual Analysis

William Ramsey

I. Prototypes and Conceptual Analysis

When philosophers write on the philosophical significance of cognitive and brain sciences, they typically expound on the bearing this research has on *issues* and *topics* in one or another area of philosophy. Thus, philosophers working in cognitive science are generally concerned with the relevance of cognitive research to such philosophical questions as, say, whether or not perception is theory-laden or whether or not belief forming strategies are rational. In this chapter, I intend to do something a little different. Rather than discuss the importance of cognitive research for some traditional philosophical *topic*, I want to focus on the implications of this research for the *way* philosophy often gets done. More specifically, I want to take a look at what many psychologists are currently saying about the way we represent concepts and discuss some consequences of their views for the age-old philosophical enterprise of conceptual analysis—that is, the search for precise definitions specifying necessary and sufficient conditions for abstract notions. As one psychologist has recently concluded, "there is a gap between the psychological and philosophical work on this problem" (Smith 1990: 51). Here, my efforts are going to be devoted to narrowing this gap. My goal will be to convince you that if much of what these psychologists are saying is true, then analytic philosophers need to seriously rethink this popular *modus operandi.*

To do this, I propose to proceed as follows. In the next section, I will give a brief characterization of the sort of philosophical enterprise I am calling conceptual analysis and try to make explicit some of the presuppositions that it rests upon. In section III, I will look at some recent empirical findings in psychology and provide a sketch of the more popular accounts of concept representation that these results have prompted. In section IV, I will examine the implications of the psychological theories discussed in section III for the philosophical enterprise discussed in section II. Here, I will develop and defend my claim that the assumptions which drive conceptual analysis are not empirically founded and clash with prevalent psychological theories of concept representation. If what the psychologists are saying is true, then the search for crisp definitions of various abstract notions by probing our intuitions is a seriously misguided endeavor. In section V, I will entertain an objection against my argument and show why the objection does not work. Finally, in section VI I will offer a brief conclusion and discuss possible ways the enterprise of conceptual analysis might be brought in line with the psychological research.

Before we get started, however, a couple of preliminary comments are in order. The first is that the thesis I will defend is a conditional one concerning what follows *if* certain empirical accounts of concept representation are correct. Since my claim is about the *relation* between a branch of empirical research and philosophical analysis, I will make no real effort to defend the empirical accounts themselves. Secondly, although no one as far as I know has tried to run the sort of detailed argument I am going to present, it is worth noting that many of the themes I will be discussing have been floating around philosophical circles for some time. Perhaps the best know expression of these sentiments is Wittgenstein's discussion of family resemblance concepts in the *Investigations*, though similar ideas can be found in the writings of other philosophers, including Hilary Putnam (1962), Peter Achinstein (1968), Harold Brown (1988), Terence Horgan (1990) and, in particular, Stephen Stich (1990, 1992), whose recent work inspired this chapter. The following can be read as an attempt to ground these ideas in an empirical base and give them a full-blooded argument.

II. Conceptual Analysis and Its Underlying Assumptions

It would be a bit of an understatement to claim that conceptual analysis has been an important aspect of Western philosophy. Since the writings of Plato in which Socrates and his cohorts repeatedly attempt to discern the true essence of matters such as piety and justice, philosophers have been in the business of proposing and (more typically) attacking definitions for a huge range of abstract notions. These include such concepts as knowledge, causation, rationality, action, belief, person, justification, and morality (to name just a few). As one author notes,

> What philosophers throughout their history have sought are those character-
> istics of what they were examining, whether it be *knowledge, truth, neces-*
> *sity, mind, recklessness, value,* or *time,* in virtue of which it is what it is;
> those characteristics which are necessary to it and give its essence. (White
> 1975: 103)

Even philosophers who do not regard the analysis of some concept as their *pri-mary* goal, nevertheless, either explicitly or implicitly, often undertake some form of conceptual analysis as a step toward achieving some further end. Hence, there can be little question concerning the significance of this enterprise to analytic philosophy. But how does this enterprise get carried out and, perhaps more importantly, what are its underlying assumptions about the way we represent concepts?

Two Criteria for Definitions

Answering the first question—how does conceptual analysis get done?—is, at first glance, relatively easy: philosophers propose and reject definitions for a given abstract concept by thinking hard about intuitive instances of the concept and trying to determine what their essential properties might be. However, this characterization is really too vague to tell us anything useful. Perhaps a better way to gain insight into conceptual analysis is to consider what is normally expected of the definitions put forth. By looking at the criteria philosophers use for definitions, we can get a firmer grasp on what philosophers are up to and perhaps uncover some of the presuppositions lurking behind this enterprise.

Naturally, there are a number of different criteria commonly invoked by philosophers searching for definitions. Here, I will focus upon only two that, although rarely mentioned, nevertheless have a major influence on the way conceptual analysis often gets done. The first of these requirements is that the definitions be relatively straightforward and simple. Indeed, a popular syntactic form assumed for definitions is that of a small set of properties regarded as individually necessary and jointly sufficient for the concept in question. Hence, more often than not philosophical definitions take a syntactic form in which the notorious (at least among copy editors) "iff" is followed by a short *conjunction* of properties. Thus, X is knowledge if and only if X is justified, true belief or X is acting freely if and only if X is doing what he or she wants. As with explanatory theories in science, a popular underlying assumption of conceptual analysis is that overly complex and unwieldy definitions are defective, or ad-hocish, even when no better definition is immediately available. If an analysis yields a definition that is highly disjunctive, heavily qualified, or involves a number of conditions, a common sentiment is that the philosopher has not gotten it right yet. Accordingly, different analyses are typically regarded as *competitors*, and, for the most part, few people take seriously the idea that the correct analysis might be one involving a disjunctive combination of these alternate definitions. To borrow a technical phrase from Jerry Fodor, analyses of this complex sort are commonly regarded as "yucky." For many philosophers, a proposed definition should be short and simple.

A second criterion definitions are generally expected to meet is a concern not about their form, but their degree of robustness. If a definition is to count as a *real* definition, then it is generally assumed that it cannot admit of any intuitive counterexamples. Hence, as we all learned in introductory philosophy, the standard way to gun down a proposed analysis is to find either a noninstance of the concept that possesses the definitional properties in question—thereby showing that the defining properties are insufficient to capture the concept—or an instance of the concept that does not possess the definitional properties—thereby showing the defining properties are not necessary. If counterexamples of this sort can be found, then the proposed definition is typically regarded as inadequate. This sentiment is nicely expressed in the following passage from a popular text on philosophical method:

> [W]e shall tentatively consider a definition satisfactory if, after careful reflec-

tion, we can think of no possible examples in which either the defined word truly applies to something but the defining words do not, or the defining words truly apply to something but the defined word does not. When we can think of such an example, then we have found a counterexample to the alleged definition showing that we do not have an accurate reportive definition. If we can find no counterexample to a definition, then we may regard it as innocent until a counterexample is found to prove otherwise. (Cornman, Lehrer, and Pappas 1982: 18)

Hence, definitions sought by philosophers engaged in conceptual analysis typically must pass at least two tests: they must be relatively simple—generally a conjunction of individually necessary and jointly sufficient properties, and it must not admit of any intuitive counterexamples. With this in mind, we can now turn to the question of psychological presuppositions.

Psychological Presuppositions of Conceptual Analysis

At first blush, it might seem a little odd to suppose that conceptual analysis involves *any* presuppositions about the way our minds work. After all, if people are interested in defining notions like justice or causation, then it is justice or causation that they are concerned with—not human psychology. Nonetheless, when we look more closely at the criteria for definitions that I have just sketched, we can indeed find lurking in the background certain assumptions about human cognition. Perhaps the easiest way to see this is to consider the significant role intuitive categorization judgments play in this type of philosophy. Notice, for example, that for either type of counterexample to actually count as a counterexample, there are going to have to be fairly strong and widely shared intuitions that some particular thing or event either is or is not an instance of the concept in question. In other words, the process of appraising definitions requires comparing and contrasting the definitional set of properties with *intuitively* judged instances and noninstances of the target concept. Without these intuitive categorization judgments, conceptual analysis as a practice could never get off the ground.

Because of this important role of intuitive judgments, conceptual analysis cannot avoid being committed to certain assumptions about the nature of our cognitive system. One such assumption is that there is considerable overlap in the sorts of intuitive categorization judgments that different people make. Without this consensus, an intuitive counterexample for one individual would fail to be an intuitive counterexample for another individual, and no single definition could be agreed upon. Moreover, given that definitions are expected to express simple conjunctions of essential properties and allow no intuitive counterexamples, there also appears to be the fairly strong presumption that our intuitive categorization judgments will coincide perfectly with the presence or absence of a small but specific set of properties. In other words, lurking in the background of this enterprise is the assumption that our intuitions will nicely converge upon a set whose members are all and only those things that possess some particular collection of features. Given that philosophers expect to find tidy conjunctive definitions, and given that they employ *intuitions* as their guide in this search, the presupposition seems to be that our intuitive categorization judgments will correspond precisely with simple clusters of properties.

A reasonable question to ask at this stage is: where do these assumptions come from? After all, prima facie one would suppose that it is an open question whether or not our intuitive judgments can guide us to a relatively simple set of defining characteristics for abstract concepts. What exactly warrants these presuppositions?

One possible answer to this question rests with the idea that philosophers are employing an underlying folk theory of the mind or, perhaps more specifically, a folk theory about the way we represent concepts. Since Plato, a recurring theme in philosophy has been that we possess "tacit" knowledge of some domain that may not be directly accessible to our consciousness, but nonetheless is manifested through intuitive judgments and can be accessed by probing these intuitions. Similarly, outside of philosophy, Chomsky (1965, 1972) and other linguists have proposed that speakers possess tacit knowledge of their native language that takes the form of an internally represented, "psychologically real" grammar. For both Plato and Chomsky, it is recognized that this tacit knowledge is not immediately accessible to consciousness. But since this underlying competence is thought to drive our intuitive judgments, a common assumption is that it can be "uncovered" or made explicit by probing and exploiting these intuitions. For example, Chomskians assume that we can ascertain a set of syntactic rules for English by looking closely at the intuitive linguistic judgments of competent English speakers because, according to them, these judgments are generated by an actual, cognitively represented grammar of English. On this view, intuitive judgments serve as data against which we can test hypotheses about the nature of the underlying structures that produce them.

Along similar lines, it seems that the easiest way to account for the assumptions that underlie conceptual analysis is by supposing that lurking in the background is a similar—though perhaps itself tacit—theory about the way we represent concepts. In other words, categorization intuitions are assumed to lead us to tidy sets of necessary and sufficient properties because, it is further assumed, these intuitions are generated by underlying representations *of* necessary and sufficient properties. On this view, it is assumed that we have tacit knowledge of the essence of abstract concepts, that the essence is a small set of necessary and sufficient conditions, and that we can uncover this knowledge by appealing to our intuitive categorization judgments. I will call this theory of concept representation the "classical" view. Although relatively few philosophers engaged in conceptual analysis explicitly endorse the classical view, it strikes me as the most plausible and charitable way to make sense of this enterprise. Appealing to our intuitive categorization judgments to support or undermine a given analysis of a concept is much the same as appealing to our intuitive grammaticality judgments to support or undermine a given account of the grammar for a language. If linguists can do it, why not philosophers?

Yet, although it may be true that this view of concept representation is the most natural way to explain the assumptions of conceptual analysis, it is important to keep in mind that conceptual analysis does not *require* this view of concept representation. It only requires the much weaker assumption that the representation scheme for concepts, whatever form it might take, yields intuitive judgments that correspond with small sets of necessary and sufficient conditions. While the classical view of concept representation may be the easiest way to support this weaker hypothesis, one could try to defend it by some other means. Indeed, I suppose one could avoid defending it altogether and simply take it as an article of faith that our intuitive judgments will behave in this way. Since every philosophical endeavor must start with some assumptions, this would not be a completely unreasonable strategy. It would not be unreasonable, that is, as long as there is no compelling motivation for doubting these assumptions.

The central claim of this chapter is that, in fact, there *is* motivation for doubting both the classical theory of representation and assumptions that our intuitive judgments will yield simple and fully intuitive definitions for abstract concepts. If the sorts of stories psychologists now tell about concept representations and categorization judgments turn out to be correct, then the philosopher's two criteria for definitions—that they are straightforwardly simple and admit of no counterexamples—cannot be jointly satisfied. To get a better sense of where the difficulties lie, we must now turn to those psychological accounts.

III. Empirical Accounts of the Nature of Concepts

The classical view of concept representation discussed in the last section has enjoyed popularity not just in philosophy. It was, until fairly recently, the accepted view of our conceptual system in cognitive psychology as well. However, beginning with the revolutionary work of Eleanore Rosch (1973, 1975a, 1978; Rosch and Mervis, 1975), there has been a growing number of psychologists who believe the classical view is an inaccurate picture of the way we organize conceptual information. As one source notes, "psychologists are currently forsaking the classical view in droves" (Smith and Medin 1981: 33). Perhaps the easiest way to explain how the classical account fell on hard times in cognitive psychology is to first look at a number of findings regarding the nature of intuitive categorization judgments. After this, we will be in a better position to examine important aspects of the more popular theories of concept representation that have supplanted the classical view.

Empirical Findings Concerning Categorization Judgments

In a number of different studies, psychologists have demonstrated what is now regarded as a very robust cognitive phenomenon: in a wide range of categorization judgments—including those for abstract concepts (Hampton 1981)—class membership does not appear to be a straightforward all-or-nothing matter. Instead, it seems that for most concepts some instances are judged to be much better examples of the target concept than other instances. In other words, our categorization intuitions appear to reflect a taxonomic system in which most categories have graded membership.

This aspect of our categorization judgments, commonly referred to as "typicality" or "prototype effects," has been demonstrated in a number of experimental designs. When asked to judge how good an example of a given concept a particular item is, subjects tend to assign very different rankings to different items in a fairly consistent manner (Rips, Shoben, and Smith 1973; Rosch 1973). Thus, for a given concept (e.g., BIRD) some instances will be ranked as much better examples (e.g., robin) than other instances (e.g., owl or ostrich). Moreover, this ranking of instances from the typical to atypical is reflected in a number of other studies. For example, when asked simply to list instances of some category, subjects regularly list the typical instances first and the atypical instances last (Rosch 1975a; Rosch, Simpson, and Miller 1976). Similarly, subjects are much quicker in judging typical instances as members of the target category than atypical instances (McCloskey and Glucksberg 1978; Rips, Shoben, and Smith 1973; Rosch 1973). Other studies reveal that the typical instances of a concept are learned more easily (Rosch 1973; Rosch, Simpson, and Miller 1976), have a greater influence on decision making (Cherniak 1984; Rips 1975), are more frequently cited than other instances (Barsalou 1983, 1985), and are judged to be *less* similar to atypical members than the latter are to them (Tverski and Gati 1978).[1] When subjects are asked to list attributes for different instances of a given concept, it has been found that the lists of instances with high typicality rankings have significantly more attributes that are common to other members of the concept than instances with low typicality rankings. By contrast, highly typical instances share fewer attributes with members of other concepts than do the less typical instances. For some concepts, no attribute applied to all of the instances considered (Rosch and Mervis 1975). Also, there is considerable evidence that a number of different factors—such as frequency of instantiation, similarity to some ideal, overall familiarity, and context of presentation—all play a role in influencing our categorization judgments, and that the interplay of these factors generates a great deal of flexibility and indeterminacy in our intuitions. For example, several investigators have provided evidence suggesting that the salience of a given feature for categorization judgments can vary in different contexts, thereby yielding different intuitions about the same sort of case in different contexts (Barsalou 1985; Rosch 1978; Roth and Shoben 1983).[2]

What do findings such as these tell us about the nature of our conceptual framework? Some psychologists, such as Rosch, have been very hesitant about endorsing any particular model of concept representation on the basis of these findings, suggesting instead that these results constrain but do not determine representation and processing models. However, even the cautious Rosch allows that "[a] representation of categories in terms of necessary and sufficient attributes alone would probably be incapable of handling all of the presently known facts" (1978: 40-41). The source of these and other anticlassical sentiments, which are now widespread in cognitive psychology, is not difficult to find. Assuming that categorization judgments are a product of our conceptual scheme, one would expect very different findings if that conceptual scheme represented categories in the way suggested by the classical picture. For example, one would expect to find all instances of a concept intuitively judged as equally good examples, and no disparity in reaction times of categorization judgments, since the criteria for category membership would apply equally well to all and only those instances.[3] The categorization studies show that this is not the case. Similarly, one would expect to find that, for any given concept, subjects would tend to list a common set of definitional features for all category members. The studies of attribution assignment undermine this expectation as well.

Because of these and similar considerations, many psychologists have become increasingly skeptical about the classical view. Of course, as with any empirical domain, refuting a theory of concept representation once and for all is not an easy thing to do, and there are a number of things that can and have been said on behalf of the classical view in response to this prima facie counterevidence.[4] However, as is often the case in science, the situation here demands an appeal to the *best* explanation, and efforts to save the classical theory have largely been dampened by the success cognitive psychologists have had in constructing alternative accounts that comport much better with the data. It is safe to say that, with a few exceptions, psychologists today believe that the classical picture of concept representation is no longer in the running.

What do these alternative accounts of concept representation look like? Since space does not permit an exhaustive survey of the many nonclassical models enjoying current popularity, I will instead outline some of the more standard themes and principles common to these models in an effort to give a brief sketch of their general form.

Contemporary Theories of Categorization and Concept Structure

To account for typicality effects and other findings mentioned in this section, many psychologists have adopted the view that concepts are represented by *prototypes* and that categorization judgments come about through the comparison of individual instances with this prototype representation (or, perhaps more accurately, comparing a representation of the instance with the prototype representation). While there are several different models that employ this basic assumption, we can understand the general idea by focusing on one standard type of theory, commonly called the "probabilistic" or "feature-based" account (Smith and Medin 1981). The central claim of this view is that the prototype is an abstracted set of features, and categorization judgments are a function of the number and significance of the features shared between the prototype and the instance in question. If some thing or event and the prototype representation share a sufficient number of salient features, then this gives rise to the intuitive judgment that the thing or event is an instance of the target concept. If the two do not share a sufficient number of features, then the instance is not so judged. Further variations on the theme include the proposal that prototypical features are assigned different weights or degrees of salience. So, for instance, a model might assign the weight of 30 for "feathered," 25 for "winged," 15 for "flies," and so on, and then assume that anything possessing enough relevant features to approach or surpass a sum of, say, 50 would be judged as an instance of the concept BIRD. On this view, a positive judgment could be generated by any one of a number of different combinations of properties that approaches or exceeds something like a threshold. In this way, the probabilistic approach supports a highly disjunctive view of concept instantiation, although the degree of disjunctiveness may vary between concepts. The view is nicely summarized by Medin and Smith as follows:

> The probabilistic view assumes that concepts are abstractions, or summary representations, but argues that for a property to be included in the summary it need have only a substantial probability of occurring in instances of the concept, i.e. it need only be characteristic of the concept, not defining. An object will then be categorized as an instance of some concept A if, for example, it possesses some criterial number of properties, or sum of weighted properties, included in the summary representation of A. Categorization is thus a matter of assessing similarity rather than applying a definition. (Medin and Smith 1984: 117)

Naturally, this simple characterization immediately prompts a number of questions: What determines which properties form the summary prototype? How many properties must the prototype and the example share for an instantiation judgment? And how are the weights assigned to the features included in the prototype representation? Fortunately, we need not be overly preoccupied with these questions here; suffice to say that attempts to address these and related concerns have spawned a number of thriving research programs in cognitive science. For example, on one version of this story, the features that are included in the summary representation are the more salient ones that have substantial probability of occurring in conjunction with other properties. On this view, the features that make up the summary prototype—and therefore make up the concept's representation—are those that are both common and unique to a given cluster of entities (Rosch 1978; Rosch and Mervis 1975; Smith and Medin 1981). Other versions hold that the relevance of a given property for categorization judgments is due to a variety of factors, some of which are sensitive to variations in context. On this variant, possession of certain properties would incline us toward a positive categorization judgment in some contexts but not in others (Barsalou 1985, 1987; Lakoff 1987; Malt and Smith 1982; Smith and Medin 1981).

These and numerous other variations on the prototype theme are now quite prevalent in cognitive psychology. If we consider once again the findings discussed in the first part of section III, we can see why they are commonly regarded as superior to classical accounts. Virtually all of the various typicality effects are easily accommodated by the prototype story. The prototype view accounts for the finding that some instances of a concept are judged to be better examples than other instances, since this is exactly what one would expect if categorization is determined by the sharing of features between a prototype and an instance. Naturally, some instances are going to have more features (or more heavily weighted features) in common with the prototype than others, and this would give rise to the gradedness in judgments of concept membership. Similarly, these models can account for differences in reaction times. If categorization judgments come about through the matching of an instance's features with those of a prototype representation, then one would expect to reach a sufficient number of matches for a positive judgment much more quickly for those cases where the instance and the prototype overlap a great deal. Probabilistic models can also explain why there are intuitively unclear instances of a concept. This occurs either because the instance's summed feature value is very close to what might be thought of as a threshold for a positive judgment, or because the set of features exceed those needed for more than one concept (Smith and Medin 1981: 69). As McCloskey and Glucksberg point out,

> For a category conceived of in this way, a potential exemplar's[5] degree of membership is determined by the proportion of the category's properties that it shares. Items sharing a large proportion of the category's properties have a high degree of membership in the category, while items sharing few of these properties have a low degree of membership. Degree of membership thus varies continuously, and no sharp boundary separates category members from nonmembers. (McCloskey and Glucksberg 1978: 467)

Since my argument is a conditional one, I will leave further defense of the prototype models for the cognitive psychologists. For our purposes, the important thing to note is that all of these models share the central Wittgensteinian idea that there is no one property or set of properties an item must possess to be judged as an instance of a target concept. Instead, possession of a significant number of prototypical features is sufficient to generate intuitions that it is an instance of a given category. Furthermore, the relevance or salience of these properties need not be a fixed constant and can vary over contexts. While this sketch barely scratches the surface of all that can be said about this family of theories,[6] it should suffice to give their general flavor.[7]

IV. Conceptual Analysis and Prototype Theories

Having assembled all the key elements for my case against conceptual analysis in the last two sections, we are now in a position to see just how the argument goes. In section II, I suggested that a possible underlying motivation for conceptual analysis is the classical view of concept representation, according to which we represent abstract concepts by representing a small set of singly necessary and jointly sufficient properties. Since prototype theories of concept representation of the sort just sketched directly contradict classical accounts, it might be thought that this alone is enough to show the incompatibility of prototype theories and conceptual analysis. But as I noted in section II, conceptual analysis does not actually *require* the classical theory be correct. Hence, if we are to develop a case against conceptual analysis on the basis of prototype theories, then a little more work is needed. But not much more.

As we saw in section II, what the philosophical practice of conceptual analysis *does* need is the assumption that our intuitive judgments about categorization and class membership can yield a definition for abstract concepts that (1) takes the form of a small conjunctive set of essential properties and (2) coheres with all relevant intuitions and allows no counterexamples. But if the sort of theories of concept representation discussed in the last section are correct, then it is highly doubtful that both of these criteria for definitions could ever be jointly satisfied. The reason is that, *ex hypothesi,* our categorization judgments are subserved by a taxonomic scheme that generates categorization intuitions that are too variegated and diverse to be captured by simple and nondisjunctive definitions. If being an intuitive instance of X is simply a matter of having a cluster of properties that is sufficiently similar to some prototype representation, and if there are a number of different ways this can be done, some of which may vary over different contexts, then any crisp definition comprised of some subset of these properties and treating them as necessary and sufficient is never going to pass the test of intuition. It will *always* admit of intuitive counterexamples because the range of diversity sanctioned by our conceptual representation scheme will be much greater than that allowed by any tidy, straightforward definition. Hence, the search for a simple, nondisjunctive definition of a given philosophical concept that accords with all of our intuitions and admits of no counterexamples is a hopeless enterprise, there simply is no such thing.

Another way to see this point is to consider the psychological underpinnings of counterexample philosophy in light of the prototype theory of concepts. As we noted earlier, philosophers invoke two types of counterexamples to shoot down a proposed analysis, one that illustrates that the properties in the analysans are not necessary, the other illustrating that such properties are not sufficient. Consider the first type of counterexample. Since on the prototype account any one of a number of different sets of properties will suffice to generate a judgment of instantiation, we should always be able to discover intuitive instances of the concept that do not possess all of the alleged necessary properties of a simple conjunctive definition. Indeed, since philosophers are generally willing to count imaginary cases as counterexamples (no matter how bizarre), a clever philosopher can just *construct* a counterinstance by contriving a case with a set of features excluding one or more of the proposed definitional properties but whose summed weights nevertheless suffice to produce an instantiation judgment. On the prototype view, intuitive counterexamples will always be forthcoming for any definition specifying necessary features.

Turning to the other type of counterexample—of the sort illustrating that the definition is not sufficient—things are a bit more complicated. Prima facie, one would think that if the prototype story were correct, it would be very difficult to come up with counterexamples of this sort. The reason is that while the prototype account may not involve any *necessary* properties, it certainly does seem to allow that various clusters might always prove *sufficient* for instantiation judgments of the concept. Nevertheless, there are aspects of the prototype account that suggest that counterexamples of this sort are relatively cheap, too. One such aspect is the context dependency of a given feature's significance for categorization judgments. If the salience of features for categorization judgments is context sensitive, then it should be possible to find or construct examples embedded in certain circumstances where the allegedly definitional features are all present but, because of the context, have a summary weighting that is too low for an instantiation judgment. Another possibility is that, for some concepts, the salience of some features in an instance might be canceled out by the possession of other features more germane to a different concept. Hence, although a given instance might contain a set of features that would normally lead one to judge it as a member of a particular category, it might wind up being judged as an instance of a different category because it happens to possess properties that are much more important for the latter (Smith and Medin 1981).

It is important to see that the point here is not that these intuitive counterexamples are not actual intuitive counterexamples to the proposed definitions. Rather, the point is that from the outlook of contemporary views of concept representation, counterexamples to classical definitions are cheap and abundant. While the counterinstances do indeed reflect the inadequacy of the proposed definition, it is not for the reasons traditionally assumed by practitioners of conceptual analysis. The definition is faulty not because there is some other simple set of necessary and sufficient conditions that can do a much better job of defining the concept in question. Rather, the definition fails because, according to prototype accounts of concepts, *there is no simple, tidy collection of properties that is possessed by all and only intuitive instances of the concept; any definition expressed in this way is doomed from the outset.* It just is not possible, on this view, to come up with a definition that is both a simple conjunction of "essential" properties and, at the same time, captures all of our intuitions.

V. A Potential Objection and Reply

Before concluding, I'd like to consider an objection against this type of argument that I have heard voiced on a number of occasions. Although I do not think the objection works, it is nevertheless helpful because it helps make sharper exactly what is at issue in this discussion.

The objection is that I am guilty of a form of illicit psychologism—that I have confused questions about *what* something really is with questions about our ordinary *thoughts about* what it is. Philosophers engaged in conceptual analysis are really concerned with discovering the true essences of matters such as knowledge and causation, not with the way we happen to represent them. Hence, psychological theories about our conceptual scheme are largely irrelevant to this *metaphysical* enterprise.

Indeed, a version of this complaint has been lodged not just against my argument, but against the very anticlassical, prototype theories upon which my argument is based. In a recent exchange, Georges Rey (1983, 1985) has argued that the psychologists advocating the prototype view have "hopelessly confused metaphysical issues of conceptual *identity* with (roughly speaking) epistemological issues of conceptual access" (1983: 238). As I understand it, Rey's objection runs as follows. Prototype theorists who attack the classical view fail to appreciate an important distinction between, on the one hand, features that ordinarily serve a pragmatic function of facilitating everyday categorization judgments, and, on the other hand, more "essential," definitional features that determine what the thing *really* is. Furthermore, we know from the work of Kripke and Putnam that the defining features of a concept need not be actually represented in the mind/brain, except, perhaps, by a few of the relevant experts. Despite their ignorance of the defining features, however, ordinary folk nevertheless often assume such features exist and could be added to their representation upon further investigation. Although Rey does not argue that this point fully rescues the classical view, one could conceivably save the classical view by arguing that typicality and instability effects arise because subjects employ the nonessential, identificational properties when making intuitive categorization judgments. This leaves open the possibility of a more definitional set of features that could be (or have been) discovered by the relevant experts and that would *really* tell you whether or not something was an instance of some concept. Indeed, recent versions of the prototype story admit just such a possibility, where it is suggested that our initial prototype representation becomes augmented with certain "core" properties acquired from the relevant experts and that take on a definitional status (Armstrong, Gleitman, and Gleitman 1983; Medin and Smith 1984).

But if all this is correct, then have I not overstated the case against the analytic philosopher engaged in conceptual analysis? For if the Kripke-Putnam thesis is right, and truly essential features can be discovered by experts for natural kind categories, then why not suppose that they can be discovered for philosophical concepts as well? If scientists can ascertain a set of necessary and sufficient properties for natural kind concepts, despite our having a prototype-based representation, then why not suppose philosophers can do the same thing for the abstract notions of philosophy? It seems that I have confused the metaphysical with the epistemological in just the way Rey cautions against.

The problem with this objection, as I see it, is that it assigns blame to the wrong party. For if there is any illegitimate connection between metaphysical matters and epistemological matters—that is, between what a thing "really" is and the way we represent it—it is the practitioner of conceptual analysis, and not me, who forges this linkage. The point can be seen most clearly if we consider the different ways in which the scientist and the philosopher go about the business of ascertaining definitional features.

According to Kripke (1972) and Putnam (1975), investigators in the natural sciences attempt to uncover "hidden" defining properties of natural kinds—such as a certain physical, chemical, or genetic makeup—through various sorts of empirical investigations. Just why it is that these sorts of features strike us as definitional for natural kind concepts is itself an interesting question that I will not pursue here.[8] What I do want to point out is that while the *types* of defining properties sought by science might have an intuitive ground, the actual defining properties themselves—the specific atomic, chemical, or genetic properties—are not based on intuition. The claim that water is H_2O certainly has no intuitive ring to it. As Rey himself is careful to note, these sorts of essential properties come to be represented only as a *consequence* of scientific investigation, and for many people, they are not represented at all. But this means that the definitions of science are not completely dependent upon our intuitive categorization judgments and may transcend our prototype representations for natural kinds in a variety of ways. Indeed, it is not at all uncommon for the scientific analysis to yield classifications that are quite counterintuitive. Although we once intuitively classified whales and porpoises as fish, contemporary classification schemes tell us it is not so. But we do not generally regard these counterintuitive cases as *counterexamples* to these scientific taxonomies. Instead, we adopt the view that science has revealed to us that our ordinary categorization judgments were mistaken. Hence, in his or her search for definitions, the scientist is allowed to step outside the bounds provided by our intuitive categorization judgments.

But now contrast this mode of investigation with that of conceptual analysis in philosophy. For starters, unlike the situation with natural kinds, it is far from clear what *types* of properties would count as more or less "definitional" for the various abstract concepts in philosophy. It is not as though notions such as causation and knowledge have a microstructure or genetic makeup. Moreover, the philosopher engaged in conceptual analysis is operating under a different set of assumptions than the scientist. As we saw in section II, the philosopher often assumes that the definitional properties can be uncovered by probing our existent, pretheoretical (what are sometimes referred to as "uncorrupted") intuitions. Hence, whatever properties govern our pristine intuitive categorization judgments are going to weigh much more heavily in assessments of competing analyses. If a given definition does not accord with our intuitive judgments (i.e., admits of intuitive counterexamples) then it is usually the definition, and not the intuitions, that is considered faulty. Because conceptual analysis takes intuitive categorization judgments as its central data, it is limited by our ordinary representation of concepts in a way that scientific investigation is not. So it is conceptual analysis, and not my argument, that forces us to base *what* a thing is upon the way we represent it. And since, *ex hypothesi*, it is a prototype representation that governs everyday categorization judgments, then it will be such a representation that guides and constrains any search for definitions performed through conceptual analysis.

Consequently, any distinction between a prototype representation that facilitates ordinary categorization judgments and a more definitional representation comprised of features discovered and relayed by empirical investigators—despite whatever legitimacy it might have for natural kind concepts—is not going to carry much weight when we consider concepts defined by traditional conceptual analysis. For these latter concepts, *philosophers* are the relevant experts. And if philosophers search for definitional properties by looking at intuitive categorization judgments, then their definitions will never go beyond those properties that comprise the ordinary, prototype representation that governs these judgments. But if that is so, then, as I have argued in section IV, it will be impossible to discover a definition that is both simple and admits of no counterexamples.[9]

VI. Concluding Remarks

Before wrapping up, it is worth reflecting for a moment on just how *un*surprising much of this should be to philosophers. The failure of analytic philosophy to produce an uncontroversial, completely satisfactory analysis of the vast majority of abstract concepts should by itself suggest that something is amiss. Moreover, even within the philosophical literature there have been cases suggesting difficulties with intuitions of the sort predicted by the prototype view. Consider Bernard Williams's (1970) well-known discussion of personal identity. Here, a proposed set of conditions for personal identity yields positive intuitive judgments when described in one way, but, as Williams points out, basically the same set of conditions tend to elicit contrary judgments when described somewhat differently. This is, of course, just what one would expect if the categorization judgments are context sensitive in the way suggested by prototype theory. As noted earlier, it is far from clear what warranted the assumption that our intuitive categorization judgments should converge in a way that would produce a clean set of necessary and sufficient conditions. Since this is an empirical question concerning matters of cognition and conceptual representation, it certainly is not something that lends itself to a priori proof.

But now what are we to make of conceptual analysis in light of these considerations? As I see things, philosophers have two main options. The first is to try to undermine the prototype accounts of concept representation that I have suggested challenge the presuppositions of conceptual analysis. Since the question of how we represent concepts and categories is largely an empirical one, philosophers who adopt this strategy had better be prepared to do serious and careful empirical research, comparable to that which motivated psychologists to abandon the classical view in the first place. I believe a much more reasonable option for philosophers to pursue would be to revise their basic assumptions and expectations about definitions of abstract concepts. As I have tried to show, if the prototype stories are correct, then the two primary expectations philosophers typically place on analyses of concepts—simplicity and avoiding all counterexamples—cannot both be satisfied. Hence, at the very least it looks like one of these criteria will need to be abandoned, or at least significantly relaxed. On the one hand, philosophers who demand analyses in the form of conjoined "essential" properties will need to abandon the assumption that such an analysis will accommodate *all* our intuitions and be willing to accept the existence of intuitive counterexamples. On the other hand, if philosophers are going to insist on air-tight analyses that admit of no intuitive counterexamples, then they must abandon the hope for tidy definitions and develop a tolerance for highly disjunctive and heavily qualified definitions. Naturally, whichever strategy we adopt will depend a good deal on the sort of work we want our analyses to do for us. Yet even here, in deciding which of the two criteria we ought to relax, recent empirical work has a role to play. For example, although there appears to be considerable overlap between intuitive judgments of different subjects with regard to highly typical and highly atypical instances, it has been demonstrated (Barsalou 1987) that there is a good deal of variance in rankings among different individuals for the moderately typical cases. Indeed, for single individuals, the typicality rankings for a given concept has been shown to progressively change over an extended period of time (with little change in the period of one day and significant change in the period of one month). Some researchers, such as Barsalou, believe that this reflects considerable instability in our conceptual representation scheme. If this is correct, then any fixed definition—even one that is highly disjunctive—may fail to capture all of the intuitions all of the time since these intuitions would not be universal or static. Consequently, abandoning simplicity in order to accommodate all intuitions may be a misguided strategy, and a more promising approach might be the one of preserving simplicity and recognizing that we cannot capture all intuitive judgments. It is worth noting that the latter tactic is not entirely foreign to philosophy. For instance, in certain respects it is quite similar to Carnap's (1950) eloquent discussion of concept *explication,* where *revision* of our intuitive categorization judgments is explicitly endorsed for the sake of simplicity. Similarly, in response to the various intuitive counterexamples to utilitarianism, Smart (1965, 1990) suggests that it is our intuitions, and not the utilitarian account of morality, that should be questioned or ignored. If the prototype story of concept representation is correct, then the strategies suggested by these philosophers—in particular, decreasing the importance of intuitive counterexamples—merit far more consideration and application than they have received.

Notes

An earlier version of this chapter appeared in *Topoi* 11 (1992): 59-70. Reprinted with kind permission from William Ramsey and Kluwer Academic Publishers.

Thanks are due to John Bickle, Marian David, Terence Horgan, Stephen Stich, John Tienson, Paul Weithman, and an anonymous referee for several helpful comments and suggestions. Earlier versions of this paper were presented at Central Michigan University, the University of Memphis, the University of Mississippi, and the Second International Conference on Cognitive Science at San Sebastian, Spain. A great deal of useful feedback was provided by these audiences.

1. Although we ordinarily think of similarity as a symmetrical relation, in a variety of cognitive episodes it does not exhibit this character. For further discussion, see Tversky and Gati (1978).

2. For a helpful overview of these findings, see Smith and Medin (1981, Chapter 3), Medin and Smith (1984), and Lakoff (1987, Chapter 2).

3. This is assuming, of course, that there is no trouble in discerning whether or not the instance in question has some definitional property.

4. For an interesting discussion of some of the ways one might try to rescue the classical view, and the difficulties with these strategies, see Smith and Medin (1981, Chapter 3).

5. Here the term 'exemplar' refers to an instance of a target concept.

6. It should be noted that most of the recent connectionist models of memory and cognition fall into the prototype paradigm as well. See, for example, Rumelhart et al. (1986) and Smolensky (1988).

7. Although somewhat dated, Smith and Medin (1981) is still the classic treatment of prototype theories.

8. One answer might be that these types of properties come to be more heavily weighted in our prototype representations for natural kind concepts because of their relevance to causal powers. For an interesting discussion of the relation between taxonomy, physical structure and causal powers, see Fodor (1987, Chapter 2).

9. Although defining scientific kinds is not hostage to all of our ordinary categorization intuitions, the ensuing definition may eventually work its way into popular culture and thereby influence our intuitive judgments in various ways, along with the older prototype representation (with the latter giving rise to typicality effects) (Rey 1983; Armstrong, Gleitman, and Gleitman 1983). Our contemporary understanding of simple substances such as water or the various concepts of mathematics may work in this way. The crucial thing to keep in mind, however, is that in these cases the defini-

tion is *learned* from others who have either discovered it through empirical investigation or simply stipulated it at the outset. Although we may indeed represent straightforward and simple definitions for a variety of concepts, this alone will not help the advocate of conceptual analysis if we do so only because someone else has empirically discovered or decreed the defining properties in question. Since either technique allows intuitive counterinstances for definitions, neither one plays by the rules insisted upon conceptual analysis. Of course, if simple core definitions already existed in all of us (perhaps along with a prototype representation used for identification purposes) that could be uncovered by reflecting on our categorization intuitions, then something like the classical view would be right after all, and the antecedent of my conditional argument (i.e., prototype theories are correct) would be false.

Chapter 11

Philosophical Theory and Intuitional Evidence

Alvin Goldman and Joel Pust

I. Intuitions as Evidence

Philosophers frequently appeal to intuitions in constructing and arguing for philosophical theories. A theory is commonly judged lacking when it fails to "capture" our intuitions and judged acceptable insofar as it captures more of our intuitions than other extant theories. This suggests that philosophers take intuitions to have a kind of evidential value. But what are intuitions, what hypotheses, exactly, do they evidentially support, and why should they have this evidential value? More generally, what is the proper role for intuitions (if any) in the "validation" of a philosophical theory? Many roles philosophers have assigned to intuition do not fall within our purview. For example, we do not examine the role of intuition in the acquisition of mathematical or logical knowledge. Indeed, we restrict our present inquiry to the role of intuitions in philosophical "analysis." This is not to suggest that philosophical analysis exhausts the mission of philosophy, nor that it comprises the most important part of philosophy. It is simply the segment or facet of philosophy where the appeal to intuition seems to us most relevant (not to say unproblematic).

Although different approaches to intuition have different detailed accounts of what intuitions are, we assume, at a minimum, that intuitions are some sort of spontaneous mental judgments. Each intuition, then, is a judgment "that p," for some suitable class of propositions p. An intuitional report is the verbal report of a spontaneous mental judgment. In principle, the verbal report of an intuition can be erroneous, either through imperfect self-knowledge, verbal error, or insincerity. Here we assume, however, that all verbal reports of intuitions are accurate, that is, correctly convey what intuition is experienced. The question facing a philosopher, then, is how and why to treat spontaneous mental judgments, either one's own or those of an informant, as evidence for a philosophical hypothesis.

There seems to be a traditional picture among philosophers of how intuitions might serve as evidence, at least among philosophers favorably disposed toward intuitions as sources of evidence. This picture can be captured with the concept of a *basic evidential source*.[1] Many classes of mental states comprise basic evidential sources, including visual seemings, auditory seemings, memory seemings, and perhaps introspective seemings. In each case, there is a class M of contentful mental states such that being in one of these mental states is prima facie evidence for the truth of its content, at least when the (token) state occurs in favorable M-circumstances. Thus, visual states are a basic evidential source because when a person experiences a state of seeming to see that p and is in favorable visual circumstances, this is prima facie evidence for the truth of p. Auditory states are a basic evidential source because when a person experiences a state of seeming to hear that p and is in favorable auditory circumstances, this is prima facie evidence for the truth of p. Memory is a basic evidential source because when a person has an ostensible memory state of seeming to recall that p and is in favorable mnemonic circumstances, this is prima facie evidence for the truth of p. Introspection might also be a basic evidential source, where introspective states are states having contents of the form, "I now have a conscious mental state of such-and-such type."

Under what conditions, exactly, does a class of states M qualify as a basic evidential source? Minimally, the following condition seems to be required:

(RI)   Mental states of type M constitute a basic evidential source only if M-states are reliable indicators of the truth of their contents (or the truth of closely related contents), at least when the M-states occur in M-favorable circumstances.[2]

The reliable indicatorship requirement is simply the requirement that when M-states occur (in M-favorable circumstances), their contents are *generally true*. When one seems to see that a telephone is on the desk, and when this occurs under circumstances of adequate light, sufficient proximity, and no obstruction, then it is usually true that a telephone is on the (contextually indicated) desk. When one seems to recall that one had cereal for breakfast, and there is no substantial interference from other episodes in memory, it is usually true that one did have cereal for breakfast.

Two other features standardly characterize basic evidential sources: (1) a counterfactual dependence, and (2) a causal medium. The notion of counterfactual dependence is defined by David Lewis as follows:

Let A_1, A_2, . . . be a family of possible propositions, no two of which are compossible; let C_1, C_2, . . . be another such family (of equal size). Then if all the counterfactuals $A_1 \Box\rightarrow C_1$, $A_2 \Box\rightarrow C_2$, . . . between corresponding propositions in the two families are true, we shall say that the C's *depend counterfactually* on the A's. We can say it like this in ordinary language: whether C_1 or C_2 or . . . depends (counterfactually) on whether A_1 or A_2 or . . . (Lewis 1986b: 164-165)

In the standard case of a basic evidential source M, the M-states depend counterfactually on the truth of their contents, at least insofar as M-favorable conditions obtain. For example, in favorable visual conditions, if the object in a person's visual field were red, the person would seem to see that something is red; if the object were yellow, the person would seem to see that something is yellow; and so forth. Similarly for propositions concerning shape: if the object were square, the person would seem to see that something is square; if the object were circular, the person would seem to see that something is circular; and so forth.[3] Note that counterfactual dependences can *explain* reliable indicatorship relations. The fact that an M-state with the content p—that is, M(p)—occurs only if p is true may be explained by the fact that if any contrary state of affairs p* were true, the contrary state M(p*) would occur rather than M(p).

In standard cases of basic evidential sources there is also a distinctive causal route from the family of states of affairs that make the M-contents true or false to the family of M-states. In vision, for instance, the distinctive causal route includes light being reflected from the truth-making state of affairs (or the objects involved in that state of affairs), traveling to the perceiver's retinas, which then send signals or information via the optic nerves to the visual cortex. In many cases of basic evidential sources (e.g., memory), we still lack a firm scientific understanding of what the causal route consists in. Nonetheless, we often have substantial evidence *that there is* such a causal route. Indeed, if we believed that there is no such causal route, there would be grounds for doubting that there are counterfactual dependences of the indicated sort. And if there were no counterfactual dependences of the indicated sort, there would be grounds for doubting that the reliable indicatorship relation obtains. We shall not insist that either a counterfactual dependence or a causal route be present in order to have a basic evidential source. Only the reliable indicatorship relation is proposed as a necessary condition for a basic evidential source. As just indicated, however, if it is known or suspected that there is no relevant causal route or counterfactual dependence, there are grounds for doubting the existence of a reliable indicatorship relation, and hence for doubting the existence of a basic evidential source.

Let us return now to intuitions. A traditional philosophical view of intuition, we believe, is that intuitions constitute a basic evidential source (or perhaps a family of basic evidential sources). For this reason, many traditional philosophers hold that when someone has an intuition with the content p, this is prima facie evidence for the truth of p. In other words, I(p) is prima facie evidence for p. We are tentatively disposed to accept this proposal. That is, *if* intuition is a basic evidential source, I(p) is prima facie evidence for the truth of p. As formula (RI) indicates, however, intuition only qualifies as a basic evidential source if intuitional states (intuitings) are reliable indicators of the truth of their contents (or closely related contents) when they occur in favorable circumstances. It remains to be seen whether intuition indeed satisfies (RI).

Being a basic evidential source is not the only possible way intuitions might qualify as evidence for some sort of philosophical theory or conclusion. Being a basic evidential source is a very special way of providing evidence, and states of all sorts, including mental states, might provide evidence without being tokens of a basic evidential source. A mental state of dizziness, for example, might be evidence that a patient has a certain disease or clinical condition, at least it might be evidence in the hands of a physician or diagnostician with suitable background information. But this does not show that dizziness is a token of a basic evidential source. First, dizziness does not seem to be a *contentful* mental state, which is necessary for being a basic evidential source. Second, even if it were contentful, its content would surely not include the clinical condition inferred by the diagnostician. Like dizziness, intuitions might also be used as evidence without being tokens of a basic evidential source. Most of our discussion, however, will examine intuition as a candidate for a basic evidential source, partly because that is the traditional philosophical approach and partly because, on the view we shall advance, it probably *is* a basic evidential source.

Under standard philosophical methodology (SPM), the content of a typical intuition is a proposition about whether a case or example is an instance of a certain kind, concept, or predicate.[4] In other words, the contents of intuitions are usually singular classificational propositions, to the effect that such-and-such an example is or is not an instance of knowledge, of justice, of personal identity, and so forth. Thus, intuited propositions are standardly of the form, "Example e is (is not) an instance of F," and intuitions are spontaneous mental assentings to such classificational propositions. More fully, the propositional content of a singular intuition might have the form, "Example e is an instance of G (e.g., justified true belief) but not an instance of F (e.g., knowledge)."

Philosophers, of course, do not primarily aim to establish the truth or falsity of singular propositions, at least not of this sort. They usually seek to defend or criticize some general theory, such as, the theory that knowledge is justified true belief, or that personal identity consists in psychological continuity. Establishing or refuting such theories is the main aim of philosophical activity, at least under the mission of philosophical analysis. An adequate reconstruction of philosophical methodology here requires a two-step evidential route. In the first step, the occurrence of an intuition that p, either an intuition of one's own or that of an informant, is taken as (prima facie) evidence for the truth of p (or the truth of a closely related proposition). In the second step, the truth of p is used as positive or negative evidence for the truth of a general theory. The first step is epistemologically central for the topic of intuition, so it will be the main object of our scrutiny. Later, however, we shall also have things to say about the second step.

Without explicit elaboration, philosophers seem to proceed on the assumption that intuitions—at least intuitions of singular classificational propositions—comprise a basic evidential source. That is ostensibly why philosophers regard the first step of the two-step route as warranted. The question that needs to be raised, therefore, is whether intuition really is a basic evidential source, in particular, whether it satisfies condition (RI). Answering this question requires closer attention to the exact content of singular classificational propositions and the exact interpretation of philosophical analysis. As we shall argue, different interpretations of philosophical analysis can offer better or worse prospects for rationalizing the working assumption of SPM that intuition is a basic evidential source.[5]

Before turning to possible interpretations, let us ask what would constitute favorable versus unfavorable circumstances for the working of intuition. What types of circumstances render intuitions unreliable, in something like the way that poor lighting conditions can render visual seemings unreliable, or background noise can render auditory seemings unreliable? There are two plausible candidates in the case of intuitions, and they illuminate how and why careful philosophical practitioners proceed as they do.

If an informant is asked for an intuition about a real live case, but she is ill-informed or misinformed about the case, her intuition as to whether the case is or is not an instance of F may be of little worth. Suppose, for instance, that Sally intuits that Oliver Stone *knows* that the Kennedy assassination was a conspiracy, partly because Sally takes the case to be one in which Stone's belief is *true*. If the latter assumption is mistaken, that is, if the conspiracy hypothesis is false, Sally's intuition that Stone knows is hardly a reliable indicator that he really does know. The possibility of incorrectly representing the facts of the case is a prime reason why philosophers construct hypothetical examples. This gives them the opportunity to stipulate relevant features of an example, so the informant will not be in the dark. Only then can an intuition be a reliable indicator of its content's truth. Things can go wrong even with hypothetical cases, however. The informant may misunderstand the description, or lose track of certain stipulated features of the case. So misinformation and confusion are analogues of poor lighting conditions, or occlusion of the stimulus, which are unfavorable circumstances for the exercise of vision. Just as in the case of vision, however, the fact that unfavorable circumstances can occur does not prevent intuition from qualifying as a basic evidential source. If one seeks to use the source as evidence, however, one wants it to be exercised only in favorable circumstances (insofar as possible).

A second possible source of error is theory contamination. If the person experiencing the intuition is a philosophical analyst who holds an explicit theory about the nature of F, this theory might warp her intuitions about specific cases. So, at any rate, it is widely assumed (and we shall support this assumption in section II). For this reason, philosophers rightly prefer informants who can provide *pre-theoretical* intuitions about the targets of philosophical analysis, rather than informants who have a theoretical "stake" or "axe to grind." Thus, when intuition is considered as a candidate for a basic evidential source, the condition of having a prior theoretical commitment might be an unfavorable circumstance for its proper (i.e., reliable) exercise.

II. Some Approaches to Philosophical Theory

Let us turn now to possible approaches to philosophical conclusions and ways intuitions might evidentially bear on them. Our taxonomy is intended to provide a small set of simple and perspicuous paradigms rather than a detailed review of the literature. The options we delineate do have some currency among contemporary writers, however, as we shall illustrate.

Broadly speaking, views about philosophical analysis may be divided into those that take the targets of such analysis to be in-the-head psychological entities versus outside-the-head nonpsychological entities. We shall call the first type of position *mentalism* and the second *extra-mentalism*. Both mentalists and extra-mentalists agree that intuitions themselves are conscious psychological states, but they differ on whether the targets of philosophical inquiry—that for which intuitions are supposed to provide evidence—are psychological or nonpsychological. In the case of mentalism, the mental entities in question are not conscious mental entities; otherwise, it would presumably be unnecessary to use indirect inferential techniques to get at them. Rather, they are nonconscious entities or structures to which introspective access is lacking.

We identify three forms of extra-mentalism: (1) the *universals* approach, (2) the *modal equivalence* approach, and (3) the *natural kinds* approach. The first approach says that philosophical analysis aims to elucidate or lay bare the contents of certain abstract, Platonistic entities, namely, certain universals. The analysis of 'S knows that p', for example, is really concerned with identifying the content or structure of a certain universal: knowledge. The second approach says that philosophical analysis aims to provide, for each philosophically interesting predicate, another predicate (or compound predicate) that is modally equivalent to it, that is, has the same intension.[6] For example, in the case of knowledge, analysis tries to find a predicate that applies to the same set of ordered n-tuples in each possible world as 'knows' does. The third approach construes philosophy as aiming to provide theories of certain *natural kinds*. Epistemology, for example, tries to provide a theory of the natural kind, knowledge.

As a paradigmatic proponent of the first extra-mentalist approach we need look no further than Plato himself. Plato's forms are classic examples of external entities that are exemplified or instantiated by particulars. They are also depicted as objects of nonperceptual intellectual apprehension, a prototype of how many philosophers construe intuition. Working within a broadly Platonistic tradition, a universals extra-mentalist might say that when someone has an intuition that e is an instance of F, what she has is an intellectual apprehension that a certain universal, F (or Fness), is instantiated by e. On this view, classificational intuitions involve the detection of a relation (instantiation or noninstantiation) between a universal and an actual or possible particular. A twentieth-century philosopher who espoused such a view was Bertrand Russell (1912, chap. 9). Although it is hard to pinpoint contemporary writers who endorse it, strands of it are certainly to be found in the literature. For example, without explicitly invoking universals, Matthias Steup hints at this position when he writes: "when we engage in a philosophical examination of such things as knowledge and justification . . . what we are interested in is not what ideas of knowledge and justification people carry in their heads, but rather what people have in common when they know something, when they are justified in believing something" (Steup 1996: 21). Both Alvin Plantinga (1993, chap. 6) and Jerrold Katz (1981, chap. 6) view intuition as a rational apprehension or "grasping" of extramental entities or states of affairs.

Clearly, the universals approach assumes that intuition is a basic evidential source, a source that gives us access to universals and their relations in roughly the same way as perception gives us access to physical objects and events. But could intuitions meet the RI constraint if their contents are construed as being about universals? How, on this view, might an intuition be a reliable indicator of a singular classificational truth? Let us introduce the notion of an *associated philosophical gloss* of a proposition. If we consider an ordinary classificational proposition like "e is an instance of knowledge," an associated philosophical gloss of it, modulo the universals approach, might be: "The universal KNOWL-EDGE is such that e is an instance of it." Presumably, naive informants' judgments do not explicitly refer to universals in this way. Nonetheless, an intuition with the content "e is an instance of F" might be a reliable indicator of the truth of its associated philosophical gloss, namely, that the universal F is such that e is an instance of it. The truth of this classificational fact might in turn provide evidence for the constitution of the universal. Thus, the evidential reconstruction of the role of intuitions on this approach would run as follows. The philosopher obtains informants' singular classificational intuitions and takes them as (prima facie) evidence that the target universal is or is not instantiated by such-and-such examples. This is premised on the assumption that intuition is a basic evidential source. A constructive analytic philosopher would collect the positive and negative instances and frame a hypothesis about the constitution of the target universal. A "destructive" philosopher would use the same positive or negative instances critically: to refute some hypothesis about the constitution of the target universal.

The chief difficulty for this approach comes with the assumption that intuition is a basic evidential source, a source of information about universals. Is there any reason to suppose that intuitions could be reliable indicators of a universal's positive and negative instances (even under favorable circumstances)? The problem is the apparent "distance" or "remoteness" between intuitions, which are dated mental states, and a nonphysical, extra-mental, extra-temporal entity. How could the former be reliable indicators of the properties of the latter? This is similar to the problem Paul Benacerraf (1973) raises about the prospects for mathematical knowledge on any Platonistic view of mathematics. Benacerraf, however, assumes that a causal connection with the object known is necessary for knowledge. We deliberately have not imposed such a requirement for a basic evidential source. Nor have we imposed the requirement of a counterfactual dependence between states of affairs that make an intuition's content true and the occurrence of such intuitions. We have only imposed the reliable indicatorship constraint. However, as mentioned in section I, wherever it is obscure, as it is here, how a causal relation or counterfactual dependence of the right sort could obtain, there are grounds for serious doubt that the reliable indicatorship relation obtains. Some philosophers (e.g., Plantinga 1993: 120-121) might reply that abstractness per se does not exclude causal relations. Nonetheless, we certainly lack any convincing or even plausible story of how intuitions could be reliable indicators of facts concerning universals. Thus, the universals approach offers an extremely thin reed on which to base philosophical methodology.

We turn next to the modal equivalence approach. The crucial point here is that the correctness of a philosophical theory depends on the contours of modal space, construed in a fully extra-mentalist, mind-independent fashion. When Edmund Gettier (1963) published his two counterexamples to the justified-true-belief analysis of knowledge, and almost all epistemologists shared the same intuitions about them, the modal equivalence approach interprets these intuitions to show that there are two possible cases in modal space to which the predicate "justified true belief" applies but the predicate "knowledge" does not apply. That these cases in modal space have these properties is evidentially supported by the indicated intuitions, on the supposition that intuition is a basic evidential source. An associated philosophical gloss of the intuitions' contents, modulo this approach, would take the form, "e is a case in the space of possibilities (i.e., in some possible world) that is an instance of G but not F." By getting evidence for such truths, it is demonstrated that "knowledge" and "justified true belief" are not modally equivalent.

The sticking point for this approach is essentially the same as the one facing the Platonistic universals approach. Intuitions are mental occurrences. Why are these mental occurrences with contents about objects in modal space reliable indicators of what is genuinely in modal space? As with the first approach, there appears to be a substantial gap between an intuiting, a type of psychological event, and the contours of objective modal space. It does not matter whether one takes possible worlds to be abstract objects or "concrete," spatio-temporally isolated objects (Lewis 1986a). There is still a substantial gap between the "inhabitants" of such objects and people's actual intuitions. How is this gap supposed to be bridged? To repeat, we are not immediately concerned with either a causal gap or the absence of a counterfactual dependence; we are concerned with a reliable indicator relationship. But given the dim prospects for either a causal connection or a counterfactual dependence, it is hard to see how there could be a reliable indicator relationship. Thus, there would be plenty of grounds to doubt that intuition qualifies as a basic evidential source if its contents were construed in terms of objective modal space.

The third approach, natural kinds extra-mentalism, has been advocated by Hilary Kornblith (1995, this volume) and Michael Devitt (1994). They hold that philosophical inquiry aims to provide a theory about the nature of certain natural kinds. Kornblith, for example, says that "the investigation of knowledge, and philosophical investigation generally" ought to be conducted on the model of the investigation of natural kinds (this volume, p. 134). The proper targets of philosophy are knowledge, meaning, and the good *themselves*, rather than the folk concepts of knowledge, meaning, or the good. Natural kinds theorists are not entirely clear about whether they conceive of natural kinds as a species of universals, but if so, they might construe them as non-Platonistic entities à la David Armstrong (1989).

Natural kinds extra-mentalists endorse a two-step evidential route in philosophical theorizing. The first step is executed by consulting persons thought to be experts about F, and eliciting from them their singular classification intuitions about F. The suggested philosophical gloss here seems to be that an intuition provides evidence for truths of the form "e is an instance of natural kind F." The second stage of the method is an empirical investigation of the concrete tokens picked out by the singular intuitions, the aim being to reveal the underlying nature of the property of being an F. This stage may lead to a theory that requires extensive revision of some intuitive judgments, or lead to the conclusion that various folk predicates do not latch onto any legitimate natural kind and should therefore be abandoned.

Our first dissatisfaction with the natural kinds approach stems from our doubt that all targets of philosophical analysis, or even most of them, qualify as natural kinds. Presumably something qualifies as a natural kind only if it has a prior essence, nature, or character independent of anybody's thought or conception of it. It is questionable, however, whether such analysanda as knowledge, justification, and justice have essences or natures independent of our conception of them. In our opinion, the lack of natural kind status would not place the topics of knowledge, justification, or justice outside the scope of philosophical analysis. Nor do we think that the corresponding predicates should be abandoned if they fail to pick out natural kinds.

Our second dissatisfaction with the natural kinds approach mirrors our worries about the other forms of extra-mentalism. The problem is: How can intuition get any reliable purchase on the constitutions of both a natural kind and an example so as to decide whether the latter matches the former? We assume here, as before, that the role or task of intuitions is to render (accurate) classification judgments. If the judgments are about natural kinds and their putative instances, a cognizer must first discern the underlying nature of the natural kind, then discern the underlying nature of the example, and then decide whether these match. It is not clear how intuition could contribute to the reliable execution of these tasks. It seems out of the question, then, that intuition could qualify as a basic evidential source under the natural kinds approach. The situation is especially problematic in the case of intuitions about hypothetical examples. Since these are not actual, concrete examples open for empirical inspection, how is intuition supposed to detect their underlying natures to see whether they qualify as instances of the target natural kind? As we have stressed, it is a pervasive feature of SPM that it employs intuitions about hypothetical cases and takes them to be on a par with (or better than) actual cases. The natural kinds approach apparently lacks any way of explaining this feature of SPM.

As indicated earlier, some proponents of the natural kinds approach advocate the use of only *experts'* intuitions. This is at variance, however, with SPM, which regards the intuitions of all people, or all linguistically competent people, as relevant. Furthermore, in the case of real natural kinds, experts are consulted about whether a given specimen is an instance of gold because those experts presumably know best what gold's nature is. But under SPM, nobody is assumed to know beforehand (in any explicit fashion) what F is. The whole purpose of appealing to intuitions is to get information about instances and noninstances of F in order to discover what F is. This seems quite at variance with the procedure advocated under the natural kinds approach.

Natural kinds proponents might concede many of our points. They might cheerfully grant that intuition is not a basic evidential source, and they might agree that their proposed methodology does not precisely match SPM. They might insist, however, that they are not *trying* to provide a rationalization for SPM, because they regard SPM as misguided in certain major or minor respects. If this is indeed their attitude, then their form of extra-mentalism simply does not fulfill the sort of objective with which we started, namely, to show, if possible, how SPM makes proper use of intuitional evidence and how intuition might qualify as a basic evidential source.

It is time to turn to mentalism, our favored approach. Mentalism interprets philosophical analysis as trying to shed light on the *concepts* behind philosophically interesting predicates, where the term 'concept' refers to a psychological structure or state that underpins a cognizer's deployment of a natural-language predicate.[7] Thus, Jones's concept of apple is the psychological structure that underlies her deployment of the predicate 'apple', and Jones's concept of knowledge is the psychological structure that underlies her deployment of the predicate 'knows' (or 'has knowledge').[8] (We ignore complications arising from multivocal words in natural languages.) The structures in question presumably include some sorts of mental representations, as well as some kinds of processing routines. The mental representations are assumed to have semantic contents, to which the theorist might appeal. Whether these contents are "narrow" or "wide," that is, determined in an individualist or antiindividualist fashion, is a topic on which we remain neutral.

Unlike the extra-mentalist approaches surveyed earlier, our form of mentalism is very congenial to the notion that intuition might be a basic evidential source. Under mentalism, moreover, its status as a basic evidential source can be sustained in a fully naturalistic framework. To see this, consider first what is the associated philosophical gloss of an intuition's content, according to mentalism. We interpret the gloss to be: "e satisfies my concept that I express through the predicate 'F'." This gloss is not intended to be the precise propositional content of an intuition, which we take to be, "e is an instance of F." But the gloss is certainly a closely related content. Moreover, given criterion (RI), intuition could qualify as a basic evidential source as long as the occurrence of intuitions with the content "e is an instance of F" are reliable indicators of the truth of the associated proposition, namely, "e satisfies my concept that I express through the predicate 'F'." Is it plausible that this reliable indicatorship relation should obtain? Definitely.

It is easy to see that intuitions with the indicated types of contents can be reliable indicators of the truth of their associated glosses. That is because there might well be an appropriate counterfactual dependence between e's satisfaction or nonsatisfaction of the concept expressed through 'F' and what the intuition "says" about e. The concept associated with a predicate 'F' will have many dispositions, but among them are dispositions to give rise to intuitive classificational judgments such as "example e is (is not) an instance of F." Thus, it is not only possible, but almost a matter of *definition*, that if the concept possessor were fully informed about the relevant features of e, then if e satisfied the concept he expresses through 'F', his intuitive response to the question of whether e satisfies this concept would be affirmative; and if e did not satisfy the concept he expresses through 'F', then his intuitive response to the question of whether e satisfies this concept would be negative. In other words, a concept tends to be manifested by intuitions that reflect or express its content. (This is a point made by George Bealer, and the general approach pursued here is similar to that advanced in Bealer 1987, 1996a, this volume.)[9] The indicated set of dispositions is the relevant counterfactual dependence that underwrites reliability. Moreover, although we do not currently know the precise causal route that connects concept structures with their conscious manifestations, it is extremely plausible, from any reasonable cognitive-science perspective, that there should be such a causal route. Thus, the satisfiability of the reliability condition seems quite safe.

We said a moment ago that it is "almost" a matter of definition that concepts have the indicated dispositions. Why "almost"? The reason, of course, is the possibility of unfavorable circumstances, or interfering conditions. An intuition might be generated or influenced, for example, by an explicit but mistaken *theory* about the concept of 'F' rather than by the concept of 'F' itself. For this reason, there could be a discrepancy between the intuition and the concept. This possibility, however, merely shows that intuitions are not *perfect* indicators of their associated glosses' truth. They can still be quite reliable, however, and, of greater relevance, they can be perfectly reliable *when occurring in favorable circumstances*. Thus, the prospects are excellent that intuitions are a basic evidential source under the mentalist construal.[10]

Some additional remarks about the mentalist interpretation are in order. First, some people might worry about the metalinguistic character of the mentalist approach, which surfaces in the portion of the gloss that alludes to a *predicate* 'F'. Is it really plausible, they might wonder, that the propositional contents of intuitions concern linguistic predicates like 'know' rather than knowledge itself? Our first response is to note that the metalinguistic element in our approach only enters in the *gloss* of the intuition's content, which need not precisely reproduce the sort of content an intuiter herself would choose to report. Second, since SPM typically involves the posing and answering of classificational questions in linguistic terms, it is clear that the process of generating an intuition involves the accessing of concepts via their cognitive relationship with (representations of) linguistic items. Thus, it is entirely appropriate to view an intuition as the manifestation of a psychological structure (viz., a concept) that can be identified by its relation to a predicate of a natural language.

Another question about the mentalist approach takes its point of departure from the assumption that concepts have *contents*. If the mentalist approach traffics in contents, which are ostensibly abstract entities, how different is it, in the end, from the universals approach? Two remarks are relevant here. First, we remain neutral on the ontological status of mental contents, so we are not committed to entities of the same status as Platonistic universals. Second, unlike the universals approach, mentalism has no burden of trying to explain how intuitions could somehow interact with, or reliably reflect, "free-floating" abstract entities. The contents of which mentalism speaks are contents embedded in, or borne by, psychological structures, which are neural or neurally realized states. Interactions between psychological states of these kinds and intuitional events (which are also neural or neurally realized events) are not fundamentally mysterious or problematic in the way that some sort of "apprehension" or "detection" of universals is problematic.

It is worth noting that even if intuitions did not have credentials to qualify as a basic evidential source, they could still have evidential significance for philosophy under the mentalist approach. Just as in the case of dizziness, one might make a justified abductive inference from intuitions as "observed" effects to concepts (with specified contents) as postulated causes. Since the aim of philosophical analysis according to mentalism is to identify the contents of certain concepts, this would be a (complex) one-step inferential route. Furthermore, it would be a straightforward kind of explanatory inference of the kind familiar

from the sciences. Thus, using intuition as evidence would not carry any mysterious, nonscientific baggage. That is also true under our defense of intuition as a
basic evidential source. Its evidential claims are no more mysterious, from a scientific or naturalistic point of view, than those of perception or memory.

Our exposition of mentalism may suggest that philosophical analysis is concerned with the concepts of single cognizers. More commonly, however, it is
concerned with the linguistic or conceptual properties of a community. Can this
be accommodated under mentalism? The default assumption of SPM is that
competent speakers of a given natural language have roughly the same conceptual contents lying behind their mastery of a particular predicate. That is, the
contents of different people's concepts of 'F' are at least roughly the same. The
usual aim of philosophical analysis, then, is to identify the one shared content.
Information about the concepts of single cognizers is evidentially relevant to the
nature of the collectively shared content so long as the chosen informants are
suitably typical members of the community, and there is a genuinely shared content. It must be acknowledged, however, that people might have markedly different contents associated with one and the same predicate. In that case, philosophical analysis must be satisfied with using intuitions to get at each person's distinct concept; it must be prepared, if necessary, to abandon the assumption that
the content of one person's concept of 'F' can be generalized to others.[11] However, there are notable philosophical examples, such as the Gettier examples,
which evoke the same intuitive responses from virtually all hearers who understand them, responses that even fly in the face of (formerly) well-entrenched theories. This strongly suggests that at least some predicates of philosophical interest have robust contents that span a wide spectrum of the linguistic community.

The mentalist approach to philosophical analysis might appear to threaten the
objectivity of classificational questions. Antecedently one might have thought
that whether an entity or state e qualifies as an instance of F is an objective matter of fact. Isn't such objectivity undercut by the mentalist approach to philosophical analysis, with its palpable subjectivity? No, we do not accept this conclusion at all. If the content of a particular concept expressed by 'F' is sufficiently determinate, then it is an objective matter of fact whether or not e is an
instance of 'F'. This fact of the matter is fixed by a combination of the content
of the concept and the features of e. To be sure, different people may have different conceptual contents associated with the same predicate 'F'. Hence, the question of whether e is an instance of 'F' is in an important sense ambiguous. Once
the concept (content) is fixed, however, the correct answer to the question is
uniquely determined by the facts concerning e.

Finally, we should add that philosophical theory need not be restricted to the
analysis of concepts (or even the analysis of tacit folk theories) as we have depicted it. First, at least certain concepts might have interesting *historical rationales* for their development or evolution, and it may be highly relevant to philosophy to identify those rationales. In fact, some historical rationales may be
viewed as a crucial adjunct of the current working concept. An example of this
will be given in section III. Second, philosophical analysis is primarily concerned with elucidating our folk concepts, but philosophy can also prescribe re-
visions in those concepts. In metaphysics, for example, conceptual analysis tries

to lay bare our folk-ontological categories. But there is also room for prescriptive metaphysics, which would seek to improve upon folk ontology through a combination of scientific discovery and broad philosophical reflection (see Goldman 1989a, 1992a). However, intuitions are less likely to play so prominent a role in the latter sector of philosophical theory.

III. Philosophical Analysis and the Psychology of Concepts

Mentalism depicts philosophical analysis as trying to pinpoint the contents of certain concepts, in the indicated psychological sense of 'concept'. But since inferences about these contents are inferences to psychological structures and processes, it would hardly be surprising if the enterprise we have described could benefit from research by psychologists and other cognitive scientists on the subject of concepts and their mental deployment. In this section, we provide a set of examples—all epistemological examples—to illustrate how such benefits might accrue. What we wish to suggest is that the investigation of "conceptual" matters (in the sense here intended) is properly, at least in part, an empirical investigation, in contrast to the traditional philosophical view that sharply opposes the conceptual and the empirical.

The potential benefits from cognitive science that we shall stress enter at the second step of SPM. Having gathered intuitions about a target predicate from one or more informants, a philosopher aims to determine the conceptual content that generates these intuitions. What is the specific content (and perhaps structure) of the informants' concepts that would explain the accumulated intuitions? Although it may be a definitional truth for a given concept that it would generate the actually collected intuitions, that concept need not be the only one with this property. In general, many different concepts—that is, concepts with nonequivalent contents—could give rise to the same (finite) set of intuitions. The philosophical analyst aims to choose from the set of possible concepts the one that best explains the collected intuitions. We shall argue that empirical psychology and linguistics can provide valuable information to assist the philosophical analyst in making a well-motivated choice.

Our first example concerns the impact of context on informants' judgments and intuitions, and the way theorists should take context effects into account in weighing competing analyses of epistemic concepts. We focus here on the concept of knowledge, since a number of recent proposals about knowledge are strongly contextualist (Cohen 1988; DeRose 1992, 1995; Goldman 1976, 1989b; Lewis 1979). A number of different things might be meant in labeling an approach to knowledge "contextualist." Here we have in mind approaches that ascribe a heavy role to the mental "set" of the knowledge *attributor*, a set that can be influenced by various contextual events. One theory that appeals to psychological context is the *relevant alternatives theory* (in some of its variants). According to this approach, the concept of knowledge implies that a subject does not know that p unless she can rule out all relevant alternatives to p. But which alternatives are relevant? According to a contextualist version of the approach, relevance is not fully determined by a rule or criterion embedded in the concept of knowledge and applied to the situation of the subject. Rather, relevance is judged by the sorts of scenarios or possibilities that are mentally "accessible" or "available" to the attributor. If an attributor has never thought of a Cartesian demon alternative, or a brain-in-the-vat alternative, or does not saliently access such an alternative at the time of judgment, he will cheerfully attribute knowledge of p to Jones in favorable circumstances. But if one of these unexcluded possibilities is saliently accessed, the intuitive feeling that Jones does not know will be fairly strong. The plausibility of this approach obviously rests on the plausibility of the idea that what is mentally available or accessible can play a large role in determining an attributor's intuitions, or inclinations, to affirm or withhold knowledge attributions. This is where psychology enters the picture. Psychological research has established that the availability of various alternatives or considerations powerfully influences an evaluator's judgments.

Suppose you are asked the following question, as hundreds of thousands of survey respondents around the world have been asked (see Campbell 1981):

> Taking all things together, how would you say things are these days? Would you say you are very happy, pretty happy, not too happy?

As Norbert Schwarz (1995) discusses, you presumably draw on some mental representation of how your life is going these days to answer this question. But do you really "take all things together"? If not, which of the myriad aspects of your life do you draw on? Chances are that you rely on the ones that come to mind most easily at this time. So your answer might be quite different at some other time if other aspects of your life come to mind. This is precisely what is found in a variety of studies.

In one of these studies, Strack, Martin, and Schwarz (1988) explored the influence of dating frequency on college students' general life satisfaction. Previous research had suggested that frequent dating might be an important contributor to general happiness. However, the apparent relevance of dating frequency depended on the order in which questions were asked, and hence on which facts were activated in the subject's mind. When respondents had to answer the general happiness question *before* they were asked a question about their dating frequency (a question that would bring dating to mind), both measures correlated only r = -.12. When the general happiness question was asked *after* the dating frequency question, the correlation increased to r = .66. Similarly, Strack, Schwarz, and Gschneidinger (1985) instructed some subjects to recall and write down a very negative event in their lives while other subjects were instructed to recall and write down a very positive event. Merely having these events in mind for purposes of comparison strongly influenced their judgment of the current quality of life. Ratings of well-being were higher for those who recalled a past negative event than for those who recalled a past positive event. Similarly, Schwarz and Strack (1991) found that subjects evaluated their own life more favorably when they met a handicapped person and listened to him describe his severe medical condition. The influence of the handicapped confederate was even more pronounced when he was visible to the respondent while the latter filled out the happiness report. Such findings emphasize the role of temporary accessibility in the choice of comparison standards.

How is this pertinent to the analysis of knowledge? If an epistemologist is trying to choose from among competing theories, some of which make heavy appeal to attributor context and some of which do not, these psychological findings are highly relevant. They give greater plausibility to theories assigning a large role to attributor context than those theories would have in the absence of such findings. It is much more plausible to hypothesize that intuitions about knowledge are heavily context driven if other sorts of judgments and evaluations are shown to be so driven.

We turn next to a different theme that bears on epistemic concepts, in this case both knowledge and justified belief. Traditional epistemology spoke of "sources" of knowledge, where the typical sources included perception, memory, reasoning, and introspection. The notion of a source or cause remains in contemporary theories that speak of belief-generating "processes." One question is whether the folk concepts of knowledge and justified belief crucially involve notions of causes or sources. Here it is good to have evidence that might confirm or disconfirm the idea that sources or origins comprise a general category that pervades commonsense thought. Evidence in favor of this notion is in fact found in cognitive science research. The linguists Clark and Carpenter (1989) provide a variety of evidence that supports the primitiveness of the source category. For example, two- and three-year-old children mark sources by using 'from' in ways that adults would not. Damon, looking at pieces of a sandwich he had pushed off the edge of his plate, says: *These fall down from me.* Chris, talking about a character in a book, says: *He's really scared from Tommy.* The conceptual origin of the source notion may be that of spatial location, but this is projected onto a variety of nonspatial domains (e.g., Jackendoff 1983; Talmy 1983). Given the wide range of source concepts, it would not be surprising that epistemic concepts like knowledge and justification should also reflect a concern for credal sources. Specifically, a belief qualifies as justified or as knowledge only if it has an appropriate source or combination of sources.

Goldman (1992b) advanced this sort of hypothesis earlier, using slightly different terminology. In that earlier terminology, also used by Ernest Sosa (1991), sources are divided into (intellectual) "virtues" and "vices." Virtuous sources are epistemically good ways of forming belief; vicious sources are epistemically bad ways. The proposal of that earlier paper, and of this one as well, is that wielders of predicates like 'justified' and 'know' represent them not in terms of a rule, criterion, or algorithm for distinguishing virtuous and vicious sources, but rather in terms of a mentally stored list of virtuous and vicious sources. This might strike the innocent philosopher's ear as slightly odd, since philosophers commonly expect concepts to be specified by something like a definition, in particular, a set of necessary and sufficient conditions. This traditional approach is certainly *not excluded* by mentalism. Inspiration for a different approach, however, may be drawn from psychology.

Research on the psychology of concepts has convinced most workers in the field that few common concepts are represented by means of a definition or a set of necessary and sufficient conditions. This so-called "classical" view has been much disparaged (see Smith and Medin 1981). A more listlike approach is found in the exemplar theory, which says that people represent ordinary concepts by means of a stored set of (representations of) previously encountered instances or tokens of the predicate in question (Medin and Schaffer 1978; Hintzman 1986; Estes 1994). For example, 'bird' might be mentally represented by the total set or a subset of the birds that the person has previously encountered. When the question is raised whether a new object is or is not a bird, some subset of the stored bird exemplars is retrieved and compared to the target object for similarity. If the similarity reaches a given threshold, the object is classified as a bird. The foregoing is a fairly pure version of the exemplar theory. Other versions would allow more abstraction, involving, for example, representations of *types* of birds. In both cases, however, a similarity-determining operation is a critical facet of the classification procedure. The same holds in our hypothesis about how informants judge whether a target belief is justified or unjustified. The source of the target belief is compared for similarity to the informant's list of virtuous and vicious sources. If the source matches virtues only, the belief is categorized as justified. If the source matches vices, the belief is categorized as unjustified. For example, a perceptually caused belief will intuitively be found to be justified. A belief caused by wishful thinking will be classified as unjustified, at least if the informant has wishful thinking on his or her list of epistemic vices. Of course, actual or hypothetical beliefs might involve antecedently unfamiliar sources. When that occurs, it is the similarity of the posited source to previously stored virtues and vices that critically influences the informant's judgment. Using this approach, a number of troublesome cases in the literature have been handled adequately; that is, the theory predicts the sorts of intuitions that philosophers actually experience (see Goldman 1992b).

Epistemologists familiar with the earlier paper might recall that the theory was billed as a new and improved version of reliabilism. But our present formulation of it has not even mentioned considerations of reliability. Where, if at all, does reliability enter the picture? On the present proposal, reliability would enter the picture at the *historical rationale* phase. In other words, we postulate that the linguistic community has identified certain epistemic sources as virtues and other epistemic sources as vices because the community judges the former to be generally reliable (i.e., conducive to truth) and the latter to be generally unreliable. Thus, reliability is the benchmark used for discriminating among approved and disapproved epistemic sources. This benchmark, however, is not represented or utilized by ordinary wielders of the concept of justification. They may only represent the types of sources themselves. Thus, we get a sort of two-stage reliabilism, in which reliability plays a role only in determining virtuous and vicious sources, not in directly deciding which beliefs are justified or unjustified. There is a close parallel here with what we might call descriptive rule utilitarianism. Such a descriptive theory would say that, historically, types of actions like honesty and dishonesty were denominated right and wrong respectively because of their utilitarian consequences. When ordinary agents imbibe moral culture, they need not learn the distinguishing criterion, but only the list of action types that are right or wrong. Newly contemplated courses of action are judged right or wrong by comparing them for similarity with the act-types antecedently stored as moral virtues or vices. Although we do not endorse descriptive rule utilitarianism, we find the two-stage hypothesis very congenial. This same two-stage sort of theory strikes us as attractive in the epistemic domain as well.

The mentalist approach to philosophical analysis is bound to encounter criticism, perhaps the same line of criticism that has been leveled against the epistemological theories outlined above. Certain critics claim, in effect, that the proposals are not genuine epistemological theories because they do not explain the nature of epistemic justification or knowledge. Ernest Sosa (1993) raises this issue when he claims that the "exemplar" approach to justification

> gives us an account of how an evaluator properly goes about evaluating a belief as justified. . . . But it does not tell us . . . what is involved in a belief's being epistemically justified—*not just what is involved in an evaluator's evaluating it as justified, n.b., but what would be involved in its actually being justified.* (Sosa 1993: 61, emphasis in original)

The objection suggested by this passage is developed at greater length by Peter Markie (1996). Markie claims that the mentalist account of our judgments of justification does not offer any explanation of what *makes* a belief justified or a process justification conferring. Instead, it offers us only a psychological hypothesis about how people make epistemic judgments, about how they come to classify beliefs into epistemological categories. For this reason, Markie claims that the mentalist version of the reliability theory of justification is perfectly consistent with positions usually thought opposed to reliabilism. This is, he alleges, because the current proposal is merely a psychological hypothesis about the mechanisms by which people categorize beliefs. It is not, as philosophical theories of justification are, an account of what makes a belief justified. The general position advocated by these critics seems to be that people's beliefs about justification or their concept thereof (in the mentalist's sense of "concept") are an entirely separate matter from the nature of justified belief, what really constitutes justified belief.[12] The claim of these critics, then is that mentalist theories simply do not answer the *philosophical* question that they ought to answer. Such a theory ought to explain what justification *is*, not how people decide whether something merits the appellation "justified."

Our response is twofold. First, the charge seems, at least on one reading, incorrect. The mentalist does offer an account of what makes a belief justified. The mentalist claims that what makes a belief justified is possession of those properties by virtue of which a deployer of the justification concept, who is aware of all relevant properties of the target belief, would classify it as justified. An account of exactly what those properties are is the very thing that a developed mentalist proposal will provide. If, for example, the concept of justified belief really does consist in a list of belief-producing sources, then what *makes* a belief justified is the fact that it is produced by one or more of those sources (or sufficiently similar ones). In other words, to *be* justified simply *is* to be produced by some such processes.[13]

Second, the charge of philosophical irrelevance is clearly motivated by extramentalism of some kind, for example, the natural kinds approach. The charge rests on a distinction between the real nature of justified belief and our psychological concept of justified belief. Because extra-mentalism claims that the object of philosophical inquiry is a nonpsychological object, it may appeal to such a distinction. Undoubtedly there is a distinction between the psychological concept of water and the real nature of water. Thus, an account of our concept of water would not necessarily be a correct account of the independent entity. But we have argued that the natural kinds approach is an inappropriate account of many of the targets of philosophical analysis. So, while we are aware that some may be dissatisfied with the modesty of the aims of mentalist methodology,[14] it seems to us to be a coherent project with a clear story to tell about how intuitions serve as evidence for the kinds of theories it proposes.[15] Unlike the extra-mentalist approaches we have surveyed, mentalism makes good sense of the standard methodology of philosophical analysis.

Notes

Pust's contribution to this paper is drawn from his work-in-progress on a doctoral dissertation, "Intuitions as Evidence," at the University of Arizona. For helpful discussion of earlier drafts of this paper, we thank Michael Bergmann, Chris Daly, John Armstrong, and discussants at the Notre Dame conference on intuitions and a University of Arizona colloquium.

1. A clear contemporary proponent of this view is George Bealer. See especially Bealer (1996a).

2. We formulate (RI) as a necessary condition rather than a necessary-and-sufficient condition because, among other things, mere de facto reliability may be insufficient to qualify a class of states as a basic evidential source (cf. Bealer 1996a). We do not wish to try to settle this issue here. Stating (RI) as a necessary condition leaves the question of sufficiency open.

3. In Goldman (1977) perceptual modalities are characterized partly in terms of counterfactual dependences.

4. General principles may also be included among the propositional contents of intuitions, for example, the principle that knowledge is closed under known entailment. We concentrate on singular propositional contents, however, because they are most intensively used in philosophical practice.

5. Our approach obviously takes *intuitings* that p to be (prima facie) evidence, or data, in philosophical methodology. How, then, do we respond to a philosopher like Lycan (1988) who insists that the *intuiteds* (that is, the propositions intuited) not the intuitings, are the philosophical "data"? We find Lycan's approach unconvincing because the intuited propositions per se have no evidential weight. Why should those propositions, rather than the many contrary propositions that are not intuited, have special evidential weight? Clearly, what gives a proposition evidential force is *being intuited*. Evidential force arises from the fact that an intuiting is a sort of mental state that reliably indicates (in favorable circumstances) its content's truth. Thus, it must be the intuiting of p that is the crucial datum, not the intuited proposition p per se.

6. The second predicate must also be "better understood" in some sense. This poses issues about the paradox of analysis that we shall not address here.

7. More generally, the target of philosophical analysis may be a (tacit) folk *scheme* or folk *theory*, not just a folk *concept*; the psychological unit, in other

words, may be larger than that of a concept. Our discussion will proceed, however, in terms of concepts.

8. We do not believe that all concepts are so closely tied to language, but those of interest to philosophical analysis are so tied.

9. Our approach also seems to comport with Peacocke (1992).

10. This is not meant to imply that intuition is a basic evidential source for propositions about mathematics, logic, or the like. We remain noncommittal on these domains, especially since their contents may not lend themselves to a mentalist interpretation. Our thesis only concerns the prospects of intuition vis-à-vis singular classificational propositions of the kind illustrated.

11. We shall not speculate about which predicates are likely to have interpersonally shared contents.

12. This objection seems to be a direct descendant of earlier philosophical criticisms of psychological accounts of concepts. Georges Rey (1983, 1985), for example, has charged that many psychological accounts of concepts tend to confuse metaphysical issues with epistemological or psychological ones. Rey notes that the term 'categorization' can refer to how things in the world are correctly classified or to how people engage in the process of classification—correctly or incorrectly. An account of the former is the task of the nonpsychological sciences and an account of the latter is the task of psychology. Since the proper account of concepts in the metaphysical sense is provided by the portion of science that deals with the kind in question, commonsense beliefs or intuitions about X are irrelevant to the nature of X. This distinction and the accompanying division of labor seems to be behind Sosa's and Markie's criticism. It should be noted that this proposed distinction is quite acceptable to most psychologists, even if they profess interest only in the nonmetaphysical issues. Edward Smith (1989), for example, endorses the distinction in language matching Markie's objection when he claims that "a metaphysical categorization considers what *makes* an entity an instance of a particular kind, whereas an epistemological categorization considers *how an agent decides* whether the entity is of a particular kind" (Smith 1989: 57, emphasis added).

13. Where the analyzed concept is revealed to be highly contextualist, however, this straightforward answer to the critic will not be available. But where a concept is highly contextualist, no straightforward answer can reasonably be expected.

14. One of us, Pust, counts himself as not yet fully satisfied.

15. Other critics have conceded the coherence of the mentalist project but found it to be of very little interest. Stephen Stich (1990), for example, asks why anyone genuinely concerned about how they ought to form beliefs should care about the folk concept of justified belief. Our distinction between a concept's content and its rationale may provide some answer to Stich's query. (For another set of answers, see Markie [forthcoming].) Although there is no guarantee that we will reflectively value forming beliefs in the ways deemed justified by the folk, there seems little doubt, pace Stich, that the historical rationale behind the folk concept, namely, true belief formation, retains its power to move us. Even if our current list of sources is an imperfect realization of the historical rationale, there is always room to revise and improve that list in accordance with the historical desideratum, which continues to attract us.

Part III

Defending the Philosophical Tradition

Chapter 12

Intuition and the Autonomy of Philosophy

George Bealer

What is the relation between science and philosophy? I hold that philosophy is in principle autonomous. When one understands what is intended by this, one will see that the claim is modest and that there are good reasons for accepting it. The view consists of two theses:

The Autonomy of Philosophy
Among the central questions of philosophy that can be answered by one standard theoretical means or another, most can in principle be answered by philosophical investigation and argument without relying substantively on the sciences.

The Authority of Philosophy
Insofar as science and philosophy purport to answer the same central philosophical questions, in most cases the support that science could in principle provide for those answers is not as strong as that which philosophy could in principle provide for its answers. So, should there be conflicts, the authority of philosophy in most cases can be greater in principle.

These theses are *modal* claims; they posit only the *possibility* of autonomous and authoritative philosophical knowledge, perhaps on the part of creatures in cognitive conditions superior to ours. To refute these theses, one must show that this sort of knowledge is *impossible*. Bear in mind just how hard it is to show something to be *impossible*. After all, impossibility claims are equivalent to necessity claims: it is impossible that P iff it is necessary that not P. To show that something substantive is necessary, one must engage in at least some philosophical argumentation. The Autonomy and Authority theses are thus not matters for science to decide. They are philosophical questions and, I believe, demand philosophical methods for their resolution. In my view, much of the project is a conceptual investigation—investigation of the concepts of intuition (the topic of this book), evidence, concept possession, and so forth. The epistemic status of this conceptual investigation is akin to the classic conceptual investigation of effective calculability (or computability) in the 1930s. It would be a misunderstanding to think of the latter as empirical. Likewise for the Autonomy and Authority theses. One might be unhappy with these theses, but they flow from the concepts, as our conceptual investigation will reveal. Once one has accepted the concepts, one is committed to accepting the relations among them.

Intuition is the key to the defense of the Autonomy and Authority theses. From the logical and semantical paradoxes we know that intuition can be mistaken. So the (early modern) infallibilist theory of intuition is incorrect. But, despite their fallibility, intuitions on my view nevertheless have a certain kind of strong modal tie to the truth. This tie is not "local," however, since individual intuitions can be mistaken. Nor is the tie an ordinary holistic tie: I accept the possibility that some hypothetical subject's best efforts at the theoretical systematization of his intuitions might be mistaken. Rather, the tie is relativized; specifically, it is relativized to theoretical systematizations arrived at in relevantly high quality cognitive conditions. Such conditions might be beyond what individual human beings can achieve in isolation. It is plausible that we approximate such cognitive conditions only in sustained cooperation with others, perhaps over generations. And even here, it is an open question whether we will ever approximate them sufficiently closely.

In section I, I will try to clarify the notion of intuition which is evidentially relevant to philosophical argumentation. Many philosophers enjoy the pastime of "intuition bashing," and in support of it they are fond of invoking the empirical findings of cognitive psychologists.[1] Although these studies evidently bear on "intuition" in a less discriminating use of the term (e.g., as a term for uncritical belief), they tell us little about intuition in the relevant sense. When empirical cognitive psychology turns its attention to intuition in this sense, it will be no surprise if it should reveal that a subject's intuitions can be fallible locally. From the paradoxes, we already knew that they were. Nor will it be a great surprise if more sustained empirical studies should uncover evidence that a subject's intuitions can be fallible in a more holistic way. Countless works taken from the history of logic, mathematics, and philosophy already give some indication that this might be so. Will empirical studies reveal that intuitions lack the strong modal tie to the truth that I mentioned a moment ago? Surely such a discovery is out of the question. Human beings only approximate the relevant cognitive conditions, and they do this only by working collectively over historical time. This quest is something we are living through as an intellectual culture. Our efforts have never even reached equilibrium and perhaps never will. The very idea of our conducting an empirical test (i.e., a psychology experiment) for the hypothesized tie to the truth is misconceived. Moreover, even if our intellectual culture were always to fail, that would not refute the thesis of a strong modal tie. The cognitive conditions of human beings working collectively over historical time might fall short. The thesis that intuitions have the indicated strong modal tie to the truth is a philosophical (conceptual) thesis not open to empirical confirmation or refutation. The defense of it is philosophical, ultimately resting on intuitions.[2]

Some people might accept that the strong modal tie thesis about intuition— and the associated Authority and Autonomy theses—are nonempirical but hold that they do nothing to clarify the relation between science and philosophy as practiced by *human beings*. After all, these theses yield only the possibility of autonomous, authoritative philosophical knowledge on the part of creatures whose cognitive conditions are suitably good. What could this possibility have to do with the question of the relation between science and philosophy as actually practiced by us?

The answer is this. The investigation of the key concepts—intuition, evidence, concept possession—establish the possibility of autonomous, authoritative philosophical knowledge on the part of creatures in those ideal cognitive conditions. The same concepts, however, are essential to characterizing our own psychological and epistemic situation (and, indeed, that of any epistemic agent). The relation between science and philosophy in our own case is to be understood in terms of how we depart from the cognitive ideal: to the extent that we approximate the ideal, we are able to approximate autonomous, authoritative philosophical knowledge. I believe that, *collectively, over historical time, undertaking philosophy as a civilization-wide project*, we can obtain authoritative answers to a wide variety of central philosophical questions.

There are two largely independent defenses of the Autonomy and Authority of Philosophy—the Argument from Evidence and the Argument from Concepts. These two arguments correspond directly to the two central questions of modern epistemology, namely, the ground of knowledge of truths and the origin of ideas. The Argument from Evidence (the topic of section II) runs as follows. Intuitions qualify as evidence, and the correct explanation of this fact is that intuitions have a strong (albeit indirect and fallible) tie to the truth when the subjects are in suitably good cognitive conditions. That tie to the truth is sufficient to underwrite the Authority and Autonomy theses. The Argument from Concepts (the topic of section III) consists of a series of examples and subsidiary arguments leading up to an analysis of what it is to possess a concept determinately. According to the analysis, it is constitutive of determinate concept possession that in suitably good cognitive conditions intuitions regarding the behavior of the concept have a strong tie to the truth. Given that most philosophically central concepts can be possessed determinately, the potential for associated intuitions is sufficient to underwrite the Autonomy and Authority of Philosophy.[3]

Before beginning, I should indicate what I mean by the central questions of philosophy. Nearly all philosophers seek answers to such questions as the nature of substance, mind, intelligence, consciousness, sensation, perception, knowledge, wisdom, truth, identity, infinity, divinity, time, explanation, causation, freedom, purpose, goodness, duty, the virtues, love, life, happiness, and so forth. When we think of the sorts of things that would qualify as answers to questions of this sort, three features stand out—universality, generality, and necessity.

The questions of philosophy are universal in the sense that, regardless of the biological, psychological, sociological, or historical context, they (and their answers) would be of significant interest to most any philosopher, *qua* philosopher (at least once they had been introduced to the underlying concepts and their basic relations to one another). These questions are general in the sense that they—and their answers—do not pertain to this or that individual, species, or historical event. Typically, the central questions of philosophy—and their answers—are phrased in quite general terms without mention of particular individuals, species, and so forth. These questions are necessary in the sense that they call for answers that hold necessarily. In being interested in such things as the nature of mind, intelligence, the virtues, and life, philosophers do not want to know what those things just happen to be, but rather what those things *must* be, what they *are* in a strong sense. It is not enough that the virtue of piety happened to be what Euthyphro exhibited: a philosopher wants to know what piety must be.

Many philosophical questions that are of pressing importance to humanity lack one or more of the three features—universality, generality, and necessity. Nevertheless, the relation between central and noncentral philosophical propositions (truths, questions) may, I believe, be understood on analogy with the relation between pure mathematics and applied mathematics. In most if not all cases, noncentral philosophical propositions are immediate consequences of central philosophical propositions plus auxiliary propositions that have little philosophical content in and of themselves. In actual practice, of course, various philosophical questions do not fit so neatly into this picture, but I think that in principle they can be made to fit. Or so I will assume.

I. Intuition

Standard Justificatory Procedure

I begin by reviewing some plain truths about the procedure we standardly use to justify our beliefs and theories generally.[4] The first point is that we standardly use various items—for example, experiences, observations, testimony—as evidence for other items, for example, theories. It should be emphasized that one does not need to adopt "evidentialism" as an *analysis* of knowledge—or of justification or warrant—in order to think that evidence is a good thing epistemically. A theory of evidence does not commit one to holding that knowledge—or justification or warrant—is to be analyzed in terms of evidence. It is also worth emphasizing that evidence—as opposed to justification and warrant—is a topic not yet examined carefully in the epistemological literature, though it has been examined to some extent by philosophers of science.

Now at one time many people accepted the traditional doctrine that knowledge is justified true belief. But now we have good evidence that this is mistaken. Suppose someone has been driving for miles past what look like herds of sheep. At various points along the journey, our person *believes* that a sheep is in the pasture. Since the situation appears to be perfectly normal in all relevant respects, certainly the person is *justified* in believing that there is a sheep in the pasture. Suppose that it is indeed *true* that there is a sheep in the pasture. Is this enough for knowledge? No. For suppose that the thousands of sheep-looking things the person has been seeing are a breed of white poodle that from that distance look just like sheep and that, by pure chance, there happens to be a solitary sheep hidden in the middle of the acres of poodles. Clearly, the person does not know that there is a sheep in the pasture. (This example is adapted from Goldman 1976.) Examples like this provide good evidence that the traditional theory is mistaken. We find it intuitively obvious that there could be a situation like that described and in such a situation the person would not know that there is a sheep in the pasture despite having a justified true belief. This intuition—that there could be such a situation and in it the person would not know—and other intuitions like it are our evidence that the traditional theory is mistaken.

So, according to our standard justificatory procedure, *intuitions* are used as evidence. Now sometimes in using intuitions to justify various conclusions, it is somewhat more natural to call them *reasons* rather than *evidence*. For example, my reasons for accepting that a certain statement is logically true are these: it follows intuitively from certain more elementary statements that intuitively are logically true; I have clear intuitions that it follows, and I have clear intuitions that these more elementary statements are logically valid. Standardly, we say that intuitions like these are *evident* (at least prima facie). For convenience of exposition let us extend the term 'evidence' to include reasons that are evident in this way.[5] So in this terminology, the standard justificatory procedure counts as evidence, not only experiences, observations, and testimony, but also intuitions. It shall be clear that this terminological extension does not bias our discussion. Readers who object to this practice should hereafter read 'evidence' as 'reasons that are evident'.

When I say that intuitions are used as evidence, I of course mean that the *contents* of the intuitions count as evidence. When one has an intuition, however, often one is introspectively aware that one is having that intuition. On such an occasion, one would then have a bit of introspective evidence as well, namely, that one is having that intuition. Consider an example. I am presently intuiting that if P then not not P. Accordingly, the content of this intuition—that if P then not not P—counts as a bit of my evidence; I may use this logical proposition as evidence (as a reason) for various other things. In addition to having the indicated intuition, I am also introspectively aware of having the intuition. Accordingly, the content of this introspection—that I am having the intuition that if P then not not P—also counts as a bit of my evidence; I may use this proposition about my intellectual state as evidence (as a reason) for various other things.

To see the prevalence of the use of intuitions in philosophy, recall some standard examples beyond the above Gettier-style examples: Chisholm's abnormal-conditions refutation of phenomenalism, Chisholm's and Putnam's refutations of behaviorism, the use of multiple-realizability in refuting narrow identity theses, the Twin-Earth arguments for a posteriori necessities and externalism in mental content, Burge's arthritis argument for antiindividualism in mental content, Jackson's Mary example, and so on. Each of these involve intuitions about certain possibilities and about whether relevant concepts would apply to them. It is safe to say that these intuitions—and conclusions based on them—determine the structure of contemporary debates in epistemology and philosophy of mind. As these examples illustrate, it is intuitions about concrete cases that are accorded primary evidential weight by our standard justificatory procedure; theoretical intuitions are by comparison given far less evidential weight.

Philosophical investigation and argument approximate the following idealization: canvassing intuitions, subjecting those intuitions to dialectical critique, constructing theories that systematize the surviving intuitions, testing those theories against further intuitions, and so on until equilibrium is approached.

This procedure resembles the procedure of seeking "reflective equilibrium" but differs from it crucially. In the latter procedure, an equilibrium among beliefs—including empirical beliefs—is sought. In the present procedure, an equilibrium among intuitions is sought. (See the next subsection for the difference between beliefs and intuitions.) Empirical beliefs—and the experiences and observations upon which they are based—are sometime used to raise and to resolve doubts about the quality of the background cognitive conditions (intelligence, attentiveness, constancy, memory, etc.). But these empirical resources are not inputs for the procedure itself; intuitions—not empirical beliefs—constitute the grist for its mill. When I speak of not needing to rely *substantively* on empirical science, this is one of the points I have in mind. As indicated, the foregoing is an idealization. In real life, these stages are pursued concurrently, and they are performed only partially. The results are usually provisional and are used as "feedback" to guide subsequent efforts. Moreover, these efforts are typically collective, and the results of past efforts—including those of past generations—are used liberally. Speech and writing are standardly used. In this connection, phenomenal experience and observation are sometimes used to raise—and also to resolve—doubts about the quality of the communication conditions (speaker and author sincerity, reliability of the medium of transmission, accuracy of interpretation, etc.). But these empirical resources are not inputs for the procedure itself. When I speak of not needing to rely substantively on empirical science, this is another one of the points I have in mind.

Perhaps the most important departure from this idealization is that in seeking answers to central philosophical questions, we also make fairly frequent use of empirical evidence—specifically, we invoke actual "real-life" examples and actual examples from (the history of) science. In virtually all cases, however, use of such examples can be "modalized away." That is, such examples can, at least in principle, be dropped and in their place one can use *rational* intuitions affirming corresponding (not to say identical) *possibilities* that have equivalent philosophical force. (I defend this claim in Bealer 1996b.) Consider the example of blind-sight. We have actual cases of subjects with accurate beliefs regarding objects in their physical visual field but without (beliefs about) any conscious sensory awareness of those objects. But for the purpose of settling central questions of philosophy (e.g., about the essential nature of consciousness and sense perception), it is enough that the phenomenon of blind-sight be *possible*. And intuitively it is. The experiments are required to establish that it *actually* occurs; but to establish that it is *possible*, intuition suffices.

Certain phenomenological possibilities might constitute an exception to the idea of "modalizing away" empirical evidence: perhaps for certain kinds of experience (e.g., certain Gestalt phenomena), the actual experience is required in order to know that that kind of experience is possible. If so, this would not upset my main theses. The reason is that this use of experience differs markedly from the use science makes of experience. When I say that philosophy need not rely substantively on science, one of my intentions is to allow this use of experiences to establish mere phenomenological possibilities. Although this point is important, I will not address it further in this chapter; indeed, at certain points I will talk as if the method needed to establish answers to central philosophical questions is nothing but a special case of the method of pure a priori justification. For the indicated reason, this might not be quite right, and appropriate adjustments would need to be made.[6]

Phenomenology of Intuitions

My next step is to discuss the notion of intuition relevant to the context of justification in logic, mathematics, and philosophy. We do not mean a magical power or inner voice or special glow or any other mysterious quality. When you have an intuition that A, it *seems* to you that A. Here 'seems' is understood, not in its use as a cautionary or "hedging" term, but in its use as a term for a genuine kind of conscious episode. For example, when you first consider one of de Morgan's laws, often it neither seems true nor seems false; after a moment's reflection, however, something happens: it now just seems true. The view I will defend is that intuition (this type of seeming) is a sui generis, irreducible, natural (i.e., non-Cambridge-like) propositional attitude that occurs episodically.

When we speak here of intuition, we mean "rational intuition." This is distinguished from what physicists call "physical intuition." We have a physical intuition that, when a house is undermined, it will fall. This does not count as a rational intuition, for it does not present itself as necessary: it does not seem that a house undermined *must* fall; plainly, it is *possible* for a house undermined to remain in its original position or, indeed, to rise up. By contrast, when we have a rational intuition—say, that if P then not not P—it presents itself as necessary: it does not seem to us that things could be otherwise; it must be that if P then not not P. (I am unsure how exactly to analyze what is meant by saying that a rational intuition presents itself as necessary. Perhaps something like this: necessarily, if x intuits that P, it seems to x that P and also that necessarily P. But I wish to take no stand on this.)

The distinction between rational intuition and physical intuition is related to a terminological point. In recent philosophy there has been an unfortunate blurring of traditional terminology. Rational intuitions about hypothetical cases are often being erroneously called *thought experiments*. This deviates from traditional use, and it blurs an important distinction that we should keep vividly in mind. Traditionally, in a thought experiment one usually elicits a physical intuition (not a rational intuition) about what would happen in a hypothetical situation in which physical, or natural, laws (whatever they happen to be) are held constant but physical conditions are in various other respects nonactual and often highly idealized (e.g., so that it would be physically impossible for observers to be present or it would be physically impossible for anyone to conduct the experiment). A classic example is Newton's thought experiment about a rotating bucket in an otherwise empty space. Would water creep up the side of the bucket (assuming that the physical laws remained unchanged)? Rational intuition is silent about this sort of question. Rational intuitions concern such matters as whether a case is possible (logically or metaphysically), and about whether a concept applies to such cases. For example, in the Gettier example we have a rational intuition that the case is possible, and we have a rational intuition that the concept of knowledge would not apply to the person in the case. In Tyler

Burge's arthritis case, we have a rational intuition that the example is possible and a rational intuition that in the example the patient would believe that he has arthritis in his thigh. Similarly, in Putnam's Twin-Earth example. None of these are thought experiments in the traditional sense; to call them thought experiments is, not only to invite confusion about philosophical method, but to destroy the utility of a once useful term.

Intuition must be distinguished from belief—belief is not a seeming; intuition is. For example, there are many mathematical theorems that I believe (because I have seen the proofs) but that do not *seem* to me to be true and that do not *seem* to me to be false; I do not have intuitions about them either way. Conversely, I have an intuition—it still *seems* to me—that the naive comprehension axiom of set theory is true; this is so despite the fact that I do not believe that it is true (because I know of the set-theoretical paradoxes).[7] There is a rather similar phenomenon in sense perception. In the Müller-Lyer illusion, it still *seems* to me that one of the two arrows is longer than the other; this is so despite the fact that I do not believe that one of the two arrows is longer (because I have measured them). In each case, the seeming persists in spite of the countervailing belief.

Of course, one must not confuse intuition with sense perception. Intuition is an *intellectual* seeming; sense perception is a *sensory* seeming (an *appearing*). By and large, the two cannot overlap: most things that can seem intellectually to be so cannot seem sensorily to be so, and conversely. For example, it cannot seem to you sensorily that the naive comprehension axiom holds. Nor can it seem to you intellectually (i.e., without any relevant sensations and without any attendant beliefs) that there exist billions of brain cells; intuition is silent about this essentially empirical question. There are, however, certain special cases in which intellectual seeming and sensory seeming can evidently overlap. For example, it can seem sensorily that shades S_1 and S_2 are different, and it can seem intellectually that S_1 and S_2 are different. Nevertheless, if it is possible for someone to have the intuition that A (i.e., if it is possible for it to seem intellectually to someone that A), typically it is possible for someone to have the intuition that A while believing that not A (or, at least, doubting that it is true that A) and while having no particular experiences, sensory (imaginative) or reflective, relevant to the truth of the proposition that A.

This brings up a closely related distinction between belief and intuition. Belief is highly plastic; not so for intuition. For nearly any proposition about which you have beliefs, authority, cajoling, intimidation, and so forth can, fairly readily, insinuate at least some doubt and thereby diminish to some extent, perhaps only briefly, the strength of your belief. But seldom, if ever, do these things so readily diminish the strength of your intuitions. Just try to diminish readily your intuition of the naive comprehension axiom or your intuition that your favorite Gettier example could occur. Although there is disagreement about the degree of plasticity of intuitions (some people believe they are rather plastic; I do not), it is clear that, as a family, they are inherently more resistant to such influences than are the associated beliefs.

It might be thought that intuition can be reduced to some sort of spontaneous inclination to belief.[8] There are counterexamples to such a reduction, however.

As I am writing this, I have spontaneous inclinations to believe countless things about, say, numbers. But at this very moment I am having *no* intuition about numbers. I am trying to write, and this is about all I can do at once; my mind is full. If I am to have an intuition about numbers, then above and beyond a mere inclination, something else must happen—a sui generis cognitive episode must occur. Inclinations to believe are simply not episodic in this way. For another sort of counterexample, consider a posteriori necessities that (on the received theory) lie beyond the reach of our rational intuition: for example, that gold has atomic number 79, that heat involves microscopic motion, and so forth. Presumably, by suitably modifying the brain we could cause a subject to acquire the sort of spontaneous inclination featured in the proposed reduction. We could, for example, cause someone to have a spontaneous inclination to believe that gold has atomic number 79. (Such inclinations would be akin to the sort of irrational inclinations posited by some social theorists, for example, "hardwired" inclinations to believe that other races are inferior.) Likewise for other a posteriori necessities. But the person still would not be able to intuit these necessities, for in that case they would be a priori, not a posteriori, as everyone takes them to be.

On another reductionist approach, intuitions are identified with a "raising-to-consciousness" of nonconscious background beliefs.[9] This proposal, however, has a number of problems. Suppose that, out of the blue, you ask me whether the naive comprehension axiom and the axioms and rules of classical logic all hold. I would thereupon have the conscious belief that they do *not* all hold. A plausible explanation is that, having studied the paradoxes in the past, I reached the conclusion that these cannot all hold, and that conclusion became one of my standing background beliefs. Upon being questioned just now, this negative background belief was then raised to consciousness. Thus, the proposal helps to explain certain conscious beliefs. But what about intuition? I have intuitions to the effect that the naive comprehension axiom plus the axioms and rules of classical logic *do* all hold. These positive intuitions would be explained on the proposed raising-to-consciousness model only if I also had associated positive background beliefs to that effect. But in that case, these positive background beliefs would have to be in *explicit contradiction* to another one of my background beliefs (namely, that the indicated principles do *not* all hold). More importantly, if my positive intuitions were explained by the supposed positive background beliefs, then given that I also have the associated negative background belief (that the indicated principles do *not* all hold), I ought, by symmetry, also have the intuition that the indicated principles do *not* all hold. But I have no such intuition, nor am I disposed to have one. In the same vein, given my educational background, I have a host of nonconscious background beliefs regarding various mathematical theorems about which I am not disposed to have any intuitions. Likewise, I have a host of nonconscious background beliefs regarding contingent matters (e.g., that I was not born on Mars) about which I am not disposed to have any intuitions.

The proposal also runs into problems with the phenomenon of novelty. At any given time, there are a number of novel questions about which one has no belief one way or the other (even a nonconscious background belief) but about which one would have a clear-cut intuition. In cases like this, one typically forms the belief associated with the intuition as soon as the intuition occurs; not the other way around. Here is an example. Consider average twenty-year-old college students with no background in logic,˙ linguistics, or philosophy. *At least according to our standard belief ascription practices*, we would not say that they right now believe that there are two readings of 'Necessarily, the number of planets is greater than seven', one on which it is false and one on which it is true given that there are nine planets. Nor would we say that they have the contrary belief. They have no nonconscious background belief one way or the other regarding this question. When they come to your lecture dealing with this, they are going to acquire new beliefs, not raise to consciousness ones they already had.[10] This at least is what our standard belief ascription practice dictates. Now suppose we confront them with the question. After some reflection, the good students come to see both readings; they have the intuitions. And therewith—not before—they come to have the associated beliefs. The conclusion is that intuition may not be identified with (or explained in terms of) a raising-to-consciousness of nonconscious background beliefs. None of this is to say that there are no nonconscious mechanisms that play some role in the formation of intuitions. (We will return to this idea in a moment.) The point is that intuition is not in any simple way the manifestation of one's background beliefs.

Intuitions are also quite distinct from judgments, guesses, and hunches. There are significant restrictions on the propositions concerning which we are able to have intuitions. By contrast, there are virtually no restrictions on what we can judge, guess, or have a hunch about. Judgments are a kind of occurrent belief; as such, they are not seemings. Guesses are phenomenologically rather more like choices; they are plainly not seemings. And hunches are akin to merely caused, ungrounded convictions or noninferential beliefs; they too are not seemings. For example, suppose that during an examination in beginning logic, a student is asked whether the following is a logical truth: if P or Q, then it is not the case that both not P and not Q. The student might have a hunch that it is. But something else could happen: it could actually *seem* to the student that it is. Phenomenologically, this kind of episode is quite distinct from a mere hunch. Or suppose that I ask you whether the coin is in my right hand or whether it is in my left. You might have a hunch that it is in my left hand, but it does not *seem* to you that it is. You have no intellectual episode in which it seems to you that I have a coin in my left hand. When I show you that it is in my right hand, you no longer have a hunch that it is in my left. Your merely caused, ungrounded conviction (noninferential belief) is automatically overridden by the grounded belief that it is in my right hand, and it is thereby displaced. Not so for seemings, intellectual or sensory: they are not automatically displaced by grounded contrary beliefs. (Recall the naive comprehension axiom and the Müller-Lyer arrows.)

Many items that are, somewhat carelessly, called intuitions in casual discourse in logic, mathematics, linguistics, or philosophy are really only a certain sort of memory. For example, it does not *seem* to me that $25^2 = 625$; this is something I learned from calculation or a table. Note how this differs, phenomenologically, from what happens when one has an intuition. After a moment's reflection on the question, it just *seems* to you that, if P or Q, then it is not the case that both not P and not Q. Likewise, upon considering the example described earlier, it just *seems* to you that the person in the example would not know that there is a sheep in the pasture. Nothing comparable happens in the case of the proposition that $25^2 = 625$.

For similar reasons, intuition must also be distinguished from common sense. True, most elementary intuitions are commonsensical. However, a great many intuitions do not qualify as commonsensical—just because they are non-elementary. For example, intuitions about mathematical limits, the infinite divisibility of space and time, the axiom of choice, and so forth are hardly commonsensical. Conversely, we often lack intuitions (i.e., rational intuitions) about matters that are highly commonsensical. For example, the following propositions are commonsensical: a house undermined will fall; items priced substantially below market value are likely to be defective; it is unwise to put your finger in electrical sockets. But rational intuition is silent about these matters. Such considerations suggest that common sense is an amalgamation: widely shared, more or less useful empirical beliefs; practical wisdom; rational intuitions; and physical intuitions. Common sense certainly cannot be *identified* with rational intuition.

Some philosophers identify all intuitions with linguistic intuitions. But this is plainly wrong if by 'linguistic intuition' they mean intuitions about words (e.g., English words) and their application. A moment's reflection reveals what is wrong with this idea: most of our intuitions simply do not have any linguistic content. Consider your intuition that, if snow is white, then it is not the case that snow is not white, or consider your intuition that the person in the sheep example would not know there is a sheep in the pasture. These intuitions simply do not concern English words and their applicability. The point can be dramatized by the fact that non-English speakers have these intuitions, whereas non-English speakers do not have intuitions about English words and their applicability. (This is not to say that there is not an intimate tie between linguistic intuitions and certain classes of nonlinguistic intuitions, but that is an altogether different matter.)

Some philosophers think of intuitions, not as linguistic intuitions, but instead as conceptual intuitions. Nothing is wrong with this if 'conceptual intuition' is understood broadly enough. But there is a common construal—traceable to Hume's notion of relations of ideas and popular with logical positivists—according to which conceptual intuitions are all analytic (in the traditional sense of conceptual containment, or truth by definition plus logic, or convertibility into logical truths by substitution of synonyms). (Of course, the onus is on philosophers who accept this view to clarify what they mean by 'analytic'.) But this theory of intuition is quite mistaken, for countless intuitions cannot be counted as analytic (on the traditional construals).[11] For example, the intuition that phenomenal colors are incompatible, that moral and aesthetic facts supervene on the (totality of) physical and psychological facts, that a given determinate (e.g., a particular phenomenal shade) falls under its determinables (e.g., being a phenomenal shade), that the part/whole relation is transitive over the field of regions, or that congruence is a symmetric relation.

Possibility intuitions are another extremely important class of intuitions which are not analytic (on the traditional construals of the term). (E.g., the intuition that the Gettier examples are possible, etc.) True, some philosophers have claimed that possibility intuitions are just intuitions of consistency. This would be reasonable if possibility were just consistency: since the proposition that p is consistent is traditionally counted as analytic, the proposition that p is possible would be analytic as well. But there are compelling objections to identifying possibility with consistency. First, all the other traditional examples of nonanalytic impossibilities (e.g., compatible but distinct phenomenal colors; nonsupervening aesthetic facts; nonreflexive congruence relations; etc.) would still be erroneously counted as possible according to the proposal. Furthermore, if by 'consistency' one means freedom from provable contradiction (relative to a formal system), Gödel's incompleteness theorem refutes the identification of possibility with consistency: no contradiction can be proved either from the Gödel self-unprovability sentence (relative to the formal system) or from its negation, but one of these two sentences expresses an impossibility.[12] Finally, since scientific essentialist impossibilities (e.g., that water contains no hydrogen, that gold is a compound, etc.) are consistent (on the prominent construals of consistency), they would erroneously be counted as possible according to the proposal.[13] Clearly, possibility intuitions cannot be identified with consistency intuitions. This point is extremely important to philosophical method, for the typical philosophical counterexample requires a possibility intuition (that such and such condition is possible) as well as an ordinary concept-applicability intuition (that in such and such situation a relevant item would, or would not, count as an F). Without possibility intuitions, philosophy would be fatally crippled.[14]

This is perhaps the place to note that, phenomenologically, there is no relevant difference between analytic and nonanalytic intuitions. Consider two transitivity intuitions: (1) the intuition that, if spatial region x is part of spatial region y and spatial region y is part of spatial region z, then spatial region x is part of spatial region z; (2) the intuition that, if biological organism x is a descendant of biological organism y and biological organism y is a descendant of biological organism z, then biological organism x is a descendant of biological organism z. There is no relevant phenomenological difference between these two transitivity intuitions despite the fact that the former would traditionally be counted as synthetic and the latter would be counted as analytic (insofar as it is a consequence of a standard definition). Nor is there any relevant "formal" difference between these two intuitions. These facts should give pause to "Humean empiricists" who would attribute evidential force to our analytic intuitions but not our synthetic intuitions: for the question of whether a given intuition is analytic or synthetic is a theoretical question that cannot be settled until late in one's philosophical investigation. The only cogent way to proceed is to admit all intuitions as evidence, at least provisionally. (I should note that this is only one of many serious problems facing "Humean empiricism.")

Earlier we considered a proposal to reduce intuitions to a raising-to-consciousness of one's nonconscious background beliefs. Although we found this proposal unsatisfactory, we did not rule out the idea that some other sort of nonconscious mechanism plays some role in the formation of intuitions at least in human beings; rather, the point was that an intuition is not a raising-to-consciousness of a nonconscious background belief. Suppose, then, that we posit a nonconscious mechanism, not a body of nonconscious background beliefs, but something else perhaps resembling one. Suppose that this mechanism somehow encodes a (recursively specifiable) theory and that the mechanism's outputs are thought of as theorems that the mechanism generates. Although I would reject the idea that intuition is identical to the raising-to-consciousness of these outputs, there is no reason to think that they might not play some role in explaining (some features of) human intuition. There is, however, an empiricist version of this proposal that we can be sure is mistaken. According to it, the encoded "theory" has the structure of an acceptable empirical theory, that is, an acceptable theory whose evidential base consists entirely of (reports of) the subject's phenomenal experiences and observations.

Many things are wrong with this proposal. To the extent that such an explanation resembles the rising-to-consciousness theory discussed earlier, it would be subject to many of the problems mentioned there. A more significant problem, however, is that it fails to explain the evidential status of our *modal* intuitions— arguably the most important class of intuitions for philosophy. Given Quinean arguments, no truly acceptable purely empirical theory would contain modals at all. So the proposed explanation would be unable to explain any of our modal intuitions.[15] (Maybe modals are "hardwired" nonempirical components of the nonconscious theory. We will return to this idea in the section II.)

Let us sum up. The thesis that I am led to is that intuition is a sui generis, irreducible, natural (i.e., non-Cambridge-like) propositional attitude that occurs episodically. Although the foregoing discussion hardly proves this thesis, it makes it very plausible.

Very well, but of what epistemic worth are intuitions? Many philosophers believe that the empirical findings of cognitive psychologists such as Wason, Johnson-Laird, Rosch, Nisbett, Kahneman, and Tversky cast doubt on their epistemic worth. But, in fact, although these studies bear on "intuition" in an indiscriminate use of the term, they evidently tell us little about the notion of intuition we have been discussing, which is relevant to justificatory practices in logic, mathematics, philosophy, and linguistics. As far as I have been able to determine, empirical investigators have not attempted to study intuitions in the relevant sense; for example, they have not been testing whether the subjects' intellectual episodes satisfy the several criteria isolated above: intellectual (vs. sensory) seemings that present themselves as necessary; distinct from "physical intuitions," thought experiments, beliefs, guesses, hunches, judgments, common sense, and memory; comparatively nonplastic; not readily overridden by countervailing beliefs; not reducible to inclinations, raisings-to-consciousness of nonconscious background beliefs, linguistic mastery, reports of consistency; and so forth. Clearly, it will be a delicate matter to design experiments that successfully test for such criteria.

When empirical cognitive psychology eventually studies intuition, it will certainly uncover the fact that a subject's intuitions can be fallible locally. But as I indicated above, the paradoxes showed that. Likewise, more sustained empirical studies might uncover evidence that a subject's intuitions can be fallible in a more holistic way; we already know that the theoretical output of logicians, mathematicians, and philosophers working in isolation can be flawed. But these negative facts pale by comparison with a positive fact, namely, the on-balance agreement of elementary concrete-case intuitions among human subjects. Indeed, the on-balance agreement among our elementary concrete-case intuitions is one of the most impressive general facts about human cognition.

II. The Argument from Evidence

I come now to the first argument for the Autonomy and Authority of Philosophy. Granted that our standard justificatory practice presently *uses* intuitions as evidence, why should this move exclusionist philosophers (e.g., radical empiricists) who just boldly deny that intuitions really *are* evidence? In "The Incoherence of Empiricism" (1993) I argued that these exclusionary views lead one to epistemic self-defeat. In this chapter, I will just assume that these arguments succeed and that we cannot coherently deny that intuitions have evidential weight. What explains why intuitions are evidence? In "The Philosophical Limits of Scientific Essentialism" (1987) I argued that the only adequate explanation is some kind of truth-based, or reliabilist, explanation. In *Philosophical Limits of Science* (forthcoming) I develop this argument in greater detail, dealing there with various alternative explanations—pragmatist, coherentist, conventionalist, and practice-based. I show that these explanations are based on principles that are open to straightforward counterexamples: if the principles were accepted, clear cases of nonevidence would have to be admitted as evidence in the situations envisaged in the examples. There is also a rule-of-evidence theory (reminiscent of Roderick Chisholm), that is, a theory that simply codifies rules for what counts as evidence in various sorts of circumstances. But this theory does not offer an *explanation* of why the sources of evidence described in the rules are sources of evidence: the rules merely *describe*; they do not *explain*. In the present context, I will assume that the case against each of these nontruth based approaches is telling and that we must turn to a truth-based, or reliabilist, explanation. This assumption will appeal to many readers independently of the indicated arguments.

Reliabilism has been associated with analyses of knowledge and justification. Our topic, however, is not knowledge or justification but rather evidence. This difference is salutary, for here reliabilism promises to be easier to defend. But not as a *general* theory of evidence: sources of evidence traditionally classified as *derived* (vs. basic) sources are subject to counterexamples much like those often used against reliabilist theories of justification. For example, testimony would still provide a person with evidence (reasons to believe) even if it were really just systematic undetectable lying. So reliability is not a necessary condition for something's qualifying as a source of evidence.[16] (The same problem would beset observational beliefs in a world in which all epistemic agents suffer systematic hallucination as a matter of nomological necessity.) Nor is reliability a sufficient condition for something's qualifying as a source of evidence: as in the case of justification, such things as nomologically reliable clairvoyance, telepathy, dreams, and hunches are prima facie counterexamples.

The natural response to these counterexamples is to demand only that *basic* sources of evidence be reliable: something is a basic source of evidence iff it has an appropriate kind of reliable tie to the truth.[17] Then we would be free to adopt some alternative treatment of nonbasic sources; for example, something is a nonbasic source of evidence relative to a given subject iff it would be deemed (perhaps unreliably) to have a reliable tie to the truth by the best comprehensive theory based on the subject's basic sources of evidence.[18] Let us agree that phenomenal experience is a basic source. Given this, the above counterexamples would not then fault this analysis of derived sources of evidence. In the case of undetectable lying, testimony would now rightly be counted as a source of evidence, for the subject's simplest comprehensive theory based on his experiences would deem it to have a reliable tie to the truth (even if it in fact does not because of the envisaged lying). In the case of spurious derived sources (reliable clairvoyance, telepathy, dreams, hunches, etc.), if one has not affirmed their reliability by means of one's simplest comprehensive theory based on one's basic sources, their deliverances would rightly not qualify as evidence.

In this setting, reliabilism is restricted to basic sources of evidence: something is a basic source of evidence iff it has an appropriate kind of reliable tie to the truth. There are two fundamental questions to answer. First, what is the character of the indicated reliable tie to the truth? Is it a contingent (nomological or causal) tie? Or is it some kind of strong necessary tie? Second, what sources of evidence are basic?

Contingent Reliabilism

On this account, something counts as a basic source of evidence iff there is a nomologically necessary, but nevertheless contingent, tie between its deliverances and the truth. This account, however, is subject to counterexamples of the sort that faulted the original sufficiency condition above (nomologically reliable telepathy, clairvoyance, guesses, hunches, etc.). Consider a creature who has a capacity for making reliable telepathically generated guesses. Phenomenologically, these guesses resemble those people make in blind-sight experiments. The guesses at issue concern necessary truths of some very high degree of difficulty. These truths are known to the beings on a distant planet who have arrived at them by ordinary a priori means (theoretical systematization of intuitions, proof of consequences therefrom, etc.). These beings have intelligence far exceeding that of our creature or anyone else co-inhabiting his planet. Indeed, our creature and his co-inhabitants will never be able to establish any of these necessary truths (or even assess their consistency) by ordinary a priori means. Finally, suppose that the following holds as a matter of nomological necessity: the creature guesses that p is true iff p is a necessary truth of the indicated kind and the creature is guessing as to whether p is true or false. But, plainly, guessing would not qualify as a basic source of evidence for the creature, contrary to contingent reliabilism.

A similar counterexample concerns a creature who is hardwired to make guesses about the truth or falsity of certain noncontingent propositions of some extremely high degree of difficulty. These propositions comprise a list of about one billion. The true propositions on this list fit into no neat theoretical systematization known to any living creature. Nor is any living creature intelligent enough to settle by ordinary means (theoretical systematization of intuitions and proof of consequences therefrom) whether the propositions that the creature guesses to be true are true—or even whether they are consistent. The creature is hardwired thus: it is nomologically necessary that, for each of the indicated propositions p, the creature, upon considering the question whether p is true, guesses that p is true iff p is true. But, plainly, guessing would not qualify as a basic source of evidence for the creature, contrary to contingent reliabilism.

One way of trying to rule out the counterexamples would be to add to contingent reliabilism a further requirement involving *evolutionary psychology*: in the course of the evolution of the species, a cognitive mechanism's contingent tie to the truth must have been more advantageous to the survival of the species than alternative sources that would not have had a tie to the truth. But this additional requirement does not help. Each of the examples can be adapted to yield a counterexample to the revised analysis. Specifically, we need only make the examples about a hypothetical species in whom the extraordinary powers for making true guesses have played a positive (but always undetected role) in the species' evolution. Certainly this would be possible. But there would be no temptation to say that guessing would in the circumstance be a basic source of evidence. Thus, the revised analysis does not provide a sufficient condition.[19] Similar counterexamples could be constructed even if it were required that the disposition to make reliable guesses be implanted in accordance with a good "design plan."

Modal Reliabilism

Given that some form of reliabilist theory is needed to explain our basic sources of evidence and given that contingent reliabilism fails to do this, we are left with modal reliabilism. According to this view, something counts as a basic source iff there is an appropriate kind of strong modal tie between its deliverances and the truth. Each of the above problems confronting contingent reliabilism is traceable to the fact that contingent reliabilism posits only a contingent tie between the deliverances of a basic source and the truth. For example, the reliability of (evolutionarily advantageous) telepathically generated guesses is only contingent; likewise, for the reliability of (evolutionarily advantageous) hardwiring-generated guesses. These problems do not arise if we require basic sources of evidence to have a strong modal tie to the truth. This is precisely what modal reliabilism says. These diagnostic facts thus provide further support for the thesis that modal reliabilism is correct.

This outcome should strike many philosophers (including, most traditional empiricists) as just right. These philosophers accept that phenomenal experience (feeling pain, its appearing that this is a table, etc.) is intrinsically more basic than, say, observation and testimony—in the words of Quine, the phenomenalistic is "epistemologically prior" to these sources. These philosophers, however, need an explanation for this fact. (Traditional empiricists, for example, take this fact as a dogma lacking explanation.) At the same time, these philosophers recognize that, for beings in good cognitive conditions, the on-balance reliability of phenomenal experience is not a mere contingent matter. Surely this fact should be relevant to explaining why phenomenal experience is a basic source of evidence, why it is "epistemologically prior" to observation and testimony. Modal reliabilism is simply a theory that reworks these plausible claims into a positive account. But we do not base our case for modal reliabilism on plausibility. It is based on the foregoing argument. A general theory of basic evidence must be reliabilist. Contingent reliabilism, however, is beset with fatal problems. To avoid them, we are forced to modal reliabilism: a candidate source of evidence is basic iff its deliverances have an appropriate kind of strong modal tie to the truth. Phenomenal experience is a basic source because it has *that* kind of modal tie to the truth.

Our Basic Sources of Evidence

Before we try to say more precisely what sort of modal tie this is, let us turn to the second question that was raised earlier but not answered. Namely, what sources of evidence are basic?

Taking it for granted that phenomenal experience is a basic source, how should we classify intuition? Is it a derived or a basic source? This question can, I believe, be answered directly by means of intuitive considerations.[20] Intuitively, intuition is a basic source of evidence.[21] For example, suppose a person has an intuition, say, that if P then not not P; or in your favorite Gettier example that the person in question would not know; or that a good theory must take into account all the evidence; and so forth. Nothing more is needed. Intuitively, these intuitions are evidentially as basic as evidence gets. They are intuitively as basic as experiences, much as tactile experiences are intuitively as basic as visual experiences. This ought to be the end of the matter. But, for a certain sort of radical empiricist, such intuitive considerations might not persuade precisely because it is a dogma of these empiricists that intuition is not a basic source; only experience is.

Let us remember where we are in the dialectic. We have agreed that intuition—including modal intuition—is a source of evidence, and that empiricists who reject this are in a self-defeating position. The empiricists with whom we are now dealing are those who accept intuition as a source of evidence and who are in the midst of trying to explain why it is a source. Their strategy is to suppose that only experience is a basic source and that intuition must therefore be a derived source, where something is a derived source of evidence relative to a given subject iff it is deemed (perhaps mistakenly) to have a reliable tie to the truth by the simplest comprehensive theory based on the subject's basic sources of evidence. The first count against these empiricists who accept that intuitions are evidence is that their supposition (that experience is the only basic source of evidence) goes against intuitions that intuition is basic. But we are ignoring this internal conflict for now. The second count against our empiricists is that the envisaged explanation fails. We have already seen the underlying problem. Once all Quinean techniques of regimentation are brought to bear, the simplest comprehensive explanation of our empirical evidence is a theory that is free of all modals—and, indeed, all intensional elements. Consequently, that comprehensive theory will not deem there to be a reliable tie between our modal intuitions and the truth. But, according to the empiricist strategy, modal intuitions would be evidence iff the subject's simplest comprehensive empirical theory deemed there to be a reliable tie between them and the truth. So our empiricists are unable to explain why modal intuitions—arguably the most important family of intuitions—have evidential weight. Relatedly, given the prevalence of modal intuitions among intuitions generally and given that modal intuitions would not be deemed to have a reliable tie to the truth, the reliability of intuitions generally would be called into question. In this event, intuitions would not have the evidential force our empiricists agree they have. We are thus led to the conclusion that the empiricist strategy fails, and that there is no alternative but to take intuition to be a basic source of evidence.[22]

Before we return to modal reliabilism, there is a preliminary problem that must be dispensed with, namely, the so-called "generality problem."[23] Consider the relation holding between x and p such that x believes p, and p is the proposition that there is no largest prime. For the sake of argument, let us count this relation as a propositional attitude. Then the deliverances of this propositional attitude will have a strong modal tie to the truth: *necessarily*, whenever this propositional attitude holds between a subject and a proposition, that proposition will be true. But surely it is not the case that the mere belief that there is no largest prime is to count as basic evidence that there is no largest prime. For all we know, the belief might have been induced by hypnosis! Does this case count as a counterexample to modal reliabilism? No. The reason is that this propositional attitude is not even a candidate for a basic source of evidence. Something can be a candidate basic source only if it is a natural (i.e., non-Cambridge-like) propositional attitude. Intuition, appearance, introspection, belief, desire, guessing, wondering all qualify. Contrast these with the relation holding between x and p such that x believes p, and p is the proposition that there is no largest prime. The range of this relation is artificially restricted, in this case to a single necessary proposition. The relation is Cambridge-like, not a natural propositional attitude (indeed, not even a genuine *species* of belief). The advantage of a theory like modal reliabilism, which offers a free-standing analysis of what it is to be a basic source of evidence, is that it can avail itself of this plausible solution to the "generality problem" in terms of natural propositional attitudes. This is possible only if intuition is a natural propositional attitude. That is why the earlier phenomenological points about intellectual seeming are so important.

The Character of the Modal Tie

To avoid the problems besetting contingent reliabilism, we arrived at a *general scheme* for analyzing what it takes for a candidate source of evidence to be basic: it is basic iff its deliverances have an appropriate kind of strong modal tie to the truth. This biconditional is not itself an analysis: it is not intended that *just any* strong modal tie be sufficient for something's being a basic source of evidence. Rather, this scheme provides us with an *invitation* to find the weakest modal tie that does the job—that is, the weakest modal tie that lets in the right sources and excludes the wrong ones. The explanation of why intuition is a basic source of evidence then goes as follows. By definition, a candidate source of evidence is basic iff it has *that* sort of modal tie; intuition does have that sort of modal tie; hence, intuition is a basic source of evidence. Likewise for phenomenal experience: it too has that sort of modal tie; hence, it is a basic source of evidence. And we have an explanation of why other candidate sources (observation, testimony, etc.) are not basic: they are not basic because they lack that sort of modal tie.

We thus have an invitation to find the weakest modal tie that does the job. One candidate is the kind of modal tie posited by traditional infallibilists. The resulting analysis would be: a candidate source is basic iff, necessarily, all deliverances of the source are true. But this is not satisfactory for two reasons. First, we have good reasons to reject infallibilism both in the case of intuition (e.g., the paradoxes) and in the case of phenomenal experience (e.g., Russell's locally uniform spectrum), so the infallibilist analysis would wrongly exclude intuition and phenomenal experience as basic sources of evidence. Second, as we will see, there are weaker modal ties that do the job.

One of them is an infallibilist tie relativized to ideal cognitive conditions. On the resulting analysis, a candidate source is basic iff, necessarily, for anyone in ideal cognitive conditions, the deliverances of that source would be true. Accordingly, for anyone in ideal cognitive conditions, basic sources provide a guaranteed pathway to the truth regarding the deliverances of the source. Of course, we humans are not in *ideal* cognitive conditions, so there is no guarantee that all of the deliverances of *our* basic sources are true. But, if we limit ourselves to suitably elementary propositions, then relative to them we *approximate* ideal cognitive conditions. For suitably elementary propositions, therefore, deliverances of our basic sources would provide in an approximate way the kind of pathway to the truth they would have generally in ideal conditions. For those of us capable of real theorizing—that is, subjects whose cognitive conditions (intelligence, memory, attentiveness, constancy, etc.) are good enough to enable them to process theoretically the deliverances of their basic sources—the size of the class of relevantly elementary propositions would not be inconsiderable.[24]

While this relativized infallibilist analysis does the job, it too posits a very strong modal tie. Our larger analytical strategy, however, invited us only to posit the weakest modal tie that does the job, and there is indeed a weaker one. It is a tie that is holistic in character and holds, not with absolute universality, but as Aristotle would say, *for-the-most-part*. To wit, a candidate source is basic iff for cognitive conditions of some suitably high quality, necessarily, if someone in those cognitive conditions were to process theoretically the deliverances of the candidate source, the resulting theory would provide a correct assessment as to the truth or falsity of most of those deliverances. Whereas the previous analysis required that the deliverances of a basic source themselves be true, this weaker analysis requires only that most of the theoretical assessments as to the truth or falsity of those deliverances be true.[25] The previous remarks about approximations then carry over mutatis mutandis. Consider subjects (like ourselves) who are capable of processing their basic sources theoretically. The result of that processing, for elementary deliverances, provides in an approximate way the kind of pathway to the truth it would provide generally in the aforementioned high quality cognitive conditions. This is the sort of pathway whose reliability increases the more elementary those deliverances are.

This analysis does the job. It tells us in a natural and non-ad-hoc way what is common to our traditional basic sources—intuition and phenomenal experience. And it tells us what is lacking in all other candidate sources—those that are nonbasic and those that are not even sources of evidence, basic or nonbasic. Moreover, I can think of no weaker modal tie that does the job. (If there should happen to be a weaker tie that does the job, I expect that it too would be sufficiently strong to underwrite the applications we shall want to make.) Finally, there is nothing mysterious about this sort of modal tie; indeed, it is implied by the analysis of concept possession (see section III below).

Some further features of the proposed analysis might be worth pointing out. Consider again some subjects who are in cognitive conditions like ours and who, like ourselves, are capable of processing their basic sources theoretically. We have seen that, when such a subject processes the deliverances of its basic sources, the pronouncements that the resulting theory makes on those deliverances are increasingly reliable the more elementary those deliverances are. It does not *follow* from this that *any* of these deliverances, even maximally elementary deliverances, would be utterly demon-proof. But the more and more elementary the deliverances are, the fewer the potential sources of error. At the limit, the only surviving potential source of error would be a Cartesian evil demon or something on a par with one. If skeptical prospects like this are indeed genuine metaphysical possibilities (I need not take a stand on whether they are), then they would if realized undermine one's quest for the truth regarding even the most elementary deliverances. Faced with this worry, one could simply give up. But if one gives up, one is bound not to succeed. The way to keep open the possibility of success is to proceed as if this sort of skeptical prospect is not realized. In this case, one would succeed as long as the skeptical prospect is not realized. And if it is realized, one would be no worse off for having tried. Relying on maximally elementary deliverances of basic sources is thus the best possible *general* strategy theorizers could have for obtaining a class of reliable beliefs regardless of the context they find themselves in: these deliverances are reliable in every possible context that is demon-free.[26] The situation is analogous when theorizers seek to enlarge this class at the risk of corresponding reductions in reliability: basic sources provide theorizers with the best possible general strategy for getting to such substantial classes of truths. This strategy is "context-free" (or "world-independent") in that it works for any subject capable of real theorizing no matter how the rest of the world is. One's basic sources may in turn be used as a yardstick for assessing whether candidate (nonbasic) sources qualify as genuine sources of evidence. Basic sources are thus by nature ideally suited to be "regress stoppers": they have their authority intrinsically, and it is an authority exceeded by no other. These features are precisely what one would want from basic sources of evidence.[27]

My claim is that something like the above analysis is right. Of course, the analysis (and others like it) would be vacuous if it were not possible for some subjects to be in cognitive conditions of the high quality indicated in the analysis and to arrive at the indicated sort of theory of the deliverances of each basic source (phenomenal experience and also intuition). In the case of intuitions, this possibility, and the modal tie to the truth that such a theory would have, are all that are needed to underwrite (the possibility posited in) the Authority and Autonomy of Philosophy. I will not elaborate this connection here, but I assume it is fairly clear in broad outline.[28] The foregoing, then, is the Argument from Evidence.

A shortcoming of traditional empiricism was that it offered no explanation of why phenomenal experience is a basic source of evidence; this was just an unexplained dogma. By the same token, traditional rationalists (and also moderate empiricists who, like Hume, accepted intuition as a basic source of evidence) did not successfully explain why intuition is a basic source of evidence. Modal reliabilism provides a natural explanation filling in these two gaps left by the traditional theories. The explanation is in terms of the indicated modal tie between these sources and the truth. But why should there be such a tie to the truth? Neither traditional empiricism nor traditional rationalism provided a satisfactory explanation. The theory of concept possession promises to fill in this gap. Such a theory is at the heart of the Argument from Concepts.

III. The Argument from Concepts

There are at least two different but related senses in which a subject can be said to possess a concept. The first is a nominal sense; the second is the full, strong sense. The first may be analyzed thus:

> A subject possesses a given concept at least nominally iff the subject has natural propositional attitudes (belief, desire, etc.) toward propositions which have that concept as a conceptual content.[29]

Possessing a concept in this nominal sense is compatible with what Tyler Burge calls misunderstanding and incomplete understanding of the concept (Burge 1979). For example, in Burge's arthritis case, the subject misunderstands the concept of arthritis, wrongly taking it to be possible to have arthritis in the thigh. In Burge's verbal contract case, the subject incompletely understands the concept of a contract, not knowing whether or not contracts must be written. (Hereafter I will use 'misunderstanding' for cases where there are errors in the subject's understanding of the concept and 'incomplete understanding' for cases where there are gaps—"don't knows"—in the subject's understanding of the concept.) Possessing a concept in the nominal sense is also compatible with having propositional attitudes merely by virtue of appropriate attributions on the part of third-person interpreters. For example, we commonly attribute to animals, children, and members of other cultures various beliefs involving concepts that loom large in our own thought. We do so without thereby committing ourselves to there being a causally efficacious psychological state having the attributed content that plays a role in "methodological solipsistic" psychological explanation. Our standard attribution practices, nonetheless, would have us deem such attributions to be appropriate. Advocates of this point of view hold that these attribution practices reveal to us essential features of our concept of belief (and, indeed, might even be constitutive of it). Everyone should at least agree that people could have a word 'believe' that expresses a concept having these features. In what follows, the theory I will propose is designed to be compatible with this practice-based view but will not presuppose it. These, then, are some weak ways in which a person can possess a concept. And there might be others belonging to a natural similarity class. This, too, is something our theory will be designed to accommodate but not to presuppose.

With these various weak ways of possessing a concept in mind, we are in a position to give an informal characterization of possessing a concept in the full, strong sense:

> A subject possesses a concept in the full sense iff (i) the subject at least nominally possesses the concept and (ii) the subject does *not* do this with misunderstanding or incomplete understanding or just by virtue of satisfying our attribution practices or in any other weak such way.

In ordinary language, when we speak of "understanding a concept," what we mean is possessing the concept in the full sense. In what follows, this ordinary-language idiom will help to anchor our inquiry, and I will use it wherever convenient.[30] It will also be convenient to have available the technical term 'possessing a concept determinately', which is just another way of expressing the notion of understanding a concept (i.e., possessing a concept in the full sense).

Now just as a person can be said to understand a concept (to possess it in the full sense), a person can be said to misunderstand a concept or to understand a concept incompletely and so on. Similarly, a person can be said to understand a proposition, to misunderstand a proposition, to understand a proposition incompletely, and so forth.

Now, intuitively, it is at least possible for most of the central concepts of philosophy to be possessed determinately—substance, mind, intelligence, consciousness, sensation, perception, knowledge, wisdom, truth, identity, infinity, divinity, time, explanation, causation, freedom, purpose, goodness, duty, the virtues, love, life, happiness, and so forth. It would be entirely ad hoc to deny this. Later on, this possibility will be used as a premise—called the *possibility of determinate possession.*

We have characterized determinate possession informally—negatively and by means of examples—and we evidently have an ordinary-language idiom for this notion. We readily see what this notion is, and it seems important theoretically. A legitimate philosophical project would therefore be to give a positive general analysis of the notion. Indeed, it cries out for one. I believe that a general analysis is feasible and, specifically, that concept possession is to be analyzed in terms of the very kind of truth-tracking pattern in one's intuitions that figured in the modal reliabilist explanation of the evidential status of intuitions. My strategy will be to begin with a series of intuitive examples that serve to isolate some ideas that will play a role in the eventual analysis.

The Multigon Example. Suppose that a sincere, wholly normal, attentive woman introduces *through use* (not stipulation) a new term 'multigon'. (This example is taken from Bealer 1987.) She applies the term to various closed plane figures having several sides (pentagons, octagons, chiliagons, etc.). Suppose her term expresses some definite concept—the concept of being a multigon—and that she determinately possesses this concept. Surely this is possible. By chance, however, the woman has neither applied her term 'multigon' to triangles and rectangles nor withheld it from them. The question has not come up. But eventually she does consider the question of whether it is possible for a triangle or a rectangle to be a multigon. When she does, her cognitive conditions continue to be normal—she is intelligent, attentive, possessed of good memory, free from distraction, and so forth—and she determinately understands the question. Now let us suppose that the property of being a multigon is either the property of being a closed straight-sided plane figure or the property of being a closed straight-sided plane figure with five or more sides. (Each alternative is listed under 'polygon' in my desk *Webster's*.) Then, intuitively, when the woman considers the question, she would have an intuition that it *is* possible for a triangle or a rectangle to be a multigon iff the property of being a multigon = the property of being a closed straight-sided plane figure. Alternatively, she would have an intuition that it is *not* possible for a triangle or a rectangle to be a multigon if the property of being a multigon = the property of being a closed straight-sided plane figure with five or more sides. Intuitively, if these things did not hold, the right thing to say would be that either the woman does not really possess a determinate concept or her cognitive conditions are not really normal.[31]

The Chromic Example. Suppose a woman has through use (in, say, her diary) introduced a new term 'chromic'. She applies the term to phenomenal qualia, specifically, to shades of phenomenal color—red, blue, purple, and so forth—but withholds it from phenomenal black and phenomenal white. Suppose the term 'chromic' expresses some definite concept—the concept of being chromic—and that she determinately possesses this concept. Again, this is surely possible. Suppose, however, that the woman has not yet experienced any shades of phenomenal gray. When she finally does, it is a central shade of phenomenal gray, and the experience of it is clear and distinct—vivid, unwavering, and long-lasting. During the course of the experience, the question whether the shade is chromic occurs to her. When it does, her cognitive conditions are wholly normal (she is fully attentive, etc.), and she determinately understands the question. Suppose, finally, that the property of being chromic is either the property of being a nonblack nonwhite phenomenal color or the property of being a nonblack nonwhite nongray phenomenal color. In this case, intuitively, the following would hold: the woman would have the intuition that the shade *is* chromic iff the property of being chromic = the property of being a nonblack nonwhite phenomenal color. Alternatively, she would have the intuition that the shade is *not* chromic iff the property of being chromic = the property of being a nonblack nonwhite nongray phenomenal color. That is, just as in the multigon case, the woman's intuitions would track the truth vis-à-vis the relevant test question. As before, if this were not so, we should say instead that the woman does not really possess a determinate concept or her cognitive conditions are not really normal.

What is distinctive about the chromic example is that the woman determinately possesses the concept of being chromic at a time when the decisive cases involve items—namely, shades of phenomenal gray—that lie beyond her experience and conceptual repertory. She determinately possesses the concept of being chromic even though, prior to experiencing phenomenal gray, she cannot even entertain the relevant test questions, let alone have truth-tracking intuitions regarding them. Surely such a thing is possible. There is no requirement that, in order to possess a concept determinately, a person must *already* have experiential and/or conceptual resources sufficient for testing the possible extensions of the concept. Determinate concept possession is in this sense "Hegelian"—a present feature revealed only in the future.

Here is a variant on the example. It might be that it is *nomologically impossible* for the woman (or, for that matter, anyone else) to experience phenomenal gray: as a matter of nomological necessity, attempts to overcome this deficiency (e.g., electrodes, drugs, neurosurgery, etc.) only lead to irreversible coma and death. But this would not prevent the woman's term 'chromic' from determinately expressing a definite concept, the concept of being chromic. Consistent with all of this, there is a certain *metaphysical possibility*, namely, the metaphysical possibility that the woman—or someone whose epistemic situation is qualitatively identical to hers—might have an increased potential for phenomenal experiences (namely, for phenomenal gray). This could be so without there being any (immediate) shift in the way the woman (or her counterpart) understands any of her concepts or the propositions involving them. In this improved situation, there would be no barrier to the woman's coming to understand and to consider the test question determinately. Intuitively, it is metaphysically possible for all this to happen.[32] And, intuitively, if it did, then just as in the original example, the woman (or her counterpart) would have truth-tracking intuitions vis-à-vis the test question.

Of course, the same sort of thing could happen in connection with nomologically necessary limitations on aspects of the woman's cognitive conditions (intelligence, attentiveness, memory, constancy, etc.): it could be that, because of such limitations, it is nomologically impossible for her to have truth-tracking intuitions vis-à-vis relevant test questions. It would nonetheless be metaphysically possible for her (or a counterpart whose epistemic situation is qualitatively identical) to have improved cognitive conditions. Intuitively, in such a situation, she would then have the relevant truth-tracking intuitions. She would determinately possess the concept iff such intuitions were metaphysically possible.

Finally, all this would hold mutatis mutandis if the examples concerned, not a solitary person (as above), but whole groups of people who determinately possess relevant concepts. These people would determinately possess a given target concept iff it were metaphysically possible for them to have the associated truth-tracking intuitions.

The moral is that, even though there might be a nomological barrier to there being intuitions of the sort we have been discussing, there is no metaphysically necessary barrier. (Remember: these intuitions need not be those of the original subjects; they may be those of people whose epistemic situation is qualitatively identical to that of the original subjects.) This leads to the thought that determinate concept possession might be explicated (at least in part) in terms of the metaphysical possibility of relevant truth-tracking intuitions (in appropriately good cognitive conditions and with appropriately rich conceptual repertories). The idea is that determinateness is that mode of possession that constitutes the categorical base of this possibility. When a subject's mode of concept possession shifts to determinateness, there is a corresponding shift in the possible intuitions accessible to the subject. In fact, there is a shift in both *quantity* and *quality*. The quantity grows because incomplete understanding is replaced with complete understanding, eliminating "don't knows." The quality improves because incorrect understanding is replaced with correct understanding.

Using these ideas, I will now formulate a progression of analyses, each beset with a problem that its successor is designed to overcome—converging, one hopes, on a successful analysis.

Subjunctive Analyses

Our discussion of the multigon example suggests the following:

> x determinately possesses the concept of being a multigon iff:
>> x would have the intuition that it is possible for a triangle or a rectangle to be a multigon iff it is *true* that it is possible for a triangle or a rectangle to be a multigon.

In turn, this suggests the following:

> x determinately possesses the concept of being a multigon iff:
>> x would have intuitions which *imply* that the property of being a multigon = the property of being a closed straight-sided plane figure iff it is *true* that the property of being a multigon = the property of being a closed straight-sided plane figure.

We have been assuming that in the example x possesses the target concept determinately in all respects except perhaps those that would decide this sort of test property-identity. Suppose, however, that we remove this background supposition. We would then want to generalize on the above idea. The natural generalization is the following:

> x determinately possesses a given concept iff, for associated test property-identities p:
>> x would have intuitions which imply that p is true iff p is true.

If f is the given concept, the associated test property-identities p are propositions to the effect that the property of being f = the property of being A, or the denials of such propositions (where A is some formula).[33] When we transform this proposal into a direct definition of *determinateness*, the mode of understanding involved when one understands determinately, we obtain the following:

> determinateness = the mode m of understanding such that, necessarily, for all
> x and property-identities p which x understands m-ly,
>   p is true iff x would have intuitions which imply that p is true.

The intention here is that 'm' ranges over *natural* modes of understanding (i.e., non-ad-hoc Cambridge modes of understanding).

A Priori Stability

A problem with this analysis is that it relies on the subjunctive 'would', but there are well-known general objections to subjunctive analyses. The solution is to replace the subjunctives with a certain ordinary modal notion. I will call this modal notion *a priori stability*. Consider an arbitrary property-identity p that someone x understands m-ly. Then, x settles with a priori stability that p is true iff, for cognitive conditions of some level l and for some conceptual repertory c, (1) x has cognitive conditions of level l and conceptual repertory c and x attempts to elicit intuitions bearing on p and x seeks a theoretical systematization based on those intuitions and that systematization affirms that p is true and all the while x understands p m-ly, and (2) necessarily, for cognitive conditions of any level l' greater than l and for any conceptual repertory c' that properly includes c, if x has cognitive conditions of level l' and conceptual repertory c' and x attempts to elicit intuitions bearing on p and seeks a theoretical systematization based on those intuitions and all the while x understands p m-ly, then that systematization also affirms that p is true.[34] A diagram can be helpful here.

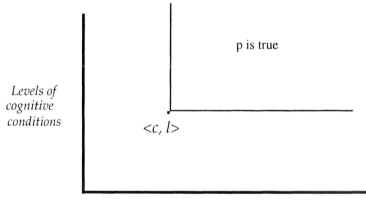

Conceptual repertories

The idea is that, after x achieves $< c, l >$, theoretical systematizations of x's intuitions always yield the same verdict on p as long as p is understood m-ly throughout. That is, as long as p is understood m-ly, p always gets settled the same way throughout the region to the "northeast" of $< c, l >$. When this notion of a priori stability replaces the subjunctives in our earlier analysis, we arrive at the following:

> determinateness = the mode m of understanding such that, necessarily, for all x and property-identities p that x understands m-ly,
> > p is true iff it is possible for x to settle with a priori stability that p is true.

The biconditional has two parts:

(a)   p is true *if* it is possible for x to settle with a priori stability that p is true.

and

(b)   p is true *only if* it is possible for x to settle with a priori stability that p is true.

The former is a *correctness* (or soundness) property. The latter is a *completeness* property. The correctness property tells us about the potential *quality* of x's intuitions: it is possible for x to get into a situation such that from then on x's intuitions yield only the truth regarding p, given that x understands p m-ly. The completeness property tells us about the potential *quantity* of x's intuitions: it is possible for x to have enough intuitions to reach a priori stability regarding the question of p's truth, given that x understands p m-ly. According to the analysis, determinateness is that mode of understanding that constitutes the categorical base for the possibility of intuitions of this quantity and quality.

A qualification is in order. As the analysis is stated, x must be able to go through the envisaged intuition-driven process arriving at the conclusion that p is true. It is enough, however, that an *epistemic counterpart* of x (i.e., someone in qualitatively the same epistemic situation as x) be able to go through the envisaged process with that outcome, while understanding p m-ly. Let us understand the proposal and its sequels in this way.

Accommodating Scientific Essentialism

Even with this qualification, however, there is a problem with the completeness clause: it conflicts with scientific essentialism—the doctrine that there are property-identities that are essentially a posteriori (e.g., the property of being water = the property of being H_2O). Plainly, the completeness clause in the analysis goes too far, for it requires that such things can be settled a priori. The completeness clause thus needs to be weakened.

Granted, we do not have a priori intuitions supporting such scientific essentialist property-identities. Even so, whoever determinately understands these property-identities should at least have associated Twin-Earth intuitions, that is, intuitions regarding Twin-Earth scenarios of the sort that underwrite arguments for scientific essentialism. For example, if someone determinately understands the proposition that the property of being water = the property of being H_2O, that person ought to have the following Twin-Earth intuition: if all and only samples of water here on earth are composed of H_2O, and if the corresponding samples on a macroscopically identical Twin Earth are composed of XYZ ($\neq$ H_2O), then those samples would not be samples of water.

If the person has intuitions of this sort, the person also ought to have various modal intuitions concerning the sorts of *counterpart entities* that are possible. For example, the person ought to intuit that it is possible for there to be a Twin Earth on which there is a counterpart of water whose composition consists of counterparts of hydrogen, oxygen, and the sharing of two electrons. Naturally, this generalizes.

These considerations lead to the following idea. Although a person who determinately understands a given natural-kind property-identity cannot settle a priori whether it is true, nonetheless the person ought to be able to settle a priori whether there is at least a *counterpart* of the property-identity that is true. Being able to settle such things a priori is a necessary condition for understanding the *categorial content* of the constituent concepts. And, of course, understanding the categorial content of a concept is a necessary condition for determinately possessing it. The idea is that this condition, taken together with the correctness condition, is jointly necessary and sufficient for determinateness.

This suggests the following analysis in which the completeness clause (b) is weakened so that it only requires categorial understanding:

> determinateness = the mode m of understanding such that, necessarily, for all x and property-identities p understood m-ly by x,
> (a)   p is true *if* it is possible for x to settle with a priori stability that p is true.
> (b)   p is true *only if* it is possible for x to settle with a priori stability that p has a counterpart which is true.[35]

Before proceeding, I should note that there is an important family of test propositions p that are entirely immune to scientific essentialism, namely, those I call *semantically stable*: p is semantically stable iff, necessarily, for any population C, it is necessary that, for any proposition p' and any population C' whose epistemic situation is qualitatively identical to that of C, if p' in C' is the counterpart of p in C, then p = p'. (There is of course an analogous notion of a *semantically stable concept*.)[36] Thus, if p is a semantically stable property-identity, the weakened completeness clause in the revised analysis entails the strong completeness clause of the earlier analysis:

> (b)   p is true *only if* it is possible for x to settle with a priori stability that p is true.

This fact is significant for epistemology, for most of the central propositions in the a priori disciplines—logic, mathematics, philosophy—are semantically stable and, therefore, immune to scientific essentialism.[37]

Accommodating Anti-Individualism

To avoid the clash with scientific essentialism, we weakened the completeness clause so that it bears on only the categorial content of our concepts. This weakening, however, creates a predictable problem having to do with the *noncategorial* content of our concepts. Suppose x is in command of nothing but the categorial content of a certain pair of concepts, say, the concept of being a beech and the concept of being an elm. He would then be in a position resembling that of Hilary Putnam, who was entirely unable to distinguish beeches from elms. In this case, x certainly would not possess these concepts determinately (although the above analysis wrongly implies that he would). A symptom of x's incomplete understanding would be his complete inability—*without relying on the expertise of others*—even to begin to do the science of beeches and elms. What is missing, of course, is that x's "web of belief" is too sparse. An analogous problem of misunderstanding would arise if x were too often to classify beeches as elms and/or conversely.

In order for x to achieve determinate possession, x's web of belief would need to be improved. But how? We can answer this question by making use of the idea of *truth-absorption*. If x were to absorb ever more true beliefs related to beeches and elms (perhaps including relevant social and linguistic facts), eventually x's incomplete understanding (or misunderstanding) would shift to determinate understanding. And, in general, if an arbitrary person x has categorial mastery of certain of his concepts but nonetheless does not understand them determinately, then by absorbing ever more true beliefs x eventually will switch out of his deficient mode of understanding and thereby come to possess the relevant concepts determinately. By contrast, people who already determinately possess their concepts can always absorb more true beliefs without switching out of their determinate possession.

These considerations suggest the following revision:

determinateness = the mode m of understanding such that, necessarily, for all x and all p understood m-ly by x,

(a)   p is true *if* it is possible for x to settle with a priori stability that p is true.

(b.i)   p is true *only if* it is possible for x to settle with a priori stability that p has a counterpart that is true.   (for property-identities p)

(b.ii) p is true *only if* it is possible for x to believe m-ly that p is true.
                                                                (for p believable by x)[36]

Why do improvements in the web of belief suffice to eliminate indeterminateness in the usual beech/elm cases? The reason (given the truth of scientific essentialism) is that there can be nothing else in which determinateness could consist in cases like this; the question of whether this is a beech or an elm is simply beyond the ken of a priori intuition. Absent intuition, web of belief is the default position on which determinateness rides. But when there is a potential for a priori intuitions, they are determinative.

The Final Analysis

In the course of our discussion, we found it convenient to shift from our focus from determinate understanding of *concepts* to determinate understanding of *propositions*. The analysis of the former notion, however, has always been only a step away:

> x determinately possesses a given concept iff x determinately understands some proposition that has that concept as a conceptual content.

This analysis invokes the notion of determinately understanding a proposition. To understand a proposition determinately is to understand it in a certain *mode*—namely, determinately. The hard problem was to say what distinguishes this mode from other natural modes of understanding. My strategy for answering this question was to quantify over natural modes of understanding, including determinateness itself (much as in Ramsified functional definitions of mental properties one quantifies over properties, including the mental properties being defined). The goal in this setting was to isolate general properties that determinateness has and other natural modes of understanding lack. My proposal was the following:

> determinateness = the mode m of understanding with the following properties:
> (a)   correctness
> (b.i)   categorial completeness
> (b.ii)   noncategorial completeness.

(a) A mode m has the correctness property iff, necessarily, for all individuals x and all propositions p that x understands in mode m, p is true *if* it is possible for x (or someone initially in qualitatively the same sort of epistemic situation as x) to settle with a priori stability that p is true, all the while understanding p in mode m. (b.i) A mode m has the categorial completeness property iff, necessarily, for all individuals x and all true (positive or negative) property identities p that x understands in mode m, it is possible for x (or someone initially in qualitatively the same sort of epistemic situation) to settle with a priori stability that there is some true Twin-Earth style counterpart of p, all the while understanding p in mode m. (b.ii) A mode m has the noncategorial completeness property iff, necessarily, for all individuals x and all true propositions p that x understands in mode m and that x could believe, it is possible for x to believe p while still understanding it in mode m.

Of course, this analysis might need to be refined in one way or another.[39] The thesis I wish to be committed to is that some analysis along these general lines can be made to work.[40]

IV. Conclusion

At the beginning of section III we characterized the notion of determinate possession informally—negatively and by means of examples. With this informal characterization in view, intuitive considerations then led us to the *possibility of determinate possession*, the premise that it should be at least possible for most of the central concepts of philosophy to be possessed determinately.[41] Our ensuing discussion of examples then led us to the idea that this informal notion of determinate concept possession might be analyzed in terms of the possibility of a certain high level of cognitive conditions such that, when one is in such cognitive conditions, one's intuitions would acquire correspondingly heightened quantity and quality. Given our earlier finding that it should be possible for most of the central concepts of philosophy to be possessed determinately, we are then led to the conclusion that it should be possible for there to be intuitions concerning the behavior of philosophically central concepts that have this heightened quantity and quality. Now, on the one hand, this heightened quantity will be enough to ensure the Autonomy of Philosophy—a sufficient supply of intuitions regarding the behavior of philosophically central concepts to allow one to answer most of the answerable central questions of philosophy without having to rely substantively on the sciences. On the other hand, the quality is heightened enough to ensure the Authority of Philosophy—intuitions approximating the truth to such an extent that empirical inquiry would, by comparison, always be subject to greater risks or error. This in outline is the Argument from Concepts, our second argument for the Autonomy and Authority of Philosophy.

I will close by sketching the connection between our two arguments—the Argument from Evidence and the Argument from Concepts. The Argument from Evidence, our first argument, also led to the Autonomy and Authority of Philosophy. In the course of giving that argument, we noted a shortcoming in traditional empiricism and traditional rationalism, namely, that neither successfully explains why intuition and phenomenal experience should be basic sources of evidence. Modal reliabilism filled this explanatory gap: the explanation is that these two sources have the right sort of modal tie to the truth. In the case of intuitions, this strong tie was sufficient to underwrite (the possibility posited in) the Authority and Autonomy of Philosophy. We saw, moreover, that neither traditional empiricism nor traditional rationalism successfully explains why there should be such a tie between these basic sources and the truth. The analysis of determinate concept possession fills this gap: In the case of intuition, determinate possession of our concepts entails that there must be such a tie. But determinate concept possession also guarantees that there be a corresponding tie in the case of phenomenal experience. Our intuitions are what seem to be so concerning the applicability of concepts to cases presented to pure thought. If our intellectual seemings have the indicated modal tie to truth, then we could hardly be mistaken regarding what seem to be the contents of our phenomenal experiences. In this way, the analysis of determinate concept possession promises to complete the picture begun by our two main epistemological traditions—rationalism and empiricism. If this is so, the fact that one and the same analysis can play this dual role provides additional reason to accept it.

Notes

1. For example, Wason, Johnson-Laird, Rosch, Nisbett, Kahneman, and Tversky.

2. The Autonomy and Authority of Philosophy view—and the arguments supporting it—are thus far more moderate than the views of L. Jonathan Cohen (1981, 1986). Cohen is committed to the impossibility of empirically testing for significant patterns of irrationality on the part of individual human beings (and groups of human beings), I am not. Indeed, the kind of modal tie to the truth I posit is consistent with the possibility of persistent error in intuition-based theories arrived at by humans engaged in a civilization-long intellectual project. Nonetheless, there are two weaker points on which Cohen and I would agree. First, whether the possibility just mentioned is truly realized is something for which there are no *empirical tests* performable by *that* civilization. I think that there is a conceptual barrier to this. (This does not rule out the possibility of a superior species performing such a test on a given civilization.) Second, even if our intellectual culture were always to fail to arrive at comprehensive intuition-based theories that are largely true, that would not refute the Autonomy and Authority theses and the thesis of the strong modal tie that underlies those theses. The cognitive conditions of human beings working collectively over historical time might fall short. That would not show that the requisite cognitive conditions are not possible for other beings. No empirical tests could ever rule out this mere possibility. (Scientific essentialism is the only hope for empirically ruling out mere possibilities. We will see that it provides no threat in the present case.)

3. In Bealer (1987) I adopted this overall argument strategy and, in particular, defended the concept-possession account of intuition's tie to the truth. In that early paper I did not yet see how to formulate a noncircular general analysis of the notion of concept possession and so was unable to show in detail that concept possession implies the indicated truth tie. R. Warner (1989) advocates a concept-possession approach to our a priori knowledge of logic. C. Peacocke (1992) offers a series of piecemeal strategies for analyzing what it is to possess particular concepts or families of concepts, but he suggests no method for how to give a noncircular general analysis. In subsequent work Peacocke adopted a concept-possession approach to a priori knowledge, but he now has backed away from that approach. A. Goldman and J. Pust (this volume) defend a concept-possession account of intuitional evidence. Although they do not take up the question of how to analyze what it is to possess a concept, they argue convincingly that the concept-possession approach is inevitable.

4. I have presented a portion of the material in this section in Bealer (1993); I can see no way to present the rest of the present chapter without reviewing it again here. I will, however, use the occasion to make a number of additional points and further clarification.

5. Empiricists should not object to this practice. After all, if something counts as evidence, it also counts as a reason that is evident. At the same time, empiricists believe that only experiences and/or observations qualify as reasons that are evident. Finally, empiricists would count a person as justified only if the person has taken into account the evident reasons.

6. It is commonly said that intuitions are easily shaped by experience. This claim is ambiguous. Meant one way, it is surely right. Various experiences are needed in order to possess our concepts determinately, especially concepts that are introduced in connection with empirical theories. Without such experiences, we would not possess various concepts, or at least would not possess them determinately. (In Burge's arthritis example, the person possesses the concept of arthritis insofar as he has various beliefs involving the concept, but he does not possess the concept determi-

nately.) Understood another way, however, the claim is questionable. Here the claim is that experiences cause us to shift from intuiting various affirmative propositions to intuiting their negations, or conversely, and these shifts are not associated with coming to possess (or ceasing to possess) our concepts determinately. My view is that, necessarily, this kind of shifting is severely constrained at least as the subject's cognitive conditions (intelligence, attentiveness, constancy, etc.) improve.

The indicated ambiguity in the notion of shaping-by-experience is associated with an ambiguity in the terms 'empirical' (or 'a posteriori') and 'a priori'. A theory may be said to be empirical insofar as experience is required in order to possess determinately the concepts involved in the belief or theory. Alternatively, a theory may be said to be empirical insofar as experience is required to justify the theory. The Autonomy and Authority theses pertain only to the second sense of 'empirical': answers to most central philosophical questions can be arrived at without substantive reliance on empirical theories, and in most cases it is possible for there to be answers arrived at by standard philosophical methods that have an authority that is greater in principle than that which answers provided by empirical theories could have.

7. I am indebted to George Myro for this example and for the point it illustrates, namely, that it is possible to have an intuition without having the corresponding belief.

8. Ernest Sosa (1996) has considered the idea of a *general* reduction of seemings to a certain sort of unprompted inclination to believe. A special attraction of this reduction is that, if correct, it would work, not just for intellectual seemings (intuitions), but also for sensory seemings (appearances). Unfortunately, there are counterexamples. Suppose someone S is looking at a duck-rabbit drawing in normal observation conditions. As it happens, S has two dispositions. The first concerns what would happen if S were coached in a certain way (i.e., if he were told to look for the duck): if told to *look for the duck*, it would appear to S that this is a *duck*. The second disposition concerns what would happen if S were coached in *no* such way (this is the kind of disposition central to Sosa's proposal): if S is not coached in any way (e.g., if not told to look for the duck), it would appear to S that this is a *rabbit*, and S would accordingly believe that this is a rabbit. Clearly, S could have both dispositions simultaneously. Now suppose we tell S to *look for the duck*. This would trigger the first disposition. Accordingly, it appears to S that this is a duck; it does not appear to S to be a rabbit. All the while, however, the second disposition (the sort of inclination featured in the proposed reduction) is still there: if S were not coached in any way, he would believe that this is a rabbit. So we have a case in which the inclination occurs and the appearance does not. But, according to the analysis, the appearance (sensory seeming) is supposed to consist in the inclination.

In reply, advocates of the counterfactual analysis of seemings might strengthen their analysis by adjoining introspection as a further condition: not only must S have the indicated sort of inclination-to-believe-absent-coaching but also S must be introspectively aware of having it. There are three problems with this strengthened analysis. First, is it really plausible that unsophisticated subjects (infants, animals) can have an appearance (a sensory seeming) only if they have an introspective awareness of an inclination-to-believe-absent-coaching? Second, suppose that S is told to look for the duck; accordingly, it appears to S that this is a duck. All the while, however, S is disposed absent coaching to believe that this is a rabbit; moreover, S could all the while be introspectively aware of this disposition. If so, the original counterexample stands. Third, introspection is itself a kind of seeming: I am introspecting that S iff it *seems* (i.e., seems reflectively) to me that S. (Like other seemings, reflective seemings can occur in the absence of the corresponding beliefs. E.g., it can seem to me that I am thinking rapidly even though I believe I am not—say, on the grounds that I believe that I have taken a drug that distorts one's subjective sense of time.) So, if this condition were adjoined to a general analysis of seeming, it would trigger a vicious regress.

9. Hilary Kornblith, for example, advocates such an approach.

10. Or immediate consequences of beliefs they already had.

11. There is one way in which this assessment might turn out to be false: if a certain very bold metaphysical thesis were true (a kind of Leibnizian identity of indiscernibles for universals), namely, if there were natural asymmetries throughout the space of universals, then conceivably every universal would have an implicit-turned-direct definition (perhaps infinitary) whose underlying constants were all logical notions (in a rich sense of 'logic' that includes as logical the notion of a natural property and kindred notions). If so, then every necessary truth could, by substitution of such definitions, be converted into a necessary proposition all of whose constituents were logical notions. This necessary proposition would be a logical truth on one construal of 'logical truth' (i.e., a proposition is a logical truth iff every proposition having the same logical form—i.e., the form determined by the constituent logical notions—is a necessary truth). Thus, if 'logical', 'logical truth', and 'definition' are understood in the indicated ways and if the bold metaphysical thesis were true, every necessary truth could be converted into a logical truth by substitution of definitions. So on that construal of 'analytic', every necessary truth would be analytic. In the text I will write as though this view is mistaken.

Of course, there are other construals of 'definition', 'logical', and 'logical truth' according to which there would still be necessities that cannot be converted into logical truths by substitution of definitions. And so in those senses, there would be necessities that are not analytic.

12. Suppose, on the other hand, that 'consistent' is taken to mean having no contradiction as a semantic consequence. Then, the Gödel theorem problem is avoided. But, assuming that logicism is mistaken, there is still Kant's original problem: individual arithmetic falsehoods (e.g., that $5 + 7 \neq 12$) would be consistent even in the semantical sense and would therefore be wrongly counted as possible according to the present view. Moreover, even if logicism were correct, we would get to virtually the same conclusion by considering—not numbers and addition and multiplication on them—but rather equi-spaced instants on the time line and associated operations on them. The relevant instants and operations could be referred to with primitive names, that is, rigid designators, introduced by means of reference-fixing descriptions. Even if the latter involved standard arithmetic vocabulary, the associated primitive names would have no such content.

13. This would not hold if all true scientific essentialist impossibility statements ⌜It is impossible that A⌝ were consequences of scientific definitions and 'consistent' were understood so as to take into account definitions (including scientific definitions).

14. Some people think that modality reduces to probability: ⌜It is possible that A⌝ is equivalent to ⌜The probability that A is nonzero⌝, and ⌜It is necessary that A⌝ is equivalent to ⌜The probability that A is 1⌝. But this is quite mistaken. On an objectivist conception, causal or physical necessities have probability of one, but they are not logical or metaphysically necessities. On a subjectivist conception, the subjective probability of an a posteriori natural kind identity—say, that water = H_2O—is less than one, but this proposition is metaphysically necessary.

15. Here are two unsuccessful responses to this problem. First, the proposed explanation might be emended thus: any *immediate modal consequence* of the nonconscious empirical theory can be raised to consciousness, and when it is, the result is an intuition having that modal content. But this emended explanation would at most ex-

plain modal intuitions such as the following: possibly p; possibly possibly p; and so forth—where p is a *nonmodal* proposition that is an immediate consequence of the nonconscious empirical theory. The problem is that this class of possibility intuitions does not include the possibility intuitions that are most important philosophically, namely, possibilities that are not actual.

Second, advocates of the proposed explanation might try to exploit the notions of consistency, inconsistency, and logical truth, somehow using them as proxies for the modal notions of possibility, impossibility, and necessity. The advantage of this approach is that, unlike modal notions, the notions of consistency, inconsistency, and logical truth might be empirically acceptable. But our earlier reflections about the differences between possibility and consistency spell defeat for all versions of this proposal.

16. Testimony-based justification thus seems to be a problem for the sophisticated ("normal worlds") theory proposed by Alvin Goldman (section 5.5 "Reliabilism," in Goldman 1986), at least as I understand his theory. The reason is that our telling of systematic lies to an isolated individual is compatible with a world's being "normal" in Goldman's sense.

17. The notion of a basic source of evidence is an intuitive notion that can be picked out with the aid of examples and rough-and-ready general principles. The following examples are typical. Depending on one's epistemic situation, calculators can serve as a source of evidence for arithmetic questions; tree rings, as evidence for the age of trees; and so forth. It is natural to say that these sources are not as basic as phenomenal experience, intuition, observation, and testimony. By the same token, it is natural to say that testimony is not as basic as observation, and likewise that observation is not as basic as phenomenal experience. Phenomenal experience, however, is as basic as evidence can get. Here are some typical rough-and-ready principles. A source is basic iff it has its status as a source of evidence intrinsically, not by virtue of its relation to other sources of evidence. A source is basic iff no other source has more authority. A source is basic iff its deliverances, as a class, play the role of "regress stoppers." Although examples and principles like these serve to fix our attention on a salient intuitive notion, they do not constitute a definition. That is our goal in the text.

18. This account of derived sources is perhaps only an idealization. See C. Peacocke (1986) for a suggestive discussion of how idealizations might work in epistemology. Note that I need not commit myself to the account of nonbasic sources in the text. For an alternative account see note 26. What is important for the present argument is that there be some account of derived sources that is consistent with a reliabilist account of basic sources.

19. Anti-Panglossian examples and also Swamp-Man examples show that it does not provide a necessary condition, either. But I will not go into that matter here.

20. Appealing to intuitions in judging this question is in no way circular, for it has already been established that intuitions are evidence. All we are doing here is appealing to intuitions to adjudicate the question of which sort of evidence intuition is, basic or nonbasic.

21. Hume (1777) probably allows that intuition is a basic source of evidence, for he holds that "intuitive certainty" is a primitive kind of knowledge. See Section IV, Part I, *An Enquiry Concerning Human Understanding*. Hume's radicalism in this area arises in connection with his views on the nature of the modalities and the extent of our intuitions concerning them.

22. Once it is agreed that intuition is a basic source of evidence, there is another point we can make against contingent-reliabilism. It makes an (otherwise avoidable) mystery of the fact that our intuitions actually have a reliable tie to the truth. If con-

tingent reliabilism were correct, it would be a contingent fact that our intuitions have such a tie. How could this (allegedly) contingent fact be explained? The most promising explanation would be one provided by an *evolutionary psychology*: just as evolutionary pressures selected in favor of perceptual mechanisms that track the truth rather than ones that do not, so also evolutionary pressures select in favor of intuitional mechanisms that track the truth rather than ones that do not. The unwarranted Panglossianism aside, there would still be a problem. Assume (for reductio) that contingent reliabilism is correct. Then it would be possible for intuitions—specifically, modal intuitions—to have been systematically in error. It is easy to describe a possible species like this whose biological fitness would be wholly equal to ours (specifically, their means/ends reasoning as fit) but whose modal intuitions would be systematically shifted in such a way that these intuitions would usually be mistaken. From an evolutionary point of view, it would then be an unexplainable mystery why these alternative beings do not exist and why, instead, only we beings with reliable modal intuitions exist.

23. In this and the succeeding paragraphs I benefited from a critical exchange with Ernest Sosa.

24. For the sort of theorizers who are able to engage in end-game self-approving theorizing, these cognitive conditions would perhaps need to be even higher, and so in turn the class of relevantly elementary propositions would be larger. Of course, what counts as "elementary" and "approximate" is vague. Although the lines are fuzzy, the larger explanatory point is clear.

25. I require only that *most* derivable consequences of the indicated a priori theory be true. I do not say *all*, for I do not want to rule out in principle unresolvable logical and philosophical antinomies. Nor do I want to rule out the possibility that Burge-like incomplete understanding might contaminate selected intuitions. What is ruled out is that this sort of thing could be the norm.

26. Maximally elementary deliverances of basic sources thus have the following characteristic: either they are demon-proof and so necessarily reliable; or else they are the next best thing—reliable in every possible context that is demon-free.

Incidentally, I provisionally defined one's nonbasic sources of evidence to be those deemed reliable by one's best theory based on one's basic sources. There is an alternative approach. Just now, when I tried to explain the role basic sources play, I reasoned thus: if there were an evil demon, I could have no success in my quest for the truth, so I might as well suppose that there are no demons; that way I maximize my chances for succeeding in my quest. Perhaps this style of reasoning could be applied a series of times, once for each kind of relative basicness. First, for completely basic sources, where the only sort of threat would be an evil demon (or something on a par with one). Second, for observation, where besides evil demons there is a threat from bad observation conditions. Third, for testimony, where besides demons and bad observation conditions, there is a threat from liars. And so forth.

27. And these features are precisely those given by the general principles invoked in note 17 to help single out the intuitive concept of a basic source of evidence. Notice that the above discussion is itself context-free in the sense just isolated: regardless of context anyone engaged in real theorizing (especially end-game self-approving theorizing) cannot but feel its intuitive pull.

Incidentally, William Alston worries that all efforts to show that observation has a tie to the truth are guilty of "epistemic circularity" in the sense that they must appeal to observation as evidence right in the course of the argument. But this is not so, for we can show the reliability of observation using our basic sources of evidence—phenomenal experience and intuition. Can we show without an analogous "epistemic circularity" that phenomenal experience has a tie to the truth? Yes, intuition-based arguments show it. Can we show without "epistemic circularity" that intuitions them- selves have a tie to the truth? No, any argument to that effect must, I believe, use intu- itions as evidence. (For example, the sort of argument in the text did.) But there is nothing vicious about this "circle." For, by the argument of section I and other argu- ments in that vein, denying that intuitions are evidence leads to epistemic self-defeat; it is impossible to have a coherent epistemology without admitting intuitions as evi- dence. (We can also show it is impossible to have a coherent epistemology without admitting phenomenal experience as evidence.) When one does admit intuitions as evidence, the kind of tie to the truth one is able to show for intuitions and phenome- nal experience is a strong *modal* tie. (Note that phenomenal experience cannot show this even for phenomenal experience.) The fact that this is a strong *modal* tie to the truth entitles these basic sources to serve as the general touchstone for evaluating the reliability of candidate sources of evidence.

28. The only serious reason to doubt that the implication holds comes from scien- tific essentialism, the doctrine that there are essentially a posteriori necessary truths (e.g., water = H_2O, etc.). In Bealer (1996a) I argue that this provides no barrier. The reason is that scientific essentialism holds only for semantically unstable terms ('water', 'heat', 'gold', 'beech', 'elm', etc.)—that is, terms that could mean some- thing different in some population of speakers whose epistemic situation is qualita- tively identical to ours. An expression is semantically unstable iff the external envi- ronment makes some contribution to its meaning. By contrast, the terms used to for- mulate (most of) the central questions of philosophy are semantically stable; the ex- ternal environment makes no contribution to their meaning in this way: 'is identical to', 'is', 'necessarily', 'possibly', 'true', 'valid', 'property', 'quality', 'quantity', 'relation', 'proposition', 'state of affairs', 'object', 'category', 'conscious', 'sensation', 'pleasure', 'pain', 'emotion', 'think', 'believe', 'desire', 'decide', 'know', 'reason', 'evidence', 'justify', 'understand', 'explain', 'purpose', 'good', 'fair', 'ought', etc.

29. This notion of conceptual content is defined in my forthcoming book, *Philo- sophical Limits of Science*. In the simplified setting in which all propositions are hyper-fine-grained we would have the following more familiar analysis: x possesses a given concept at least nominally iff x has natural propositional attitudes (belief, de- sire, etc.) toward propositions in whose logical analysis the concept appears. Inci- dentally, if you question whether there really is this weak, nominal sense of possess- ing a concept, you may treat the analysis just given as a stipulative definition of a technical term. Doing so makes no difference to the larger project.

30. It is not essential to our inquiry that the ordinary-language idiom fit exactly the informally characterized notion of possessing a concept in the full sense. If it does not, my eventual proposal should be viewed as an analysis of the informally characterized notion, what I will call "determinate possession." There is a long tradi- tion of isolating a theoretically important notion informally by means of examples and then turning to the theoretical project of giving a positive general analysis of it. Indeed, there is a tradition of doing this even when there is no ordinary-language id- iom that exactly fits the notion in question. We see this kind of project in Aristotle in connection with the notions of substance, eudaimonia, and so on; in St. Augustine and Russell in connection with the notion of acquaintance; in Kripke in connection with his notion of epistemic possibility; and so forth. If need be, my project should be viewed in the same way. Having made this qualification, however, I will assume that the ordinary-language idiom does fit the notion of possessing a concept in the full sense, and I will proceed to use this idiom whenever convenient.

31. What would happen if the person had one of these intuitions—say, that a tri- angular multigon is not possible—but upon seeing a triangle the person formed a

perceptual belief that the presently seen triangle *is* a multigon? Would this go against what I say in the text? No, for the person's cognitive conditions would clearly be *abnormal*.

32. In the present example we can be sure that the envisaged conditions are metaphysically possible, for *we* are beings in such conditions. But this is only an artifact of the example. When we generalize on the above set-up, facts about actual human beings drop out. Thinking otherwise would be a preposterous form of anthropocentrism.

33. There is a residual question regarding the restriction to property-identities p. Concerning this restriction, the formulation might be exactly right just as it stands. On a certain view of properties, however, an additional qualification would be needed. I have in mind the view according to which (1) all necessarily equivalent properties are identical and (2) for absolutely any formula A (no matter how ad hoc and irrelevant A's subclauses might be), a property is denoted by all expressions of the form: the property of being something such that A. If this view were correct, there would be true property-identities of the following sort: the property of being f = the property of being f such that P, where P is any arbitrary necessary truth. In this case, the proposed analysis would commit us to the possibility of settling a priori *every* necessary truth. This is too much. This undesirable consequence can be avoided in one of two ways. The first is to deny (1) or (2) or both; there are some interesting arguments supporting this move. The second way is to accept (1) and (2) but to adopt an enriched logical theory that is able to mark the distinction between property-identities that are ad hoc in the indicated way and those that are not. There are already several logical theories of this sort in the literature. In what follows I am going to assume that the unwanted consequence can be avoided by one or another of these means.

34. When I speak of higher level cognitive conditions, I do not presuppose that there is always commensurability. In order for the proposal to succeed, I need only consider levels of cognitive conditions *l'* and *l* such that, with respect to *every* relevant dimension, *l'* is definitely greater than *l*.

35. The notion of counterpart is defined as follows: p' is a counterpart of p iff$_{def}$ it is possible that there is a population C such that it is possible that, for some population C' that is in qualitatively the same epistemic situation as C, p' plays the same epistemic role in C' as p does in C.

36. These notions were isolated in my "Mental Properties" (1994) and examined further in "*A Priori* Knowledge and the Scope of Philosophy" (1996a) and "On the Possibility of Philosophical Knowledge" (1996b).

37. This theme is explored further in the papers just mentioned and in my *Philosophical Limits of Science* (forthcoming).

38. Perhaps 'believes' should be strengthened to 'rationally believes' and p restricted to propositions that x can rationally believe. In this connection, bear in mind that the testimony of a trusted informant is often sufficient for rational belief.

39. We have identified determinateness as *the* mode m of understanding that has both the correctness and completeness properties. Plausibly, there is not just one mode m like this. (For example, if there is a relation of acquaintance like that posited in traditional epistemology, there is presumably an associated mode of understanding; if so, it would have both the correctness and completeness properties.) But such modes of understanding would be species of a genus, and that genus would be the general mode of understanding, determinateness. This would lead us to revise the analysis one last time as follows: determinateness = the genus of modes m of understanding with the correctness and completeness properties.

40. If you have doubts about the analysis, bear in mind that the analysis is compatible with the idea that determinateness might come in degrees, achieved to a

greater or lesser extent. What the analysis aims at is the notion of completely determinate possession. If you find yourself disagreeing with the analysis on some point
or other, perhaps the explanation is that you have in mind cases involving something less than completely determinate possession.

41. Since, as mentioned in note 28, the terms we use for expressing the central
concepts of philosophy are semantically stable, environmental factors play no role
in the determinate possession of these concepts. Accordingly, the special restrictions that have bearing on concepts expressed by semantically unstable terms have
no bearing here.

Chapter 13

Rationality and Intellectual Self-Trust

Richard Foley

To what extent should we intellectually trust ourselves? Questions of intellectual trust arise with respect to one's faculties, procedures, methods, senses, and ways of reasoning, and they also arise with respect to the opinions that these faculties, methods, procedures, and so forth generate. Moreover, there is a relation between the two; if I trust my faculties, methods, and so forth, I will tend to trust also my opinions, and vice-versa; trust in one tends to transfer to the other.

Questions of intellectual trust arise with respect to others and also oneself. It is more unusual but they can also arise with respect to one's future self and one's past self. My concern is with intellectual trust in one's current self—in particular, with trust in one's current opinions, cognitive faculties, intellectual procedures, and so forth.

Most of us most of the time do intellectually trust ourselves by and large. Any remotely normal life requires a fair amount of self-trust, and for that matter trust in others as well. An adequate philosophical account of intellectual trust, however, will tell us something more; it will tell us something about what necessitates intellectual trust, how extensive it should be, and what can interfere with it.

I am especially interested in seeing how these issues look from a first-person perspective, as opposed to a third-person perspective. My primary concern will not be to look at inquirers from the outside and to ask what degree of self-trust they must have if they are to be reliable and have knowledge. Instead, I will be examining how issues involving self-trust look from the internal perspective of someone who wants to be a responsible believer, with intellectual integrity. Moreover, I will be examining these issues from a purely epistemological point of view, which is to say I will be concerned with what degree of self-trust it is reasonable for individuals to have insofar as their goal is to have accurate and comprehensive beliefs (as opposed, for example, to having beliefs that will make them happy).

Within the history of modern epistemology, there are two broad traditions concerning intellectual trust, with plenty of variety within each tradition and no sharp division between them (the differences between epistemologists within the two traditions being a matter of degree).

One of these traditions is what I shall call the "Lockean tradition." According to Lockeans, before one is entitled to trust an opinion or a faculty, one needs a specific positive reason for thinking it reliable. Lockeans seek to minimize the role of unexamined and unargued-for self-trust in our intellectual lives.

The second tradition is "Reidean." According to Reideans, one is entitled to rely on one's opinions and also upon the faculties, methods, procedures, and so forth. that produce them unless one has concrete reason for distrusting them. Their motto is "innocent until proven guilty." This approach emphasizes the unavoidability, indeed the omnipresence, of the self-trust in our intellectual lives.

What is there to say about the two traditions? The first and most obvious thing to say is that the former creates the threat of a regress. I am not entitled to trust opinion/faculty A unless I have a reason to do so. What gives me this reason? Opinion/faculty B? If so, then what gives me a reason to trust opinion/faculty B? C? If so, then what stops this regress? The traditional answer is foundationalism. Some faculties or methods are self-certifying or some opinions self-evident.

This answer has come under withering attacks over the last forty years, perhaps the most influential being those of Wilfrid Sellars. His critiques and those of the philosophers who followed him produced a widespread rejection of traditional foundationalism. The rejection has not been universal of course, but it has been sufficiently widespread that we are now well into what can be termed a "postfoundationalist" era. In this postfoundationalist era, a variety of new approaches to the problems of epistemology have been proposed as alternatives to traditional foundationalism—coherentism, probabilism, externalism, reliabilism, naturalized epistemology, socialized epistemology, and others.

Simultaneously, and often related to these new approaches, philosophers have proposed new, or sometimes have retooled old, ways of thinking about radical skeptical hypotheses (the evil demon hypothesis, the dream hypothesis, etc.). One of the primary benefits of traditional foundationalism was supposed to have been that it provided us a refutation of such hypotheses. With the fall of traditional foundationalism, it was natural to ask, how should we now think about radical skeptical hypotheses?

Many answers have been proposed, but the following are three of the most familiar:

(1)   Such hypotheses, and the worries they might appear to generate, are self-referentially incoherent, since in using these hypotheses to raise radical skeptical worries would-be skeptics need to presuppose the general reliability of the very faculties and methods that they are challenging. (Cavell 1979: 230)

(2)   Such hypotheses are metaphysically impossible, given the nature of belief or language or reference (e.g., Putnam, Davidson); the nature of belief, language, or reference make it altogether impossible for our opinions to be largely in error. (Davidson 1973-74, 1986; Putnam 1987.)

(3)   Such worries are unnatural; they are the products of a mistaken philosophical tradition, and hence they can be safely dismissed. (Rorty 1979.)

I am not going to discuss these proposed treatments of skepticism at any length. Instead, I will simply state my own opinion, which is that radical skeptical hypotheses and the worries they dramatically illustrate are neither inevitably incoherent, nor metaphysically impossible, nor even inevitably unnatural.

To be sure, in everyday contexts entertaining general skeptical doubts is peculiar, because doing so requires a detachment from ordinary concerns. There is no natural way to raise radical skeptical doubts when discussing with your mechanic the problems you are having with your car. If you want your car's chronic overheating problem fixed, you will not be disposed, even if you are a philosopher, to wonder aloud whether your memories of the car's repeated breakdowns might be completely mistaken. A fortiori you will not discuss with your mechanic, except perhaps as a joke, whether you have adequate reasons for thinking that your car exists. On the other hand, in the context of an inquiry into our role as inquirers, especially if the inquiry is a philosophical one that takes as little as possible for granted, skeptical worries can arise without force. We worry whether our cognitive equipment and our ways of employing this equipment are sufficiently well suited to our environment to be reliable.

The way for postfoundationalist epistemologists to respond to such worries is not to pretend that they can legislate against them metaphysically or that they can show them to be self-referentially incoherent or that they can dismiss them as unnatural worries. It is rather to recognize that what makes epistemology possible also makes skeptical worries unavoidable, namely, our ability to turn our methods of inquiry and our opinions into objects of inquiry. Within the context of such an inquiry, the worry that our beliefs might be widely mistaken is as natural as it is ineradicable. We want to be able to defend our faculties and methods, even our most fundamental ones, but the only way to do so is by using these faculties and methods, which means that we will never succeed in altogether ruling out the possibility that our opinions are largely mistaken. This is a generalization of the Cartesian circle, and it is a circle from which we can escape no more than could Descartes.

Skeptical worries are in this sense inescapable, and the appropriate reaction to them is not denial or despair but acceptance. It is no great loss to acknowledge our permanent vulnerability to error, and to acknowledge with it also that inquiry always requires a significant leap of intellectual faith, a large dose of intellectual self-trust, the need for which cannot be eliminated by further inquiry.

Admitting this even has its advantages. It discourages intellectual smugness and correspondingly encourages a respect for differences of opinion. If we keep in mind the possibility that our way of looking at the world might be seriously mistaken, we will be less inclined to issue self-satisfied dismissals of views at odds with our own. (Foley 1993, especially Chapter 2.)

A Reidean conclusion falls out of this very quick discussion of the last three hundred years of epistemology. Namely, once we abandon the aspirations of traditional foundationalism, the only realistic answers to questions of how to arrange and how to organize our intellectual lives are ones that involve large elements of unargued-for intellectual self-trust. This is the broad position on self-trust that I endorse.

However, this Reidean conclusion leaves unanswered many of the most interesting questions about intellectual self-trust. A healthy degree of self-trust may be our only realistic option in arranging our intellectual lives, but not unlimited self-trust. So, the pressing questions are, what degree of intellectual self-trust is appropriate, and what kinds of considerations can legitimately undermine self-trust?

As a first step toward answering these questions, I propose that the degree of self-trust one should have in an opinion is proportionate to the degree of confidence one has in the opinion and with what I will call the "depth" of the opinion. Similarly, the degree of trust one should have in a faculty, method, or procedure should be proportionate to the confidence one has in the reliability of that faculty, method, or procedure, and the depth of this confidence.

Confidence is not a guarantee of truth or reliability, but for the first-person questions I am raising (questions about what intellectual issues look like from one's own perspective), it is the place to begin. One begins with what one feels surest of. The relevant kind of confidence is epistemic—confidence in the accuracy of my opinions, as opposed, for example, to confidence that I can defend these opinions against attacks from others.

Even so, mere confidence is not enough. Depth is also important. Some opinions, even ones that are confidently held, are not deeply held. They are instead the doxastic counterparts of whims, impulses, and urges, which in practical reasoning are not to be treated with the same seriousness as full-blooded, less fleeting, and more deeply seated drives, wants, and needs. Analogously, in theoretical reasoning, shallowly held opinions are not to be taken as seriously as more deeply held ones.

What separates deeply held from shallowly held opinions is not mere revisability over time. Most of our opinions, whether deeply held or not, are revisable. With perhaps a few exceptions; there are conceivable turns of events and evidence that would cause us to abandon or modify them.

On the other hand, some opinions—again, even some confidently held ones—are so shallow, so tenuously held, that new evidence is not needed to undermine or reduce our confidence in them. A little reflection is all that is needed.

By contrast, other opinions are not so vulnerable to reflection. Some are the products of considerable thought, deliberation, and reflection, and hence further reflection would not be likely to alter them. Others are acquired with little thought but are nonetheless deeply held. For example, many of our perceptual beliefs are automatically or quasi-automatically acquired and yet reflection would not prompt us to revise them; they are reflectively stable.

Like confidence, depth is a matter of degree, varying in large part with how internally controversial the opinion (or set of opinions) is. Some opinions are such that, given one's other opinions, even a moment's reflection would be enough to undermine them. Others are such that only lengthy reflection would undermine them. Still others are such that no amount of reflection would undermine them (since there is no internal motivation to alter them).

So, to repeat, my thesis is that not every opinion is equally credible, equally appropriate to trust, or equally suitable for deliberating, theorizing, and decision making. The rough rule is that the more confidently held and the more deeply held an opinion is, the more reasonable it is for us to rely on it.

This is a general account, applying to full-fledged beliefs as well as to belief-like states, for example, intuitions. Intuitions are immediate unreflective judgments about an event, problem, or collection of information. In philosophy there is wide use of intuitions about hypothetical cases, modal intuitions, ethical intuitions, intuitions about the applicability of a concept or predicate, and so on. Just as with full-fledged beliefs, we can ask of intuitions: should we trust them, and if so, how much? Given the above thesis, the answer is, "it depends." It depends on the confidence we have in them and their depth, for example, would one's immediate reaction be sustained on reflection? Qua intuitions there is nothing epistemically special about them.

Many of the objections against using intuitions in philosophy and other kinds of theoretical reasoning are not objections against intuitions per se but rather objections that, when valid, apply equally to other sorts of intellectual judgments. For example, some objections are at bottom attempts to show that for many of us certain kinds of intuitions are not deep. They would not survive careful reflection on the data, including empirical data available to us from cognitive science. But if this is so, it is an objection against shallow intuitions, not intuitions per se.

Another objection is that intuitions are often not universally shared. But then again, neither are very many other kinds of intellectual judgments. If an intellectual judgment is not widely shared, then this is one of the things one has to reflect on, whether the judgment is an intuition or not. In some cases, the fact that there is no agreement may be devastating to one's confidence in the intuition. In other cases, the lack of agreement may be easily explained away.

Yet another objection is that intuitions can be shaped by the way the issue is framed, or by one's recent history, or one's mood, or one's culture. This is no doubt often true, just as it is often the case with respect to our other judgments. And so, the possibility that an intuition has been shaped by such factors is once again one of the issues we must reflect upon. In some cases our confidence in the intuition may be undermined by such reflection, but in other cases not.

There are other belieflike phenomena: hunches, forebodings, premonitions, and suspicions. They too should be treated in the same way as full-fledged beliefs and intuitions: we should rely on them to an extent corresponding to their confidence and depth.

A general account of rationality, or at least an account of what can be termed "egocentric rationality," lies behind my proposal regarding the degree of self-trust it is appropriate for one to have in an opinion, faculty, method, or procedure.

The notion of rationality—and associated notions of reason, reasonability, justification, and so on—come down to us historically (both within philosophy and in other contexts) with a variety of senses. With some oversimplification, the senses can be divided into two broad categories. One sense of rationality (reason, justification, etc.) tends to be externalist, objective, and closely connected with knowledge (i.e., with what is required for us to stand in a relation of knowledge to our environment), and the other tends to be internalist, more subjective, and closely connected with responsible believing (i.e., with what is required for us to put our own intellectual house in order).

Both senses are important for thinking about our intellectual lives, and both senses are important for understanding the history of epistemology. Indeed, many of the great modern epistemologists (e.g., Locke and Descartes) assumed that a single unified notion of rationality could capture both senses. In particular, they thought that if we were responsible believers, we could also be assured of being knowers.

Most epistemologists no longer think that there are intellectual guarantees of this sort, in large part because the great foundationalist projects of modern epistemology have failed. However, the lesson is not that one or the other aspect of Cartesian and Lockean projects has to be entirely abandoned and that we have to choose between the sense of rationality that tends to be externalist, objective, and closely connected with knowledge and the sense that tends to be internalist, subjective, and closely connected with responsible believing. The lesson, rather, is that there are simply different projects for epistemologists to pursue, and that these distinct projects must not be confused with one another.

The project I am interested in, to repeat, is the one that is concerned with what is required for us to put our own intellectual house in order. Being rational in this sense requires that I make myself invulnerable to intellectual self-criticism, to the extent possible. It is a matter of having opinions that would stand up to further reflection and deliberation, that is, having opinions that are capable of withstanding my own critical scrutiny (Foley 1993).

This notion of rationality implies that I am permitted in the name of rationality to rely upon my existing intellectual resources—my opinions, faculties, methods, and so forth—in forming new opinions and revising old ones. Hence, by its very nature it is a notion of rationality that emphasizes the importance of my trusting these resources. The trust is not absolute, of course, but only prima facie. Moreover, the appropriate degree of trust should vary with the degree of confidence one has in the opinion (or set of opinions, or faculty) and the degree of depth of the opinion (or set of opinions, or depth of confidence in the faculty).

There is a close connection between this kind of rationality and the kind of rationality that philosophy typically embodies. Egocentric rationality is essentially a matter of putting one's own intellectual house in order, of getting all the pieces (beliefs, concepts, etc.) to fit together as well as possible and to do so in such a way that one satisfies oneself intellectually, such that further reflection, even deep reflection, would not undermine the stability. Additional evidence, information, or data might undermine it, but not further reflection on the opinions and evidence that one already has.

But notice, this is a pretty accurate characterization of philosophy, and philosophical rationality, as well. Some important details aside, philosophy is reflection aimed at putting one's intellectual house in order, especially with respect to our most fundamental concepts, and of doing so without further empirical investigation. This does not necessarily mean that philosophy is nonempirical. It just means that in doing philosophy one wants to do as well as possible in getting one's concepts to fit together in a coherent way and in a way that is optimal for understanding current data, current theories, and current intellectual problems.

One need not be closing off the possibility that future information and future intellectual developments may make one's current ways of getting the categories, concepts, and so forth to fit together look uninteresting, or irrelevant, or unsubtle enough. Rather the idea can be that one is doing the best one can, given one's present tools (one's present opinions, concepts, etc.) to provide a coherent intellectual picture, or at least a coherent overall conceptual organization.

This conception of philosophy does not see its purpose as the uncovering of timeless, stable truths. Its purpose is instead closer to what Robert Frost said of poetry: It aims at a momentary stay against confusion.

Philosophy so conceived also contrasts with scientific reasoning, which tends to be more diachronically focused: science is more concerned with generating empirical data and formulating hypotheses that will get us to the next step, one that will either further confirm or further refine or alter our views about a specified range of phenomena.

Thus, philosophy—or more precisely, philosophical rationality—is a special case of egocentric rationality. Hence, what I have said about egocentric rationality in general—about the need for self-trust and about the appropriate degree of trust being a function of confidence and depth—applies to philosophy as well.

This is the beginnings of an account of intellectual self-trust, and of its importance for philosophy as well as for our intellectual lives in general. It is only a beginning, however—only a very general framework.

A question that a complete account of intellectual self-trust needs to address is, how much and what kinds of internal intellectual conflict can comfortably coexist with self-trust? The most extreme kind of internal intellectual conflict would be to have explicitly contradictory beliefs—to believe simultaneously and in the same sense (e.g., consciously, as opposed to consciously and unconsciously) P and not P. I say 'would' because there is a literature concerned with whether, given the nature of belief, it really is possible to have full-fledged, explicitly contradictory beliefs. I am going to ignore this kind of conflict.

Another kind of internal intellectual conflict, or at least internal tension, occurs when one has inconsistent beliefs, since it is impossible for all of one's beliefs to be true. It is not particularly unusual for us to have inconsistent beliefs. Unbeknownst to me, I may believe some necessary falsehoods. If so, my beliefs as a whole are inconsistent. Or I may believe A, B, C . . . N, which together, unbeknownst to me, imply not P. But I believe P. Again, my beliefs are inconsistent.

So, it is not all that unusual for us to have inconsistent beliefs, and it is not all that philosophically interesting either. The more interesting cases, at least for epistemology, are ones in which I am aware that my beliefs are inconsistent. Lottery cases and preface cases are the most well-known examples. Again, there is a considerable literature.

I am also going to ignore these cases in order to concentrate on another kind of conflict, one that need not rise to the level of inconsistency but that does involve a conflict between levels of beliefs—in particular, between one's first-order beliefs and one's beliefs about one's cognitive capacities and abilities in forming these first-order beliefs.

The specific cases I have in mind are ones in which I acquire empirical information that threatens to undermine my trust in the reliability of one or more of my cognitive capacities, methods or procedures, and in the opinions they generate. The general form of these cases is as follows: I have a confident and deep opinion that P, but I then acquire information that this opinion belongs to a class of opinions about which people in general are unreliable, and at least at first glance there is no reason to think I am different from most people.

Here is an example: In a wide range of studies, the one-hour personal interview has been shown to be unhelpful in improving the accuracy of opinion. For example, it has been shown unhelpful to medical schools in predicting the likely success of applicants should they be admitted, where the success they are trying to predict is a high grade-point average. Likewise, it has been unhelpful to colleges and universities in predicting likely success of applicants in teaching, where the success they are trying to predict is defined by high student evaluations. Similarly, personal interviews have been shown unhelpful to parole boards in predicting recidivism among convicted criminals, where recidivism is defined by future convictions. In each of these cases, the one-hour interview does not help improve predictions; it does not help individuals, or committees, identify who will be successful in medical school, who will be good teachers, or who will not commit future crimes. Indeed, far from improving predictive performance, holding interviews usually worsens it. For example, committees using statistical measures (university grades, ranking of undergraduate institution, etc.) alone do better than committees using these statistical measures plus interviews. (For a summary of some of the findings, see Dawes 1994.)

The number of such studies over the last ten to fifteen years has multiplied and the results are almost always the same. Indeed, it is an exaggeration but only a very slight one to say for that for any predictions of future behavior that have been studied, personally interviewing the subjects for one hour harms rather than aids predictive accuracy.

These are remarkable findings. If they were taken seriously, they would have enormous social implications. After all, millions of hours of work time and billions of dollars are expended in the United States alone on personal interviews.

The usual explanation of the worsened predictive performance is that irrelevant information (e.g., personal appearance and mannerisms) swamps relevant information. Or even if the information is not totally irrelevant (that is, even if appearance and mannerisms do to some extent affect teaching evaluations, likely success in medical school, and the likelihood of a convictions for a crime), the information gets weighted more heavily than it should.

Many issues can be raised about this literature, including some that challenge its cogency. The issue I want to focus on, however, is the egocentric one—namely, how should I react to this literature if I am the one forming opinions on the basis of interviews? Should it undermine my trust in my ability to form reliable opinions. If so, to what extent?

I will make the example more concrete. I interview Smith and on the basis of this interview and other background opinions about teaching and students I have opinion x about Smith's likely success in the classroom, as measured by teaching evaluations. Then I recall the literature on interviewing. Assume for the discussion here that the literature makes it reasonable for me to believe that after personal interviews, interviewers have a strong tendency to make worse predictions about the applicants' future job performance, educational success, and so on. Moreover, suppose I have no reason to think I am different. This may give me a reason to avoid interviews as a predictive technique. But suppose I cannot. My job requires it. It required me to interview Smith. Now that I have done so, the question is, should I trust my interview assessment, my opinion x? When I directly consider the issue of whether Smith is likely to be a successful teacher, I have confidence in opinion x. However, when I go up a level and consider that this opinion was formed after a personal interview with Smith and that people in general are unreliable in their postinterview assessments and that there is no reason, at least at first glance, to think I am different from most people, my opinion begins to look different.

Not much hinges on this particular example or on the particular set of studies about interviewing on which the example is based. If you have doubts about the example or the studies lying behind it, it is not difficult to come up with other examples and other studies. There is now an extensive literature in cognitive psychology that describes our tendencies to make mistakes of judgment and reasoning in a variety of situations. So, take your favorite example in this literature—neglect of base rates, overconfidence bias, probability blindness, anchoring phenomena—and construct your own analogous problem case.

A vigorous debate has built up around this literature. However, very little of the debate is about the personal, egocentric epistemological issues that are my concern. The debate rather has focused on such questions as, what do these studies tells us about the rationality of humans in general. Do they suggest widespread irrationality? The initial reading of the studies was that they document widespread epistemic irrationality. They show that people are less than ideally accurate cognizers and processors of information and hence are less than ideally rational.

However, there have been various objections to this reading. One of the most interesting is an evolutionary response that denies there is any irrationality in these cases, or at least any deep systematic irrationality. The appearance of deep irrationality disappears, it is claimed, once we widen the context, and the way to widen the context is to look for the evolutionary advantages of the cognitive structures and dispositions that generate the mistakes that the subjects in the studies make. Specifically, we are told to look for the evolutionary advantages of these structures and dispositions for our hunter-gatherer ancestors in the environment in which they found themselves and in which these structures and dispositions evolved (by most accounts, the late Pleistocene). Looking for such advantages will provide us with good hints as to the usefulness of these cognitive structures and dispositions. The underlying assumption here is that our cognitive structures (the fundamental ones anyway) were selected for, and hence they are, if not optimal, at least much better than random with respect to promoting survival.

One counterresponse to this evolutionary response is that it is not so much mistaken as not to the point. Suppose we grant that the cognitive structures that produce the pattern of mistakes documented in recent studies were well designed for hunter-gatherers in the Pleistocene and hence in some broad (pragmatic) sense were rational for them in that context and environment. All this may be so, but we are not hunter-gatherers operating in a Pleistocene environment. We are not so constantly preoccupied, at least not directly, with the business of survival. So, structures and dispositions that served our ancestors well and were in some pragmatic sense rational for them need not also be rational for us.

Indeed, in the modern world we are occasionally occupied with concerns that, if not purely intellectual, are at least largely intellectual. This is so in basic science, in philosophy, and in many other intellectual areas as well. This is not to say that there may not be pragmatic pay-offs of these intellectual inquiries. It is only to say that the immediate end is epistemic; the main point is to get things right—to have accurate and comprehensive beliefs about the domain at issue. Moreover, if in the midst of deciding, debating, discussing these intellectual matters, inquirers uncovered they had been making mistakes of the sort documented in recent studies, if for example they found they had been ignoring base rates, they themselves would correct the mistake and would (correctly) consider it irrational not to do so. They would not be content with the idea that such mistakes on their part are rational in some wide sense, that is, that they are the products of structures and dispositions that were selected because they tend to enhance prospects for survival.

Why is this? Why would they (correctly) regard such an observation as irrelevant? Because in doing their science or in doing their theorizing, they are in a context in which their goals are (relatively) pure intellectual ones. Their goals are not pragmatic (survival, for example) but rather to have accurate and comprehensive beliefs about the domain at issue.

In any event, whatever one thinks of these various moves and countermoves about the literature that documents our tendencies to make various sorts of intellectual mistakes, it is clear that most of the debate has focused on general and impersonal issues concerning the rationality of humans in general rather than on the first person and sometimes even intensely personal questions that are my concern. Questions and debates about the rationality of humans in general are important and intriguing, but a more immediate issue is, how am I to react to this literature in arranging my own intellectual life?

One possible reaction can be characterized as "the sanguine response:" I am different from most people. Most people have a tendency to make mistakes of the kind in question but I do not. For example, other people are bad interviewers, letting irrelevant factors influence their judgments, but I am not. I am different. So, with respect to Smith, I need not be wary of my postinterview assessment.

Unfortunately, this response looks like mere bluster unless there is some evidence indicating I really am different. Occasionally there may be such evidence. As more studies are conducted on our tendencies to make mistakes, the findings are becoming more subtle and encourage the making of distinctions. Not every group, we are finding, is equally vulnerable to making the mistakes in question. Those trained in economics are less likely to commit "sunk costs" mistakes, for example. They constitute a kind of protected class, as it were. These more focused studies thus offer me the possibility of an escape from the worries that the general studies produce. I may be in the protected class.

On the other hand, the literature on interviewing, to this date, has unearthed no such protected class. There is no well-defined group whose predictions are not damaged by one-hour interviews. But the more important observation is that even if future studies do identify a protected group, there are no assurances that I will belong to it. So, the general problem I am concerned with here has not been side-stepped.

Another possible reaction is "the bleak response:" If I am not in a protected class, my only reasonable option in the interviewing case is to discount entirely the interview. After all, I have evidence to think that most people are unreliable in their postinterview assessments and I have no evidence to think I am different. So, the only reasonable options are to revert to my preinterview opinion, or if this is not possible (perhaps I had no preinterview opinion) to withhold judgment.

The strategy, in other words, is to protect myself from the harmful effects of the interview, and to do so by numbing myself intellectually with respect to the interview, so that it has no effect on my opinion. The goal is the intellectual equivalent of looking the other way.

Perhaps I do not have to do so forever. As the salient features of the interviewee fade with time, so too the harmful cognitive effects of the interview may also fade. (The memory of the warm charming personality fades and reliable evidence begins once again to be emphasized.) So with time, it may be that the strategy of totally ignoring the interview will no longer be necessary. That is, with time it may be that I can think about the interview without being so swayed by its irrelevant features. But in the meantime, according to this response, the only reasonable option is for me to ignore the interview completely, relying on my preinterview opinion or withholding judgment altogether.[1]

A better response steers a course between complete blustering and complete discounting: My having evidence indicating that most people have a tendency to be unreliable in their postinterview predictions does not necessarily preclude me from making reasonable predictions about the interviewee, even if I do not have specific evidence that I am in a protected class. I do not necessarily have to ignore the interview, nor do I have to wait for the effects of the interview to fade or acquire additional evidence. Further deliberation, further reflection, and further self-monitoring is also an option.

In particular, I can deliberate and reflect, taking the warnings of the literature seriously but also taking pains to guard myself against the tendencies and effects that the literature warns me against. Alternatively, even if I believe that I cannot entirely avoid these tendencies, I can nonetheless adjust for them and recalibrate my opinion. We often engage in such recalibrations. Here is an everyday example: I am marking a student paper that argues for a position that I regard as untenable. I realize that I have a tendency to be overly critical of arguments in defense of this position, since I regard the conclusion as so implausible. So, in marking the paper I monitor myself against bias. However, I may also realize there is a part of me that cannot help but regard as weak any arguments for the position in question. So, after reading the paper, I recalibrate, correcting for my own bias, and assign a grade accordingly.

Recalibration is a realistic option only if I have some vague idea about the source of my unreliability. Consider an analogy. Cigarette smoking is irrationally dangerous given that we know smoking has a tendency to cause cancer. Of course, not everyone who smokes heavily gets cancer, and if we knew what factors caused some smokers to contract cancer, then it might be safe for us to smoke if we knew we were free of those factors; otherwise, smoking is too dangerous. Similarly in the interviewing cases and other such cases: If I have no idea what causes me and others to be unreliable, I cannot monitor myself for these factors and hence recalibration is not a realistic option.

Fortunately, I do have a sense of what the main sources of unreliability are: It is the manner and the appearance of the interviewees. Hence, recalibration is at least a possibility. I can try to correct for the flattering manner, or the brusque manner, or the appealing appearance, or the unappealing one. Moreover, the resulting opinion can be a reasonable one for me to have. If I perform the recalibration to my own deep satisfaction, such that further reflection would not prompt me to retract, I am entitled to my opinion.

Consider a hypothetical extension of the above studies. Assume that we have in hand not just studies that indicate that interviews worsen predictive performance but in addition studies that indicate that performance is not improved even when the interviewers are warned in advance about the inaccuracies created by personal interviews and explicitly asked to guard against them. I know of no empirical studies of precisely this sort. However, it would not be hugely surprising if advance instruction and warnings did not altogether eliminate the negative effects of interviewing.[2]

Under these conditions, it may be even more tempting to think that the only reasonable option is to discount entirely the interview. Self-monitoring and recalibration might seem hopeless, since the ability to self-monitor and recalibrate has itself been shown to be futile or of only limited benefit. So, reverting to previous opinion or withholding are the only reasonable options.

But once again, this is a too rigid response. The fact that I have to rely on challenged abilities and procedures to reach an opinion, if I am to have an opinion at all, does not completely eliminate the possibility of my rationally having an opinion. To be sure, I cannot ignore the warnings posed by the (hypothetical) study; I cannot simply assume that unlike most others, I do have the ability, when forewarned about the harmful affects of the one-hour personal interview, to reliably self-monitor or to recalibrate. On the contrary, this is one of the issues about which I must deliberate and on which I must take a stand. In many cases, perhaps even most, deliberation and reflection may lead me to conclude that it is too risky for me to allow the interview to have any effect on my opinion, in which case reverting to previous opinion or withholding are indeed the only reasonable options. There are possible exceptions, however. I am not always and everywhere forced, on pains of irrationality, to reach this conclusion.

Of course, much will depend on the nature of the (hypothetical) studies that indicate predictions are not improved even when interviewers are informed about the problems created by personal interviews and asked to guard against them. If these studies provide no clues as to why self-monitoring is not generally effective, then I will have nothing to guide me in trying to guard myself against unreliable self-monitoring. (Recall the smoking analogy above.) On the other hand, the studies themselves may very well suggest hypotheses about what it is that typically goes wrong in these attempts to self-monitor. If so, I can try to monitor my self-monitoring in hopes of protecting myself against these problems, or failing this I can try to recalibrate. Moreover, if the resulting opinion is both confidently held and deep, such that further reflection would not undermine it— not even further reflection on the literature that informs me of the general unreliability of self-monitoring—then I am entitled to this opinion and am entitled also to rely on it in further deliberations and decisionmaking. I am entitled to rely on it despite the fact that in forming the opinion I have had no choice but to employ procedures and abilities that are being challenged.

This stance may strike some as overly complacent, but in fact it is little more than an acknowledgment of the unavoidably central role of self-trust in our intellectual lives. One way of illustrating this role is to draw out the close analogy between the worries created by the hypothetical empirical study I have been discussing and the worries created by radical skeptical hypotheses, worries that motivated (and plagued) many of the great projects of modern epistemology. The worries are exactly similar in structure.

For example, consider the worries that Descartes faced with respect to his method of doubt, the ones that led to his struggles with the Cartesian circle: Descartes recommended that we believe only that which is impossible to doubt, and he asserted that if we do so we can be assured of not falling into error. But he then asked, might not that which is psychologically impossible for us to doubt nonetheless be false? When I consider a proposition P directly, it may be impossible for me to doubt its truth. But when I consider myself and my opinions from the outside, as it were, it seems as if I cannot altogether dismiss the possibility that what is psychologically impossible for me to doubt might nonetheless be false.

Descartes' strategy for dealing with this worry, notoriously, was to use the method of doubt to establish that God exists and then to establish also that God would not allow us to be deceived about propositions that it is impossible for us to doubt. In other words, he appealed to what he regarded as indubitable propositions—that God exists and that God would not allow us to be deceived—to argue that indubitability assures us of truth, hence the circle.

Nevertheless, the problem with this cluster of arguments is not their circularity. The problem is rather that they are bad arguments. As individual arguments they do not succeed. Indeed, as far as I can determine, no one in the entire history of philosophy other than Descartes himself has thought that his proof of God's existence is really altogether indubitable, and not many have even thought that it is altogether indubitable that a good God might not allow falsehoods to be psychologically impossible to doubt. So, no one really thinks that Descartes' arguments succeed, but the problem, I repeat, is not their circularity. Descartes' overall strategy is a perfectly appropriate one. There is nothing wrong with Descartes resorting to the method of doubt to reply to worries about the method. On the contrary, he had no choice but to do so. The method of doubt is forwarded by him as the fundamental method of inquiry. So, if he is going to respond to worries about the method, he had better use it.

The truth is that some questions deserve to be begged. They have to be begged if they are to be answered at all. First and foremost among such questions are ones about our own intellectual faculties, methods, procedures, and abilities. To answer such questions, we often have no choice but to rely on those same faculties, methods, procedures, and abilities. This is so whether the challenge is based on a thought experiment, as it was with respect to Descartes' method of doubt, or on empirical studies.

Moreover, it is not always a trivial matter to be able to beg a question. It is not always the case that a set of faculties, methods, procedures, and abilities, when employed consistently, will generate evidence that confirms the reliability of those same faculties, methods, procedures, and abilities. On the contrary, if applied consistently, the faculties, methods, procedures, and abilities can generate evidence that undermines their pretensions of reliability. Indeed, this is a most tried-and-true skeptical strategy. (See Foley 1993, especially: 75-88.)

The most important point to keep in mind, however, is the simplest one. Namely, skeptics do not win merely by invoking their challenge. In particular, a skeptical challenge does not automatically succeed merely because it is challenging faculties, methods, procedures, and abilities which, if they are to be defended at all must be defended using those very same faculties, methods, procedures, and abilities.

There is a further analogy between the problems facing Descartes and his method of doubt and those posed for us by empirical studies documenting our tendencies to make mistakes. Although there is nothing wrong with Descartes resorting to the method of doubt to answer challenges to the method—on the contrary, he has no choice but to do so if the method is to be defended at all—this circularity does prevent him from getting the absolute guarantees of truth he sought. Since he is using the indubitable to defend the indubitable, he cannot possibly succeed in altogether extinguishing skeptical worries. Moreover, this would be so even if his individual arguments had succeeded—that is, even if he succeeded in showing it to be indubitable that God exists and that God would now allow falsehoods to be indubitable.

This problem of not being able to entirely extinguish skeptical doubts is not just Descartes' problem. It is also our problem. We too want to be able to defend our faculties and methods, but the only way to do so is by using these faculties and methods, which means that we will never succeed in altogether ruling out the possibility that our opinions are largely mistaken. This is a generalization of the Cartesian circle, and it is a circle from which we can escape no more than could Descartes. However, it is not a condition of our being rational, at least in the important egocentric sense that concerns me, that we be able to escape this circle and obtain such guarantees.

The same lessons apply, mutatis mutandis, to the empirically based worries that I have been discussing. There are no assurances that in trying to guard against the tendencies that the literature warns us against that I will be able to do so successfully. Similarly, there are no assurances that in trying to recalibrate, if this is my strategy, that I will able to do so accurately. Reliability and accuracy are not assured us by being rational. What this means is that a large dose of intellectual faith in ourselves is an inevitable part of our intellectual lives. If we had guarantees of the sort that traditional foundationalists such as Descartes sought, such self-trust would not be so necessary. But we do not and so it is.

There is a final analogy that is worth pursuing briefly, an analogy between the cases of internal intellectual conflict I have been discussing and cases of intellectual conflict with others. The basic analogy is this: In thinking about the general tendency of humans to make mistakes of a certain kind and then applying this to myself and my opinions (e.g., the interviewing example), I am looking at myself from the outside. I am taking an external stance with respect to myself, at least to the extent possible. The warning that I give myself, based on the literature, is, as it were, a warning from the outside, from an external vantage point. It is a warning to the effect that I am not to place confidence in how things look to me from the inside. (For example, I am not to be so sure of my postinterview opinions.) The question I have been addressing is, what am I to make of this warning?

Framing the issue in this way holds out the hope that the cases I have been discussing can be handled in a way that is structurally analogous to the way that intellectual conflicts with other people are handled.

Testimony sometimes produces challenges to a particular opinion that I have. Your testimony about P conflicts with my own opinions. However, other challenges are more general, as when for example you (or some group) tells me that my whole way of approaching a certain set of issues is mistaken, and mistaken not in detail but fundamentally.

When faced with such testimony, I cannot simply ignore or discount it. Mere bluster is not appropriate, especially insofar as I accept the notion that your cognitive equipment and faculties are broadly similar to mine. Thus, insofar as I have intellectual trust in myself, I am pressured, on threat of coherence, to trust you as well and hence to give some credence to your opinions. Of course, the trust need not and should not be absolute and unconditional, but rather only limited and prima facie.

Nevertheless, when faced with an intellectual conflict produced by your testimony, if I am to have any opinion at all, I have no choice but to make what I can from my perspective of the conflict and of your testimony, even if this means making use of faculties, procedures, opinions, and so forth that you are challenging and hence that are at issue. I have no choice but to reexamine as best I can my way of thinking about the issues and to monitor myself in light of your challenges. This may sometimes lead me to conclude that reversing my previous opinions is the best option; other times it may lead me to conclude that withholding judgment is the best option; but sometimes it may lead me to conclude that the best option is to retain by and large my previous opinions, with at most only minor adjustments or recalibrations of those opinions.

This might seem a hopeless or irrational or an irreparably partial way to proceed, since in effect it is to allow one of the parties to the conflict to arbitrate the conflict. But it is altogether misleading to think about such conflicts in terms of a model of neutral, impartial arbitration between conflicting parties. This is especially misleading insofar as the concern is with the first-person question, What am I to believe in the face of this conflict? Insofar as this is the question, I have no choice but to make what I can of the conflict using the faculties, procedures, opinions, and so forth I have confidence in, even if these faculties, procedures, and opinions are the very ones you are challenging.

Precisely the same set of points holds with respect to the more impersonal conflicts or tensions produced by the empirical studies I have been discussing. As with the challenges arising out of intellectual conflicts with others, I am not entitled simply to dismiss these empirical challenges. I cannot simply assume that I am reliable and leave the matter at that. I must instead reexamine as best I can my way of thinking about the issues and monitor myself in light of these empirical challenges. However, I have to do this, and I am entitled to do this, from my own perspective, using the faculties, procedures, opinions, and so forth I have confidence in, even if these faculties, procedures, and opinions are precisely the ones the empirical studies are challenging.

This conclusion illustrates yet again the importance, the centrality, and the irreplaceability of the first person perspective in thinking philosophically about our intellectual lives. Descartes and Locke were wrong about many things, but they were not wrong about this.

Notes

1. Of course, my job may require me to declare one way or the other—for example, to declare whether Smith is likely to be a successful teacher. But this is a separate issue. We often declare what we do not really believe, and this need not amount to lying (although of course lying is also common enough). The phenomenon I am referring to is one of forced judgement, where with respect to one's public stance withholding is not an option. The situation is analogous to that of individual jurors in a criminal trial; they are required to vote guilty or not guilty; they do not have the option of withholding, although, interestingly, the jury as a whole does have this option—the hung jury.

2. For example, the literature on anchoring suggests it is difficult to undo cognitive mistakes once they have occurred, even when people are told of the mistakes, that is, even after they are debriefed. So, forewarning may not eliminate harmful effects either. On the other hand, Richard Nisbett has led studies (1993) that provide evidence for thinking that some of the mistakes reported in the literature (ignoring base rates for example) are correctable with the right sort of instruction.

Chapter 14

Minimal Intuition

Ernest Sosa

Is there any future in philosophy? I mean to ask not about the job market, but about armchair theorizing. How viable is a priori reflection as found, for example, in philosophy, analytic or otherwise? That is our main question.

Intuition and deduction, according to Descartes, are our "two most certain routes to knowledge" on which we must "exclusively rely in our acquisition of knowledge." Since that great Age of Reason, however, reason has fallen on hard times. Denigrated by powerful movements, from romanticism to postmodernism, even within academic philosophy it has been scorned by philosophers otherwise as far apart as the existentialists and the positivists.

In recent decades the critique of reason and intuition has acquired a more serious, more scientific cast. Psychological results now impugn the epistemic worth of rational intuition, and indeed human rationality itself. In what follows I consider the viability of armchair theorizing and of intuition itself as a source of epistemic justification. I ask what the vaunted empirical results can really establish about the worth of such reflection and intuition. And I compare intuition with other such sources of justification as introspection and perception.

We begin by defining our terms. According to my dictionary, intuition is "apprehension without reasoning," but this ill fits current usage. As the terms are now used, at least in philosophy, although perceptual and introspective apprehensions need involve no reasoning, they are not "intuitions." Seeing that this is a hand amounts to apprehension without reasoning, but not to "intuition." And the same goes for introspecting a throbbing headache.

Remembering that Washington crossed the Delaware is also a noninferential apprehension without being an intuition. Let us put such memory aside. Let us focus, not on belief *retention*, but on other sources of present belief. Beliefs retained through memory must have been acquired in some other way. Beliefs can have sources other than memory, moreover, even when not first acquired. I may know, based on some seconds of free fall, that my plane is about to crash. But my knowledge that it is crashing, when it does hit the ground, is not just due to memory, even though it is not a belief that I only then *acquire*. After all, I knew already that it was about to crash. In any case, we focus here on sources of belief other than memory. We put aside beliefs that are *at the time* due solely to retentive memory.

What then *is* intuition? Shall we define it simply as noninferential belief due neither to perception nor to introspection? This broad sense lets in the intuitions of geometry and logic but also the hunches of a gambler. And that seems appropriate enough: gamblers do have intuitions, even if too often they are dashed.

It will be agreed that some such intuitions are knowledge. For that is to say only this: that sometimes one knows something that one does not then infer or perceive or introspect. What specifically might be so known? That $2 + 2 = 4$, for example, that no sphere is a cube, that nothing is numerically self-diverse, even that one exists. Are these not things that one knows? Are they not known without being inferred or perceived or introspected?

Thus conceived, intuition can be as humble and primitive as are the instinctive expectations of an animal or an infant. Our interest is, however, in more abstract and theoretical intuitions, like the intuition that space is Euclidean. In philosophy we might just focus on propositions that are *necessary*. Thus instinctive expectations will not count, nor will one's belief that one exists, nor the belief that our space is Euclidean. None of these counts as necessarily true, so none can be grasped by intuition in our present sense.

Intuition thus conceived will be dismissed by those who reject the category of necessary truth, so we define a weaker notion as follows:

(I1)   At t, S intuits that p iff (a) at t S believes that p without (then) inferring that p as a conclusion, nor perceiving that p, nor introspecting that p (nor *merely* remembering that p); and (b) the proposition that p is an abstract proposition.[1]

Intuition is thus viewed as a basis of armchair theorizing about the abstract. Here I do not define what it is for a proposition to be abstract. Fortunately, our working grasp of the concept seems good enough for present purposes. As a first step toward explication, however, I would suggest that abstract propositions abstract away from any mention of particulars. Thus, we may allow, as abstract, propositions quite specific and determinate in the properties or relations that they involve.

However plausible (I1) is as an account of intuitive *belief*, there is a better account of intuition. On this alternative account, intuition is analogous, *not* to perceptual belief, but rather to a kind of "ostensible" perception. A pencil immersed in water, for example, is "ostensibly perceived" as a bent pencil. One has a sensory experience as if one saw a bent pencil, despite being certain that it is straight. One therefore has *no* belief, no matter how faint, that the pencil is bent, and yet the ostensible perception of a bent pencil remains, nonetheless.

Something similar is experienced in the grip of paradox. One is sure that (a) if from a place with a sand dune one removes a grain with no other effect on the sand, then a sand dune will remain in that place; and one is equally sure that (b) a place entirely devoid of sand contains no sand dune. Each of these seems indeed a proper object of rational intuition. Each is an abstract proposition believed just in virtue of being understood; no perception, introspection, or reasoning is required. Even if the sorites reductio forced me to abandon my belief in (a) or (b), however, each to me would retain an intellectual appearance of intuitive correctness. This intellectual appearance seems analogous to the perceptual appearance that the pencil is bent even when one knows it to be straight. How are we to understand it?

Before one is shown the relevant reductio, one *would* naturally believe the naive comprehension axiom, just in virtue of understanding what the axiom itself says: that each meaningful predicate or property determines a corresponding set, even if its cardinality is zero. This axiom seems extremely plausible intuitively, absent perception, introspection, or relevant reasoning. Such immediate plausibility attaches to some abstract propositions, and need involve no belief.

Nevertheless, such seemings or appearances, whether sensory or intellectual, may still be *inclinations* to believe based on direct experience (sensory) or understanding (intellectual), and regardless of collateral reasoning. Here, accordingly, is our modified definition.

(I2) At t, it is intuitive to S that p iff (a) if at t S were merely to understand fully enough the proposition that p (absent relevant perception, introspection, and reasoning), then S would believe that p; (b) at t, S does understand the proposition that p; and (c) the proposition that p is abstract.[2]

Can one be immediately, introspectively aware of the intuitive appeal of a proposition? Pretheoretically it would seem so. In this respect experiential and intellectual seemings are on a par. One can tell directly and introspectively that one ostensibly perceives the stick as bent, despite being sure it is straight. Similarly one can tell directly how intuitive one finds the comprehension axiom, despite being sure that it is false. An acceptable definition of intuition should be compatible with such pretheoretical intuitions. Is (I2) in harmony with them? It would seem so, since whether or not one *would* react mentally in a certain way is often enough something one *can* tell introspectively, with no relevant reliance on perception, memory, or reasoning. Thus, while suffering a braggart, one may know directly that "if he had boasted one more time, I would have been annoyed."[3] This is direct knowledge, or anyhow direct belief about a conditional involving one's mental state, the sort of conditional in our definition of intuition, (I2). Definition (I2) hence jibes with our apparent ability to tell directly whether or not one finds it intuitive that p.

It might be held that intuition is an occurrent, episodic phenomenon and cannot amount simply to a dispositional state. I am not myself entirely convinced of this, but if it is thought important, we can modify (I2) accordingly, to yield the following:

(I3) At t, S has an intuition that p iff (a) if at t S were merely to understand fully enough the proposition that p (absent relevant perception, introspection, and reasoning), then S would believe that p; (b) at t, S does understand the proposition that p; (c) the proposition that p is an abstract proposition; and (d) at t, S thinks occurrently of the proposition that p (in propria persona, not just by description).

Bearing in mind that we could always strengthen our conception of intuition from (I2) to the stronger (I3), here we work with the weaker conception, which is a good enough approximation for our purposes.

Few would dispute that one knows at any given time quite a lot that one finds "intuitive." Our earlier examples will serve for a start: that $2 + 2 = 4$; that no sphere is a cube; that nothing is numerically self-diverse. Here are some things we are *not* committed to in agreeing that there is such knowledge:

(i)   We are *not* committed to the objectivity of necessity; we need not even affirm that there are any necessary truths.

(ii)   We are *not* committed to any ontological Platonism; the use of 'the proposition that', and the like, can be regarded as pleonastic.

(iii)   We are *not* committed to any irreducible intentional grasp or ontological acquaintance; no such grasp need be involved in our "intuition": an intuited proposition is simply one that *would* be believed if understood, absent relevant perception, memory, introspection, and reasoning.

Since we are not committed to any of these controversial views; since it is not controversial that $2 + 2 = 4$; since it is not controversial, surely, that this is something one *would* believe upon understanding it; and since it is not controversial that one *need not* perceive or introspect or infer it, in order to believe it; therefore, it is not controversial that in the sense of (I2) it is intuitive to one that $2 + 2 = 4$. Nor is it controversial that we *know* that $2 + 2 = 4$. So it is not controversial that we know a proposition that is for us intuitive.

It may be countered that we have secured uncontroversial agreement at the cost of emptiness and triviality. How could such a thin conception of intuition be of much use? When we say that a belief is thus intuitive, we are saying only that it is something abstract that one *would* believe upon merely understanding it. How could this possibly help explain the epistemic justification or aptness of such beliefs and how they can amount to knowledge? Moreover, it may be argued that specific psychological results cast serious doubt on our supposed intuition and its alleged epistemic role.

In order to assess these objections we can compare intuition, on one side, with introspection and perception on the other. How positive a conception have we of introspection and perception? Introspective belief is belief about a present conscious state of one's own, or so let us assume. As for perceptual belief, let us focus on visual perception of shape and color, and on perceptual beliefs about shapes or colors based on corresponding visual experiences. If that is our positive characterization of introspection or perception, could we do at least as well for intuition? Could we say that rationally intuitive belief is belief of an abstract proposition based merely on understanding it?[4]

A reckless introspector who thinks he undergoes a certain complex subjective experience is not automatically guaranteed that his belief is epistemically justified or apt. Even if one is right to consider one's visual image dodecagonic, one's belief may still have low epistemic quality if one often confuses dodecagons with decagons.

Similar reflections apply to perception as well. If I take something seen at dawn in a fog to be white and round, my perceptual belief may fail to be epistemically justified or apt, even if it turns out to be true.

Neither introspection nor perception is automatically a source of epistemically justified, true belief. We can go wrong when introspecting or perceiving. And the same is true of intuition. We do make mistakes when we take ourselves to intuit that p. Moreover, as Descartes saw, there is an important component of intuition in simple arguments of the form "Since p1, . . . , pn, therefore q." So mistakes in reasoning might sometimes involve mistakes in intuition.

A growing body of psychological literature details how even in conditions of apparent full normality, with high alertness and ample reflection time, subjects systematically go wrong in their reasoning and in the intuitions involved. Doubts arise about some of these results, but an impressive lot of them seem safe from such doubts. What should we conclude about the epistemic scope and value of intuition?

Actually, we have long known of the fallibility of apparent rational intuition, even in the best conditions of alertness, normality, and reflection time. It is hard to improve on the conclusive case provided by the paradoxes known since antiquity. What we can now contribute, therefore, is to extend the known scope of our evident fallibility. Suppose we do succeed in this, as I am prepared to grant upon considering some of the relevant literature. We humans are indeed sometimes systematically in error when we apparently intuit while normal, alert, and amply reflective. Our reasoning *competence* seems flawed; not just our performance. What follows from this? Does it seriously undermine our continued use of intuition?

Any such conclusion would be premature. Thus, compare the following. It is evident that human perception is fallible. More, it is known that human perception is systematically misleading in certain conditions. What should we conclude about our faculty of perception? In conditions known to psychologists, a normal subject would be systematically misled unless aided by collateral information. Before discovering ways in which perceptual conditions can be misleading, one is liable to go astray systematically in a variety of perceptual beliefs. Absent collateral information, human perception falls far short of epistemic perfection. Moreover, the flaws are not just accidental and occasional; they are systematic and widely shared. In the light of this, what do we conclude about the epistemic value of perception? Surely it would be precipitous and imperceptive to condemn perception wholesale on the basis of such fallibility. Would it not be comparably precipitous and imperceptive to condemn intuition wholesale?

Accordingly, the case from the psychological results against the value of intuition seems weak in the extreme. This in no way denigrates the scientific experiments involved, or their results. It only casts doubt on a certain use of them by philosophers.

There remains the charge that our concept of intuition is just empty and trivial. The point now is that nothing defined so abstractly and negatively could be of much use in enhancing or explicating the epistemic status of any of our beliefs, including abstract beliefs of logic, mathematics, and philosophy.

When we attribute to ourselves reliable faculties of perception or introspection in explaining how we know various things, however, must we have a detailed account of the operative mechanisms if such explanation is to enhance our reflective knowledge? That seems too stringent a requirement.

Suppose, on the other hand, that one *can* properly self-attribute perceptual or introspective knowledge despite lacking any very determinate scientific account of the operative psychological mechanisms. In that case, might not the same be true of intuition?

Recall our account of intuition:

(I2)   At t, it is intuitive to S that p iff (a) if at t S were merely to understand fully enough the proposition that p (absent relevant perception, introspection, and reasoning), then S would believe that p; (b) at t, S does understand the proposition that p; and (c) the proposition that p is abstract.

We had concluded that many propositions thus intuited are also known: for example, that $2 + 2 = 4$; that no cube is a sphere; that nothing is numerically self-diverse. If the appeal to intuition is to help explain in some way *how* one knows any of these things, then intuition must presumably be a reliable "source" of true belief, but here its thinness becomes problematic. How can anything so thin help explain anything?

Recall, however, Descartes' reasoning about the *cogito*:

I am certain that I am a thinking thing. Do I not therefore also know what is required for my being certain about anything? In this first item of knowledge there is simply a clear and distinct perception of what I am asserting; this would not be enough to make me certain of the truth of the matter if it could ever turn out that something which I perceived with such clarity and distinctness was false. So I now seem to be able to lay it down as a general rule that whatever I perceive very clearly and distinctly is true. (Descartes 1984: 24)

Descartes reflects, first, that only its clarity and distinctness makes it certain to him that he thinks, but, second, that this could not be so unless the clarity and distinctness of a belief reliably guaranteed its truth. And the courage of his convictions moves him to draw the entailed conclusion.

Suppose we do take ourselves to know the propositions listed: that $2 + 2 = 4$, and so forth, as, I assume, we all do. Suppose it is clear to us that these do not derive from perception or introspection or reasoning, which again seems uncontroversial. If we persist in thinking that we still do know such facts, presumably it cannot be just a coincidence that we are right in believing them. It must be more than a coincidence that, with regard to these facts, we get it right: that we would believe that p only were it so that p. Not only must we be so constituted and positioned, so related to the subject matter, that we *would* get it right, or tend to get it right; in addition, it cannot be just an accident *that* we are now so constituted and related.[5] Thus, compare: If in a house of mirrors I happen to stand before the one true mirror, then even if I thereby mirror in my beliefs the facts reflected in that mirror, I still do not thereby *know* those facts if I would have believed similarly had I been standing before any of the distorting mirrors all around. Knowledge requires a belief that mirrors the fact believed and does so nonaccidentally in relevant respects. This in turn requires that the mirroring or tracking involved derive from the exercise of an epistemic virtue seated in the subject and exercised in appropriate circumstances. For many sorts of perception we have impressive understanding of the mechanisms that seat the relevant faculties in the subject. Quite a lot is known, for example, about the structures in a subject's eyes, brain, and nervous system, that seat in that subject her faculties of visual perception. About introspection, however, we know much less.

Each of perception and introspection seems at least receptive to the following schema:

> S ø's that p *only if* S believes that p in virtue partly of these facts: (a) that S understands the proposition that p, and (b) that the proposition that p is true and of a certain sort s, one appropriate for ø'ing.

Thus in a case of visual perception:

> S sees that this is white and round *only if* S believes that this is white and round in virtue partly of these facts: (a) that S understands the proposition that this is white and round, and (b) that this proposition is both true and one that attributes a color and shape to a seen and indicated object, and is hence of a sort appropriate for sight.

And in a case of introspection:

> S introspects that she has a headache *only if* S believes that she has a headache in virtue partly of these facts: (a) that S understands the proposition that she has a headache, and (b) that the proposition in question is both true and one that attributes a present mental state to the attributor, and is hence of a sort appropriate for introspection.

What shall we say analogously of intuition? Try this:

> S intuits that $2 + 2 = 4$ *only if* S believes that $2 + 2 = 4$ in virtue partly of these facts: (a) that S understands the proposition that $2 + 2 = 4$, and (b) that the proposition in question is both true and abstract, and is hence of a sort appropriate for intuition.

Obviously not all abstract truths can be known by unaided intuition. Hence it would seem important to distinguish the specific factor d that makes the truth of an abstract proposition reliably discernible on inspection. Such a discernibility factor d would help us understand better how it is that intuition provides knowledge of the abstract.

Notice now the parallel between intuition and introspection. To intuit is to believe an abstract proposition merely because one understands it and it is of a certain sort IT. To introspect is to believe a proposition about a concurrent mental state of one's own that one believes merely because one understands it and it is of a certain sort IS. Given the great variety of propositions one can intuit and the individual differences in the degree to which people have that capacity, it is not easy to fix on a sort IT that will cover such variety while being neutral among the individual differences. But then the same seems true of introspection. It seems no less difficult to specify the relevant sort IS that will do the corresponding job for introspection. And the same holds of perception as well. In none of these cases would it be easy, or perhaps even *possible,* to specify a sort d such that it is true propositions of sort d specifically that one would believe upon understanding them, and thereby know.

Both perception and introspection impose contingent requirements on a subject/proposition pair S/P at a time t, beyond S's understanding P, if S is to know P through the respective faculty. If S perceives that p, for example, then the fact that p must be leading causally through appropriate channels to S's belief that p. Introspection does not require such channels but it does require the *truth* of P, which in the case of introspection will be contingent. Intuition is distinctive in requiring nothing concrete except perhaps for S's understanding of P.

Not all understood abstract propositions can be known by intuition. Some need to be proved. What distinguishes those that *can* be known intuitively? We might try simplicity, but that is unpromising, since insightful mathematicians, like Ramanujan, are capable of exceedingly complex intuitions.

Again, our problem is not peculiar to intuition. The same applies to introspection. Some of one's mental states are discernible on simple inspection. But others are not so easy to discern. What is the difference? Here again a simple appeal to simplicity is not promising.

Most often introspective beliefs slip in uninvited and unannounced, but occasionally they derive from deliberate and conscious inspection of the contents of one's consciousness. Does a belief gain positive epistemic status simply by deriving from such inspection? Here are some reasons for doubt. I might attribute to myself an outstanding ability to recognize shapes, even though in fact my accuracy falls well within the normal range. Presumably my confidence would entail comparable confidence in my ability to introspect the shapes of my visual images, even though here again my accuracy is similarly undistinguished. If I (ostensibly) introspect that a visual image of mine is a dodecagon, but half the time I confuse dodecagons with decagons, does the fact that my belief derives from introspection lend it much credibility? Surely not, in which case only a certain *sort* of introspection will yield such credibility. What sort? Compare my introspective belief that an image at the center of my visual field, whose contours are quite distinctly discernible, is triangular, or square, or . . . , or even hexagonal, or octagonal. Within this range, it seems very plausible that attentive introspection does lend considerable credibility to the fact introspected. And within this range it is also very plausible that nearly all of us enjoy a high degree of accuracy in our introspective beliefs. This correlation cannot be just a coincidence. Is it not clear enough that the *reason* why introspection yields credibility within the normal range, from *triangular* up to *octagonal* or thereabouts, resides precisely in the fact that introspection within that range is highly reliable? Intro-spective beliefs beyond that range forfeit credibility, except for believers endowed with special shape-detection powers, who *would* attain thereby a high enough success ratio and correlated credibility.

That one introspects that p, therefore, does not suffice to render one's belief epistemically justified. Only a special *sort* of introspection yields such credibil-ity. What sort? Propositions in the relevant field must tend to be such that one *would* believe them if and only if they were true, and this itself must be no acci-dent or mere coincidence. One must be gifted with a sensitivity to propositions in that field whose truth one mirrors or tracks. Presumably there is something about the normal range of shapes that enables one to tell that one tends to mirror the presence or absence of shapes in that range. It must be such sensitivity that helps one stay within the proper limits of one's relevant introspective faculty.

What mechanism could be at work in making us thus reliable? Must there be some gestalt enabling us to determine one's reliability on the basis of its pres-ence or absence? I can discern no such gestalt. Both with regard to intuition and with regard to introspection, nevertheless, we seem able to tell the limits of our abilities. Somehow we can tell the sorts of propositions that lie *within* the proper scope of our respective faculty, and to believe accordingly. Perhaps our discernment is largely implicit. Perhaps our cues form a motley lot. Even so, we generally restrict our corresponding beliefs within their proper limits. And when we do go wrong, we adjust in ways that enable us thereafter to avoid systematic errors. We monitor our belief formation, at least implicitly, and make adjust-ments that improve its systematic reliability.

Putting aside memory and reasoning, we have three familiar modes of belief acquisition: introspection, perception, and intuition. Introspection is directed in-wards, to the present contents of one's consciousness, including both experiences and attitudes. Perception is directed outwards, to perceptible aspects of the envi-ronment, such as shapes and colors open to inspection through normal eyesight. Both introspection and perception concern particular facts, which involve one or more contingent entities specifically. Intuition gives us direct insight into the general and abstract.

Objections of two main sorts are often brought against intuition. First, it is argued that in known circumstances intuition systematically leads us astray. Second, if we define a minimal conception of intuition safe from doubts attach-ing to more substantial accounts, it is argued that this minimal conception is just too thin to be of much epistemic use.

These objections against intuition have counterparts against introspection and perception. Perception is systematically misleading in well-known circum-stances. Yet we do not dismiss perception just because of that. We do not con-clude that one is blind just because one is color blind. We do not dismiss vision altogether simply because it is subject to systematic illusions. By parity of rea-soning, therefore, it would be an overreaction to dismiss intuition just because it misleads us systematically in certain known circumstances.

Introspection too falls short of perfection; it is not fail-safe. There are cases in which introspection does and would lead us aright, but also cases in which it would too often lead us astray. Only if the case at hand is of the former sort does introspection yield epistemic justification. What distinguishes that sort of case? What distinguishes it, aside from the fact that it is the sort of case in which the subject's introspection is not misleading? There seems no reason to believe in any sui generis special attitude of introspection, in any special, unified introspection that falls little short of perfection in specifiable conditions.[6] The range of cases within which introspection is reliable seems more plausibly regarded as motley. But why should this be a problem for introspection?

Compare facial recognition and voice recognition. Any normal subject can tell reliably, for each face or voice in a vast range, that it *does* belong to someone she knows; and for each face or voice in another large range, that it does *not* belong to anyone she knows. One can tell apart reliably faces and voices in two motley collections: the familiar from the unfamiliar. Must there be some special gestalt that unifies the respective collections? Must there be some special, sui generis propositional attitude that justifies one's belief that this is a face or voice I recognize, in all cases where that belief is justified? Surely not.

If so, if such unification through a special gestalt or a special sui generis attitude is not required for justified face or voice recognition, why should it be required for justified introspection? And why require it for justified intuition?

Justified intuitive or introspective belief requires that the belief in question derives from the exercise of *reliable* intuition or introspection: that is, from the exercise of the respective faculty in a situation wherein the subject *would* most likely get it right. This requires features in the presence of which the subject's faculty is reliable enough, *and* to which the subject's employment of the faculty is sensitive, so that in their presence he would employ it, while in their absence he would not. Nevertheless, the set of features in question may still be motley. Take again face or voice recognition. Here the set of features may be just the relevant visually or aurally perceptible features by means of which we can tell that we see a face or hear a voice. And those features form a rather motley set. "This I have seen before," think we immediately of a familiar face, but not, or not so fast, of an undistinguished facade or a nondescript landscape.

Our exercise of a cognitive faculty or intellectual virtue requires a *practical sensitivity* to features relevant to its reliable exercise. One somehow registers their presence or absence, which affects whether or not one assents. The relevant features involved can be complex and variegated, however, so as to make *theoretical awareness* of our procedure tentative and generic. Such awareness can be attained at various levels of determinacy. One may see that a tomato is red, for example, in which case one's belief derives (a) from perception, (b) from visual perception, and (c) from visual color perception; to mention only three levels of increasing specificity or determinateness. For greater determinacy one might invoke transmission of light, rods and cones, and so forth. Even before our discovery of such a scientific account, nevertheless, people surely knew the colors of seen objects, and often knew *how* they knew: namely, through visual perception—knew it, therefore, at *some* level of determinacy. This despite their ignorance of the relevant science, and despite their inability to capture in some unified formula the full panoply of proposition/circumstance pairs within which their faculty is reliable.

Why should it be any different for intuition? Why require knowledge of the specific processes and mechanisms involved, things that remain undiscovered for much of our perceptual and introspective repertoire? What is more, the set of abstract contents apt for intuiting seems motley, *not* unified intrinsically by any sui generis feature of the relevant contents, and *not* unified relationally either, through some special sui generis attitude that the subject bears to them only.

Suppose we lack any unitary gestalt covering the special sets of propositions that we intuit or introspect or perceive reliably. And suppose no special, sui generis natural attitude corresponds only to the reliable cases of our intuiting, introspecting, or perceiving. Suppose on the contrary that the relevant natural attitudes are only intuition, introspection, and perception themselves, along with certain natural more determinate or specific attitudes such as visual perception, auditory perception, and so forth, any of which is unreliable in specific cases that we cannot isolate through some unitary gestalt characteristic shared in common by these cases only. This may be thought to raise a serious problem as follows: How then can we understand our beliefs to be reliably based? What source or faculty or basis can we assign to a perceptual, introspective, or intuitive belief, enabling us to see it as a reliably acquired or sustained belief?

The best answer is itself a question: Why make such a demand? Why *require*, for the defense of intuition or introspection or perception, that one *specify* in general terms the conditions within which the respective faculty is sufficiently reliable? Yes, it would be nice if we could make that specification. Yes, it would give us a *better* understanding of how it is that we know the things we know through the exercise of the faculty. But what follows if we cannot? What follows beyond the fact that we lack some understanding that it would be nice to have?

Would it follow that there *is* no such faculty? Would it follow that it is too unreliable to be of use in enabling us to *know* through its exercise and in helping us to understand *how* we know, by citing its good offices?

Even if one's set of reliably introspectable propositions is motley, one still is *oneself* a reliable introspector, in the sense that, however motley that set is, *somehow* one is able to restrict one's introspective believing within its proper bounds. Might one not be well enough justified in believing *this itself*, so as to help constitute a coherent perspective on one's epistemic doings, a coherent perspective that enables some measure of reflective knowledge?

If that applies to introspection, it applies also to perception. As in the case of the faces and voices, the set of propositions whose truth one reliably perceives may be motley. Yet one still *somehow* restricts one's perceptual believing within its proper bounds. And, again, might one not be well enough justified in believing this itself, so as to help constitute a coherent perspective on one's epistemic doings, a coherent perspective that enables some measure of reflective knowledge?

If that all applies to introspection and to perception, finally, what precludes applying it to intuition as well? The set of propositions that one reliably intuits may be quite motley. Yet one still *somehow* restricts one's intuitive believing within its proper bounds. And, here yet again, one might be well enough justified in believing this itself, so as to help constitute a coherent perspective on one's epistemic doings, a coherent perspective that enables some measure of reflective knowledge.

Of course, we are not clueless on the factors relevant to our cognitive reliability. We know, for example, that the reliability of our eyesight suffers when it is too dark or too foggy, or when the object seen is too far or too small. We more easily introspect headaches than many of our attitudes and emotions. And we know that simple propositions of arithmetic, geometry, and logic are prime candidates for reliable intuition. The more systematic our knowledge of the conditions within which a faculty is reliable, the better our epistemic perspective on that faculty, and the better our knowledge deriving from that faculty. These are matters of degree, however, and here intuition seems not inferior to introspection or perception.

In conclusion, we have considered objections of two sorts against our minimal intuition: first an objection deriving from the fact that such intuition can be systematically unreliable with respect to specifiable sorts of questions; second, that it yields too thin a conception of intuition, one unlikely to be of much use. These objections are rebutted as follows.

First, even granting that intuition *is* systematically unreliable with respect to specifiable sorts of questions, what follows even so? Introspection and perception are also in that way and to that extent unreliable. If that sort of consideration is a serious indictment of intuition, therefore, it seems no less serious when applied to introspection or perception.

In the second place, even if our minimalist conception of intuition is quite thin, the most defensible conceptions of introspection and perception seem comparably thin. Any indictment of intuition on grounds of thinness must be brought against introspection and perception as well, by parity of reasoning. If we doubt that we can know about the abstract through intuition, therefore, we must equally doubt that we can know about the inner through introspection, or about our surroundings through perception. For the moment, that seems defense enough of intuition.[7]

Notes

1. Here we thus focus, stipulatively, on "abstract" intuition, on the sort of intuition that seems important for the armchair theorizing of philosophers. I have also recently discussed other aspects of the epistemology of intuition in Sosa 1996.

2. By "relevant" perception or introspection, I mean perception or introspection that p. By "relevant" reasoning I mean reasoning that supports or undermines belief that p. I say that S would believe that p if he understood that proposition "fully enough," by which I mean that there is a degree of understanding such that if S to that degree understood the proposition that p, then S would believe that proposition. Occasionally in what follows I leave the qualifier implicit.

3. At least one may know directly the fully introspectable correlate of that proposition: "If I took it that . . . "

4. This does not rule out that upbringing and experience play a major role in the acquisition of such intuitions; it requires only that their role, if any, be played exclu-

sively in virtue of their role in securing one's *understanding* of what one intuits. This would seem to be possible even if our concept of understanding both (a) is *vague*, and (b) fundamentally involves *degrees*.

5. Some accidents are of course compatible with one's knowing, as when one looks in a certain direction by accident and learns things that one would not have known otherwise.

6. Except possibly for *demonstrative* occurrent beliefs that "this" (ostending an image) is "thus" (ostending its determinate shade of color or its specific shape). *Such* introspective beliefs are so thin, however, that they offer little epistemically.

7. Someone might emphasize the poverty of our theoretical understanding of *how* we negotiate a walk through a crowded room. But that does not mean that we are hopelessly and totally baffled as we walk; much less does it mean that we should stop doing it.

Chapter 15

Southern Fundamentalism and the End of Philosophy

George Graham and Terry Horgan

One hallmark of twentieth-century Anglo-American philosophy has been the analysis and clarification of philosophically important ideas or concepts—concepts like *knowledge, freedom,* and *belief.* Hereafter, we shall employ the term 'ideology' (and the expression 'ideological inquiry') for inquiry into the nature and workings of human ideas or concepts, and into the semantics of the terms that express these concepts; and also for the facts that such inquiry seeks to discover.[1] For a long time during especially the 1950s and 1960s, "a priori conceptual analysis" was the popular manner, within philosophy, in which to think of ideology. A priori conceptual analysis was the metaphilosophy of ideological inquiry.

A priori conceptual analysts fell into one of two camps: first, the "high church analysts," who basically endorsed a model of analysis as designed to capture precise, informative, tractably specifiable, noncircular necessary and sufficient conditions for the application of philosophically important concepts (conditions definitive of what is sometimes called the classical view of concepts); and second, the "reformers" who believed that the specification of precise and informative necessary and sufficient conditions is, at most, only feasible for some concepts (perhaps certain concepts in mathematics or physical science), and who try to include reforms or revisionary proposals for definitions of key concepts.

Recently philosophers have worried about whether either conception of philosophical ideological inquiry could possibly capture the nature and workings of philosophically significant concepts given that they so thoroughly dissociate conceptual reflection from psychology, linguistics, and science in general. In the past two decades philosophers have raised doubts about "aprioristic" ways of knowing, as not fitting well with the sort of general overall account of the workings of human cognition that is emerging in developing science, including cognitive science and neuroscience. There is also mounting evidence that human concepts, including ones of interest to philosophers, typically lack precise boundaries and noncircular necessary and sufficient conditions (cf. Rosch 1973, 1975a, 1978; Rips 1975; Smith and Medin 1981; Bishop 1992).

We take it as beyond serious doubt that philosophers should attempt to clarify and analyze philosophically important concepts. Ideology is central to philosophy. But we think, as do increasingly many others, that the burial of a priori conceptual analysis is at hand; for certain key methodological assumptions at its core are likely false. We also think that most attempts to formulate a model of ideology as a broadly a posteriori or empirical interdisciplinary enterprise either make ideology seem totally indistinguishable from field linguistics and cognitive anthropology, thus denuding it of philosophy, or make it so weak and tepid that it is difficult to conceive how it could ever have the sort of central role in philosophy that it has had in this century.[2]

One aim of the present chapter is to do better: to offer a postanalytic metaphilosophical interpretation of the nature and role of ideological inquiry in philosophy. We will describe and try to motivate a general metaphilosophical position we call *postanalytic metaphilosophy*. We will also describe, illustrate, and try to motivate a species of this genus that we ourselves advocate: *southern fundamentalism* (SF). The title of this chapter refers, not to any impending termination either for philosophy itself or for ideological inquiry as central within it, but rather to the overarching *goal(s)* of philosophy. We come not to dismiss the broad conception of philosophy that emphasizes the clarification of philosophically important concepts, but to reanimate and redirect this vision of the philosophical enterprise.

I. Postanalytic Metaphilosophy

The general version of philosophical ideological inquiry we wish to defend is not *totally* different from conceptual analysis as traditionally conceived. But ideology itself should be distinguished from traditional philosophical assumptions *about* ideology—for instance, (i) that philosophically interesting concepts usually can be given precise, noncircular, informative, "analyses" or "explications"; (ii) that statements expressing these analyses are analytic truths; and (iii) that we can produce these analyses via a priori reflection. On our view, ideology is really a broadly *empirical*, interdisciplinary, enterprise encompassing such fields as psychology, linguistics, social anthropology, and philosophy. This nonaprioristic conception of ideology is at the heart of postanalytic metaphilosophy.

Empirical Inquiry from the Armchair

What do *philosophers* have to contribute to ideological inquiry? In addressing this question, it is illuminating to consider the sources of empirical data in theoretical linguistics concerning competing theories of natural-language syntax. The empirical data for syntactic theory include certain judgments and judgment dispositions of competent language users—in particular, judgments and dispositions concerning the grammaticality or ungrammaticality of various sentence-like strings, and concerning grammatical ambiguity or nonambiguity of various sentences. Such judgments are relevant simultaneously to psychological theories of human language processing, and also to linguistic theories about the syntax of language itself. Native speakers, after all, can be expected to have judgment dispositions about these matters that reflect a solid mastery of their own language (or their own regional dialect, at any rate). So, when native speakers are intersubjectively consistent and also uniformly confident about such syntactic judgments, then normally the best psychological explanation will be that these judgments reflect the natives' syntactic competence, their mastery of the syntactic norms or syntactic structures underlying their language. And this psychological hypothesis, in turn, has a direct implication for linguistic theory—namely, that under an adequate theory of syntax for the natives' language (or dialect), those syntactic judgments will turn out generally correct.

Similar observations hold with respect to hypotheses or theories concerning ideology. Certain robust patterns of judgment among competent users of concepts and language will be plausibly explained as manifesting the users' conceptual/semantic competence.[3] Here, too, as with grammaticality judgments, much of the relevant data is close at hand, some of it in the form our own introspectively accessible linguistic intuitions about how to describe various actual and envisioned scenarios. (Other kinds of close-at-hand data can be relevant too—for instance, facts about the pragmatic and social/institutional purposes served by the concepts and terms in question.) Since the evidence such data provides is empirical, it is of course defeasible. But it is data, nonetheless, and can function as empirical evidence about questions of ideology in much the same way that syntactic judgments provide empirical evidence for theories of syntax.

Consider, for instance, the following thesis about the ideology of our concept *water*: Necessarily, a quantity of liquid is water only if it is has chemical composition H_2O. In "The Meaning of 'Meaning'," Hilary Putnam (1975) convinced virtually the entire philosophical community of this thesis, by asking us to consult our intuitions about how to describe his Twin-Earth scenario. (Saul Kripke's influential arguments for related ideological theses work similarly.) We were surely right to be convinced, because the deliverances of our own descriptive intuitions very likely reflect the proper workings of our own conceptual/semantic competence with the notion of water, and hence are very likely correct.

The point of the past few paragraphs has been to emphasize the evidential relevance, for questions of ideology, of data that are relatively close at hand, so close that competent speakers can obtain the data from our armchairs (*die vom Armchair aus zuhandenen Daten*). Being armchair-obtainable does not prevent the data from being empirical and hence epistemically defeasible; this also makes such data eminently accessible to us philosophers, even though our methods do not involve wearing white coats or conducting field linguistics. When questions of ideology are at issue, thought experiments really *are* experiments; they generate important (though defeasible) empirical data. Intuitive judgments or armchair-obtainable data should enjoy (in Owen Flanagan's [1991] helpful phrase which we adapt here) "squatter's rights" as we embark on the process of seeking broad coherence. This does not mean that such data get to squat forever or that they are indefeasible. But it does mean that our intuitive judgments should enjoy a high degree of prior epistemic reliability or warrant—namely, that under an adequate theory of the ideology of philosophically significant concepts, those judgments will turn out generally correct.

Much of what has actually gone on within traditional conceptual analysis can

be viewed, retrospectively, as constituting this kind of empirical ideological inquiry, even though it has often been conducted under mistaken methodological
assumptions. For example, "counterexampling" a proposed conceptual analysis,
by describing an imagined scenario for which the analysans term seems intuitively applicable and the analysandum expression does not (or vice versa),
teaches us something about the ideology of the concept under scrutiny. There
virtually always *are* counterexamples to proposed analyses, it seems; the idea
that the concepts really have the kinds of necessary/sufficient conditions analyses
being sought is apparently mistaken. But the exercise of generating counterexamples to putative analyses is often ideologically illuminating anyway. We understand the concept of *knowledge* better, for instance, upon appreciating the
kinds of scenarios in which justified true belief that *p* does not constitute knowledge that *p* (cf. Bishop 1992). And of course, philosophers tend to be quite *good*
at this thought-experimentation dimension of ideological inquiry, since it figures
so centrally in philosophical practice.

The Role of Ideology in Philosophy

"The aim of philosophy, abstractly formulated," wrote Wilfrid Sellars, "is to understand how things in the broadest possible sense of the term hang together in
the broadest possible sense of the term" (1963b: 39-40). Sellars' claim enjoys
immense historical support. Presumably, as the activities of many of the greatest figures in the history of philosophy illustrate, there are important fundamental features of human experience that are studied in science, expressed in social
institutions, and represented in human beliefs and other attitudes. Philosophy
tries to bring these beliefs and attitudes into broad coherence with one another—
to bring them, as John Rawls and others would put it, into wide reflective
equilibrium. Very often, acquiring this kind of understanding or equilibrium
involves investigating the *ideology* of certain key concepts involved in the specific philosophical issue or problem under scrutiny. Ideological inquiry has long
played a central role in philosophy, and it should retain this central role even if
the specific doctrines about ideology embodied in a priori analytic philosophy are
mistaken.

Most any familiar philosophical issue or problem could be cited to illustrate
the point. Take, for instance, the question of whether humans ever choose or act
freely. When investigating this philosophical issue, one invariably finds oneself
asking about the ideological workings of our concept of freedom itself. In particular, one finds oneself asking whether the concept of freedom is such that a decision or an action is free only if it is not causally determined by prior events.
Such ideological questions persist and remain central to philosophical inquiry
about human freedom, even if (as seems likely) the notion of freedom lacks any
precise and informative "singly necessary/jointly sufficient condition structure"
of the kind sought in high church analysis.

As another example, consider the question whether commonsense intentional
psychology (so-called *folk* psychology, or FP) is compatible with the thesis
(call it *mechanism*) that humans are complex physico-chemical systems all of
whose physical changes and bodily motions are explainable in purely physico-

chemical terms (cf. Malcolm 1968). Under what conditions, if any, would FP be true even if (as seems probable to us, given current evidence) mechanism is true? Is it likely that the requisite compatibility conditions are satisfied, given the current state of scientific knowledge about the inner workings of humans? In investigating these questions, one finds oneself asking about the ideological workings of FP concepts, vis-à-vis the neurobiological or physico-chemical levels of description. Is the concept of belief, say, such that there must necessarily be a smooth fit between folk psychological and neuroscientific levels of explanation and description? Some philosophers, like Paul and Patricia Churchland, maintain that the concept of belief, if it is to apply to anything at all, must apply to a smoothly reducing state-type. Their ideological thesis is that FP, in order to be compatible with neurobiology, must be *reducible* to neurobiology via systematic type-type identities between FP state-types and neurobiological state-types. This alleged compatibility constraint is quite demanding; so, if the Churchlands' ideological thesis is correct, then (as they emphasize) FP might very well be radically false. On the other hand, if FP's ideological commitments are actually more modest than the Churchlands maintain, then FP might be compatible with mechanism even if the former cannot be reduced to neurobiology.[4] Again, an ideological question is right at the heart of an important philosophical issue. Even though the methodological assumptions of a priori conceptual analysis are evidently mistaken, ideological questions still retain a central role in philosophy.

Ideological Polarity and Philosophical Puzzlement

Philosophically interesting concepts frequently exhibit a certain internal tension, involving a tendency to "pull in opposite directions" ideologically. This feature, which we will call *ideological polarity*, is one major source of philosophical puzzlement, and often figures quite centrally in philosophical problems.

The problem of freedom and determinism provides a vivid and striking example of ideological polarity in the concept of free agency. On one hand, ordinary practice and ordinary epistemic standards pull in the direction of compatibilism: people readily and frequently attribute freedom of decision and action to one another on the basis of evidential standards quite unrelated to the question whether human decisions and actions are causally determined by prior events. On the other hand, virtually no reflective person, when explicitly confronted with the question whether freedom and causal determinism are compatible, can fail to feel the intuitive pull of the contention that if a choice or action is causally determined by the laws of nature and the antecedent state of the world, then it is not freely chosen or freely performed (cf. Graham 1993: 158-171).

The problem of psychophysical "explanatory exclusion" (Kim 1989) provides another example. Assume, as seems very likely true on current evidence, that mechanism is true—so that all human behavior (described as "raw motion") is explainable, in principle, in purely physico-chemical terms. Suppose, in addition, that intentional mental state-types are not identical to neurobiological state-types. On one hand ordinary practice and ordinary epistemic standards pull in the direction of saying that intentional mental state-types have causal/explanatory relevance anyway; that is, people's behavior is also explainable in terms of beliefs, desires, and related mental state types (qua mental). But on the other hand, there is an undeniable intuitive pull in the contention that the in-principle neurobiological explainability of all human physical motions excludes mental properties from having any genuine causal/explanatory relevance of their own—assuming that they are not just *identical* to neurobiological properties. The pull of this exclusionary intuition we take it, is at least part of the reason why philosophers like the Churchlands maintain that type-type reducibility is a condition for the compatibility of folk psychology and neuroscience. In their view reduction underwrites interlevel property-identities; and if mental properties are identical to (causally explanatory) neurobiological ones, then of course these properties avoid explanatory exclusion.

The fact that people's conceptual/semantic intuitions are pulled in competing directions in many philosophical problems is itself an important part of the overall body of ready-at-hand empirical data that ought to get accommodated in an adequate empirical account of the ideology of the operative concepts and terms. It is a fact that should be *respected* in one's ideological theorizing. This does not mean that all contentions with prima facie intuitive pull should end up being vindicated as *correct*, of course; in many cases that outcome will be impossible, since the competing contentions are often just incompatible. It does mean, however, that a credible metaphilosophical position should provide the resources for *explaining* the intuitive pull of the contentions it rejects as false— ideally, for explaining how this intuitive pull, despite being mistaken, nonetheless does somehow emanate from our semantic/conceptual competence anyway, and reflects something important in the nature and workings of our concepts themselves. Put another way: Someone who is conceptually and semantically competent *ought* to find philosophical problems intuitively puzzling, and hence, an adequate ideological story about the key concepts and terms in a philosophical problem ought to explain that puzzlement as somehow emanating from the nature of the concepts themselves.

A guiding analogy, in thinking about how such explanations could go, might be the case of persistent perceptual illusions, such as the Müller/Lyer illusion:

The illusion that the second line is shorter than the first persists, even after one comes to firmly believe that this is not so. Moreover, this is true for any *normal* perceiver. An adequate scientific explanation of the illusion should not only explain why this is so; in addition (and here's the key point), it should explain this by reference to the very design features of the visual system that undergird *correct* perceptual judgments. Something in the nature and workings of the human perceptual system (and its cognitive overlay) should account for the illusion.

Likewise, an adequate account of the ideology of philosophically puzzling concepts should make it possible to explain why any normal (and suitably motivated) cognizer will, when confronted with a given philosophical problem, experience philosophical puzzlement intuitively. Even if certain intuitively plausible contentions get rejected, under the account, they are intuitively plausible nonetheless, and will likely remain so even after being rejected. A credible treatment of the operative concepts should lend itself to a plausible explanation of this intuitive persistence, and of the ideological polarity it reflects.

Principles of Postanalytic Metaphilosophy

What then should be our metaphilosophical conception of philosophy, given these considerations and given the demise of apriorism? What should postanalytic metaphilosophy say about the philosophical enterprise itself, and about ideology as a component of that enterprise? We submit that it should say *at least* the following things. First, philosophy should retain the synoptic aim of understanding how things, in the broadest sense of the term, hang together in the broadest sense of the term. Second, philosophy should eschew the goal of providing "conceptual analyses," and should give up the idea that its own methodology is aprioristic.[5] Third, philosophy should treat ideological issues as central, albeit broadly empirical. Fourth, philosophy should operate via wide reflective equilibrium—a methodology that is nonaprioristic and attends to current scientific knowledge and strives to accommodate it. Fifth, philosophy should regard armchair-obtainable data about ideological questions as empirical, and hence defeasible. Sixth, philosophy should regard such data as having *strong* prima facie evidential status—similar to the evidential status, in linguistics, of introspective intuitions about grammaticality and syntactic ambiguity. We will call this the *principle of accommodation*, the idea being that the judgments that constitute such data should in general get accommodated as correct under an adequate ideological account, rather than turning out mistaken. Seventh, if a philosophical problem involves concepts that exhibit ideological polarity (as reflected in conflicting beliefs, or belief-tendencies, involving that concept), then an adequate account of the concept's ideology should explain the "ideological pull" of any of these belief-tendencies that turn out, according to the account, to be mistaken. We will call this the *principle of respect*, the idea being the rejected judgments should be treated respectfully, by having their prima facie plausibility both acknowledged and explained.

It is arguable that this postanalytic approach to philosophy is not really new at all, but actually revives an ancient and venerable conception of philosophical inquiry. Consider the following passage from Aristotle:

> We must, as in all other cases, set out the appearances (*phainomena*), and first of all go through the puzzles. In this way we must prove the reputable views (*endoxa*) about these ways of being affected; if possible all (of them), but if not all, then most and the most authoritative (of them). For if we both unravel (*luetai*) the difficulties and leave the reputable views alone, we will have proved the case sufficiently. (*Nicomachean Ethics* VII.1, 1145b2-8)

Close-at-hand empirical data about matters of ideology, data that includes facts about ordinary people's conceptual/semantic intuitions, provides powerful empirical evidence about those matters. Philosophical theory construction ought therefore to proceed by a wide reflective equilibrium methodology that aims to accommodate such data as well as possible. Aristotle's *endoxa* (sometimes translated as "common beliefs") are naturally viewed as data of just this close-at-hand kind. Aristotle's view that an adequate philosophical treatment of a given philosophical puzzle or problem should strive to accommodate the *endoxa* as well as possible (especially those that are most authoritative, exerting the strongest pull on our semantic/conceptual intuitions about what is right to say), is naturally viewed as expressing a commitment to a reflective-equilibrium methodology that assigns heavy weight to the principle of accommodation.

Ideological polarity, too, and its role in philosophical puzzlement, also figures prominently in Aristotle's conception of philosophy. This is revealed in the passage just quoted: some *endoxa* may conflict with others, thus generating puzzlement, and normally in such a situation the less authoritative ones get trumped by the more authoritative ones in the philosophical position that correctly unravels the puzzle. But in addition, Aristotle also emphasizes the importance of explaining the intuitive pull of the views that get rejected. He says:

These, then, are the sorts of puzzles (*aporiai*) that arise; some of these (claims) must be undermined, and others left intact. For the unraveling (*lusis*) of the puzzle is discovery. (*Nicomachean Ethics* VII.3, 1146b6-8)

We must not only state the truth but also the cause of the error—for this contributes toward producing conviction; for whenever a reasonable explanation is given of why a false view appears true, this makes us more confident of the true view. (*Nicomachean Ethics* VII.14, 1154a22-25)

The principle of respect thus plays an important complementary role alongside the principle of accommodation, in the reflective equilibrating process whereby philosophical puzzles get unraveled. The Stagirite, in addition to his many other notable accomplishments, was evidently a postanalytic philosopher!

Philosophy, regarded as a nonaprioristic enterprise, must of course pay attention to other domains of knowledge, and in particular to results and developments in science. The sort of reflective equilibrium sought in philosophy should indeed be *wide*—which means, among other things, that philosophy should take science seriously into account. The ideological dimension of philosophy, too, should operate by wide reflective equilibrium, and hence should be informed by empirical results and theories in linguistics, cognitive science, an other related fields. But ideological inquiry, even though it should be scientifically informed, certainly can and should remain a central part of philosophy per se. The empirical data of ideology are largely ready-at-hand, and the armchair is a fine place both for generating such data and for generating and testing ideological hypotheses via wide reflective equilibrium.

II. Southern Fundamentalism

In earlier writings (Graham and Horgan 1988; Horgan and Graham 1991; Horgan 1993a) we have articulated and defended a specific version of realism about folk psychology: a version contending (i) that the ideological or conceptual commitments of FP are substantially weaker than is widely believed (by both eliminativists and certain prominent FP realists); and hence (ii) that the integrity of FP would not actually be threatened by any of the potential scientific scenarios typically envisioned by eliminativists (e.g., a scenario in which FP turns out not to be type-type reducible to neuroscience, or a scenario in which there turns out not to be a language of thought). We have used the expression 'southern fundamentalism' for this brand of FP realism. Here we will use the expression in a much broader way: as a label for a general metaphilosophical position.

Southern fundamentalism, in this broad sense, is a species of what we have above called postanalytic metaphilosophy (PAM); the generic claims of PAM are a part, but not the whole, of SF. SF embraces PAM's principles, which are largely methodological, and adds to them two substantive claims about matters of ideology. These claims are each *empirical* ideological assertions. They are metaphilosophical in the sense of being quite broad in scope: they apply to philosophically central concepts *in general*, and not merely to specific concepts that are central in certain specific philosophical issues or problems.

We will set forth the two claims this section and then defend them by arguing that they are highly credible given the methodological principles of PAM—especially the principle of accommodation and the principle of respect. If these arguments are right, then the two claims acquire a certain derivative methodological status themselves, by virtue of their generality: they become *working hypotheses* that have substantial prima facie credibility, whenever some specific ideological investigation is undertaken in philosophy. That is, they become "default assumptions" in ideological inquiry.

Ideological Austerity, Ideological Opulence, and the Fundamentalist Creed

We begin by briefly amplifying the southern fundamentalist position toward folk psychology, and then characterizing SF's two key claims as a generalization of this position.

In philosophical debates about the status of FP, both eliminativists and certain realists tend to take for granted that FP is ideologically committed to some or all of the following claims of *vertical absorbability*, a *language of thought*, and *horizontal absorbability*, respectively:

(VA) Folk psychology is reducible to natural science, via systematic type-type identities between FP properties and certain properties posited in natural science.

(LT)   Humans have internal mental representations that (i) possess language-like syntactic structure, and (ii) possess the propositional content of putatively attributable FP attitudes.

(HA)   Folk psychology is destined to become a part of mature cognitive science.

We have elsewhere called these *putative true-believer conditions* (PTB's). And we have called *opulent* the conception of FP's ideology that claims that FP is committed ideologically to such PTB conditions, which claims that the concepts of FP are such that FP cannot be true unless there are systematic type-type identities (VA), a language of thought (LT), and scientific integration (HA).[6] By contrast, we ourselves have defended what we call the *austere* conception of FP's ideology, which asserts that under the correct account of the nature and workings of FP concepts, FP simply is not committed to these PTB conditions. The very austerity of FP concepts allows that a creature might fail to possess, for example, a language of thought and yet rank as a true believer. (In section III below we will briefly rehearse our arguments for this austere conception.)

We turn now from debates about FP to philosophical issues in general. For many philosophical questions, there are various competing construals of the commitments or ideological presuppositions of the key concepts involved, and these vying construals often can be positioned relative to one another, in order of increasing opulence. SF's first empirical claim is this: *in general*, the correct ideological account of any given philosophically interesting concept will fall toward the austere end of the associated range of competing ideological construals. That is, SF asserts that the key concepts in philosophical problems will normally be relatively austere ideologically; the commitments of statements employing these concepts will normally be no more opulent than is required by the purposes for which the concepts are employed in thought, in discourse, and in social practices and institutions. In general, therefore, the *correct* position concerning any given philosophical problem or issue will be one that treats the key concepts involved as relatively austere; positions that instead treat the concepts as relatively opulent will normally be mistaken. (It is important to appreciate, however, that even concepts that are *relatively* austere, in the sense just roughly described, might still be quite opulent by some *nonrelative* measure of "extent of ideological commitment.")[7]

We have already mentioned how SF works concerning realism/eliminativism debates about FP: SF asserts that the ideology of FP is sufficiently austere that FP is compatible with mechanism even if FP is not type-type reducible to neuroscience; indeed, FP is not committed to any of the PTB conditions (VA), (LT), or (HA). Concerning the problem of freedom and determinism, for another instance, the SF position would be that *compatibilism* likely will turn out generally correct: if so, freedom-attributions, as ordinarily employed, are not committed to the falsity of causal determinism vis-à-vis human choice and action; hence the contention that humans make free choices and perform free actions is not incompatible with the hypothesis of causal determinism.

Needless to say, it is perfectly possible to adopt an ideological/semantical austerity thesis concerning *some* concepts involved in *some* philosophical problems, while also adopting an ideological opulence thesis concerning *other* concepts involved in other problems. But southern fundamentalism embraces the general hypothesis that philosophically interesting concepts will tend to be austere rather than opulent. We will call this first claim of SF the *principle of ideological austerity.*

The austere/opulent distinction also arises in connection with ideological polarity. Often when a philosophically important concept exhibits polar tension (thereby generating philosophical puzzlement), the tension involves the competing pull of two ways of construing the concept: one austere, the other opulent. In the problem of freedom and determinism for instance, the tension is between an austere "compatibilist" pull in connection with the concept of freedom, and an opulent "incompatibilist" pull. In the problem of psychophysical explanatory exclusion, the tension is between (i) an austere "compatibilist" pull in connection with the concepts of causation and causal explanation, the idea being that human behavior can be given various kinds of causal explanations at various different levels of description; and (ii) an opulent "incompatibilist" pull, the idea being that if mental properties are not just identical to neurobiological ones, then the fact that all human physical motions are causally explainable, in principle, in neurobiological terms excludes mental properties from having genuine causal/explanatory relevance.

SF, being a species of postanalytic metaphilosophy, incorporates PAM's principle of respect. A southern fundamentalist thus must recognize, and must take very seriously, the burden of explaining plausibly those polarity-involving belief-tendencies that get rejected as mistaken. And, given the ideological austerity principle, SF is committed to the contention that in general, the mistaken belief-tendencies in philosophy will be the "opulence tendencies"—the tendencies responsive to the "opulent pull" associated with the problematic concept(s) at the core of a given philosophical problem. SF's second principal contention, then, is this: even though ideological opulence-tendencies are normally mistaken, they are nevertheless explainable as emanating from the nature of the key concepts themselves and from human cognitive mechanisms that figure in semantic/conceptual competence with those concepts. (Recall the analogy of the Müller/Lyer illusion.) We will call this the principle of the *respectful explainability of ideological opulence-tendencies.*

We maintain that once one appreciates the kinds of evidence that supports austerity theses concerning various *specific* ideological issues in philosophy, one will see that similar *kinds* of evidence will tend to be available across the board. postanalytic metaphilosophy's principle of accommodation plays a central role here: given this principle plus the kinds of armchair-obtainable ideological data that tend to be available for most philosophically central concepts, SF's principle of ideological austerity is a highly credible ideological hypothesis. So we will argue in the next part of this section.

We also hold that certain ideological opulence-tendencies, like those involved in the freedom/determinism problem and in the problem of explanatory exclusion, can be plausibly explained in a way that comports well with postanalytic metaphilosophy's principle of respect. We maintain that once one appreciates the structure of the relevant sort of explanation, one will see the same general kind

of explanatory strategy is likely to be available across the board. So SF's second
principle, the respectful explainability of ideological opulence-tendencies, is also
a highly credible ideological hypotheses. So we will argue in the last part of this
section.

The Principle of Ideological Austerity

As we argued earlier, close-at-hand empirical data about matters of ideology, data
that include facts about ordinary people's conceptual/semantic intuitions, provides powerful empirical evidence about those matters. Philosophical theory
construction ought, therefore, to proceed by a wide reflective equilibrium that
aims to accommodate such data as well as possible. Ceteris paribus, a philosophical account that renders such intuitions correct for the most part—especially those judgments that reflect our strongest semantic/conceptual intuitions
about what is right to say, vis-à-vis various envisioned scenarios—will be
preferable to an account that renders them systematically mistaken.
(Analogously, a syntactic theory that renders correct our strong intuitive judgments about grammaticality will be preferable, ceteris paribus, to a theory that
renders certain of them systematically mistaken.)

To illustrate the workings of this postanalytic philosophical methodology,
consider the austere conception of the ideology of FP: the contention that FP is
not ideologically committed to theses (VA), (LT), or (SA). We will now summarize three interrelated, mutually reinforcing, empirical arguments (cf. Horgan
and Graham 1991; Horgan 1993a) in favor of the austere conception of FP's ideology, over against the opulent conception. All involve armchair-obtainable empirical data.

First is the argument from *recalcitrant intuitions*. When we envision scenarios in which theses (VA), and/or (LT), and/or (HA) turn out to be false, and then
ask ourselves whether it seems intuitively appropriate to describe those scenarios
by saying "Humans turn out not to have beliefs and desires," the answer is negative. On the contrary, it seems natural to say things like the following, about
these hypothetical situations: "Humans will have acquired grounds to *believe*
that their own internal states do not have language-like structure; or that FP is
not reducible to neuroscience via type-type identities; or that FP will not get ab-
sorbed into mature science." If the PTB theses are really built into the ideology
of FP or if they are part of the proper understanding of the nature and workings
of FP concepts, however, then this putative ideological fact ought to reveal itself
in our own descriptive intuitions *vis-à-vis* the envisioned scenarios: describing
the people in those scenarios as having beliefs and desires should seem semantically mistaken to us, just as it seems semantically mistaken to describe the stuff
in the oceans and lakes of Putnam's Twin Earth as *water*.[8] But it does not. So,
since we ourselves are folks, and hence have conceptual/semantic competence
with respect to the concepts and terms of FP, it is very likely that our descriptive intuitions about the envisioned scenarios are correct—and hence that the falsity of theses (VA), (LT), or (HA) would not falsify FP at all, that is, it is
likely that the ideology of FP is austere, not opulent.

Second is the argument from *ideological conservatism*. Notions like action, assertion, having reasons, and epistemic warrant all are folk psychological: they presuppose that humans are true believers. These notions play certain essential roles in human life that would surely persist even if we discovered that the theses (VA), (LT), and (SA) are false; hence, if FP were ideologically committed to such PTB conditions, this commitment would go directly contrary to certain central purposes for which FP concepts and terms are employed. But since human concepts and terms evolve in a broadly pragmatic way, in general they are not likely to have satisfaction or application conditions that are more severe or restrictive than is required by the purposes they serve. So FP is not likely to exhibit any such gratuitous, counterpragmatic, features. Hence the ideology of FP is very likely austere, rather than opulent.

Third is the argument from *current conceivability*. Although we humans can readily conceive discovering that any or all of the PTB conditions are false, we cannot even conceive of ourselves dropping folk-psychological notions like action, assertion, and epistemic warrant, and thus we cannot conceive of ceasing to regard ourselves and one another as true believers. For, to drop these notions on these grounds—or even to *try dropping* them—would be *actions*, performed for a *reason*; and notions like action and having a reason are themselves thoroughly folk-psychological. This conceivability mismatch between dropping the PTB theses on the one hand, and dropping FP on the other, is naturally accommodated under the ideological hypothesis that FP is conceptually austere: for, in that case the envisioned scenarios are ones in which the FP concepts still *would* apply to humans. Under the opulent conception of FP's ideology, however, no such accommodation is possible; instead, it remains a puzzle why we should find ourselves unable to imagine dropping concepts whose putative ideological commitments we can fairly easily conceive ourselves discovering to be false. So the conceivability mismatch provides evidence for the austere conception over against the opulent conception, since the former accommodates it whereas the latter renders it puzzling. (It should be stressed that this argument is empirical, not transcendental. Maybe non-FP-tinged successors of FP concepts could be devised, even though we presently have virtually no idea what such replacement concepts would be like. But even those philosophers who, like ourselves, do not buy transcendental arguments, should acknowledge that conceivability considerations can constitute important *empirical* data about matters of ideology.)

In the case of these three empirical arguments, as with abductive empirical reasoning in general, the fact that several distinct forms of evidence converge on the same conclusion means that their net epistemic import is even greater than the "sum" of their respective individual epistemic "weights." In our view, the empirical case for the austere conception of FP's ideology, over against the opulent conception, is very strong indeed.

We submit that similar arguments are likely to be available *in general* when ideological questions are at issue in philosophy. In general, facts about what seems intuitively "right to say" about various scenarios will tend to favor ideological austerity over ideological opulence; and in general, considerations of ideological conservatism will tend to reinforce the case for austerity. (Conceivability considerations will sometimes be relevant too, though not always.)

Take, for instance, the issue of freedom and determinism. If we leave aside the rather special, philosophical, discourse contexts in which this issue is explicitly under discussion (whereof more below), focusing instead on our linguistic/conceptual intuitions about how to employ the concept of freedom in various *typical* contexts (and on the correlative *epistemic* standards that are employed, in those contexts, with respect to freedom attributions), the intuitions strongly support the contention that the ideology of freedom is relatively austere, and in particular that ordinary freedom attributions are not ideologically committed to the falsity of causal determinism. Moreover, this austerity hypothesis receives further empirical support when we ask about the point and purpose of freedom attributions within human practice and human social institutions—in particular, the ways that such attributions are intertwined with practices of praising, blaming, and punishing. Compatibilism certainly seems a more plausible *empirical* hypothesis about the ideology of the concept of freedom than does incompatibilism. Once again, this does not mean that freedom attributions get to squat forever compatibly with determinism. There might, for all we now surmise, emerge motivated considerations for letting freedom go the way of phlogiston. But the current best conviction (on our reading of the arguments pro and con) is that the compatibilist view of the nature and workings of the concepts of freedom and determinism is the best one.

What we have said thusfar is designed to elaborate and support the first of the two key contentions of southern fundamentalism, namely, that philosophically pivotal or significant concepts will normally be relatively austere ideologically. We claim that armchair-obtainable empirical data will in general provide strong support for this contention, given the methodological dictum of postanalytic metaphilosophy we call the principle of accommodation.

The Respectful Explainability of Ideological Opulence-Tendencies

Gareth Matthews's (1980) gentle and often eloquent evocations of ideological awareness in young children are testimony to a startling fact about people's semantic/conceptual intuitions. Often they are strong, often they produce decisive judgments. Here is one example from Matthews:

> Some question of fact arose between James and his father, and James said, "I *know* it is!" His father replied, "But perhaps you are wrong." Denis (four years, seven months) then joined in saying, "But if he knows he can't be wrong! *Thinking's* sometimes wrong, but *knowing's* always right." (27)

What is interesting about the example is that Denis felt a familiar conviction—a robust semantic intuition arising from his linguistic competence. Is it possible to claim to know but be wrong? Of course it is. But is it possible to *know* and be wrong? Of course not, pronounces Denis. Denis offers us a successful case of ideological competence, since our concept *knowledge* is made up (in part) of the concept *is not wrong*.

So far we have discussed one dimension of southern fundamentalism: it advocates ideological austerity theses, over against ideological opulence theses, and it

cites data close-at-hand as powerful empirical evidence in favor ideological austerity theses. We turn now to the southern fundamentalist position about ideological opulence-tendencies, namely, that although these tendencies are generally
mistaken, they are nonetheless respectfully explainable—that is, are explainable
in a way that ties them closely to people's semantic/conceptual competence and
to the actual ideological workings of the concepts involved.

We will describe an approach to the phenomenon of ideological polarity that
we think has considerable plausibility, considerable potential generality, and
considerable promise for meeting the explanatory requirements just described. Insofar as it does, it provides evidence for southern fundamentalism's principle of
the respectful explainability of ideological opulence-tendencies. But although we
are presenting it as providing support for SF, we do not propose to make it an
official or proper part of this metaphilosophical position. The position itself
could be right even if the explanatory format we propose is mistaken or incomplete.

The approach builds upon a general point about certain philosophically important terms and concepts that is articulated, illustrated, and argued by David
Lewis (1979), namely, that these terms and concepts often are partially governed
by certain implicit, context relative, parameters. These parameters are elements
of what Lewis calls the "score in the language game." They include, for instance,
presuppositions (e.g., that France presently has exactly one king); factors determining the referent, in context, of a given definite description; factors determining the standards for contextually correct applicability of vague terms like 'bald,'
'flat' or 'hexagonal', and contextually variable factors operative in modal and
counterfactual discourse (e.g., factors that get formalized in possible-world semantics as the *accessibility relation* over possible worlds, and the *similarity ordering* over possible worlds).

Lewis makes three especially pertinent points about such implicit parameters.
First, as competent thinkers and speakers we deal with them so naturally that we
often do not even notice them. Take definite descriptions, for instance. Frequently, Lewis points out, more than one object within a contextually determined domain of discourse will be a potentially eligible referent of 'the F.'
When this happens, the proper referent will be the most *salient* F in the domain,
according to some contextually determined salience ranking. We take this implicit context relativity so much in stride that we often are not even aware of it.
Lewis gives this example:

> Imagine yourself with me as I write these words. In the room is a cat,
> Bruce, who has been making himself very salient by dashing madly about.
> He is the only cat in the room, or in sight, or in earshot. I start to speak to
> you: "The cat is in the carton. The cat will never meet our other cat, because
> our other cat lives in New Zealand. Our New Zealand cat lives with the
> Cresswells. And there he'll stay, because Miriam would be sad if the cat
> went away." At first, "the cat" denotes Bruce, he being the most salient cat
> for reasons having nothing to do with the conversation. If I want to talk
> about Albert, our New Zealand cat, I have to say "our other cat" or "our
> New Zealand cat." But as I talk more and more about Albert, and not any

more about Bruce, I raise Albert's salience by conversational means. Finally, in the last sentence of my monologue, I am in a position to say "the
cat" and thereby denote not Bruce but rather the newly-more-salient Albert.
(Lewis 1983: 241)

Second, implicit context-relative parameters frequently get altered through a
process Lewis calls *accommodation*, something is said that requires some parameter to have a new value, in order for what is said to be true (or otherwise acceptable), so that parameter thereby takes on that new value. Concerning salience and
definite descriptions, he says:

> One rule, among others, that governs the kinematics of salience is a rule of
> accommodation. Suppose my monologue has left Albert more salient than
> Bruce; but the next thing I say is "The cat is going to pounce on you!" . . .
> What I have said requires for its acceptability that "the cat" denote Bruce, and
> hence that Bruce be once again more salient than Albert. If what I say re-
> quires that, then straightaway it is so. (Lewis 1983: 242)

Third, often if a context-relative parameter is one we would naturally think of
as involving standards that can be either raised or lowered, then accommodating
upward will seem more natural than accommodating downward. Concerning context-relative standards of precision for terms like 'hexagonal' and 'flat,' for example, Lewis remarks:

> I take it that the rule of accommodation can go both ways. But for some
> reason raising the standards goes more smoothly than lowering. If the stan-
> dards have been high, and something is said that is . . . [acceptable] only
> under lowered standards, then indeed the standards are shifted down. But what
> is said . . . may seem only imperfectly acceptable. Raising our standards,
> on the other hand, manages to seem commendable even when we know that
> it interferes with our conversational purposes. (Lewis 1983: 245)

Now, a general Lewis-inspired approach to ideological polarity would invoke
the following core ideas or hypotheses. First, numerous philosophically interesting concepts involve implicit, context-relative parameters. Second, philosophical
puzzles largely arise because the very posing of the puzzle tends to change the
score in the language game in such a way that the contextual parameters are ren-
dered more *stringent*, in the new context, than they are in ordinary contexts.
Third, the intuitive sense of ideological tension largely stems from (i) these
score shifts themselves, (ii) the fact that they often occur without our noticing
them, and (iii) the fact that, as Lewis puts it, "raising our standards . . . manages to seem commendable even when we know that it interferes with our conversational purposes."

Consider, for example, the problem of freedom and determinism. The score-
shifting account would go something like the following (cf. Horgan 1979,
1985). In ordinary contexts of usage, freedom attributions and associated modal
locutions like 'could have done otherwise' are governed by discourse parameters

under which such statements are compatible with causal determinism. (Under the contextually appropriate accessibility relation, the class of possible worlds accessible from the actual world normally includes possible worlds in which the agent acts otherwise; this is so even if causal determinism prevails in the actual world.) When the philosophical problem of freedom and determinism is explicitly posed, however, the very posing of it tends to shift the modal accessibility-parameter in the language game to a *maximally strict* accessibility relation; relative to this new score in the language game, statements of the form 'Agent S could have done otherwise' are true only if there is a possible world W such that (i) W is identical to the actual world up until the moment just prior to S's act, and (ii) the actual world's laws of nature are never violated in W. So, although freedom attributions are compatible with determinism in *ordinary* discourse contexts, they tend to become incompatible with determinism in those very *philosophical* contexts in which the compatibility issue is being investigated! Our intuitive sense of puzzlement about freedom and determinism stems from our failure to notice, at the level of reflective consciousness, that contextual parameter-shifting is going on, or that contextually variable parameters are involved at all. And this puzzlement is further exacerbated by the way the contextual standards, once raised, tend to stay high.

Consider, for another example, the problem of explanatory exclusion. A scorekeeping account similar to the one just described would go as follows. Often a given phenomenon is susceptible to several kinds of explanation, at several different levels of description. When this is so, typically certain implicit context-relative parameters will determine which kind is appropriate for the purposes at hand. In the case of human behavior, any of several types of explanation might be the most appropriate—psychological, for instance; or neurobiological; or in principal, even microphysical. When psychological descriptions and explanations are the contextually appropriate ones, the contextually variable parameters governing causal/explanatory relevance are such that intentional mental properties, qua mental, do possess such relevance; they do so regardless of whether mechanism is true, and regardless of whether intentional psychology is type-type reducible to neuroscience. Just what causal/explanatory relevance amounts to is itself a vexed philosophical issue, of course. In our view the central requirement is that the properties or state-types in question should figure in sufficiently systematic patterns of counterfactual dependency (Horgan 1989, 1991, 1993b). Such patterns can perfectly well exist at various different levels of description, with contextually variable discourse parameters then determining which level is the one that is appropriate in a given context of inquiry. So the ideological commitments of the concepts employed at various levels of description, and also of the general concepts of causation and causal explanation, are sufficiently austere that higher-level, mentalistic, causal explanations of behavior are not really threatened by mechanism at all. *In context*, so the Lewis story would go, the parameters governing psychological discourse are typically such that psychological causal explanations can perfectly well be correct—even if mechanism is true and even if intentional psychology is not type-type reducible to neurobiology.

But the very posing of the explanatory-exclusion question creates an *atypical* discourse context, one in which the key parameters tend to shift in a way that generates conceptual puzzlement. One tends to undergo a series of cognitive steps something like the following. (Note that some of these are cognitive "acts of omission.")

1.   Focusing on the causal explanation of behavior at some theoretical level more fundamental than the psychological level—such as, neurochemical explanation of specific muscle movements.

2.   Accommodating, automatically and subliminally, to the parameters of explanatory relevance appropriate to this kind of explanation.

3.   Failing to notice that such accommodation has occurred, or that context relative parameters of explanatory relevance are operative.

4.   Noticing that for the kind of natural-science-level explanation under consideration, *intentional* properties (if any) of the causally operative states and structures are quite irrelevant.

5.   Shifting focus to the role of mental properties in the causal explanation of action.

6.   Failing to accommodate to the parameters of explanatory relevance appropriate for mentalistic explanation.

7.   Finding it intuitively plausible that if mental properties are not just identical to neurobiological properties, then they never have any *genuine* causal/explanatory relevance at all.

The crucial component in such a process is step 6, which paves the way for the state of philosophical puzzlement that arises at step 7. One key factor contributing to step 6 is the overarching failure to notice, at the level of reflective consciousness, that context relative parameters of explanatory relevance are operative at all, or that accommodation is going on. Another is a subliminal cognitive resistance to the kind of accommodation that actually would be required at step 5. To accommodate properly would be to acquiesce in standards of explanatory relevance that are lower, on a scale we might call "comparative degree of scientific fundamentality," than the standards already operative after step 2; and accommodation involving lowering of standards often does not go smoothly (as Lewis points out).

Now, articulating and defending in detail score-shifting accounts of ideological tension, vis-à-vis the problem of freedom and determinism and vis-à-vis the problem of explanatory exclusion, are tasks for another occasion. In addition, arguing the *general* applicability of such score-shifting accounts, vis-à-vis ideological tension within philosophy, is a *large* task for another occasion. Our purpose here, using these two philosophical problems just as examples, has been a much more modest one, namely, to suggest and illustrate one promising-looking strategy for explaining ideological opulence-tendencies in a manner that both reveals that they are mistaken and yet also reveals why they so naturally arise as a by-product of the ideological workings of the concepts themselves. We will close with some final remarks about some of the ways that the score-shifting approach fits with the principles of postanalytic metaphilosophy.

First, this approach implements the Aristotelian injunction to *give a reasonable explanation of why a false view appears true*, preferably in a manner that connects directly to the ideological workings of the key concepts themselves. If the scorekeeping accounts just sketched are on the right track, then it is not some sort of *egregious blunder*, some sort of *conceptual howler*, to think that freedom is incompatible with determinism or that neurobiological explanation excludes psychological explanation. Rather, although these views are indeed mistaken (or so we maintain), they are mistakes that reflect something real and important about our concepts themselves, namely, that the concepts are subject to contextual parameters which, in certain *atypical* discourse contexts, can get raised so high that freedom attributions really do become incompatible with causal determinism, and mental properties really do become causally/explanatorily irrelevant.

Second, the score-shifting approach is part of a nonaprioristic/wide reflective equilibrium conception of philosophical method, under which philosophical inquiry is continuous with inquiry within the various sciences. Obviously, if the scorekeeping story is to be defended it must in part be a matter of plausible-looking speculations about the psychology of language processing and the psychology of concept-wielding. Thus, the ultimate viability or nonviability of the approach depends, in part, on whether or not these speculations will ultimately mesh well with theoretical accounts within cognitive science. So be it; philosophy *is* continuous with science.

Third, the score-shifting approach to ideological tension can potentially fit well with our suggestion that philosophical puzzlement should perhaps be regarded on the model of the Müller/Lyer illusion. Even if one *accepts* the proposed explanation of the ideological tension involved in problems like freedom/determinism and mentalism/mechanism, the intuitively felt tension tends to persist anyway. Indeed, its persistence might well be *expected*, as a natural (and perhaps even unavoidable) by-product of the way our language-using and concept-forming mechanisms respond when placed in the unusual, nonstandard, discourse contexts created by the raising of such philosophical puzzles. Thus, the fact that score-shifting accounts can be accepted as plausible even if they do not make one's intuitive sense of puzzlement "dissolve" phenomenologically, should be viewed as a theoretical plus.[9] As the Stagirite so wisely remarked, whenever a reasonable explanation is given of why a false view appears true, this makes us more confident of the true view.

Fourth, and finally, if philosophically interesting concepts are relatively austere as southern fundamentalism holds, this allows that they can shift contexts without *necessarily* losing fidelity to their proper conditions of application. They can cross contextual boarders without failing in any obvious or straightforward way to apply. The austerity of concepts means that the relation between different contexts of application is much more opaque than for opulent concepts, say, where ideological commitments constrain or prohibit application in different or unusual discourse contexts, for example, is it possible for a determined choice to be free? If the relevant concepts were relatively opulent the answers to such questions could conceivably be quite obvious. If the concept *free choice* is such that there must necessarily be no causal explanation of the choice, free choice would be incompatible with determinism. We would (and should) find it unimaginable that a choice could be both free and determined. But the concepts of free and determined are austere, or so we claim, and so it is simply not obvious whether a choice could be both free and determined. It is not transparent what happens semantically when the context shifts; our convictions sit poised to move one way or another as the score changes. As the Princetonian so sagaciously noted, changing standards can interfere with conversational purposes. That should be of no surprise to philosophers who have long thought that conflicting linguistic intuitions are to be faced, not dismissed. Faced, they can perhaps be brought into wide reflective equilibrium; dismissed, they nag at us until we allow ourselves to be drawn back into ideological inquiry—into philosophy.

Notes

A previous version of this chapter appeared in *Truth and Rationality: Philosophical Issues* 5 (1994): 219-247. Reprinted with kind permission from George Graham and Terry Horgan, and Dr. Enrique Villanueva.

This is a thoroughly co-written chapter. The order of authorship is alphabetical. We are indebted to participants in the VI Sophia Conference and to the following philosophers in particular for helpful criticisms and comments on earlier drafts of this paper: Eduardo Bustos, Eduardo Rabossi, Timothy Roche, John Tienson, Mark Timmons, and James Tomberlin. We thank Timothy Roche for bringing to our attention the Aristotle passages we quoted, and for providing the translations.

1. We do not intend our use of 'ideology' to have sociopolitical connotations. Perhaps we are not the first to use the word stripped of such connotations Marcelo Dascal informs us that Augusta Comte (1798-1857) coined the term 'ideologie' (originally devoid of political connotations) to represent the construction of a theory of philosophically important concepts and theories that in some important sense was empirical or anti-apriori. Some such doctrine, according to Dascal, played an important role in guiding Comte's characterization of social science. It is our goal, Comte aside, to formulate a doctrine of ideological inquiry to serve as a model for what we call postanalytic metaphilosophy. We prefer to speak of "ideological inquiry" rather than of "conceptual analysis," to reduce the danger that metaphilosophical understanding be skewed by historical connotations of the word "analysis" (which we are about to identify).

2. Most, not all. An account of conceptual clarification parallel in some respects to the account of ideological inquiry recommended here may be found in Bishop (1992), an essay we discovered only after completing the penultimate draft of this chapter.

3. Note that a central assumption of ideological inquiry is that people are not at liberty to let concepts and the terms that express them mean or signify whatever whimsy dictates. There are *norms* that govern, at least loosely, the proper use of concepts and terms. The character of these norms is what is at issue in ideological inquiry. It is also part of what is at issue in debates over the cognitive mechanisms that

subserve different conceptual tasks, such as categorization (see Smith and Medin 1981). Competent users of concepts and language really are *competent* users. They possess information (or "tacit knowledge") about semantic/conceptual norms.

4. Ideological commitments of FP could arise either *directly*, solely by virtue of the local workings of FP concepts within FP itself, or *indirectly*, by virtue of various linkages between FP concepts and other concepts from our commonsense conceptual scheme or from science. The nature of ideological commitment is a large topic, closely intertwined with complex issues about the nature of meaning, the nature of concepts, semantic holism, the import for semantics if the analytic/synthetic distinction is untenable, and so forth. Even in the absence of any developed theoretical account of ideological commitment, however, evidence can be garnered for and against various ideological claims or hypotheses—like the Churchlands' ideological contention that FP, in order to be true of human beings (given what contemporary science tells us about humans as physico-chemical systems), must be smoothly type-type reducible to neuroscience.

5. Or, at any rate, it should give up the idea that its own methodology is exclusively aprioristic. One might balk at the notion that there is no room for anything a priori in philosophy. The notion of the a priori is by no means so sufficiently well behaved that there is a perfectly easy way to decide whether a method that is by and large empirically based contains or is free of a priori elements. This is a large topic for another occasion.

6. As remarked already (cf. note 4), these alleged ideological commitments could arise either directly or indirectly. Advocates of the opulent conception need not maintain that FP's allegedly opulent theoretical commitments arise directly, that is, solely by virtue of the internal ideological workings of FP's concepts. In particular, they need not maintain that these putative commitments are purely *analytic*, that is, are entailed by FP purely as a matter of meaning. (They need not embrace the analytic/synthetic distinction at all.) Nevertheless, they do implicitly assume that under the right account of FP's ideology, the falsity of PTB conditions would render FP itself radically false.

7. It is tempting to regard austerity as a principle of parsimony or economy applied to the ideological realm: as an attempt to limit the number of types of entities, states, or processes to which the use of certain concepts commits us. Although in this chapter we wish to leave open the precise relation between austerity and parsimony, for that requires discussion on another occasion, it is important to appreciate that parsimony is different from austerity. For instance, one parsimonious reading of folk psychology would reduce its essential explanatory ingredients to beliefs and desires, and leave out explanatory reference to other attitudes and emotions altogether, thereby limiting the range of entities in FP to which the use of FP terms commits us. Parsimony is a subtractor or reducer. By contrast, the principle of austerity is a blocker or stopper. It denies that concepts carry multiplex implicit commitments to conditions that have to be satisfied if those concepts apply. So, for example, on one opulent reading, for something or someone to count as a true believer, it must possess a language of thought; whereas on an austere reading of *belief*, a creature's title to true believerhood rests on criteria much closer to the ordinary evidentiary surface than the evidence required to determine whether such a creature possesses a language of thought. See Horgan and Graham (1991) for discussion.

8. John Heil puts the point forcefully: "If I visit Twin Earth and describe the liquid in lakes and rain puddles as water, I am in error" (1992: 33).

9. By contrast, when an ideological account treats a certain pretheoretic belief or belief-tendency as the product of some logical fallacy (or some dubious implicit assumption), the account thereby incurs a phenomenological burden; once we accept

that the specified inference pattern or assumption is indeed the basis for the belief-tendency, and we also come to see clearly why the inference pattern is fallacious (or why the implicit assumption is dubious), the belief-tendency itself should dissolve phenomenologically. (Reasoning that is initially plausible, once seen to be fallacious or dubious, should *lose* its plausibility.) Ideological opulence-tendencies, however, are often quite persistent. Lewis-style scorekeeping accounts are not only compatible with this persistence, but also appear to explain it.

Chapter 16

Why Bother with Reflective Equilibrium?

Michael R. DePaul

A Short Dialogue

Imagine I am sitting in a bar, in fact, that I am belly up to the bar. It is not the sort of pub one finds around a university—filled with academic types. It is an ordinary joint, filled with ordinary folks. If I strike up a conversation with the person beside me, at some point I'll probably be asked—

Friend: What do you do?

Me: I teach at the university.

(I have always envied colleagues from other disciplines who can dispense with this evasion: "I'm a chemist," "I'm a psychologist," or even "I'm an historian," might pass, but can you imagine coming right out with "I'm a philosopher.")

Friend: Oh! What do you teach?

(My evasion never does much good.)

Me: Philosophy.

(I cringe whenever I say this, since God only knows what ordinary folks think of when they hear "philosophy." As I say it I cannot help thinking of the sorts of books stacked on the "Philosophy" shelf in American shopping mall bookstores. But today I am lucky. I have struck up a conversation with someone who has no preconceptions at all, so a simple request for clarification follows. Historical figures are a safe bet, so I mention some of the usual suspects: Plato, Aristotle, Descartes, Kant, and, to end up with a name that might ring a bell with a mysterious and profound tone, *Wittgenstein*. Such names are enough to scare most people off. But not everyone! Today I am *not* so lucky. I am asked what sort of things these people wrote about.)

Me: Philosophers are interested in very fundamental questions, for example:
         What is it to know something? What, if anything, can we know? Is ev-

erything that happens caused? What is it for one thing to cause another? What sort of life is best for a human being? What is the nature of virtue? Of moral obligation? And so on.

(Ethics is a lot closer to home than metaphysics or epistemology, and besides, even in these secular times, most people have been exposed to religious approaches to moral questions, so it is a good bet the conversation will strike off in that direction.)

Friend: Now I understand—philosophy is like religion. You study the Bible and perhaps other religions, sacred texts, the *Bhagavadgita*, . . . What do you think about reincarnation?

(I can only take so much, even when pacified by beer!)

Me: *That just isn't right!* Philosophers do *not* approach these questions as religion does. We do *not* rely upon sacred texts or the teachings of some church.

Friend: But then how *do* philosophers go about answering these questions?

(I am afraid the prospects for an honest answer to this question are grim! I believe the method of reflective equilibrium, first described and advocated by Nelson Goodman (1965) and further developed and applied to ethics by John Rawls (1971, 1974), describes the approach the vast majority of philosophers in fact follow. More importantly, it provides an enormously influential answer—in my opinion, close to a correct answer—to the more interesting and philosophical question: How *should* we conduct philosophical inquiry? But can you imagine trying to explain and justify this method to your ordinary Jane or Joe who has been pounding nails or tightening nuts all day?)

Me: Let me try to explain. I'll use moral theory as an example, but remember that philosophical inquiry into other matters, for example, knowledge, causation, reference, or the nature of belief, is similarly conducted. The philosopher must begin her inquiry regarding morality with the moral beliefs she happens to have, such as, beliefs about what is morally good, which acts are right and wrong, or about when guilt is appropriate. Some of her judgments will concern actual things or actions, but others will be about imaginary or hypothetical cases, such as, actions performed by the characters in a movie or novel. And some of her judgments will concern general principles, for example, she will likely judge that two actions cannot differ morally without also differing in some relevant nonmoral feature. The philosopher then attempts to eliminate any beliefs or judgments formed in circumstances that obviously make error likely, such as, when she is ignorant of potentially relevant facts or her personal interest is somehow at stake.
          Her next task is to construct a "theory" that accounts for the remain-

ing judgments: her "considered" judgments. In attempting to construct this theory the philosopher's considered judgments do not function as a scientist's data is commonly thought to function, for the philosopher seeks to bring her considered judgments into balance with a theory via a process of *mutual* adjustment to *both* her theory and her considered judgments. Here's what I mean: Suppose that, after she has a good start on an acceptable theory, that is to say, she has constructed a theory that accounts for a wide range of her considered judgments, the philosopher discovers that this promising theory is in conflict with some of her other considered judgments. The philosopher is not bound to revise the theory so that it accords with these judgments. Rather, she must attempt to determine, via further reflection, whether it is the theory or the judgments that, all things considered, she finds more likely to be true, and then revise her beliefs accordingly. If the considered judgments that conflict with her provisional theory are very firmly held and seem to her to be central to her system of moral beliefs, and her reflections do not reveal that these judgments are involved in further conflicts, then it will be the theory that she will have to revise. But if the theory nicely accounts for all her most central and most confidently made considered judgments, and she finds it intuitively attractive on its own, and it seems to her to reveal the deep nature of moral obligation, and perhaps, in addition, the judgments with which this theory conflicts concern unusual cases, then it is the judgments that the philosopher will revise. And so we see that in her effort to construct a coherent system of moral judgments and theoretical principles that account for these judgments neither particular judgment nor theoretical principle is always favored. Whenever conflicts emerge, the philosopher must reflect on the connections among her beliefs and determine what to revise on the basis of what, all things considered, seems to her most likely to be correct.

Even if the philosopher manages to bring her considered judgments and moral theory into a state of balance or equilibrium via such a process of mutual adjustment, her work will not be finished. The philosopher must seek an even wider equilibrium. She must also consider the connections between her moral beliefs and principles and the other sorts of beliefs, principles and theories she accepts or rejects. This process was in fact already begun when the philosopher filtered out initial moral beliefs that were formed in circumstances that she is confident entail a high risk of error. When she filtered out these judgments she was merely revising moral beliefs that flagrantly conflict with firmly although perhaps tacitly held epistemic principles. This process can be carried further. As the philosopher works out a more and more complete system of moral beliefs, she will obviously wish to see to it that this system of beliefs attains an appropriately high epistemic status. She must, in effect, see to it that her moral beliefs and the epistemic principles she accepts are coherent. In addition, in order to bring her epistemic principles to bear upon her moral beliefs, she will almost certainly also need to consider various beliefs about moral beliefs, such as, beliefs about the circumstances in which her moral beliefs were formed, the factors that effect a person's moral judgments, the incompatible moral judgments made by others, and so on. As a result an even wider range of beliefs will be brought into play, some of which will likely lead to other areas of controversy. For example, consideration of the fact that other people make different moral judgments naturally leads to anthropological, sociological, and historical studies of different cultures and the debates about relativism and cultural diversity. Once again, however, the philosopher must seek a coherent system of belief by a process of *mutual* adjustment—neither moral nor epistemic beliefs nor any of the other beliefs that come into play are granted a privileged status.

Thus, for example, if a central, well-established, and intuitively plausible epistemic principle entails that some range of moral judgments are unjustified or irrational, then the philosopher will have to eliminate these moral judgments. But if a tentative epistemic principle yields a similar negative evaluation of central, firmly held moral judgments, then it will be the epistemic principles that will have to be revised. After all, the epistemic principles will themselves have been developed via a similar reflective process, and so will have been based in part upon considered judgments about whether beliefs formed in various circumstances would be rational or justified, and the philosopher may discover upon reflection that she is not as confident of these epistemic judgments as she is of the moral judgments with which, by way of epistemic principles, they conflict. Hence, whenever she encounters a conflict or incoherence within her system of beliefs, the philosopher must consider the conflicting beliefs, the logical and epistemic relations between these beliefs and the other propositions she accepts or rejects, and revise on the basis of what comes to seem likely to be true as a result of her reflections.

It is not too hard to see that there can be conflicts between moral beliefs and other types of beliefs as well. For example, metaphysical theories about the nature of persons or about what sorts of entities are ontologically respectable may well bear upon moral beliefs, as could various psychological theories, for example, regarding the nature of madness, or sociological theories, for example, about the role a moral theory must play in society. The important point is that the philosopher seeks to construct an ever more comprehensive system of beliefs and to bring these beliefs into equilibrium via a process of *mutual* adjustment.

(This description of the philosopher's method is quite a mouthful, but, to put things backwards, supposing my friend managed to digest it all, he would probably refuse to swallow it! The grounds for refusal are familiar.)

Friend: Now I really am confused, or perhaps I should say astonished. I suppose I shouldn't be surprised to discover that philosophers don't do anything but think about things, that they don't pour over historical documents, conduct surveys, make observations of natural phenomena in the field, perform experiments, or worry over complex calculations. But this really is a bit much! If what you say is true, the accounts that philosophers end up advancing, in your example an account of morality—an account that you have grandiosely labeled a "theory"!— apparently are entirely determined by nothing more than the philosopher's own intuitive judgments. Isn't it really quite a scandal that people who employ this frivolous method are paid good money to hold positions at the best colleges and universities, and that the results they obtain are published by legitimate journals and presses, and that generations of students have been forced to take courses taught by these people in which they must first buy and then study these books? It seems to me the philosophers have put one over on us. What excuse could there possibly be for investigating such obviously important matters as morality and the other topics addressed by philosophy in such a self-absorbed and self-indulgent manner? It's no wonder nobody cares, or far that matter knows, what philosophers have to say.

Dead Ends

Before I try to answer the question my level headed interlocutor has posed, I am going to be somewhat high-handed in this section and describe, without much argument, how I think we can expect the method of reflective equilibrium to work. Three important claims about what we cannot expect the method of reflective equilibrium to do for us will emerge. If these claims are correct, they foreclose some of the more obvious routes one might want to take in defending this method of inquiry.

Let's begin with a description of what, in essence, the method of reflective equilibrium directs the philosopher to do: (i) to reflect upon her beliefs and the logical and evidential interconnections among her beliefs, (ii) to try to construct "theories" that are intuitively appealing on their own and that account for various categories of beliefs, for example, judgments about right and wrong, epistemic judgments, or judgments regarding what refers to what, and (iii) to resolve such conflicts as are uncovered in the course of these reflections and efforts at theory construction on the basis of what comes to seem most likely to be correct as a result of still further reflection. (For a more complete and systematic description of reflective equilibrium see Daniels 1979 or DePaul 1993: ch. 1.)[1] It is no news that since, as this decription makes clear, the entire process is guided by nothing more than the inquirer's own beliefs, judgments, and what seems to the inquirer to be correct upon reflection, given enough screwy initial beliefs and unusual judgments about how to resolve conflicts, an inquirer could end up accepting just about anything in reflective equilibrium. Hence, my first and least controversial claim about what reflective equilibrium cannot do: (1) *The method of reflective equilibrium provides no guarantee that it will lead inquirers to true beliefs.*[2]

It is not, however, all that easy to accept any old screwy thing in reflective equilibrium. To do so one must be willing to make suitably screwy adjustments throughout one's entire system of beliefs. So it is not surprising that we do not very often find people who have a coherent but wacky system of beliefs. When we discover someone who holds some bizarre belief, what we usually find is that she also holds, or is disposed to accept, other more "normal" beliefs that we can use to persuade her to revise her strange belief. This is to say, what we usually find is that people who hold screwy beliefs have not reached a point of reflective equilibrium, and that they generally can be forced to revise their screwy beliefs in order to bring their beliefs into reflective equilibrium. Hence, one might hope to show that the method of reflective equilibrium is "reliable" even though it cannot guarantee the truth to every inquirer. However, although we admittedly do not often encounter people with coherent but totally bizarre systems of belief, we do not actually need to find such people to have good reason to suspect that the method of reflective equilibrium is not generally reliable. All we need is a sufficient amount of difference of (perfectly nonscrewy) opinion. It is safe to say that philosophers and other thinkers who have addressed similar questions throughout the ages have in fact employed something at least very much like the method of reflective equilibrium. Hence, I think we can safely take the various views about morality, God, how society should be structured, the nature of human persons, beauty, and so forth that have been propounded in one way or another by philosophers, religious and political leaders, novelists, poets, artists, and so on, to provide a fair indication of what sorts of views a person can accept in reflective equilibrium. And we find plenty of sufficiently great difference of opinion here for it to be a very safe bet that (2) *The method of reflective equilibrium will not even reliably lead inquirers to the truth.*[3]

One might, of course, say the same sorts of things about deductive arguments. Given strange enough premises, you can construct a deductively valid argument for any bizarre conclusion you pick. And even ignoring this sort of mere possibility of screwy conclusions being derived by deductive arguments, contrary views have actually been advanced by serious thinkers as the conclusions of deductive arguments often enough for one to argue, in the way I have regarding reflective equilibrium, that deductive arguments will not reliably lead all inquirers to the truth. But of course that is neither here nor there. The interesting thing about deductive arguments is that they are perfectly reliable *conditionally,* that is, given true premises, they yield true conclusions. Similarly, one might claim that the method of reflective equilibrium is to some degree conditionally reliable. Perhaps it is too much to expect that this method is perfectly conditionally reliable like deduction, but perhaps it might have the sort of conditional reliability we think inductive arguments have: given true premises the conclusions of such arguments are very probably true. Thus, while reflective equilibrium may not be able to guarantee that it will lead every inquirer to the truth, nor even that it will lead the majority of inquirers to the truth, it may be asserted that it will reliably lead the rights sorts of inquirers to the truth, that is, inquirers whose intuitive judgments, both in forming beliefs initially and about the resolution of conflicts, are true. I think this is true enough, and I suppose it is worth taking note of that fact. Unfortunately, it will not help answer the question posed above in the absence of some reason for thinking that *our* intuitive judgments are true. But if 'our' here refers to "us philosophers," our all to obvious differences of opinion pretty clearly indicate that our intuitive judgments are not all true. So it would seem we would need some way of picking out those of us whose intuitions *are* true before we could say for whom the method of reflective equilibrium is reliable, and it obviously is not very likely we will manage to pull that off.

Maybe instead of talking about truth, we should try to answer the question above in terms of justification. But we had better first pin down just what 'justification' is supposed to indicate here. We can initially locate the concept of justification that has received the most attention from epistemologists by factoring it out of knowledge: Knowledge is justified true belief plus (some feature designed to rule out Gettier problems); hence, justification, in this sense of the term, is whatever a true belief plus must have in order to count as knowledge.[4] One influential class of theories seeks to account for justification in terms of reliability (see, Goldman 1979, 1986). Moreover, even very many of those philosophers who reject reliability theories still hold that justification must be truth conducive (Alston 1985; BonJour 1985). If these philosophers are correct, the considerations adduced above seem to indicate that the method of reflective equilibrium will not lead all or even most philosophers to form beliefs that are justified. Of course, it is not universally agreed that justification is truth conducive; perhaps it is just a mistake to think that it is. If we forget about truth conduciveness and attend to the various theories of justification, one type of theory seems to be tailor-made for defending the method of reflective equilibrium, namely, coherence theories. However, the fit here is simply *too* good. No one with the concerns about reflective equilibrium we are out to address will be satisfied upon being told that reflective equilibrium is guaranteed to yield justified beliefs when in the sequel this claim is defended by appeal to a coherence theory of justification. Their concerns about reflective equilibrium will simply reemerge as familiar objections to coherence theories of justification. Finally, without getting involved in the various debates about the nature of epistemic justification, I think it is safe to say that even if justification is not truth conducive, it is in a certain sense "objective." One's beliefs must satisfy certain objective standards to count as justified. There are certain sorts of fallacious patterns of inference, and no matter what sort of rationalization or "justification" the inquirer might be able to construct for using them, these patterns of inference simply cannot yield justified belief. (The gambler's fallacy and hasty generalizations may provide examples of such fallacies.) But unfortunately the coherence constraints imposed by reflective equilibrium are not sufficient to guarantee that any inquirer employing the method will accept only correct epistemic standards. Hence, since reflective equilibrium does require an inquirer to live up to his or her own standards, that is, the standards that he or she accepts in reflective equilibrium, (3) *The method of reflective equilibrium cannot be counted on to yield justified beliefs.*[5]

Rationality, Reflective Equilibrium, and Alternative Methods

(I keep hearing what my friend from the bar might say.)

Friend: Am I missing something or are you giving me reasons for doubting this reflective equilibrium business? The idea was for you to explain why you're in *favor* of it.

The fundamental reason I am in favor of "this reflective equilibrium business" can be stated easily enough: Any other approach to philosophical inquiry is irrational. But this claim on behalf of reflective equilibrium obviously requires a lot of explanation and not a little justification before it will count for more than name calling. First, although rationality is still esteemed in most (although not all) circles, and it might even be generally (although not universally) agreed that philosophical inquiry *must* be rational, the term 'rationality' is used by different people in so many different senses that it would be nice if I explained how *I* am using it. Second, given that there are many conceptions of rationality floating about, I ought to explain why rationality, *as I conceive of it*, is an especially good thing. I might as well warn in advance that once you begin to understand how I think of rationality you will probably feel the need for an explanation of why rationality is valuable to be more pressing than you do now, when you are free to think of it in your own favorite way. Third, I obviously cannot simply claim that all alternatives to reflective equilibrium are irrational. I had better do something in the way of convincing you of this claim.

Having raised these three issues, I am going to explicitly focus on only one of them and hope my views regarding the other two become apparent along the way. I will argue that any method of philosophical inquiry that is an alternative to reflective equilibrium is irrational. If all goes well, along the way you will pick up a pretty good idea of the conception of rationality I am working with, even though I will not present an explicit account or analysis. Also, I hope that by portraying clearly exactly what one must do to deviate from reflective equilibrium and how such a deviation is irrational, it will become clear what is wrong with such irrationality, and perhaps begin to become clear why one might value the corresponding sort of rationality.

Friend   So! Are you going to explain why any alternative to reflective equilibrium must be irrational or not?

Well, think very abstractly of what the method of reflective equilibrium recommends and then ask yourself how a method of philosophical inquiry would have to look to be a genuine alternative to reflective equilibrium. From one perspective, reflective equilibrium seems to direct the inquirer simply to take her judgments about something, for example, knowledge, right and wrong, or the nature of belief, and attempt to construct a "theory" that accounts for these judgments. When one views reflective equilibrium from this perspective it is easy to conceive of alternative methods, and alternatives that are obviously preferable at that! But this perspective on reflective equilibrium does not afford us a fair view, for the method does not direct the inquirer simply to construct a theory that accounts for her initial intuitive judgments. Most centrally, the method directs the inquirer to do two things as she attempts to construct a philosophical theory:

(I)   Reflect upon the logical and evidential relations that hold between her initial intuitive judgments and the other beliefs and theories she accepts, between these judgments and the emerging theory she is constructing to account for them, between this emerging theory and any relevant background beliefs or theories she accepts, and so on.

(II)   Whenever these reflections uncover some sort of conflict or incoherence among beliefs, resolve the conflict by revising beliefs in the way that comes to seem most likely to be correct upon thorough reflection, that is, after taking into account everything she believes that might be relevant.

When one really focuses upon these two directives, it becomes rather more difficult to conceive of an alternative to reflective equilibrium, or more specifically, to conceive of a *rational* alternative to this method.

In order to constitute a real alternative to reflective equilibrium, a method would have to oppose reflective equilibrium with respect to one or the other of its two central directives. In order to do this, such a method must either (A) abandon reflection altogether, or (B) direct the inquirer to reflect, but to do so incompletely, that is, to leave certain beliefs, principles, theories, or what have you out of account, or (C) not allow the results of the inquirer's reflections to determine what the inquirer goes on to believe. I maintain that a method of philosophical inquiry having feature (A), (B), or (C) would be irrational. I will consider these in turn.

Abandoning Reflection

I am not sure I really need to comment on (A), since it is just about a directive not to think, but here goes. A "method" of inquiry incorporating (A) would surely be a strange beast, indeed, so strange that it is doubtful whether it would constitute a possible method of philosophical inquiry at all. Such a "method" might direct the inquirer simply to believe whatever she happens to believe, without thinking things over at all. I am inclined to think that this already constitutes a good reason for calling the method "irrational." In addition, it is terribly improbable that an inquirer following such a method would end up having any very coherent or systematic view or accepting anything much like the sort of theoretical accounts philosophers seek.[6] It would seem the only "method" that would be likely to lead an inquirer to hold a theory or systematic account without doing any reflective thinking on her own would be one that baldly presents the account or theory and directs the inquirer to believe it without further ado. It is hard for me to imagine the sort of pessimism about one's own cognitive powers that would lead one to adopt such a method. To accept directive (A) one would have to give up entirely upon one's self and either accept whatever one happens to believe without giving it any thought or blindly submit to some sort of wholly external authority and accept what that authority dictates without giving it any thought.

It might seem that I am exaggerating here, but notice that to follow the sort of method we are imagining one would have to accept the teachings of authority, here embodied in the account or theory the "method" directs one to accept, *for absolutely no reason*. To have a reason for doing so one would have had to reflect at least enough to uncover the reason, and at least to that small extent have trusted the results of one's own reflection. This was what I was trying to indicate by calling the authority "wholly external." The inquirer is not here accepting the dictates of the authority because she has come to believe that, at least regarding certain matters, the authority is either reliable or more reliable than she is. There is obviously nothing unusual or irrational about accepting an authority in such a way. We all do it countless times, for example, when we accept a pathologist's identification of a tissue sample, a theoretical physicist's nontechnical explanation of a complex mathematical theory, or the result of a mathematical operation indicated by a pocket calculator. Not only is there nothing unusual or irrational about such acceptance of authority, it is perfectly compatible with the method of reflective equilibrium. To take a simple case, if upon complete reflection a person comes to be certain that some authority is perfectly reliable about a certain range of propositions, then unless the authority should endorse some proposition within that range that the person is certain is false, the way for the person to maintain coherence within her system of beliefs is to accept the dictates of the authority and revise her other beliefs accordingly.

Another problem with abandoning reflection is that a person who fails to reflect is liable, and I think virtually certain, to end up accepting what he himself does not really find acceptable. Here is what I mean. It very commonly happens that when we reflect upon something we believe, we uncover among the other things we believe, or come to believe as a result of our reflections, reasons for doubting or rejecting our initial beliefs, reasons which, all things considered, we are much more strongly committed to than the original belief, and which would therefore lead us to abandon the original belief. Thus, I say, a person who fails to reflect and goes along believing what he has always believed is liable to believe what he himself does not find most acceptable. The danger of believing what one does not find acceptable must be even greater for one who adopts the teachings of some outside authority without reflection. But no matter how one comes to do so, I think it is irrational to believe what one finds unacceptable, and a method of philosophical inquiry that directs inquirers to put themselves into such a position cannot be rational.

Reflecting Incompletely

It might seem that methods of inquiry that incorporate (B), and thus direct merely *incomplete* reflection, do not entail the sort of irrationality—the pessimism, submission to external authority or danger of self-contradiction—I have claimed is involved when one abandons reflection. Indeed, methods of inquiry that leave out certain sorts of judgments are quite familiar and seem unobjectionable. We expect, for example, that evolutionary biologists or physicists studying cosmology will ignore any religious beliefs they might have during their scientific inquiries, and we surely would be somewhat disturbed to find that this expectation was not fulfilled. Another example might be provided by legal proceedings, were we expect decisions to be made only on the basis of what qualifies as evidence according to the relevant legal standards, not on the basis of any beliefs a judge or juror might happen to have that bear upon the case.[7] Moreover, many of the criticisms of reflective equilibrium have focused on the use the method makes of intuitive judgments, so critics pretty clearly do not want us to abandon reflection entirely, but to reflect in a more limited way, a way that gives our intuitive judgments no weight. That critics do not wish us to abandon reflection altogether of course comes as no surprise—for it would be a very odd thing to spell out a set of reasons for not forming beliefs in the way that someone is inclined to form them, and present these reasons to that person for consideration, when what you want the person to stop doing is reflecting about her beliefs altogether!

Although there are many examples of acceptable methods of limited reflection, they are not really to the point. In order to be following a genuine alternative to reflective equilibrium the inquirer must not merely set aside or eliminate certain beliefs, or even whole classes of beliefs. To be employing an alternative method the inquirer must eliminate beliefs *without any ground for doing so*. If she had a reason for leaving some of her judgments out of account, for example, those judgments do not meet her own epistemic standards, then she would *not* simply be leaving them out of account. They *would* have been taken into account, have been reflected upon, and this reflection would have revealed these judgments to be in conflict with other more strongly held beliefs or principles, and this realization would in turn have led to the revision, and perhaps the rejection, of these judgments.[8] When we focus our attention on the relevant kind of incomplete reflection, the kind that really is incompatible with reflective equilibrium, it becomes apparent that it is irrational after all, that it involves the same sort of pessimism, submission to external authority, and high risk of self-contradiction we saw when considering the complete abandonment of reflection.

It is easy to see that a method of inquiry with feature (B) puts the inquirer at risk of accepting what she does not find acceptable, and thereby contradicting herself in a sense, in much the same way a method of inquiry incorporating feature (A) does: Some of the beliefs or theories that are left out of account might very well conflict with the system of belief the inquirer is led to accept by following his method of limited reflection. If this happens, and the inquirer is in fact more strongly committed to the beliefs that were left out of account and would remain so after duly considering the conflict and how best to resolve it, then it can hardly be rational for the inquirer to accept the system of beliefs the method of inquiry led him to, since this system is contradicted by other things he believes more firmly and would continue to find preferable if he were to consider the matter. I do not believe a philosophical method that puts an inquirer into such a position is rational.[9]

It may not be apparent why I think methods of limited reflection involve pessimism and submission to external authority. But what other explanation could there be for a person ignoring certain of her judgments, even when she is very strongly committed to them and has no reason of her own for doubting them? Such a person must either be alienated from the part of herself responsible for the judgments being excluded and have given up on this part of herself without having any reason for distrusting this part, or she is submitting to some method, approach, or authority that directs her to ignore certain judgments of which she is confident, even though she cannot really believe this method, approach, or authority will lead her to the truth.

I think the point I am trying to make is important enough that I am going to risk belaboring it. I want to focus on the aspect of submission to external authority by considering what must be happening when a person sets out to criticize the method of reflective equilibrium. The inquirer employing reflective equilibrium has started out with a set of initial judgments about some area, and through a process of mutual adjustment constructed a theory that accounts for these judgments. The inquirer will also have reflected on the connections that hold between this system of theory and corresponding judgments and any other beliefs that might be relevant, and once again brought her beliefs into a stable equilibrium via a process of mutual adjustment. A critic must advance some sort of argument against some element of the resultant system of belief. To pick a pertinent example, the critic might cite studies by cognitive psychologists showing that our intuitive judgments about the area in question are unreliable, and press the inquirer not to allow these intuitive judgments any weight at all in determining the theory she ends up accepting. In all likelihood, what the critic is thinking is that the inquirer is ignorant of the relevant studies and that she accepts many of the same forms of argument and background epistemological views that he does, so that when she is made aware of the studies and the implications of these studies for her considered judgments and the theories in part supported by these judgments, she will accept the studies and implications just as the critic has.

If this is what the critic is doing, then he really is not doing anything that conflicts with the method of reflective equilibrium. He is merely providing the inquirer with information acquired in ways the inquirer accepts which conflicts with some of what the inquirer believes and expecting the inquirer to make appropriate adjustments so that her system of beliefs is again coherent. This is nothing more nor less that what reflective equilibrium dictates.

But suppose that the inquirer is not ignorant of the psychological studies and that she has already incorporated her belief in the results of these studies into her system of beliefs in a way that does not require her to give her intuitive judgments no weight in her deliberations. To do so consistently, she obviously must differ with the critic somewhere else, for example, with respect to some epistemic principle, rule of inference, or judgments about what interpretation of data is most plausible. But if her beliefs are indeed in a state of reflective equilibrium, she will have considered the opinions about which she does not agree with her critic, and there will be a coherent story to tell in support of her own views that the inquirer finds most acceptable upon thorough reflection. This is the case we must consider to get an alternative to reflective equilibrium, and to get the alternative we must imagine the critic still demands that the inquirer agree with him in this case. What would bring the inquirer to do such a thing? She would have to abandon the results of her own reflection, give up, at least in part, on thinking for herself, and simply knuckle even though she firmly believes, after careful reflection on all the relevant considerations, that doing so will lead her away from the truth and into error. I do not think it would be rational for her to do such a thing. Indeed, is this not one paradigm of what we consider to be irrational? Is it not exactly what we think happens when inquisitions and pogroms succeed most thoroughly, rather than merely in provoking cynical head nodding?

Perhaps it is unfair to imagine the critic *demanding* agreement—we have no pogroms or inquisitions. Critics simply present their arguments, aggressively perhaps, but with the sort of tame linguistic aggression one finds in graduate seminars, discussions at conferences, and in the pages of journals. What, in such polite society, would bring the inquirer to abandon the results of her inquiry? It is naive to think the answer is not pretty much the same. She would still have to give up and knuckle under even though thorough reflection had led her to believe this means accepting what is false. She may not be doing this because she has been shown "the instruments" or to avoid the ghetto. But she must be motivated by considerations she does not regard as having any more relation to attaining the truth, such as, by a desire to fit in, have others to talk with, earn degrees, publish, achieve a professional reputation, and so on.

Not Believing What Seems Most Likely to be True

A philosophical method that does not allow the results of a person's reflection to determine what she accepts, as in (C), is perhaps most obviously irrational. Such a method would have to direct the inquirer to reflect, but after she had completed her reflections, to believe something other than what these reflections had led her to consider most likely to be correct. And it surely could not be rational, if it is so much as possible, for a person who had fully reflected upon some conflict among her beliefs to believe what these reflections have convinced her is mistaken and to leave off believing what her reflections have convinced her is correct. An inquirer who did such a thing would have given up on herself as an intellectual being and not merely risked believing what she herself does not find acceptable, but in fact have accepted what she herself does not find acceptable. In addition, it seems that, when it comes down to the final resolution of conflicts among beliefs, such an inquirer must be submitting to some sort of external or alien authority, since she goes with beliefs that she herself does not consider most likely to be correct. And so we see that a method that does not allow the theory the inquirer accepts to be determined by the results of her reflection is irrational as well. (See Onora O'Neill 1992 for a useful discussion of how submission to alien authority figures in Kant's attempt to vindicate reason.)

Why Give a Damn About Being "Rational"?

Friend: OK. I see why you say that any alternative to reflective equilibrium is irrational. I might even cut you some slack and grant that reflective equilibrium is the only rational method of philosophical inquiry, since I think I see how the additional argument might go. But so what? You say it would be irrational for a person to leave some of her beliefs out of account, or to believe something that conflicts with what she is more strongly committed to. I grant you, that sounds pretty good in the abstract. Particularly a person who believes one thing when her own reflections have led her to be more strongly committed to something else seems to be contradicting herself somehow. But what if some of this person's beliefs are nothing but crazy superstitions? What if she is paranoid or obsessive and they are the result of some sort of chemical imbalance in her brain? Couldn't we fairly say that it would be irrational to take such beliefs *into* account? And wouldn't it be even worse if the person were very strongly committed to these superstitions or delusions, and revised other beliefs to conform with them? You say that to knuckle under and go along without reasons for doing so drawn from one's own system of belief is to behave in the same way as the most pathetic victims of inquisitions. But I could just as well point out that to stick with one's own superstitions or delusions against the testimony of the rest of the world and continue making whatever adjustments are necessary to maintain a coherent system of belief is to follow the path of the dogmatist or lunatic. I would say that this is irrational, but you say just the opposite. There is not much sense haggling over who gets to keep a word, so you win. Let's say 'rationality' refers to the sort of self-consistency you seem to have in mind. What I want to ask about is the value of this subjective type of rationality. Philosophers once thought that if they proceeded rationally they would be led to knowledge and truth, or at the very least to justified beliefs. But you've already admitted this doesn't hold for your sense of rationality. So why should we care about proceeding rationally in this sense? What's so bad about being irrational?

Me: I've tried to portray very clearly what a person must do in order to follow a method other than reflective equilibrium. I wanted to try to get you to form a clear picture of what one is involved in believing irrationally in the way I have described. If you have this clearly in mind, if you really see what it is that one would be doing, . . . Wasn't it Louie Armstrong who said "If you have to ask, you ain't never gonna get it." The answer should be intuitively obvious.

(This ending obviously is not entirely fair. Insofar as the question concerns merely the disvalue of the sort of irrationality I have described, I do not think it terribly unfair. There is of course more to be said. One might ask, for example, whether the disvalue of irrational belief is best understood in terms of the violation of an obligation or whether it is more a matter of failing to attain something desirable or valuable. And if it is best understood in terms of obligations, one must ask after the ground of the obligation and whether it is a moral obligation or an obligation of some other sort. Or one might wonder whether irrational belief is something to feel guilty about, ashamed of, or regret for. But these are further questions. It might be lazy of me to begin a discussion that raises them and then let them drop, but I do not think it unfair. If the question really just is whether irrational belief of the sort I have described is a bad thing, then I do not believe there is much one can say to a person who has a clear conception of exactly what such a belief involves and still cannot just see that it is a bad thing. What makes my ending unfair is that although my friend asks what is so bad about irrational belief, the way he raises this question, by pointing to the possibility that rational belief might come into conflict with other values such as believing the truth or avoiding dogmatism or even not being a little bit insane, suggests that what he really wants to raise is a comparative question. He wants to be convinced not that irrational belief is a bad thing, but that it is more important than other relevant values, for example, the value of believing the truth or, for that matter, the value of being a part of an intellectual community. He wants a reason for thinking that, when faced with the possibility that in attaining the one value we will lose the others, we should act to guarantee that we believe rationally and hope that the cost of doing this is not that we miss out on other good things. For my claim has been not merely that irrationality is a bad thing, and rationality a good thing, but that this is the value around which philosophical inquiry should be structured. Particularly when by making this claim I go against the dominant intellectual tradition that sees truth as the value that structures inquiry in general, philosophy in particular, and as the fundamental concept in terms of which all epistemic concepts (such as rationality) are to be defined, it does seem unfair to sidestep this issue. My excuse is that it is too large an issue to address within the confines of this chapter, and the truth is that I am not at all sure what to say.)

Notes

I began working on an earlier incarnation of this chapter while in Germany with a grant from the Alexander von Humboldt-Stiftung. I am grateful to the AvH for their support and to Prof. Andreas Kemmerling, my host at the Seminar für Philosophie, Logik, und Wissenschaftstheorie, Ludwig Maximillian Universität-München. I had the opportunity to present the earlier incarnation of this chapter at the Ludwig Maximillian Universität, Universität Konstanz, University of Reading, University of Kent, and the University of Notre Dame, and I received many helpful comments from members of the audience on each occasion. I also had an opportunity to present this chapter in more or less its current form to a Summer Seminar organized by the Dutch Research School for Advanced Studies in Ethics, where the comments from the audience were once again very helpful. Finally, I have benefited from detailed comments by Marian David on both of the earlier versions of this chapter.

1. Because it does not play an important role in the argument I plan to offer here, I have neglected one very significant element of reflective equilibrium. This is the consideration of alternative theories available to one that Rawls stresses when distinguishing wide from narrow reflective equilibrium. I give this element thorough consideration in DePaul 1993.

2. (1) should be interpreted to mean: it is not the case that every inquirer who employs the method of reflective equilibrium will be led to form true beliefs. It is consistent with (1), so interpreted, that some inquirers are such that if they were to employ the method of reflective equilibrium they would be led to form true beliefs. The method might be said to guarantee truth to such special inquirers.

Obviously I here assume that truth is not properly defined as what a person would accept in some ideal state, which ends up being equivalent to a state of wide reflective equilibrium. Such a definition gets us a guarantee of truth, but on the cheap.

3. There are a number of plausible ways of interpreting (2). Perhaps it is most natural to interpret it to mean that each inquirer is such that if he or she were to employ the method of reflective equilibrium, he or she would not be led to form beliefs that are mostly true. However, this is not what I mean by (2). Rather, I mean that it is not the case that the vast majority of inquirers are such that if they employ the method of reflective equilibrium, then they will be led to form true (or mostly true) beliefs. It is compatible with this interpretation, and with the considerations on the basis of which I made claim (2), that some inquirers are such that if they employ, the method of reflective equilibrium, they will be led to form true (or mostly true) beliefs. Some may take the considerations I cited to support the stronger, and perhaps more natural reading of (2), but I here make no such claim. If half of those who employ a method of inquiry are led to form one belief, and the rest of those who employ the method are led to form some incompatible belief, then we can be just about certain that the method is at best leading 50 percent of those who use it to the truth. Suppose it is the case that 50 percent of those enploying the method end up accepting the truth. What is going on? It might be that there are not any relevant differences among the inquirers employing the method, so that some feature of the method is responsible for the outcome. In this case we might be able to conclude that any inquirer who employs the method will have only a 50 percent chance of coming to form a true belief as a result. But it might also be the case that there is some relevant difference among inquirers, some feature that only 50 percent of inquirers have, and that the method will invariably lead inquirers with this feature to the truth. I have said nothing that might decide between these alternatives, so I wish (2) to be interpreted in a way that is compatible with both.

I should mention another possible, but perhaps less likely, confusion. I intend the set of "beliefs a person following the method of reflective equilibrium is led to form" to contain only those beliefs formed as a result of employing this method of inquiry. I assume the vast majority of the beliefs of the vast majority of people are ordinary perceptual, memory, introspective, and testamonial beliefs. I also assume that the vast majority of these beliefs are true. Most people who employ the method of reflective equilibrium will retain these beliefs throughout the process, but I do not think this is relevant to the reliability of this method of inquiry.

4. Plantinga (1993) identifies the epistemic concept he calls 'warrant' in this way, reserving the term 'justification' for a more deontological concept of epistemic evaluation. I have chosen to stick with 'justification' simply because that is the more commonly used term.

5. After my remarks about (1) and (2) it should be clear that I intend (3) to be interpreted as the claim that it is not the case that all or even the vast majority of inquirers who employ the method of reflective equilibrium will be led to form beliefs that are justified. For a more thorough presentation of my reasons for thinking that reflective equilibrium can guarantee neither truth, reliability or justification see DePaul 1993: chs. 1 & 2.

6. I have in mind here explicit theories and self-consciously systematic accounts. It is of course a common practice to view ordinary cognizers as having implicit theories or systematic views about various matters in order to explain certain aspects of the cognizer's behavior. Surely the most familiar example of this approach is provided by the Chomskian explanation of the ability of native speakers to recognize grammatical sentences of their own language.

7. The legal example is not entirely happy, since I think we do not really believe that the judge or juror should base her *belief* only upon the admissible evidence. Her *decision* must be so based, but in forming a belief about the case, she should use all

the evidence she has.

8. In another kind of case, perhaps this is what happens with science and religion, when either the person of an exclusively scientific temperament rejects religion or the devout religious believer rejects science: The inquirer is systematically more confident of judgments in one area than of judgments in a potentially relevant area. So the inquirer decides to work out her views in the area where she is most confident first, and only then consider how her judgments in the other area relate, consistently revising the judgments in the second area so they conform to the judgments in the first. Once again, although at a certain stage of inquiry it might seem that some judgments are simply being left out of account, and hence that some alternative to reflective equilibrium is being employed, if we consider the person's practice more broadly, we can see that this practice does indeed qualify as a sort of reflective equilibrium.

9. I should say that what worries me here is perhaps not best captured in terms of "risk." I expect any method of inquiry that is not Cartesian—moving from indubitable premises by indubitable steps—will put the inquirer at risk of error, perhaps even the error of self-contradiction. Of course, I do believe that the risk involved in methods having feature (A) or (B) represents much more than an abstract possibility. As I noted above, I think we can pretty much count on methods having feature (A) leading inquirers to accept things they do not find acceptable, and in practice I think the probability of a method having feature (B) leading to such a result is nearly as great. After all, if it were not very likely that following a method of limited reflection would lead the inquirer to different conclusions, there would not be much point in following such a method rather than a method of complete reflection, and one would not expect those who argue for the exclusion of one or another class of judgments to be so vociferous. But although I cannot quite put my finger on it, I think there is something more that is worrisome here than the fact that there is a very real possibility or even a probability that methods having feature (A) or (B) will lead inquirers astray, something about the way such methods, particularly those having feature (B), march inquirer's into trouble without acknowledging that there is any trouble.

Reference List

Achinstein, P. (1968). *The Concepts of Science*. Baltimore: Johns Hopkins University Press.

Alston, W. (1985). "Concepts of epistemic justification." *The Monist* 68: 57-89.

Armstrong, D. (1989). *Universals*. Boulder: Westview Press.

Armstrong, S. L., L. R. Gleitman, and H. Gleitman. (1983). "What some concepts might not be." *Cognition* 13: 263-308.

Bacharach, M., and S. Hurley. (1991). "Issues and advances in the foundations of decision theory." M. Bacharach and S. Hurley (eds.). *Foundations of Decision Theory: Issues and Advances*. Oxford: Basil Blackwell: 1-38.

Baddeley, A. D. (1990). *Human memory: Theory and practice*. Needham Heights, NJ: Allyn and Bacon.

Baillargeon, R. (1987). "Object permanence in 3-1/2 and 4-1/2 month old infants." *Developmental Psychology* 23: 655-664.

Baillargeon, R., E. Spelke., and S. Wasserman. (1985). "Object permanence in five-month-old infants." *Cognition* 20: 191-208.

Barsalou, L. (1983). "Ad-hoc categories." *Memory and Cognition* 10: 82-93.

_____. (1985). "Ideals, central tendency, and frequency of instantiation." *Journal of Experimental Psychology: Learning, Memory, and Cognition* 11: 629-654.

_____. (1987). "The instability of graded strticture: Implications for the nature of concepts." U. Neisser (ed.). *Concepts and Conceptual Development: Ecological and Intellectual Factors in Categorization*. Cambridge: Cambridge University Press.

Battig, W. F., and W. E. Montague. (1969). "Category norms of verbal items in 56 categories: a replication and extension of the Connecticut category norms." *Journal of Experimental Psychology* 80(3): 1-46.

Bazerman, M. H., H. A. Schroth, P. P. Shah, K. A. Diekmann, and A. E. Tenbrunsel. (1994). "The inconsistent role of comparison others and procedural justice in reactions to hypothetical job descriptions: implications for job acceptance decisions." *Organizational Behavior and Human Decision Processes* 60: 326-352.

Bazerman, M. H., S. B. White, and G. F. Loewenstein. (1995). "Perceptions of fairness in interpersonal and individual choice situations." *Current Directions in Psychological Science* 4(2): 39-43.

Beach, L. R. (1964). "Cue probabilism and inference behavior." *Psychological Monographs* 78: 1-20.

Bealer, G. (1987). "The philosophical limits of scientific essentialism." J. Tomberlin (ed.). *Philosophical Perspectives* 1. Atascadero, CA: Ridgeview Publishing: 289-365.

_____. (1993). "The incoherence of empiricism." S. Wagner and R. Warner (eds.). *Naturalism: A Critical Appraisal.* Notre Dame: Notre Dame University Press: 163-196.

_____. (1994). "Mental properties." *The Journal of Philosophy* 91: 185-208.

_____. (1996a). "*A priori* knowledge and the scope of philosphy." *Philosophical Studies* 81: 121-142.

_____. (1996b). "On the possibility of philosophical knowledge." *Philosophical Perspectives* 10. Oxford: Basil Blackwell.

_____. (forthcoming). *Philosophical Limits of Science.* Oxford: Oxford University Press.

Benacerraf, P. (1973). "Mathematical truth." *Journal of Philosophy* 70: 661-679.

Berlin, B., and P. Kay. (1969). *Basic Color Terms: Their Universality and Evolution.* Berkeley: University of California Press.

Bishop, M. A. (1992). "Conceptual clarity in philosophy." *American Philosophical Quarterly* 29: 267-277.

Bloom, P. (1994a). "Possible names: The role of syntax-semantics mappings in the acquistion of nominals." *Lingua* 92: 297-329.

_____. (1994b). "Semantic competence as an explanation for some transitions in language development." Y. Levy (ed.). *Other Children, Other Languages: Theoretical Issues in Language Development.* Hillsdale, NJ: Lawrence Erlbaum Associates.

Bloomfield, L. (1933). *Language.* New York: Holt.

BonJour, L. (1985). *The Structure of Empirical Knowledge.* Cambridge: Harvard University Press.

_____. (1994). "Against naturalized epistemology." *Midwest Studies in Philosophy* 19: 283-300.

Boyd, R. (1988). "How to be a moral realist." G. Sayre-McCord (ed.). *Essays on Moral Realism.* Ithaca, NY: Cornell University Press: 181-228.

Bransford, J. D., and J. J. Franks. (1971). "Abstraction of linguistic ideas." *Cognitive Psychology* 2: 331-351.

Brown, H. (1988). *Rationality.* London: Routledge.

Bruner, J. S., R. R. Olver, and P. M. Greenfield. (1966). *Studies in Cognitive Growth.* New York: Wiley.

Burge, T. (1979). "Individualism and the mental." *Midwest Studies in Philosophy* 4: 73-122.

Campbell, A. (1981). *The Sense of Well-Being in America.* New York: McGraw-Hill.

Campbell, J. (1995). *Past, Space and Self.* Cambridge: MIT Press.

Carey, S. (1985). *Conceptual Change in Childhood.* Cambridge: MIT Press.

Carnap, R. (1950). *Logical Foundations of Probability.* Chicago: University of Chicago Press.

Cavell, S. (1979). *The Claim of Reason.* Oxford: Oxford University Press.

Cherniak, C. (1984). "Prototypicality and deductive reasoning." *Journal of Verbal Learning and Verbal Behavior* 23: 625-642.

_____. (1986). *Minimal Rationality*. Cambridge: MIT Press.

Chomsky, N. (1965). *Aspects of the Theory of Syntax*. Cambridge: MIT Press.

_____. (1972). *Language and Mind*. NewYork: Harcourt, Brace and Jovanovich.

_____. (1980). *Rules and Representations*. New York: Columbia University Press.

Churchland, P. (1981). "Eliminative materialism and the propositional attitudes." *Journal of Philosophy* 58: 67-90.

Clark, E., and K. Carpenter. (1989). "The notion of source in language acquisition." *Language* 65: 1-30.

Clark, H. H., and P. Lucy. (1975). "Understanding what is meant from what is said: A study in conversationally conveyed requests." *Journal of Verbal Learning and Verbal Behavior* 14: 56-72.

Cohen, L. J. (1981). "Can human irrationality be experimentally demonstrated?" *Behavioral and Brain Sciences* 4: 317-370.

_____. (1986). *The Dialogue of Reason*. Oxford: Clarendon Press.

Cohen, S. (1988). "How to be a fallibilist." J. Tomberlin (ed.). *Philosophical Perspectives* 2. Atascadero, CA: Ridgeview Publishing: 91-123.

Cole, M., and B. Means. (1981). *Comparative Studies of How People Think*. Cambridge: Harvard University Press.

Cole, M., and S. Scribner. (1974). *Culture and Thought*. New York: John Wiley.

Conee, E., and R. Feldman. (1983). "Stich and Nisbett on justifying inference rules." *Philosophy of Science* 50: 326-331.

Coppee, H. (1874). *Elements of Logic: Designed as a Manual of Instruction*. Philadelphia: J. H. Butler.

Cornman, J. W., K. Lehrer, and G. Pappas. (1982). *Philosophical Problems and Arguments: An Introduction* (3rd ed.). NewYork: Macmillan.

Cummins, D. (1996a). "Dominance hierarchies and the evolution of reasoning." *Minds and Machines* 6: 463-480.

_____. (1996b). "Evidence for the innateness of deontic reasoning." *Mind and Language* 11: 160-190.

Daniels, N. (1979). "Wide reflective equilibrium and theory acceptance in ethics." *Journal of Philosophy* 76: 256-282.

_____. (1980a). "Reflective equilibrium and Archimedean points." *Canadian Journal of Philosophy* 10: 83-103.

_____. (1980b). "On some methods of ethics and linguistics." *Philosophical Studies* 37: 21-36.

_____. (1984). "Two approaches to theory acceptance in ethics." D. Copp (ed.). *Morality, Reason and Truth*. Totowa: Rowman and Allenheld: 120-140.

Davidson, D. (1967). "Truth and meaning." *Synthese* 17: 304-323.

_____. (1973-74). "On the very idea of a conceptual scheme." *Proceedings and Addresses of the American Philosophical Association* 17: 5-20.

_____. (1982). "Rational animals." *Dialectica* 36: 317-327.

_____. (1986). "A coherence theory of truth and knowledge." E. LePore (ed.). *The Philosophy of Donald Davidson*. London: Basil Blackwell: 307-

319.

_____. (1987). "Knowing one's own mind." *Proceedings and Addresses of the American Philosophical Association* 60: 441-457.

Dawes, R. M. (1988). *Rational Choice in an Uncertain World.* San Diego: Harcourt Brace and Jovanovich.

_____. (1994). *House of Cards.* New York: Free Press.

Dennett, D. C. (1978). *Brainstorms.* Montgomery: Bradford Books.

_____. (1986). "The logical geography of computational approaches: A view from the East Pole." R. Harnish and M. Brand (eds.). *The Representation of Knowledge and Belief.* Tucson: University of Arizona Press.

DePaul, M. (1993). *Balance and Refinement: Beyond Coherence Methods of Moral Inquiry.* London: Routledge.

DeRose, K. (1992). "Contextualism and knowledge attributions." *Philosophy and Phenomenological Research* 52: 913-929.

_____. (1995). "Solving the skeptical problem." *Philosophical Review* 104: 1-52.

Devitt, M. (1994). "The methodology of naturalistic semantics." *Journal of Philosophy* 91: 545-572.

Descartes, R. (1984). *The Philosophical Writings of Descartes, v. I.* J. Cottingham, R. Stoothof, and D. Murdock (eds.). Cambridge: Cambridge University Press.

Dretske, F. (1988). *Explaining Behavior: Reasons in a World of Causes.* Cambridge: MIT Press.

Ekman, P. (1971). "Universals and cultural differences in facial expressions of emotion." J. K. Cole (ed.). *Nebraska Symposium on Motivation.* Lincoln: University of Nebraska Press.

Estes, D., H. M. Wellman, and J. D. Woolley. (1989). "Children's understanding of mental phenomena." H. Reese (ed.). *Advances in Child Development and Behavior.* New York: Academic Press.

Estes, W. (1994). *Classification and Cognition.* Oxford: Oxford University Press.

Finke, R. A., M. J. Johnson, and G. C.-W. Shyi. (1988). "Memory confusions for real and imagined completions of symmetrical visual patterns." *Memory and Cognition* 16: 133-137.

Flanagan, O. (1991). "The modularity of consciousness." *Behavioral and Brain Sciences* 14: 446-447.

Flavell, J. H., F. L. Green, and E. R. Flavell. (1995). "Young children's knowledge about thinking." *Monographs of the Society for Research in Child Development* 60(1).

Fodor, J. (1975). *The Language of Thought.* New York: Thomas Y. Crowell. Reprinted by Harvard University Press (1979).

_____. (1987). *Psychosemantics.* Cambridge: MIT Press, A Bradford Book.

_____. (1990). *A Theory of Content and Other Essays.* Cambridge, MA: MIT Press, A Bradford Book.

_____. (1994). *The Elm and the Expert.* Cambridge: MIT Press, A Bradford Book.

Foley, R. (1993). *Working Without a Net.* New York: Oxford University Press.

Foote, P. (1984). "Killing and Letting Die." J. Garfield (ed.). *Abortion: Moral and Legal Perspectives*. Amherst: University of Massachusetts Press.

Frake, C. O. (1969). "The ethnographic study of cognitive systems." S. A. Tyler (ed.). *Cognitive Anthropology*. New York: Holt, Rinehart and Winston.

Franks, J. J., and J. D. Bransford. (1971). "Abstraction of visual patterns." *Journal of Experimental Psychology* 90: 65-74.

Gagne, C. L., and E. J. Shoben. (1997). "Thematic relations and the creation of combined concepts." T. B. Ward, S. M. Smith, and J. Vaid (eds.). *Conceptual Structures and Processes: Emergence, Discovery, and Change*. Washington: American Psychological Association.

Garner, W. R. (1974). *The Processing of Information and Structure*. New York: Halsted Press.

Gelman, S. A., and H. M. Wellman. (1991). "Insides and essence: early understandings of the non-obvious." *Cognition* 38(3): 213-244.

Gentner, D. (1989). "The mechanisms of analogical learning." S. Vosniadou and A. Ortony (eds.). *Similarity, Analogy, and Thought*. Cambridge: Cambridge University Press: 199-241.

Gettier, E. (1963). "Is justified true belief knowledge?" *Analysis* 23: 121-123.

Gibbs, R. W. (1989). "Understanding and literal meaning." *Cognitive Science* 13(2): 243-251.

_____. (1994). *The Poetics of Mind: Figurative Thought, Language, and Understanding*. New York: Cambridge University Press.

Gilbert, D. T. (1991). "How mental systems believe." *American Psychologist* 46(2): 107-119.

Gilbert, D. T., D. S. Krull, and P. S. Malone. (1990). "Unbelieving the unbelievable: Some problems in the rejection of false information." *Journal of Personality and Social Psychology* 59(4): 601-613.

Gilovich, T. (1991). *How We Know What Isn't So: The Fallibility of Human Reason in Everyday Life*. New York: Free Press.

Gleason, H. A. (1969). *An Introduction to Descriptive Linguistics*. London: Holt, Rinehart, and Winston.

Glucksberg, S. (1991). "Beyond literal meaning: The psychology of allusion." *Psychological Sciences* 2(3): 146-152.

Glucksberg, S., P. Gildea, and H. B. Bookin. (1982). "On understanding nonliteral speech: Can people ignore metaphors?" *Journal of Verbal Learning and Verbal Behavior* 21: 85-98.

Glucksberg, S., and B. Keysar. (1990). "Understanding metaphorical comparisons. Beyond similarity." *Psychological Review* 97: 3-18.

Goldman, A. (1976). "Discrimination and perceptual knowledge." *Journal of Philosophy* 73: 771-791.

_____. (1977). "Perceptual objects." *Synthese* 35: 257-284.

_____. (1979). "What is justified belief?" G. Pappas (ed.). *Justification and Knowledge*. Dordrecht: Reidel: 1-23.

_____. (1986). *Epistemology and Cognition*. Cambridge: Harvard University Press.

_____. (1989a). "Metaphysics, mind, and mental science." *Philosophical*

Topics 17: 131-145.

_____. (1989b). "Psychology and philosophical analysis." *Proceedings of the Aristotelian Society* 89: 195-209.

_____. (1992a). "Cognition and modal metaphysics." *Liaisons: Philosophy Meets the Cognitive and Social Sciences.* Cambridge: MIT Press: 49-66.

_____. (1992b). "Epistemic folkways and scientific epistemology." *Liaisons: Philosophy Meets the Cognitive and Social Sciences.* Cambridge: MIT Press: 155-175.

_____. (1993a). *Philosophical Applications of Cognitive Science.* Boulder: Westview Press.

_____. (1993b). "The psychology of folk psychology." *Behavioral and Brain Sciences* 16(1): 15-28.

Goodman, N. (1965). *Fact, Fiction and Forecast.* New York: Bobbs-Merrill.

Gopnik, A. (1993). "How we know our minds: the illusion of first-person knowledge of intentionality." *Behavioral and Brain Sciences* 16(1): 29-113.

Gopnik, A., and J. W. Astington. (1988). "Children's understanding of representational change and its relation to the understanding of false belief and the appearance-reality distinction." *Child Development* 59(1): 26-37.

Gopnik, A., and V. Slaughter. (1991). "Young children's understanding of changes in their mental states." *Child Development* 62(1): 98-110.

Graham, G. (1993). *Philosophy of Mind: An Introduction.* Oxford: Blackwell.

Graham, G. and T. Horgan. (1988). "How to be realistic about folk psychology." *Philosophical Psychology* 1.

Grice, H. P. (1975). "Logic and conversation." P. Cole and J. L. Morgan (eds.). *Syntax and Semantics 3, Speech Acts.* New York: Academic Press.

Gutting, G. (1982). "Can philosophical beliefs be rationally justified." *American Philosophical Quarterly* 19: 315-330.

Hallen, B., and J. O. Sodipo. (1986). *Knowledge, Belief and Witchcraft.* London: Ethnographica.

Hammond, P. (1988). "Consequentialist foundations for expected utility." *Theory and Decision* 25: 25-78.

Hampton, J. A. (1981). "An investigation of the nature of abstract concepts." *Memory and Cognition* 9: 149-156.

Harman, G. (1986). *Change of View.* Cambridge: MIT Press.

Heider, E. R. (1971). "Natural categories." *Proceedings of the Annual Convention of the American Psychological Association* 6: 43-44.

_____. (1972). "Universals in color naming and memory." *Journal of Experimental Psycholgy* 93: 111-211.

Heil, J. (1992). *The Nature of True Minds.* Cambridge: Cambridge University Press.

Henley, N. M. (1969). "A psychological study of the semantics of animal terms." *Journal of Verbal Learning and Verbal Behavior* 8: 176-184.

Hesse, M. (1966). *Models and Analogies in Science.* Notre Dame: University of Notre Dame Press.

Hintzman, D. (1986). "'Schema abstraction' in a multiple trace memory model." *Psychological Review* 93: 411-428.

Horgan, T. (1979). "'Could', possible worlds, and moral responsibility." *South-*

ern Journal of Philosophy 17: 345-358.

_____. (1985). "Compatibilism and the consequence argument." *Philosophical Studies* 47: 339-356.

_____. (1989). "Mental Quausation." J. Tomberlin (ed.). *Philosophical Perspectives* 3. Atascadero, CA: Ridgeview Publishing.

_____. (1990). "Psychologistic semantics, robust vagueness, and the philosophy of language." *Meanings and Prototypes: Studies in Linguistic Categorization*. London: Routledge: 535-557.

_____. (1991). "Actions, reasons, and the explanatory role of content." B. McLaughlin (ed.). *Dretske and His Critics*. Cambridge: Basil Blackwell.

_____. (1993a). "The austere ideology of folk psychology." *Mind and Language* 8: 282-297.

_____. (1993b). "Nonreductive materialism and the explanatory autonomy of psychology." S. Wagner and R. Warner (eds.). *Naturalism: A Critical Appraisal*. Notre Dame: University of Notre Dame Press.

Horgan, T., and G. Graham. (1991). "In defense of southern fundamentalism." *Philosophical Studies* 62: 107-134.

_____. (1994). "Southern fundamentalism and the end of philosophy." *Philosophical Issues* 5: 219-247.

Hsee, C. K. (1996). "The evaluability hypothesis: an explanation of preference reversals between joint and separate evaluations of alternatives." *Organizational Behavior and Human Decision Processes* 67: 247-257.

_____. (1997). "Less is better: when low-value options are valued more highly than high-valued options." *Journal of Behavioral Decision Making*.

Hume, D. (1777). *An Enquiry Concerning Human Understanding*.

Imai, M., and D. Gentner. (1994). "Linguistic relativity vs. universal ontology: Cross-linguistic studies of the object/substance distinction." Proceedings of the 29th Regional Meeting of the Chicago Linguistic Society.

Irwin, J. R., P. Slovic, S. Lichtenstein, and G. H. McClelland. (1993). "Preference reversals and the measurement of environmental values." *Journal of Risk and Uncertainty* 6: 5-18.

Jackendoff, R. (1983). *Semantics and Cognition*. Cambridge: MIT Press.

_____. (1991). "Parts and boundaries." *Cognition* 41: 9-45.

Johnson, M. K., S. Hashtroudi, and D. S. Lindsay. (1993). "Source monitoring." *Psychological Bulletin* 114(1): 3-28.

Kachelmeier, S. J., and M. Shehata. (1992). "Examining risk preferences under high monetary incentives: experimental evidence from the People's Republic of China." *American Economic Review* 82: 1120-1141.

Kahneman, D. (1996). "The cognitive psychology of consequences and moral intuition." Manuscript, Princeton University.

Kahneman, D., B. L. Frederickson, C. A. Schreiber, and D. A. Redelneir. (1993). "When more pain is preferred to less: Adding a better end." *American Psychologist* 4(6): 401-405.

Kahneman, D., and D. T. Miller. (1986). "Norm Theory: comparing reality to its alternatives." *Psychological Review* 93: 136-153.

Kahneman, D., and I. Ritov. (1994). "Determinants of stated willingness to pay for public goods: a study in the headline method." *Journal of Risk and Un-*

certainty 9: 5-38.

Kahneman, D., P. Slovic, and A. Tversky. (1982). *Judgment Under Uncertainty: Heuristics and Biases.* Cambridge: Cambridge University Press.

Kahneman, D., and A. Tversky. (1979). "Prospect theory: an analysis of decision under risk." *Econometrica* 47(2): 263-291.

Kaplan, M. (1994). "Epistemology denatured." *Midwest Studies in Philosophy* 19: 350-365.

Katz, J. (1981). *Language and Other Abstract Objects.* Totowa: Rowman and Littlefield.

Keil, F. C. (1989). *Concepts, Kinds, and Cognitive Development.* Cambridge: MIT Press.

Keysar, B. (1989). "On the functional equivalence of metaphoric and literal meanings." *Journal of Memory and Language* 28: 375-385.

Kim, K. (1989). "Mechanism, purpose, and explanatory exclusion." J. Tomberlin (ed.). *Philosophical Perspectives* 3. Atascadero, CA: Ridgeview Publishing.

Kornblith, H. (1994). "A conservative approach to social epistemology." F. Schmitt (ed.). *Socializing Epistemology.* Totowa: Rowman and Littlefield: 93-110.

_____. (1995). "Naturalistic epistemology and its critics." *Philosophical Topics* 23: 237-255.

_____. (manuscript). "Cogent arguments for naturalism: a reply to Kaplan."

Kripke, S. (1972). *Naming and Necessity.* Cambridge: Harvard University Press.

Kucera, H. K., and W. N. Francis. (1967). *Computational Analysis of Present-Day American English.* Providence, RI: Brown University Press.

Labov, W. (1975). "Empirical foundations of linguistic theory." R. Austerlitz (ed.). *The Scope of American Linguistics.* Ghent: Peter De Ridder Press: 77-133.

Lakoff, G. (1972). "Hedges: a study in meaning criteria and the logic of fuzzy concepts." *Papers from The Eighth Regional Meeting, Chicago Linguistics Society.* Chicago: University of Chicago Linguistics Department.

_____. (1987). *Women, Fire and Dangerous Things.* Chicago: University of Chicago Press.

Langacker, R. W. (1987). "Nouns and verbs." *Language* 63: 53-94.

Larmore, C. (1996). *The Morals of Modernity.* Cambridge: Cambridge University Press.

Lehrer, K. (1983). "Belief, acceptance and cognition." H. Parret (ed.). *On Believing: Epistemological and Semiotic Approaches.* New York: Walter de Gruyter.

_____. (1991). *Metamind.* Oxford: Oxford University Press.

Levi, I. (1991). "Consequentialism and sequential choice." M. Bacharach and S. Hurley (eds.). *Foundations of Decision Theory: Issues and Advances.* Oxford: Basil Blackwell: 92-122.

Lewicki, P. (1985). "Nonconscious biasing effects of single instances on subsequent judgments." *Journal of Personality and Social Psychology* 48(3): 563-574.

Lewis, D. (1979). "Scorekeeping in a language game," *Journal of Philosophical*

Logic 8: 339-359.

_____. (1983). *Philosophical Papers, v I*. Oxford: Oxford University Press.

_____. (1986a). *On the Plurality of Worlds*. Oxford: Basil Blackwell.

_____. (1986b). "Causation." *Philosophical Papers, v II*. Oxford: Oxford University Press.

Lichtenstein, S., and P. Slovic. (1973). "Response-induced reversals of preference in gambling: an extended replication in Las Vegas." *Journal of Experimental Psychology* 101: 16-20.

Loftus, E. F. (1993). "The reality of repressed memories." *American Psychologist* 48: 518-537.

Loftus, E. F., and R. W. Scheff. (1971). "Categorization norms for fifty representative instances." *Journal of Experimental Psychology* 91: 355-364.

Lycan, W. (1988). "Moral facts and moral knowledge." *Judgment and Justification*. New York: Cambridge University Press: 198-215.

Mackie, J. L. (1974). *The Cement of the Universe*. Oxford: Clarendon Press.

Malcolm, N. (1968). "The Conceivability of mechanism." *Philosophical Review* 77: 45-72.

Malt, B. C. and F. F. Smith. (1982). "The role of familiarity in determining typicality." *Memory and Cognition* 10: 69-75.

Markie, P. (1996). "Goldman's new reliabilism." *Philosophy and Phenomenological Research* 56: 799-817.

_____. (forthcoming). "In defense of one form of traditional epistemology." *Philosophical Studies*.

Markman, E. M. (1985). "Why superordinate category terms can be mass nouns." *Cognition* 19: 31-53.

Marr, D. (1982). *Vision: A computational Investigation into the Human Representation and Processing of Visual Information*. San Francisco: W. H. Freeman.

Matthews, G. (1980). *Philosophy and the Young Child*. Cambridge: Harvard University Press.

McCawley, J (1975). "Lexicography and the Count-Mass distinction." *Berkeley Linguistic Society* 1: 314-321.

McClennen, E. F. (1983). "Sure-thing doubts." B. P. Stigum and F. Wenstop (eds.). *Foundations of Utility and Risk Theory with Applications*. Dordrecht: Reidel: 117-136.

McCloskey, M., and S. Glucksberg. (1978). "Natural categories: Well-defined or fuzzy sets?" *Memory and Cognition* 6: 462-472.

McDaniel, C. K. (1972). *Hue Perception and Hue Naming*. Unpublished B.A. thesis, Harvard University.

McDowell, J. (1994). *Mind and World*. Cambridge: Harvard University Press.

McNeil, B. J., S. G. Pauker, H. C. Sox Jr., and A. Tversky. (1986). "On the elicitation of preferences for alternative therapies." H. R. Arkes, et al. (eds.). *Judgment and Decision Making: An Interdisciplinary Reader*. Cambridge: Cambridge University Press: 386-393.

Medin, D. and D. Schaffer. (1978). "A context theory of classification learning." *Psychological Review* 85: 207-238.

Medin, D. L., and E. E. Smith. (1984). "Concepts and concept formation." *An-*

nual Review of Psychology 35: 113-138.

Medvec, V. H., S. Madey, and T. Gilovich. (1995). "When less is more: counterfactual thinking and satisfaction among Olympic medalists." *Journal of Personality and Social Psychology* 69: 603-610.

Mervis, C. B., J. Catlin, and E. Rosch. (1975). "Development of the structure of color categories." *Developmenital Psychology* 11: 54-60.

Mervis, C. B., E. Rosch, and J. Catlin. (1975). "Relationships among goodness-of-example, category norms, and word frequency." Unpublished manuscript. (Available from the second author.)

Miller, D. T., and C. McFarland. (1986). "Counterfactual thinking and victim compensation: a test of Norm Theory." *Personality and Social Psychology Bulletin* 12(4): 513-519.

Mitchell, M., and J. Jolley. (1992). *Research Design Explained*. Fort Worth: Harcourt Brace Janovich.

Murphy, G. L., and D. L. Medin. (1985). "The role of theories in conceptual coherence." *Psychological Review* 92(3): 289-316.

Neuman, P. G. (1974). "An attubute frequency model for the abstraction of prototypes." *Memory and Cognition* 2: 241-248.

Nisbett, R. E. (ed.). (1993). *Rules of Reasoning*. Hillsdale, NJ: Lawrence Erlbaum Associates.

Nisbett, R. E., and L. Ross. (1980). *Human Inference: Strategies and Shortcomings of Social Judgment*. Englewood Cliffs, NJ: Prentice-Hall.

Nisbett, R. E., and T. D. Wilson. (1977). "Telling more than what we can know: Verbal reports on mental processes." *Psychological Review* 84: 231-259.

Nozick, R. (1995). *The Nature of Rationality*. Princeton: Princeton University Press.

O'Neill, O. (1992). "Vindicating reason." P. Guyer (ed.). *The Cambridge Companion to Kant*. Cambridge: Cambridge University Press.

Peacocke, C. (1986). "Rationality Requirements, Knowledge and Content." *Thoughts: An Essay on Content*. Oxford: Basil Blackwell.

_____. (1992). *A Study of Concepts*. Cambridge: MIT Press.

Plantinga, A. (1993). *Warrant and Proper Function*. New York: Oxford University Press.

Posner, M. I. (1973). *Cognition: An Introduction*. Glencoe, IL: Scott, Foresman.

Proust, M. (1992). *Within a Budding Grove*. C. K. S. Moncrieff and T. Kilmartin (trans.). Modern Library Edition.

Putnam, H. (1962). "The analytic and the synthetic." H. Feigl and G. Maxwell (eds.). *Minnesota Studies in Philosophy of Science, v. 3*. Minneapolis: University of Minnesota Press: 350-397.

_____. (1975). "The meaning of 'meaning'." *Philosophical Papers, v. 2: Mind, Language and Reality*. Cambridge: Cambridge University Press: 215-271.

_____. (1987). *The Many Faces of Realism*. LaSalle, IL: Open Court.

Quine, W. V. O. (1989). "Philosophy: Mind, brain and behavior." A. J. Brownstein (ed.). *Progress in Behavioral Studies, v. 1*. Hillsdale, NJ:

Lawrence Erlbaum Associates.

Quinn, W. (1993). "Actions, intentions, and consequences: The doctrine of doing and allowing." *Morality and Action*. Cambridge: Cambridge University Press.

Ramsey, W. (1992). "Prototypes and conceptual analysis." *Topoi* 11: 59-70.

Rawls, J. (1971). *A Theory of Justice*. Cambridge: Harvard University Press.

_____. (1974). "The independence of moral theory." *Proceedings and Addresses of the American Philosophical Association* 48: 4-22.

Reed, S. K. (1972). "Pattern recognition and categorization." *Cognitive Psychology* 3: 382-407.

Reitman, J. S., and G. H. Bower. (1973). "Storage and later recognition of concepts." *Cognitive Psychology* 4: 194-206.

Rey, G. (1983). "Concepts and stereotypes." *Cognition* 15: 237-262.

_____. (1985). "Concepts and conceptions: a reply to Smith, Medin and Rips." *Cognition* 19: 297-303.

Rips, L. J. (1975). Inductive judgments about natural categories." *Journal of Verbal Learning and Verbal Behavior* 12: 1-20.

_____. (1989). "Similarity, typicality, and categorization." S. Vosniadou and A. Ortony (eds.). *Similarity and Analogical Reasoning*. New York: Cambridge University Press: 21-59.

Rips, L. J., F. J. Shoben, and F. E. Smith. (1973). "Semantic distance and the verification of semantic relations" *Journal of Verbal Learning and Verbal Behavior* 12: 1-20.

Roese, N. J., and J. M. Olson (eds.). (1995). *What Might Have Been: The Social Psychology of Counterfactual Thinking*. Mahwah, NJ: Lawrence Erlbaum Associates.

Rorty, R. (1979). *Philosophy and the Mirror of Nature*. Princeton: Princeton University Press.

Rorty, R, J. B. Schneewind, and Q. Skinner (eds.). (1984). *Philosophy in History*. Cambridge: Cambridge University Press.

Rosch, E. (1973). "On the internal structure of perceptual and semantic categories." T. E. Moore (ed.). *Cognitive Development and the Acquisition of Language*. New York: Academic Press.

_____. (1974). "Linguistic relativity." A. Silverstein (ed.). *Human Communication: Theoretical Perspectives*. New York: Halsted Press.

_____. (1975a). "Cognitive representation of semantic categories." *Journal of Experimental Psychology: General* 104: 192-233.

_____. (1975b). "Universals and cultural specifics in human categorization." R. Brislin, S. Bochner, and W. Lonner (eds.). *Cross-Cultural Perspectives on Learning*. New York: Halsted Press.

_____. (1975c). "Cognitive reference points." *Cognitive Psychology* 7: 532-547.

_____. (1976). "Classifications of real-world objects: origins and representations in cognition." *Bulletin de Psychologie*: 241-250

_____. (1977). "Human categorization." N. Warren (ed.). *Studies in Cross-Cultural Psychology*, v. 1. London: Academic Press.

_____. (1978). "Principles of categorization." E. Rosch and B. Lloyd (eds.).

Cognition and Categorization. Hillsdale, NJ: Lawrence Erlbaum Associates: 27-48.

Rosch, E., and C. Mervis. (1975). "Family resemblances: studies in the internal structure of categories." *Cognitive Psychology* 8: 382-439.

Rosch, E., C. B. Mervis, W. Gray, D. Johnson, P. and Boyes-Brian. (1976). "Basic objects in natural categories." *Cognitive Psychology* 8(3): 382-439.

Rosch, E., C. Simpson, and R. S. Miller. (1976). "Structural bases of typicality effects." *Journal of Experimental Psychology: Human Perception and Performance* 2: 491-502.

Roth, E. M. and F. J. Shoben. (1983). "The effect of context on the structure of categories." *Cognitive Psychology* 15: 346-378.

Routley, R. (1981). "Alleged problems attributing beliefs, and intentionality, to animals." *Inquiry* 24: 385-418.

Rumelhart, D. E. (1979). "Some problems with the notion of literal meanings." A. Ortony (ed.). *Metaphor and Thought.* Cambridge: Cambridge University Press.

_____. (1993). "Some problems with the notion of literal meanings." A. Ortony et al. (eds.). *Metaphor and Thought* (2nd ed.). New York: Cambridge University Press: 71-82.

Rumelhart, D., P. Smolensky, J. McClelland, G. and Hinton. (1986). "Schemata and sequential thought processes in PDP models." *Parallel Distributed Processing, v. II.* Cambridge: MIT Press: 7-57.

Russell, B. (1912). *The Problems of Philosophy.* New York: Oxford University Press.

Salmon, W. (1957). "Should we attempt to justify induction?" *Philosophical Studies* 8: 33-48.

Savage, L. J. (1954). *The Foundations of Statistics.* New York: Wiley and Sons.

_____. (1972). *The Foundations of Statistics.* New York: Dover.

Schwarz, N. (1995). "Social cognition: information accessibility and use in social judgment." E. Smith and D. Osherson (eds.). *Thinking, An Invitation to Cognitive Science, v. 3.* (2nd ed.). Cambridge: MIT Press: 345-376.

Schwarz, N., and F. Strack. (1991). "Evaluating one's life: a judgment model of subjective well-being." F. Strack, M. Argyle, and N. Schwarz (eds.). *Subjective Well-Being.* Oxford: Pergamon Press.

Searle, J. R. (1983). *Intentionality: An Essay in the Philosophy of Mind.* New York: Cambridge University Press.

_____. (1990). "Consciousness, explanatory inversion, and cognitive science." *Behavioral and Brain Sciences* 13(4): 585-642.

_____. (1992). *The Rediscovery of the Mind.* Cambridge: MIT Press.

_____. (1993). "Metaphor." A. Ortony (ed.). *Metaphor and Thought.* Cambridge: Cambridge University Press.

Sellars, W. (1963a). "Empiricism and the philosophy of mind." *Science, Perception, and Reality.* London: Routledge and Kegan Paul.

_____. (1963b). "Philosophy and the scientific image of man." *Science, Perception, and Reality.* London: Routledge and Kegan Paul.

_____. (1967). *Philosophical Perspectives.* Springfield, IL: Charles C.

Thomas.

Shafir, E. (1993). "Choosing versus rejecting: Why some options are both better and worse than others." *Memory and Cognition* 21(4): 546-556.

_____. (1995). "Compatibility in cognition and decision." J. R. Busemeyer, R. Hastie, and D. L. Medin (eds.). *Decision Making from the Perspective of Cognitive Psychology (The Psychology of Learning and Motivation, v. 32)*. New York: Academic Press: 247-274.

Shafir, E., I. Simonson, and A. Tversky. (1993). "Reason-based choice." *Cognition* 49(2): 11-36.

Shafir, E., and A. Tversky. (1992). "Thinking through uncertainty: nonconsequential reasoning and choice." *Cognitive Psychology* 24(4): 449-474.

Shepard, R. N. (1962). "The analysis of proximities: multidimensional scaling with an unknown distance function. I and II." *Psychometrika* 27: 125-140, 219-246.

Shepard, R. N., A. K. Romney, and S. B. Nerlove. (1972). *Multidimensional Scaling: Theory and Applications in the Behavioral Sciences (v. I and II)*. New York: Seminar Press.

Shiffrin, R. M., and W. Schneider. (1977). "Controlled and automatic human information processing: II. Perceptual learning, automatic attending and a general theory." *Psychological Review* 84: 127-190.

Shoemaker, S. (1988). "On knowing ones own mind." J. Tomberlin (ed.). *Philosophical Perspectives* 4. Atascadero, CA: Ridgeview Publishing: 187-214.

Shope, R. K. (1983). *The Analysis of Knowing: A Decade of Research*. Princeton: Princeton University Press.

Skyrms, B. (1975). *Choice and Chance*. Belmont, CA: Dickenson Publishing.

Slovic, P. (1975). "Choice between equally valued alternatives." *Journal of Experimental Psychology: Human Perception and Performance* 1: 280-287.

Slovic, P., D. Griffin, and A. Tversky. (1990). "Compatibility effects in judgment and choice." R. Hogarth (ed.). *Insights in Decision Making: Theory and Applications*. Chicago: University of Chicago Press: 5-27.

Slovic, P., and S. Lichtenstein. (1983). "Preference reversals: A broader perspective." *American Economic Review* 73: 596-605.

Smart, J. J. C. (1965). "The methods of ethics and the methods of science." *Journal of Philosophy* 62: 344-349.

_____. (1990). "Integrity and squeamishness." J. Glover (ed.). *Utilitarianism and its Critics*. New York: Macmillan: 170-174.

Smith, E. (1989). "Three distinctions about concepts and categorization." *Mind and Language* 4: 57-61.

Smith, E., and D. Medin. (1981). *Concepts and Categories*. Cambridge: MIT Press.

Smith, E. R., and F. D. Miller. (1978). "Limits on perception of cognitive processes: A reply to Nisbett and Wilson." *Psychological Review* 85: 355-362.

Smith, E. E., L. J. Rips, and E. J. Shoben. (1974). "Semantic memory and psychological semantics." G. H. Bower (ed.). *The Psychology of Learning and Motivation, v. 8*. New York: Academic Press.

Smith, E. E., E. J. Shoben, and L. J. Rips. (1974). "Structure and process in semantic memory: a featural model for semantic decisions." *Psychological Review* 81: 214-241.

Smith, F. A. (1990). "Categorization." D. Osherson and E. Smith (eds.). *Thinking: An Invitation to Cognitive Science, v. 3*. Cambridge: MIT Press: 33-53.

Smolensky, P. (1988). "On the proper treatment of connectionism." *The Behavioral and Brain Sciences* 11: 1-74.

Sosa, E. (1991). *Knowledge in Perspective*. New York: Cambridge University Press.

_____. (1993). "Proper functionalism and virtue epistemology." *Nous* 27: 51-65.

_____. (1996). "Rational intuition: Bealer on its nature and epistemic status." *Philosophical Studies* 81: 151-162.

Spelke, E. (1991). "Physical knowledge in infancy: reflections on Piaget's theory." S. Carey and R. Gelman (eds.). *The Epigenesis of Mind*. Hillsdale, NJ: Lawrence Erlbaum Associates.

Spencer, N. (1973). "Differences between linguists and nonlinguists in intuitions of grammaticality-acceptability." *Journal of Psycholinguistic Research* 2: 83-98.

Stanovich, K. E. (1996). *How to Think Straight About Psychology*. New York: HarperCollins.

Steup, M. (1996). *An Introduction to Contemporary Epistemology*. Upper Saddle River, NJ: Prentice-Hall.

Stich, S. (1979). "Do animals have beliefs?" *Australasian Journal of Philosophy* 57: 15-28.

_____. (1983). *From Folk Psychology to Cognitive Science: The Case Against Belief*. Cambridge: MIT Press.

_____. (1984). "Relativism, rationality and the limits of intentional description." *Pacific Philosophical Quarterly* 65: 211-235.

_____. (1988) "Reflective equilibrium, analytic epistemology and the problem of cognitive diversity." *Synthese* 74: 391-413.

_____. (1990). *The Fragmentation of Reason*. Cambridge: MIT Press.

_____. (1992). "What is a theory of mental representation?" *Mind* 101: 243-261

_____. (in preparation). "Do you really care whether your beliefs are true?"

Stich, S. and Nisbett, R. (1980). "Justification and the psychology of human reasoning." *Philosophy of Science* 47: 188-202.

Strack, F., L. L. Martin, and N. Schwartz. (1988). "Priming and communication: The social determinants of information use in judgments of life-satisfaction." *European Journal of Social Psychology* 18: 429-442.

Strack, F., N. Schwarz, and E. Gschneidinger. (1985). "Happiness and reminiscing: the role of time perspective, mood, and mode of thinking." *Journal of Personality and Social Psychology* 49: 1460-1469.

Strawson, P. (1952). *Introduction to Logical Theory*. New York: John Wiley.

Talmy, L. (1983). "How language structures space." H. Pick and L. Acredolo (eds.). *Spatial Orientation: Theory, Research, and Application*. New York: Plenum Press: 225-282.

Tersman, F. (1993). *Reflective Equilibrium*. Stockholm: Almqvist and Wiksell International.

Turing, A. (1950). "Computing Machinery and Intelligence." *Mind* 59: 434-460.

Tversky, A., and I. Gati. (1978). "Studies of similarity." E. Rosch and B. Lloyd (eds.). *Cognition and Categorization*. Hillsdale, NJ: Lawrence Erlbaum Associates.

Tversky, A., and D. Griffin. (1991). "Endowment and contrast in judgments of well-being." F. Strack, M. Argyle, and N. Schwarz (eds.). *Subjective Well-Being*. New York: Pergamon Press.

Tversky, A., and D. Kahneman. (1986). "Rational choice and the framing of decisions." *Journal of Business* 59: 251-278.

_____. (1991). "Loss Aversion in riskless choice: a reference dependent model." *Quarterly Journal of Economics* (November): 1039-1061.

_____. (1992). "Advances in prospect theory: cumulative representation of uncertainty." *Journal of Risk and Uncertainty* 5: 297-323.

Tversky, A., S. Sattath, and P. Slovic. (1988). "Contingent weighting in judgment and choice." *Psychological Review* 95: 371-384.

Tversky, A., and E. Shafir. (1992). "The disjunction effect in choice under uncertainty." *Psychological Science* 3(5): 305-309.

Tversky, A., P. Slovic, and D. Kahneman. (1990). "The causes of preference reversal." *American Economic Review* 80: 204-217.

Underwood, B. J. (1966). *Problems in Experimental Design and Inference*. New York: Appleton-Century-Crofts.

VonNeumann, J., and O. Morgenstern. (1972). *Theory of Games and Economic Behavior*. Princeton: Princeton University Press.

Vygotsky, L. S. (1962). *Thought and Language*. New York: Wiley.

Ware, R. (1979). "Some bits and pieces." F. Peletier (ed.). *Mass Terms: Some Philosophical Problems*. Dordrecht: Reidel: 15-29.

Warner, R. (1989). "Why is logic *a priori*?" *The Monist* 72: 40-51.

Weiskrantz, L. (1986). *Blindsight: A Case Study and Implications*. Oxford: Oxford University Press.

White, A. R. (1975). "Conceptual analysis." C. J. Botempo and S. J. Odell (eds.). *The Owl of Minerva*. New York: McGraw-Hill.

Wierzbicka, A. (1988). *The Semantics of Grammar*. Amsterdam: John Benjamins.

Williams, B. (1970). "The self and the future." *Philosophical Review* 79: 161-180.

Williams, M. (1996). *Unnatural Doubts: Epistemological Realism and the Basis of Skepticism*. Princeton: Princeton University Press.

Wilson, T. D., and N. Brekke. (1994). "Mental contamination and mental correction: Unwanted influences on judgments and evaluations." *Psychological Bulletin* 116(1): 117-142.

Wilson, T. D., and J. L. Stone. (1985). "Limitations of self-knowledgee: More on telling more than we can know." P. Shaver (ed.). *Review of Personality and Social Psychology, v. 6*. Beverly Hills: Sage: 167-183.

Wisniewski, E. J., M. Imai, and L. Casey. (1996). "On the equivalence of superordinate concepts." *Cognition* 60: 269-298.

Wisniewski, E. J., and B. C. Love. (forthcoming). "Relations versus properties in conceptual combination." *Journal of Memory and Language.*

Wittgenstein, L. (1953). *Philosophical Investigations.* New York: Macmillan.

Zadeh, L. A. (1965). "Fuzzy Sets." *Information and Control* 8: 338-353.

Index

About the Contributors

George Bealer is Professor of Philosophy at the University of Colorado at Boulder. He is author of *Quality and Concept* (1982) and numerous articles in metaphysics, epistemology, philosophy of mind, and philosophy of language. His new book, *Philosophical Limits of Science*, will appear shortly.

Robert Cummins is Professor of Philosophy at the University of California, Davis. He is the author of *Representations, Targets and Attitudes* (1996), *Meaning and Mental Representation* (1989), and *The Nature of Psychological Explanation* (1983).

Michael R. DePaul is Associate Professor of Philosophy at the University of Notre Dame. His research focuses primarily on epistemology, metaethics, and most particularly, moral epistemology. He is the author of *Balance and Refinement* (1993).

Richard Foley works primarily in epistemology. His published work includes *The Theory of Epistemic Rationality* (1987) and *Working Without a Net* (1993). He is Professor of Philosophy, Dean of Arts and Sciences, and Dean of the Graduate School at Rutgers University.

Alvin Goldman is Regents' Professor of Philosophy and Research Scientist in Cognitive Science at the University of Arizona. He is the author of *A Theory of Human Action* (1970), *Epistemology and Cognition* (1986), *Liaisons: Philosophy Meets the Cognitive and Social Sciences* (1992), *Philosophical Applications of Cognitive Science* (1993), and *Knowledge in a Social World* (forthcoming).

Alison Gopnik is Professor of Psychology at the University of California at Berkeley. She has published extensively in developmental psychology, philosophy, and cognitive science, most recently in *Words, Thought and Theories*, co-authored with Andrew Meltzoff (1997).

George Graham is Chair and Professor of Philosophy and Professor of Psychology at the University of Alabama at Birmingham. Among his publications is *A Companion to Cognitive Science*, co-edited with William Bechtel, and *Philosophical Psychopathology* (1994), co-edited with G. Lynn Stephens (1994).

Gary Gutting is Professor of Philosophy at the University of Notre Dame. He is the author of *Religious Belief and Religious Skepticism* (1982), and *Michel Foucault's Archaeology of Scientific Knowledge* (1989); and the editor of *Paradigms and Revolutions: Appraisals and Applications of the Philosophy of Science of Thomas Kuhn* (1980) and the *Cambridge Companion to Foucault* (1994). His *Pragmatic Liberalism and the Critique of Modernity* is expected soon.

Terry Horgan is Professor of Philosophy at the University of Memphis. He has published papers (often collaborative) in metaphysics, philosophy of mind, philosophy of language, and metaethics. Among his publications is *Connectionism and the Philosophy of Psychology* (1996), co-authored with John Tienson.

Tamara Horowitz is Associate Professor of Philosophy at the University of Pittsburgh. She is co-editor of *Thought Experiments in Science and Philosophy* (1991) with Gerald Massey, and *Scientific Failure* (1994) with Allen Janis. She has written articles in the areas of epistemology and decision theory.

Hilary Kornblith is Professor of Philosophy at the University of Vermont. He is the author of *Inductive Inference and Its Natural Ground* (1994), and editor of *Naturalizing Epistemology* (1985), now in its second edition.

Carolyn B. Mervis is Professor of Psychology at the University of Louisville. Her research has concerned concepts and categorization, and more recently language development, focusing especially on William's Syndrome.

Joel Pust is Assistant Professor of Philosophy at the University of Delaware. He received his doctorate from the University of Arizona with a dissertation on the evidential role of intuitions in analytic philosophy. His primary interests are in epistemology and the philosophy of mind.

William Ramsey is Associate Professor of Philosophy at the University of Notre Dame. He is co-editor of *Philosophy and Connectionist Theory* (1991) with Stephen Stich and David Rumelhart, and is the author of numerous articles in the philosophy of psychology and cognitive science.

Eleanor Rosch is Professor of Psychology at the University of California at Berkeley. In addition to her research on the nature of concepts and the categorization of objects and events, she is interested in Buddhist psychology and the psychology of religion. She co-authored *The Embodied Mind: Cognitive Science and the Human Experience* (1991) with Francisco Varela and Evan Thompson, and she is co-editor, with Barbara Lloyd, of *Cognition and Categorization* (1978).

Eldar Shafir is Associate Professor of Psychology and Public Affairs at Princeton University. His research focuses on reasoning, decision making, and behavioral economics.

Ernest Sosa is Romeo Elton Professor in the Philosophy Department of Brown University and an adjunct Distinguished Professor in the Philosophy Department of Rutgers University. He has published papers in epistemology and metaphysics. Some of his epistemology papers are collected in *Knowledge in Perspective* (1991).

Stephen Stich is Board of Governors Professor of Philosophy and Cognitive Science at Rutgers University. His publications include *From Folk Psychology to Cognitive Science* (1983), *The Fragmentation of Reason* (1990), and *Deconstructing the Mind* (1996).

Eric Schwitzgebel is an Assistant Professor of Philosophy at the University of California at Riverside, having received his Ph.D. in philosophy at the University of California at Berkeley in 1997. He has published papers on the theory-theory of cognitive development and on classical Chinese philosophy.

Edward J. Wisniewski is an Associate Professor in Psychology at the University of North Carolina at Greensboro. He received his doctoral degree in Cognitive Science from Brown University. His research interests include language understanding, mental representations, and learning. He has published a number of papers and book chapters on these issues